BESTSELLING BOOK SERIES

National Parks of the American West For Dummies®

Cheat Sheet

The Best of America's National Parks

Arches National Park (Chapter 9)

Best vista: Petrified Dunes Viewpoint
Notable wildlife: Desert bighorn sheep, western collared lizard
Most unique experience: Touring Fiery Furnace
Top attraction: Delicate Arch
Best time to visit: October through May

Death Valley National Park (Chapter 10)

Best vista: View of Death Valley from atop Dante's View
Notable wildlife: Mules, desert bighorn sheep
Most unique experience: Standing 282 feet *below* sea level.
Top attraction: Scotty's Castle
Best time to visit: November through March

Grand Canyon National Park (Chapter 11)

Best vista: Sunset from Lipan Point
Notable wildlife: Condors, ringtail cats, Grand Canyon pink rattlesnake
Most unique experience: Mule ride into the canyon
Top attraction: South Rim
Best time to visit: Spring, fall

Grand Teton National Park (Chapter 12)

Best vista: Oxbow Bend
Notable wildlife: Elk, moose, bison, wolves, and pronghorn antelope
Most unique experience: Standing atop the Grand Teton
Top attraction: Teton Range
Best time to visit: Late summer, early fall

Mount Rainier National Park (Chapter 13)

Best vista: Emmons Glacier from Sunrise
Notable wildlife: Mountain goats
Most unique experience: Walking on a glacier in summer
Top attraction: Mount Rainier
Best time to visit: Summer, fall

Olympic National Park (Chapter 14)

Best vista: View of glaciers and Strait of Juan de Fuca from Hurricane Ridge
Notable wildlife: Harbor seals, Roosevelt Elk
Most unique experience: Visiting the beach, a rain forest, and a snowfield in one day
Top attraction: Hoh Rain Forest
Best time to visit: Summer, early fall

The Best of America's National Parks (continued)

Sequoia and Kings Canyon National Parks (Chapter 15)

Best vista: From atop Moro Rock
Notable wildlife: Black bears
Most unique experience: Standing next to General Sherman Tree
Top attraction: Giant Forest
Best time to visit: Summer, winter

Yellowstone National Park (Chapter 16)

Best vista: Upper Geyser Basin from Observation Point
Notable wildlife: Wolves, grizzly bears, bison
Most unique experience: Watching wildlife in Lamar Valley
Top attraction: Old Faithful geyser
Best time to visit: Early summer, fall

Yosemite National Park (Chapter 17)

Best vista: Yosemite Valley from top of Glacier Point
Notable wildlife: Black bears
Most unique experience: Hiking to the top of Half Dome
Top attraction: Yosemite Valley
Best time to visit: Early summer

Zion National Park (Chapter 18)

Best vista: Zion Canyon from Angel's Landing
Notable wildlife: Mountain lions
Most unique experience: Hiking The Narrows
Top attraction: Zion Canyon
Best time to visit: Spring, early fall

Top Ten Rules for a Safe and Fun Trip

🖊 Park animals are wild, not part of a petting zoo, so keep your distance from them.

🖊 Make sure that the only souvenirs you take out of a park are pictures or items you buy in a gift shop.

🖊 Pack plenty of film, flashcards, and extra batteries for your camera.

🖊 Pack plenty of sunscreen, and don't be bashful about using it.

🖊 Waterfalls can be awfully slippery, so don't try to climb them or get too close to the edges.

🖊 When visiting parks inhabited by bears, don't leave any food in your car or in your tent.

🖊 Pack rain gear — even if you don't expect rain on your trip.

🖊 Be careful where you put your hands when you're hiking — you never know when you may disturb a snake or spider.

🖊 Don't drink water from a lake or stream unless you treat or filter it first.

🖊 When traveling to a park at a higher elevation, ease into your vacation by taking it easy and acclimating on the first day.

FOR DUMMIES®

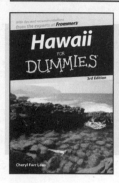

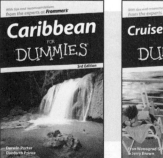

National Parks of the American West

FOR DUMMIES®

3RD EDITION

National Parks of the American West

FOR DUMMIES®

3RD EDITION

by Kurt Repanshek

WILEY

Wiley Publishing, Inc.

National Parks of the American West For Dummies®, 3rd Edition
Published by
Wiley Publishing, Inc.
111 River St.
Hoboken, NJ 07030-5774
www.wiley.com

Copyright © 2005 by Wiley Publishing, Inc., Indianapolis, Indiana

Published simultaneously in Canada

WILEY

About the Author

Kurt Repanshek, a misplaced Easterner, has been roaming the Rocky Mountains since 1985, when he arrived in Wyoming as state correspondent for The Associated Press. A freelance writer now based in Park City, Utah, he has managed to find his way to the top of the Grand Teton; paddled portions of the Green, Colorado, and the Middle Fork of the Salmon rivers, as well as Yellowstone's Shoshone and Yellowstone lakes, hiked to Phantom Ranch in the Grand Canyon, climbed Half Dome in Yosemite, and cross-country skied in the predawn cold to catch sunrise on the North Rim of the Grand Canyon, all in the pursuit of stories. He is the author of *Hidden Utah* and *Hidden Salt Lake City & Beyond* (both from Ulysses Press), and his work has appeared in *Audubon, Sunset, National Geographic Traveler,* and *Hemispheres,* among other publications.

Dedication

To my sons, Jesse and Sean: May they always share my curiosity to see what lies behind the next mountain.

Author's Acknowledgments

Believe it or not, books are not as easy to cobble together as they are to read. I'm thankful to my wife, Marcelle, for her belief that I'm a somewhat decent writer. I'd also be remiss if I didn't acknowledge her remarkable tolerance every time she heard that I still had "just one more" park to visit in the name of research. Kudos go to my editor, Lisa Torrance, a never-ending source of encouraging words and wise suggestions. Countless other folks came to my assistance time and again whenever I ran into dead-ends. Specifically, for their time, patience, and efforts, I'd like to thank David Barna and his communications staff at National Park Service headquarters in Washington, D.C., and the communications staff and various rangers at Death Valley National Park, Grand Canyon National Park, Grand Teton National Park, Mount Rainier National Park, Olympic National Park, Sequoia/Kings Canyon National Parks, Yellowstone National Park, Yosemite National Park, and Zion National Park. Finally, a big "thank you" to those many behind-the-scenes folks in the parks who ran down lodging, trail, and sightseeing information at a moment's notice.

Publisher's Acknowledgments

We're proud of this book; please send us your comments through our Dummies online registration form located at www.dummies.com/register/.

Some of the people who helped bring this book to market include the following:

Editorial

Editors: Natalie Faye Harris, Margot Weiss

Copy Editor: Jennifer Bingham

Cartographer: Elizabeth Puhl

Editorial Manager: Christine Beck

Editorial Assistant: Melissa Bennett

Senior Photo Editor: Richard Fox

Cover Photos: © J.A. Kraulis/ Masterfile

Cartoons: Rich Tennant, www.the5thwave.com

Composition

Project Coordinator: April Farling

Layout and Graphics: Melanee Prendergast, Heather Ryan

Proofreaders: David Faust, Leeann Harney, Carl Pierce, TECHBOOKS Production Services

Indexer: TECHBOOKS Production Services

Publishing and Editorial for Consumer Dummies

Diane Graves Steele, Vice President and Publisher, Consumer Dummies

Joyce Pepple, Acquisitions Director, Consumer Dummies

Kristin A. Cocks, Product Development Director, Consumer Dummies

Michael Spring, Vice President and Publisher, Travel

Brice Gosnell, Associate Publisher, Travel

Kelly Regan, Editorial Director, Travel

Publishing for Technology Dummies

Andy Cummings, Vice President and Publisher, Dummies Technology/General User

Composition Services

Gerry Fahey, Vice President of Production Services

Debbie Stailey, Director of Composition Services

Contents at a Glance

Maps at a Glance

· ·

Table of Contents

Chapter 15: Sequoia and Kings Canyon National Parks 250

Introduction

*Y*ou've managed to carve some time out of your hectic schedule and head west to one of America's national parks. That's great! You'll see some of the most breathtaking scenery in America, and you'll glimpse wildlife ranging from wolves, bears, elk, and moose to bald eagles, great blue herons, and California condors. Plus, depending on which park you visit, you may discover something interesting about America's cultural history. Stop by Yellowstone, the nation's first national park, and you can even find out how the whole park movement began.

What makes a trip to a national park so wonderful? For starters, the parks give you a chance to flee the rat race and unwind in gorgeous settings. America's national park system is more diverse than any other park system in the world. You can stroll the seashore at Olympic National Park in Washington, climb (or just admire) craggy mountains in Grand Teton National Park in Wyoming, or travel through one of the most impressive canyons on earth at Grand Canyon National Park in Arizona. At Utah's aptly named Arches National Park, you can hike among the planet's largest collection of rock arches. California and Nevada share Death Valley National Park, the lowest and hottest spot in the Western Hemisphere.

These attractions are just a few of your park options. In the year 2004, the national park system included 385 sites — parks, monuments, historical sites, recreation areas, battlefields, military parks, lakeshores, seashores, scenic rivers, and trails — scattered across America. So numerous are the sites that it would be hard to do them all justice in one book. Therefore, we've culled what I like to think are the "best of the best" of the national parks west of the Rocky Mountain Front.

Even with that limitation, you face a wide array of choices. Unless you're a life-long national parks junkie, you probably could use a little guidance to help decide which park is for you, when to go, and what to see when you reach your destination. This book is designed to anticipate your questions and point out the not-so-obvious factors in a cut-to-the-chase format.

About This Book

National Parks of the American West for Dummies, 3rd Edition, is designed to guide you through some of the park system's western gems and show you what they offer. This book isn't like a novel, which you must read from beginning to end in order to stay on top of the plot. Instead, you can simply jump to the chapter about the park that interests you and then move on.

Dummies Post-it® Flags

As you're reading this book, you'll find information that you'll want to reference as you plan or enjoy your trip — whether it be a new hotel, a must-see attraction or a must-try walking tour. Mark these pages with the handy Post-it® Flags included in this book to help make your trip planning easier!

This book isn't an encyclopedia, either. My goal is to whet your interest in the park system with a solid look at 11 of its crown jewels. I also help you choose the park and plan the vacation that's right for you.

Just as early explorers in Yellowstone returned to the East Coast with maps of their newly discovered wonderland, I assembled a map of this book, which my editor calls a table of contents. Use this map judiciously. If you're already a road warrior and you know how to find accommodations, you probably can skip Chapter 6. On the other hand, if you've never been to a national park and are concerned about hiking through forests with mountain lions (but no tigers) and bears oh my, turn to Chapter 8 for some tips on surviving — and enjoying — your park trip.

Please be advised that travel information is subject to change at any time — and this is especially true of prices. I therefore suggest that you write or call ahead for confirmation when making your travel plans. The authors, editors, and publisher can't be held responsible for the experiences of readers while traveling. Your safety is important to us, however, so we encourage you to stay alert and be aware of your surroundings. Keep a close eye on cameras, purses, and wallets, all favorite targets of thieves and pickpockets.

Conventions Used in This Book

All the individual park chapters contain the same types of information — top attractions, when to go, how to get there, where to stay, where to eat, and so on — in the same order. This format allows you to open the book to any chapter and access the information that you need quickly and easily.

In this book, I've included lists of hotels, restaurants, and attractions. As I describe each, I often include abbreviations for commonly accepted credit cards. Take a look at the following list for an explanation of each:

> AE: American Express
>
> DC: Diners Club
>
> DISC: Discover
>
> MC: MasterCard
>
> V: Visa

I've divided the hotels into two categories — my personal favorites and those that don't quite make my preferred list but still get my hearty seal of approval. Don't be shy about considering these "runners up" hotels if you're unable to get a room at one of my favorites or if your preferences differ from mine — the amenities that the runners up offer and the services that each provides make all these accommodations good choices to consider as you determine where to rest your head at night.

I also include some general pricing information to help you as you decide where to unpack your bags or dine on the local cuisine. I've used a system of dollar signs to show a range of costs for one night in a hotel (the price refers to a double-occupancy room) or a meal at a restaurant (included in the cost of each meal is an appetizer, an entrée, and a dessert). Check out the following table to decipher the dollar signs:

Cost	Hotel	Restaurant
$	$75 and under	$10 and under
$$	$76 to $100	$11 to $19
$$$	$101 to $200	$21 to $26
$$$$	$200 to 250	$27 to $35
$$$$$	$251 and more	$36 and more

Foolish Assumptions

As I wrote this book, I made some assumptions about you and what your needs might be as a traveler. Here's what I assumed about you:

- ✔ You may be an experienced traveler who hasn't had much time to explore the national parks and wants expert advice when you finally do get a chance to enjoy that particular locale.

- ✔ You may be an inexperienced traveler looking for guidance when determining whether to take a trip to the national parks and how to plan for it.

- ✔ You're not looking for a book that provides all the information available about the national parks or that lists every hotel, restaurant, or attraction available to you. Instead, you're looking for a book that focuses on the places that will give you the best or most unique experience in the national parks.

If you fit any of these criteria, then *National Parks of the American West For Dummies,* 3rd Edition gives you the information you're looking for!

How This Book Is Organized

Vacations are precious and often too short. They're certainly too short to spend flipping through a guidebook trying to figure out how and where to relax. As a result, this book is user-friendly and organized in a logical fashion. The book includes four parts; each one covers a major aspect of your trip. The parts are further broken down into chapters that delve into the nitty-gritty of trip planning or the highlights of each park.

Part 1: Introducing the National Parks of the American West

Why visit a national park? What makes them special? Which park should you visit? The chapters in this part answer these questions. In the first chapter, you'll find a quick lowdown on "the best of the best" that I've discovered during my adventures. In Chapter 2, you'll find information on the parks' historical and cultural backgrounds. Next, I touch on the diversity of the West's national parks, explain some of your vacation options, and tell you when parks are the most (and least) crowded. Deciding which park is best for you and your family is the tricky part. The subtle and not-so-subtle differences among the parks can determine which one is right for you. Although I quickly fell in love with Yellowstone's geysers and wildlife, Yellowstone may not appeal to you at all. Therefore, I get specific and explain, for example, why Kings Canyon National Park is a great choice if you're a backcountry nut, but not the best choice if you're hauling three young kids with you. I also address what kind of weather to expect and how to plan a budget.

Part 11: Planning Your Trip to the National Parks of the American West

Getting from Point A to Point B has always been a problem for me, usually because I like to detour to Points C and D along the way. Fortunately, in this book, I don't take the alternate route. In this part, I describe how you can get to the parks and find your way around after you arrive. (You can determine how much meandering you want to do.) This section also details the best and easiest ways to book accommodations. I also touch on how to cope with money while you travel. Plus, I've included information on travelers with special needs or interests. For instance, you can find information on which parks offer great kid-friendly adventures, tips for senior travelers, and helpful details for disabled travelers. In addition, I've touched on one of my favorite subjects: how *you* can get involved with educational projects inside the parks. Finally, I sprinkle in some helpful hints on how to survive your park experience (a national park is considerably less tame than an amusement park), and I offer some pointers on what things to toss in your suitcase.

Part III: Exploring the National Parks of the American West

In Chapters 10 through 18, you get the lowdown on 11 of the West's best parks — all of which are crowd pleasers and worthy of your attention. Each park chapter begins with the must-see attractions. Then I give you the scoop on what you need to do before you get to the park and how to manage your time after you arrive (whether you can stay one day or a few). I even introduce you to each park's wild kingdom, reveal the best spots for memorable photographs, and let you in on a few safety issues. Read these chapters so you'll know what to expect when you drive through the entrance gates and can explore the park on your own with confidence.

Part IV: The Part of Tens

Do you need ten reasons to visit a national park? I give plenty of justification in this part. Turn to Chapter 19 where I sum up ten incredible national park vistas, to Chapter 20 where I reveal why a national park vacation beats a trip to (insert the name of your nearest man-made, woefully expensive amusement park), or to Chapter 21 where I point out ten ways to enjoy a national park on the cheap.

In back of this book I've included an *appendix* — your Quick Concierge — containing lots of handy information you may need when traveling in the national parks, protocol for sending mail or finding taxis, and more. Check out this appendix when searching for answers to lots of little questions that may come up as you travel. You can find Quick Concierge easily because it's printed on yellow paper.

Icons Used in This Book

In the margins throughout this book, you find little doodles called *icons* (I figured Post-Its wouldn't last forever). They point out helpful (and sometimes money-saving) tips to consider before leaving home and while you're on the road. Here's how to decipher them:

Keep an eye out for the Bargain Alert icon as you seek out money-saving tips and/or great deals.

Best of the Best icon highlights the best the destination has to offer in all categories — hotels, restaurants, attractions, activities, shopping, and nightlife.

Watch for this icon to identify annoying or potentially dangerous situations, such as traffic jams, crowded outlooks, and unsafe conditions.

Parks are kid-friendly by their very nature. Still, I use this icon to point out hotels, restaurants, and activities that are particularly attractive to kids and families.

Helpful rangers can make recommendations that guide you toward a great park experience. Look for this symbol to discover spectacular views, wonderful hikes, and not-to-be-missed activities.

Find out useful advice on things to do and ways to schedule your time when you see the Tip icon.

Where to Go from Here

Go to Yellowstone. Or Yosemite. Or maybe the Grand Canyon or Mount Rainier. Or any other park mentioned in this book. (I guarantee that you won't be disappointed.) The following pages resemble a great long-distance hike — you never know what's around the next bend in the trail. So throw on a backpack, take a swig of water, and get ready to explore the national parks!

Part I

Introducing the National Parks of the American West

Darn it, Kevin! I told you to keep hold of the leash and not to throw sticks while we're in the park with Rusty!

In this part . . .

*Y*ou've finally decided to take a national park vacation.
Great! You won't be sorry. But you need a game plan.
Which park do you want to visit? When should you visit?
And how do you get there? In the first part of this book, I help
you answer those questions. I've also included a section that
delves into the cultural and historical backgrounds of the
parks to help you "get grounded" in what they're all about
before you reach the entrance gates.

Chapter 1

Discovering the Best of the National Parks of the West

In This Chapter

▶ The best ways to experience the outdoors
▶ Top places to stay and dine
▶ Favorite winter escapes and family activities

*T*he old adage "If you've seen one, you've seen them all," doesn't apply to America's national parks. Each park has its own, distinct personality. Even those that border one another — such as Yellowstone and Grand Teton, or Sequoia and Kings Canyon — have some very different elements. If you're a wildlife fan, it's easy to choose a visit to Yellowstone over a trip to Death Valley. If you want to walk sea-swept beaches, Olympic, not Mount Rainier, is the place to head. When it comes to descending into the landscape, Zion tops the list. Want to see a rock landscape out of the old Flintstone's cartoon scenery? No place comes as close as Arches with its rock arches, windows, and fins.

If you haven't already visited these places, it may be hard to know which fits with the vacation you envision. But that's okay, because I've already done all the hard work and come up with some lists that help define the very best of the national parks of the West.

 Throughout the book, you will find the "Best of the Best" icon highlighting the best the parks have to offer in all categories—hotels, restaurants, hikes, wildlife viewing, and more.

The Best Scenic Overlooks

Sometimes you can't see the forest for the trees. Sometimes you can see almost forever. Here are some of the best places for great views:

 ✔ **Dantes View:** There are two benefits to trekking to this viewpoint in Death Valley National Park. One, you escape the blistering heat of the valley floor. Two, you gain an incredible vantage point over

Death Valley. Views spread downward to the parched salt pan of Badwater and upward toward the summit of Telescope Peak across the valley. See Chapter 10.

✔ **Lipan Point:** There are numerous overlooks that provide breathtaking views into the Grand Canyon, but this one gets a gold star. Not only is it far enough from Grand Canyon Village on the South Rim to discourage crowds, but come sundown, it offers what is arguably the best view into the canyon. See Chapter 11.

✔ **Hurricane Ridge:** Look to the north, and you see the Strait of Juan de Fuca and Canada. Look to the south, and you spot glacier-coated peaks and thick coniferous forests that practically beg you to hike down into them. This ridgeline outpost in Olympic National Park clearly demonstrates why this park is a favorite for those looking to mix up their activities — mountaineering and beachcombing — during a national park vacation. See Chapter 14.

✔ **Glacier Point:** Yosemite's Half Dome gets more press, but its summit is much tougher to reach and it doesn't offer the same perspective of the Yosemite Valley. Plus, when you're standing atop Half Dome, you can't admire its ponderous profile the way you can from Glacier Point. Although you can hike to the top of Glacier Point via the Four Mile Trail, you can drive much more quickly to the summit and enjoy the view without the exertion. See Chapter 17.

✔ **Angel's Landing:** It takes a hike that at times is strenuous and that will test your fear of heights, but climbing to the top of this outcrop in Zion National Park is a real thrill. Not only can you congratulate yourself for making it to the top, but once there you can enjoy some beautiful views down into Zion Canyon. See Chapter 18.

The Best Day Hikes

A national park vacation should be an "active" vacation, one that challenges your body as much as your mind. Here's a collection of day hikes that will get you started in the right direction:

✔ **Primitive Trail from Double O to Landscape Arch:** Definitely off the beaten path, this hike in Arches National Park has little rock cairns marking a route that will at times test your trail-finding skills. But it also rewards by taking you between, and atop, rock fins, past showy displays of wildflowers (in springtime), and treating you to some solitude in this otherworldly landscape. See Chapter 9.

✔ **Hidden Falls/Inspiration Point:** Committing to this hike in Grand Teton National Park allows you to enjoy a gentle boat ride across Jenny Lake before (and after) venturing into the mountains. True, this hike is popular and can be crowded, but it pays off with several views of crashing water falls and one overlooking Jenny Lake.

You can also watch classes of hopeful climbers working on their techniques before heading up to the top of the Grand Teton. See Chapter 12.

✔ **Cape Alva/Sand Point Loop:** Temperate rain forest, grassy meadows, and sandy beaches. This hike in Olympic National Park has it all, and tosses in some petroglyphs reflecting Native Americans' impressions of whales for good measure. See Chapter 14.

✔ **Lone Star Geyser:** Most folks who head to the Upper Geyser Basin at Yellowstone National Park are satisfied to view Old Faithful and stroll along the boardwalk up to Geyser Hill. What makes the hike to the Lone Star Geyser a winner is the beautiful forest the trail roams through, the nearby Firehole River, and the payoff: a towering mound of geyserite that erupts about every three hours with a gusher of steaming water. See Chapter 16.

✔ **Half Dome:** True, this is one long day hike. But the 17 miles you'll cover from start to finish lead you uphill alongside frothing cataracts, along the edge of the Little Yosemite Valley, and up one of Yosemite National Park's signature rockfaces to an incredible viewpoint overlooking the Yosemite Valley. If you take this hike on a hot day, allow some time on your return to cool off in the Merced River before it leaps down into the Yosemite Valley via Nevada and Vernal falls. See Chapter 17.

✔ **Riverside Walk:** If you don't have the time to hike the entire length of Zion National Park's "Narrows" trail, this is a good substitute. Located at the Temple of Sinawava, this walk leads you into a massive slot canyon whose walls rise thousands of feet above the Virgin River. A summertime hike into this canyon is cooling and reveals dazzling displays of hanging gardens. See Chapter 18.

The Best Places to Sleep under the Stars

Heading into the backcountry can be one of the best aspects of a national park vacation. You can walk off into the woods in just about any direction, but here are some of my favorites:

✔ **Lizard Creek Campground:** Near Grand Teton's northern border, this out-of-the-way campground is often overlooked, so you can be sure it's not overrun with noisy campers. The forest setting on the shores of Jackson Lake is picturesque, and there's no light pollution to obscure your views of the night sky. See Chapter 12.

✔ **Shoshone, Lewis, or Yellowstone lakes:** You have to work, either by hiking or paddling, to reach the backcountry campsites that dot the shores of Yellowstone National Park's three major lakes. But I guarantee you won't be disappointed. I've seen shooting stars crease the sky on clear nights, and wildlife abounds in this natural setting. See Chapter 16.

✔ **High Sierra Camps:** Strung like jewels through the backcountry of Yosemite National Parks, these camps make venturing into the backcountry less daunting than it may seem to first-timers. There's no need to carry a tent, because the camps offer tent-cabins for shelter, and no need to carry food, because the on-site chef feeds hikers as if they were kings. See Chapter 17.

✔ **Kolob Canyon:** Located in the northwestern corner of Zion National Park, this canyon leads to Kolob Arch, which, with a 310-foot span, just may be the world's longest freestanding arch. Along the way, the trail passes a number of backcountry campsites and La Verkin Creek. See Chapter 18.

The Best Lodges to Check Into

There are lodges, and then there are *lodges!* Not all national park lodges were created equally. Here are my top picks:

✔ **Furnace Creek Inn:** Nestled on a hillside amid a sprawling grove of palm trees, this Mission-style inn has an almost palatial feel to it. While the rest of Death Valley National Park sizzles in the summer heat, this inn bakes in atmosphere. I've been tempted to spend my Death Valley visit pool-side surrounded by the inn's gardens. See Chapter 10.

✔ **El Tovar Hotel:** This historic hotel on the South Rim of the Grand Canyon coddles its guests with elegant rooms, a private sitting room that provides privacy from unregistered guests, innovative cuisine, and a staff that's always ready to pamper you. See Chapter 11.

✔ **Jenny Lake Lodge:** Surrounded by an evergreen forest in the afternoon shadow of the Grand Teton, this lakeside lodge with its accompanying cabins is a perfect romantic retreat. Although rustic in appearance, the lodge, its cabins, and their furnishings provide a wonderfully relaxing and comfortable retreat after a day in the park. See Chapter 12.

✔ **Old Faithful Inn:** The patriarch of what I like to call the "stately national park inn," this oversized log cabin in the heart of Yellowstone is infused with atmosphere, stories, and charm. Sure, some of the rooms require that you use communal bathrooms down the hall, but all give you the impression that you're staying someplace special. And with the Upper Geyser Basin out your window, you are. See Chapter 16.

✔ **The Ahwahnee Hotel:** Queens, presidents, and Hollywood elite have stayed in this striking lodge in Yosemite, and for good reason. You won't find a finer accommodation in the national park system. This hotel is pricy, but if you can afford it, you won't regret staying here. See Chapter 17.

The Best Park Dining Rooms

Just because you're in the wilderness, you don't need to go hungry. In fact, meals at some park restaurants will require you to take a hike to keep off the pounds. Some of my favorites:

- ✓ **The Arizona Room:** A short stroll from the edge of the Grand Canyon's South Rim, this dining room doesn't take reservations. Instead, your name goes on a list and when a table opens they call your name. Trust me, the wait is worth it, particularly when you time things perfectly and the sun is setting on the canyon. See Chapter 11.

- ✓ **Paradise Inn:** Perhaps it's the location on the flanks of Mount Rainier, or maybe the fact that a day spent hiking really hones the appetite, but I've never had a bad meal in the inn's historic dining room. The food, which tends to the hearty side, comes in large, tasty portions. See Chapter 13.

- ✓ **Lake Crescent Lodge:** My youngest son discovered the palette-pleasing joy of crab cakes during our stay in Olympic National Park, and the ahi tuna main course wasn't bad, either. The beautiful lake-front setting, the elegant dining room, attentive staff, and sumptuous menu that features some of the freshest seafood in the park system all combine to make this one of my favorite park restaurants. See Chapter 14.

- ✓ **Lake Hotel:** On the shore of Yellowstone Lake, this colonial-style hotel boasts a restaurant that's not only Yellowstone's best, but also one of the best in the whole national park system. The view of the shimmering lake through the dining room's windows doesn't hurt, of course, but the creative menu and the meals' preparation are the main attractions. See Chapter 16.

- ✓ **The Ahwahnee Hotel:** You don't have to be a hotel guest to eat in the elegant dining room here, and I strongly recommend you dine here at least once, to enjoy both the food and the ambience. The dining room pulls out all the stops at year's end during the annual Bracebridge Dinners that recreate an Olde English Christmas feast that is part pagentry and part culinary extravaganza. See Chapter 17.

The Best Winter Escapes in the Parks

Parks are open year-round, although many are most crowded in the summer months. If your schedule allows, be daring and schedule a winter visit. Here are some great winter activities to pursue:

- ✓ **Storm watching:** When storms roll in from the Pacific Ocean, they send humongous waves crashing into the seastacks that tower off the shore of Rialto Beach in Olympic National Park. Some people schedule their winter weekends around this incredible display of nature's forces. See Chapter 14.

✔ **Cross-country skiing:** Many national parks offer cross-country skiing come winter, but Sequoia has gigantic trees to go along with it. Kicking and gliding beneath these cinnamon-hued behemoths is the experience of a lifetime. See Chapter 15.

✔ **Wildlife watching:** When winter arrives in Yellowstone, it forces the animals out of the high country and down to the river valleys, making them much more accessible than during the summer months. The Lamar Valley is home to several wolf packs, thousands of elk, and hundreds of bison during the winter months. Snowshoeing in the park takes on added excitement when you spy a set of wolf tracks on the trail. See Chapter 16.

✔ **Snowshoeing:** The West's national parks offer endless snowshoeing opportunites. Trails are marked and rentals are available in: Grand Teton, Mount Rainier, Sequoia, Yellowstone, and Yosemite. The solitude you'll enjoy while snowshoeing down a trail, and the discoveries you'll make, are unforgettable. See Chapters 12, 13, and 15 through 17.

The Best Family Activities in the Parks

National parks are perfect for family vacations, because they offer activities for all ages. Here are some of the possibilities:

✔ **Climb a mountain:** Climbing can be a great family bonding adventure if you and your teens love the outdoors. Climbing schools at Grand Teton, Mount Rainer, and Yosemite national parks can help you conquer summits. See Chapters 12, 13, and 17.

✔ **Go for a float:** Rivers run wild through a lot of the parks, and you can find many rafting companies ready to turn you into white-water cowboys. Although the Grand Canyon is particularly renowned for its white-water raft trips, other possibilities exist in and around Arches, Grand Teton, Olympic, and Sequoia/Kings Canyon national parks. See Chapters 9, 11, 12, 14, and 15.

✔ **Lodging and learning:** The concessionaire at Yellowstone National Park offers a nice variety of "lodging and learning" programs that combine accommodations and meals with interpretive programs ranging from cross-country skiing and wolf watching in winter to family-specific summer programs that include painting, photography, animal tracking, and hiking. See Chapter 16.

✔ **Saddle up:** Horseback rides can be found in Grand Canyon, Grand Teton, Yellowstone, Yosemite, and Zion national parks. Grand Canyon, of course, also offers its famous mule rides into the canyon. See Chapters 11, 12, and 16 through 18.

Chapter 2

Digging Deeper into the National Parks of the American West

- -

In This Chapter

▶ Introducing the history and culture of the western parks
▶ Discovering the parks' most intriguing man-made attractions

- -

*A*ll parks aren't created equal. You see, the movement to create national parks didn't begin until most of the eastern half of the country was thoroughly tamed, settled, and politically subdivided. As a result, the eastern parks are rich in America's cultural history — you know, George Washington slept here, there, and over there.

The western parks, on the other hand, preserve the country's magnificent and spectacular wild side. That's not to say that western parks don't recount pages of cultural history. In fact, at Yellowstone's Albright Visitor Center you can learn about 19th century painter Thomas Moran, whose sketches and paintings of the region helped sway Congress to make Yellowstone the country's (and the world's!) first national park. At Yosemite, the Ansel Adams Gallery traces the career of the world-famous landscape photographer.

The individual park chapters focus heavily on enjoying the outdoors and the natural wonders of the western parks, so in this chapter, I give you a closer look at their history and culture.

Arches National Park

Not too surprisingly, considering its eye-catching vistas, this national park actually played a role in the environmental movement. Before the late **Edward Abbey** became an outspoken proponent for wilderness, and a bestselling author of such books as *Desert Solitaire* and *The Monkey Wrench Gang,* he was a seasonal ranger at what was then known as Arches National Monument.

Although not many have left their mark in this rugged area, a few intrepid **Ute Indians** and **pioneers** have spent time here. Just off the Delicate Arch Trail is a **Ute petroglyph panel** that includes etchings of horses and bighorn sheep. Also, near the beginning of the trail is **Wolfe Ranch.** Disabled Civil War veteran John Wesley Wolfe and his son Fred moved here from Ohio in 1898, and in 1907 John's daughter Flora, her husband, and their two children joined them. They left in 1910, after which John's cabin was destroyed by a flash flood. The cabin used by Flora's family survived and has been preserved by the Park Service. You'll see the cabin, a root cellar, and a corral.

Death Valley National Park

Americans looking for gold in California's mountains in 1849 got lost in the parched desert here trying to avoid the severe snowstorms in the nearby Sierra Nevada. One person perished along the way, and the land became known as Death Valley. In 1925, 76 years after the Forty-niners' harrowing experiences, tourism came to Death Valley. It would have begun sooner, had the valley not been consumed by lucrative **borax mining** since the late 1880s.

In one of his last official acts, **President Herbert Hoover** declared Death Valley a national monument in February 1933. With the stroke of a pen he not only authorized the protection of a vast and wondrous land, but also helped to transform one of the earth's least hospitable spots into a popular tourist destination.

In 1994, when **President Clinton** signed the **California Desert Protection Act,** Death Valley National Park became the largest national park outside Alaska, with more than 3.3 million acres.

In 2000, Congress passed a bill that returned 7,000 acres (including about 300 in the Furnace Creek area) in and around the park to the **Timbisha Shoshone,** an American Indian tribe that inhabited the area for thousands of years before the area became a national monument. This was the first time that a tribal homeland has been established within the boundaries of a national park, and nearly 50 tribal members now live in the valley year-round. The bill banned casinos, but the future of the Timbisha Shoshone's homeland may include a cultural center, lodging, and homes for tribal members. For up-to-date information, contact the Timbisha Shoshone Tribe at ☎ 760-786-2374.

 Scotty's Castle, the Mediterranean hacienda in the northern part of the park, is undeniably Death Valley's premier attraction. The elaborate Spanish tiles, well-crafted furnishings, and innovative construction with ahead-of-its-time solar water heating all wow visitors. Even more compelling is the colorful history of this villa in remote **Grapevine Canyon,** which is brought to life by park rangers in 1930s clothing.

Grand Canyon National Park

A number of different **Native American tribes** have lived in or around the canyon, and the Navajo, Havasupai, Kaibab Paiute, Hopi, Zuni, and Hualapai tribes still dwell in this area. Their predecessors left behind more than 3,000 **archaeological sites** and **artifacts** — some are 10,000 years old.

In the 1500s, **Spanish missionaries** and gold-greedy **explorers** passed through the area, but it wasn't until the 1800s that white people began settling here. **Prospectors** clambered through the canyon in search of precious minerals, and some of them stayed after their mines, plagued by high overhead costs, shut down. The first **tourists** followed, and began flooding the area after the railroad linked Grand Canyon Village to Williams, Arizona, in 1901.

Theodore Roosevelt used the **Antiquities Act** to declare Grand Canyon a national monument in 1908. Congress established Grand Canyon National Park in 1919.

Most of the historic buildings on the South Rim are concentrated in **Grand Canyon Village,** a National Historic District. **Hermits Rest,** on Hermits Rest Route, and **The Watchtower,** on the Desert View Drive, are also of historical significance.

Mary Colter, a Minneapolis schoolteacher who began decorating the shops that sold American Indian art along the Santa Fe Railroad line in 1902, designed more than a half dozen of these historic buildings. As both a decorator and a self-trained architect, Colter later designed these Grand Canyon landmarks: **Hopi House** (1905), **The Lookout** (1914), **Hermits Rest** (1914), **Phantom Ranch** (1922), **Watchtower** (1932), and **Bright Angel Lodge** (1935). Colter's work drew heavily on the architectural styles of Native Americans and Spanish settlers in the Southwest. **Charles Whittlesey** designed another historic building, the **El Tovar Hotel** (1905), in a style reminiscent of a northern European hunting lodge. On the North Rim, **Grand Canyon Lodge,** built in 1928, is on the National Register of Historic Places.

Grand Teton National Park

The first **homesteaders** began arriving in the area in the 1880s. Many discovered, though, that the frigid winters and short growing season made it difficult — indeed, virtually impossible — to eke out a living, so they abandoned the area. By 1907, cattle ranchers discovered that wealthy Eastern hunters were attracted to the area as a vacation site, and the **dude-ranching industry** secured its first foothold in **Jackson Hole,** the great valley that runs the length of the Tetons on the east side.

When cattle interests learned of a movement to convert privately owned grazing land on the valley floor into a national park, a rancorous tug-of-war began. Congress had designated the area south of Yellowstone National Park the Teton Forest Reserve in 1897 and attempted to create a larger sanctuary in 1918; however, local opposition defeated the measure. In 1923, a more well-reasoned and successful attempt was made to preserve the area for future generations when **Maud Noble,** a conservation-minded entrepreneur, and a group of other concerned locals, aided by **Yellowstone Superintendent Horace Albright,** prepared a plan for setting aside a portion of the Jackson Hole as a national recreation area. Congress first set aside 96,000 acres of mountains and forests (excluding Jackson Lake) as a national park in 1929.

John D. Rockefeller Jr. got into the act by establishing the **Snake River Land Company,** which became the vehicle through which he anonymously accumulated more than 35,000 acres of land between 1927 and 1943. His goal was to donate the property for an enlarged park, but opponents in Congress prevented the government from accepting his gift.

Finally, in 1950, the Feds and the locals reached a compromise: The government agreed to reimburse Teton County for revenue that would have been generated by property taxes, and to honor existing leaseholds, and present-day Grand Teton National Park was born.

Mount Rainier National Park

Although most of the mountains in the West were seen as obstacles by the early pioneers, Mount Rainier so captivated early settlers that as early as the 1850s, less than a decade after Seattle was founded, aspiring mountaineers were heading for its snowcapped slopes. In 1857, an army lieutenant, **August Valentine Kautz,** climbed to within 400 feet of the summit; and in 1870, **General Hazard Stevens** and **Philemon Van Trump** made the first recorded complete ascent of the mountain (trapped near the summit at dark, they survived the night huddled in ice caves formed by sulfurous steam vents, with the steam providing enough heat to keep them from freezing to death). In 1884, **James and Virinda Longmire** opened the mountain's first hotel. In 1899, Mount Rainier became the nation's fifth national park, and by 1916, the trail system now known as the **Wonderland Trail** was completed, forming a loop nearly 100 miles long around the mountain.

Mount Rainier lies toward the southern end of the Washington Cascades. Here, the crags of the North Cascades are replaced by a volcanic landscape of rolling hills punctuated by Mount Rainier, Mount St. Helens, and to the east, Mount Adams and Goat Rocks. The Cascades aren't dead, they're just sleeping, a fact driven home by the eruption of Mount St. Helens on May 18, 1980. Though Mt. Rainier's volcanic peak hasn't erupted for more than 150 years, it could erupt again at any time.

Olympic National Park

Despite its inherent ruggedness, raininess, and mysterious nature, the interior of Olympic National Park began yielding its secrets in the mid- to late-1800s. Unbridled curiosity and the inevitable desire for timber, minerals, and tourism dollars played a part in its exploration. Westward-moving **pioneers** had established homesteads on the peripheries of the peninsula as early as the mid-1800s. However, the first documented exploration of the interior didn't occur until 1885, and then it was no easy feat. It took one group of **explorers** a grueling month of hacking through dense brush to get from Port Angeles to Hurricane Ridge. Today, it takes approximately 45 minutes by car.

On the advice of these adventuresome explorers, Congress declared most of the peninsula a national forest. Then, in 1909, just before leaving office, **President Theodore Roosevelt**, an avid hunter, established Mount Olympus National Monument, in order to preserve the summer range and breeding grounds of dwindling herds of Roosevelt elk (flatter-ingly named for the president himself in a brilliant piece of prelegislative public relations). In 1938, **President Franklin Roosevelt** turned the national monument into a national park, and in 1953, the coastal strip was added. Finally, in 1981, the park was declared a **World Heritage Site.**

Sequoia and Kings Canyon National Parks

These parks owe their existence to a small band of determined mid–nineteenth century **conservationists.** Alarmed by the wholesale destruction of the region's **sequoia forests,** these farsighted people pushed to make the area a protected park. Finally, Sequoia National Park was created in 1890, along with the tiny General Grant National Park, which was established to protect **Grant Grove.** In 1926, the park was expanded eastward to include the smaller **Kern Canyon** and Mount Whitney, and in the 1960s Kings Canyon was finally protected. In 1978, **Mineral King** was added to Sequoia's half of the park.

Yellowstone National Park

Yellowstone National Park was officially created in 1872, when **President Ulysses Grant** signed legislation making it the first national park in the world. In the years afterward, it suffered from incompetent superintend-ents and shortages of cash until at last, in 1886, the U.S. Army took pos-session and helped limit poaching and establish a sense of order. In 1916, control of the park was transferred to the newly created **National Park Service.** Yellowstone became one of the first parks to come under its stewardship.

For trivia fans: French trappers named the **Yellowstone River** for its yel-lowish banks much farther north in Montana.

Yosemite National Park

Yosemite Valley, where 95 percent of park visitors head (more than four million people a year), is just a small sliver of the park, but it holds the bulk of the region's jaw-dropping features. This is the place of record-setting statistics: the **highest waterfall** in North America and three of the highest in the world (Upper Yosemite, Sentinel, and Ribbon falls), the biggest and tallest piece of exposed granite (**El Capitan**), and stands of **Giant Sequoia.**

Conservationist **John Muir** found much of his inspiration to fight for nature in Yosemite's vistas. Yet because of its beauty, recent years have brought disquieting turmoil to this wilderness haven, with increasing traffic, litter, and noise. It seems that, in many ways, Yosemite is being loved to death. But the National Park Service has implemented a transportation plan aimed at getting visitors out of their cars. They're working to reduce human impact on the Yosemite Valley by, among other things, removing asphalt and concrete, and we can already see improvements. Yosemite has also seen changes due to Mother Nature. In recent years, floods and rockslides have slightly altered the face of the valley, destroying campgrounds and some trails.

Zion National Park

Today, 150 years after the Mormon settler **Isaac Behunin** named his homestead here **Little Zion,** the park still casts a spell as you gaze upon the sheer multicolored walls of sandstone, explore narrow canyons, hunt for hanging gardens of wildflowers, and listen to the roar of the churning, tumbling **Virgin River.** The park means different things to different people: a day hike down a narrow canyon, a rough climb up the face of a massive stone monument, the red glow of sunset over majestic peaks.

Millions of years ago, a **shallow sea** covered the sand dunes here. Minerals from the sea (including lime from the shells of sea creatures) cemented sand particles together to form sandstone. Later, movements in the earth's crust lifted the land, draining away the sea but leaving rivers that gradually carved the soft sandstone into the spectacular shapes we see today.

Chapter 3

Deciding Where and When to Go

- -

In This Chapter

▶ Asking yourself what you want from your vacation
▶ Getting to know the national parks
▶ Choosing your season
▶ Looping through more than one park

- -

*H*ow do you decide which park to visit? In this chapter, I help you figure out which park is best for you by asking a few questions to pinpoint your likes, dislikes, and vacation goals. Then I give you a run-down of each park's strong points — and drawbacks. Of course, if you're like me, one park just isn't enough. So at the end of the chapter, I recommend a few loops that can get you to more than one.

Deciding What You Want from a National Park

Okay, now you get to answer some questions. Truthfully. If you take a little time to consider your preferences and options, you can identify exactly how, and where, to spend your perfect national park vacation.

Are you looking for an **active vacation,** one that works your body by climbing mountains, rafting rivers, hiking through forests, or kayaking in an ocean? Outfitters at Grand Teton National Park and Mount Rainier National Park offer mountaineering classes that might culminate in a climb. At Yellowstone National Park, you can find three wonderful lakes waiting for you to explore from a canoe or sea kayak. A great way to see the Grand Canyon is aboard a raft during a wet and wild trip down the Colorado River. And in just about any national park, you can plan a weeklong backpacking trip into the woods.

Do you want a **relaxing trip** rather than a workout? At Olympic National Park, you can rent a cabin along Lake Crescent and do nothing but enjoy the view or head over to Sol Duc Hot Springs Resort for a refreshing soak in the warm waters. Death Valley serves as a wonderful midwinter retreat, one where you can relax in a grove of palm trees with a good book, interrupted only by a dip in the pool. Sequoia National Park offers towering stands of trees with gentle paths winding below them.

Do you want an **educational getaway,** where you can delve into America's cultural or military heritage? Yosemite National Park offers a wonderful glimpse into the valley's cultural past through a pioneer cemetery and a living history exhibit on the Ahwahneeche, a tribe that at one time inhabited the Yosemite Valley. At Zion National Park, you can learn about the Civilian Conservation Corps that helped build trails and roads in some of the park. For more information on educational programs or research opportunities at the parks featured in this book, see Chapter 7.

 Are you looking for the best place for a **family vacation** that doesn't break the bank? I can't think of a park that isn't a wonderful experience for kids of all ages. See Chapter 7 for my park recommendations and for tips on traveling with families.

Do you need to plan a **wheelchair-accessible trip?** Would you or anyone in your group have a difficult time roaming through Olympic National Park's Hoh Rain Forest? Then see Chapter 7 for my park recommendations and tips for travelers with special needs.

Flipping Through Park Snapshots

Knowing that America's national park system comes pretty darn close to offering something for everyone doesn't make choosing which park to visit any easier. So, in this section, I provide a few snapshots of my favorite western parks. Breeze through these 30-second previews to get a feel for each park — both what's good and not so good.

Arches National Park (Utah)

In a state with five national parks, visitors often debate their favorites. Mine is Arches. No greater collection of rock arches exists on Earth. You can find big arches, tiny arches, arches about to give way to gravity, and arches under construction. You can also see classic redrock vistas. In late afternoon, the landscape seems to catch fire in the sweeping rays of the setting sun.

Thanks to southern Utah's relatively mild winters, Arches is a true four-season park. Although summer draws the biggest crowds, you may opt for one of the other, more temperature-friendly, seasons. Come in late fall or anytime in the winter, and you're likely to have most of the park to yourself.

 Arches is also kid-friendly. Youngsters stay happy for hours by climbing up into rock windows or playing in vast sandboxes created by sandstone erosion.

Park pros

- ✔ Visit Arches to see fantastic rock formations.

- ✔ Find more rock arches than anywhere else on Earth.

- ✔ You can see the park's highlights in one day.

Park cons

- ✔ The park can be brutally hot in summer.

- ✔ Arches has no in-park lodging and only one (relatively small) campground.

- ✔ Restaurants and accommodations in nearby Moab can be pricey.

Death Valley National Park (California/Nevada)

The hottest place in the Western Hemisphere is Death Valley National Park, but the beauty of this desert playground is that the heat isn't intolerable 365 days of the year. You can visit in summer if you think that enduring the heat is like some red badge of courage (which it literally will be, if you forget your sunblock). Or come in the winter months (November through March) when temperatures are comfortable enough for you to spend all day exploring the park and its otherworldly landscape.

If you enjoy stately national park lodges, book a room (if you can afford the rate) at the Furnace Creek Inn. This Death Valley resort is truly an elegant desert oasis complete with palm groves and a watering hole, which happens to be a wonderful swimming pool. Western history lives on in Scotty's Castle, a shrine to a once-upon-a-time cowboy who proved that living off someone else's largesse is easier than working for your own. (For the story on Scott's ill-gotten gains, see Chapter 10.)

Kids enjoy this park. They can play in its sand dunes, search for desert pupfish, or avoid the heat in a swimming pool.

Park pros

- ✔ Death Valley contains the Western Hemisphere's lowest spot.

- ✔ The stark, otherworldly landscape is intriguing.

- ✔ The valley becomes delightful when winter rains produce wild-flower blooms.

Park cons

- ✔ In summer, the park is as hot as the proverbial firecracker.

- ✔ The valley offers few accommodations.

- ✔ The landscape is dry and dusty.

Grand Canyon National Park (Arizona)

Stand on either side of the enormous Grand Canyon and the landscape unfolds in dramatic layers. Explore the canyon's floor and discover towering waterfalls that nourish hanging gardens.

Although the focus of this park is its strikingly beautiful geography, the Grand Canyon offers more than just opportunities to gape. You find mule rides, raft trips, hiking paths, and, of course, gorgeous views galore. The two rims of the canyon have distinct personalities, too. The higher North Rim (with an average elevation of 8,000 feet) is cooler, less crowded, and more remote than the more popular South Rim, which features more tourist facilities, easier access, and a longer season.

Park pros

- ✔ Encounter dramatic vistas of one of the world's most startling landscapes.

- ✔ The canyon floor is wet and wild, thanks to the rollicking Colorado River.

- ✔ Numerous activities test your limits above and below the Grand Canyon's rim.

Park cons

- ✔ The canyon bottom turns into a convection oven in midsummer.

- ✔ Getting from one rim to the other rim is a long, inconvenient process.

- ✔ The South Rim is very crowded in July and August.

Grand Teton National Park (Wyoming)

America's Matterhorn towers over the national park that anchors Wyoming's western border. If you're looking for wildlife, come to Grand Teton. Drive (or float) through this park and you encounter moose, bison, elk, antelope, and the occasional black bear. If you hike into the backcountry, you may even see a grizzly bear. Plus, bald eagles and osprey perch in the trees, otters frolic in the waters of the Snake River, and wolves (that have migrated down from Yellowstone National Park) lope through the park.

But the park features more than just wildlife. You also find world-class mountain climbing in the Tetons, numerous boating opportunities (such as power boats on Jackson Lake and drift boats, rafts, kayaks, and canoes on Snake River and other lakes), and a portal into the Old West. The Tetons' craggy, snow-capped peaks reflect the rising and setting suns. Lakes cupped at the bottom of mountains mirror the peaks, and the Snake River makes picturesque oxbow bends. You definitely won't have to work hard to compose your photographs at Grand Teton.

The nearby town of Jackson isn't officially part of the park, but it unquestionably hangs its hat on the Tetons. If you ever grow weary of the park's natural resources, head to town for a slice of the Old West.

Park pros

- ✔ Grand Teton is wildlife central.

- ✔ Mountain climbers can scale the purple mountains' majesty.

- ✔ You can paddle along alpine lakes and explore rivers with world-class trout fisheries.

Park cons

- ✔ Winter can be grueling in terms of the weather and a lack of things to do if you don't like snow.

- ✔ If you stay in Jackson, driving back and forth to the park eats up time and puts a lot of miles on your rig.

- ✔ Flat-landers may need a day or two to acclimate to the elevation.

Mount Rainier National Park (Washington)

You never really lose sight of the snow-capped volcano during your visit at Mount Rainer. Rising to 14,410 feet, the mountain *is* the park; everything revolves around it, from the hiking trails and the glaciers to the lodges, which offer wonderful views of the peak. If you like to hike, this park is made for you. You can work your way around the base of the mountain on the Wonderland Trail or take shorter hikes to glacial snouts, lookout towers, and even the snowy summit.

Highlights of the southern flank include Paradise (the site of the atmospheric Paradise Inn), an extensive visitor center, and a resident glacier. Not to be overlooked is Sunrise on the mountain's eastern slopes, a hub of hiking activity and the highest point on the mountain that can be reached by car.

The lack of park roads makes navigation difficult, especially if you need to travel from Point A to Point B. In any case, the myriad of intriguing spots discourage a windshield tour of Mount Rainier —stop your car so you can get out and look around.

Park pros

- ✔ More than 20 glaciers cover Mount Rainer.

- ✔ You can hike trails through dense forests and wildflower meadows.

- ✔ The beautiful and historic Paradise Inn is a great lodging option.

Park cons

- ✔ Winters can be incredibly cold, restricting the park to the heartiest travelers.

- ✔ Busy summer weekends, which draw throngs from nearby Seattle and Tacoma, can make Paradise hard to reach.

- ✔ A lack of roads makes navigating the mountain difficult and time consuming.

Olympic National Park (Washington)

Where else can you interrupt a seaside vacation for an afternoon trip to a snowfield? Or end a rainforest hike with a dip in a swimming pool fed by hot springs? Talk about a park with diversity!

Olympic National Park is a real crowd pleaser. At this park, you can ski, hike, boat, fish, and comb the beach or explore hot springs, waterfalls, and dense rainforests. If you're lucky (and a bit persistent), you can spot a wealth of wildlife, such as Roosevelt elk, deer, sea otters, seals, sea lions, black bears, eagles, and osprey. And don't forget the huge, slimy banana slugs that crawl through the Hoh Rain Forest.

Although road access is limited, Olympic offers enough interesting nooks that you don't need to travel all over the park to stay busy (or amazed).

Park pros

- ✔ Olympic is a three-in-one park with seashore, rainforest, and glaciers.

- ✔ Impressive *sea stacks* (cool rock outcrops) rise above offshore waves.

- ✔ Great hiking possibilities abound.

Park cons

- ✔ Foggy, wet weather can dampen a park vacation.

- ✔ In-park lodging is very limited.

- ✔ Winter rains can shut down trails and roads.

Sequoia/Kings Canyon National Parks (California)

Although these two parks are joined at the waist like Siamese twins and share a common administration, they have distinctly different personalities. Most folks are familiar only with Sequoia and its famous trees; as a result, Kings Canyon National Park is wonderfully uncrowded.

Wilderness lovers can roam spacious Kings Canyon, a ruggedly beautiful and thoughtfully underdeveloped park. Its off-the-beaten path location encourages back-to-earth vacations and discourages rampant commercialism. You may huff and puff your way into its high backcountry, but after you get there, you can cruise the High Sierra terrain in near solitude.

Although Sequoia isn't overdeveloped, if you visit the protected tall trees, you'll have plenty of company. Happily, this limits human intrusion on the park's backcountry — a fact that benefits the environment and means you can enjoy the scenery with a dose of solitude.

Park pros

- ✔ Astonishingly big trees fill Sequoia.
- ✔ The beautiful High Sierra landscape dazzles visitors who make the effort to trek into the backcountry.
- ✔ Kings Canyon is an uncrowded beauty.

Park cons

- ✔ Kings Canyon is hard to get to during the summer months and is closed to vehicular traffic during the winter months.
- ✔ Both parks have limited lodging options.
- ✔ The parks don't have eastern entrances.

Yellowstone National Park (Wyoming/Idaho/Montana)

Long considered the crown jewel of the national park system, Yellowstone definitely deserves the label. In 1872, this 2.2-million-acre preserve became the world's first national park and jumpstarted the national parks movement not only in America but also around the globe.

Thermal features (such as geysers), the Grand Canyon of the Yellowstone, and Yellowstone Lake are just some of the park's awe-inspiring highlights. The rustic charm of the Old Faithful Inn never fails to please. And I haven't even mentioned the park's wild kingdom — the most complete animal habitat in the United States. Yellowstone has been referred to as North America's Serengeti because of its diverse wildlife population, including elk, bison, moose, grizzly, black bears, wolves, mountain lions, and bald eagles. Had you visited Yellowstone in 1750, you would have found the same wildlife species that live in the park today.

The park also boasts diverse lodging options. You can pamper yourself with a stay at the charming Lake Yellowstone Hotel, go low budget in one of the bare-bones cabins surrounding Roosevelt Lodge, or hoist your house on your back and head off into the forest.

Park pros

- ✔ The world's first national park, Yellowstone is a leader in the national parks movement.

- ✔ Yellowstone features the world's largest collection of geysers, hot springs, and *fumaroles* (holes leaking volcanic vapors).

- ✔ This wild kingdom is crawling with wolves, grizzlies, bison, moose, elk, and more.

Park cons

- ✔ Some park cabins are horribly run down.

- ✔ Stretches of the Grand Loop road network are woefully dilapidated.

- ✔ Crowds descend in summer.

Yosemite National Park (California)

Ansel Adams made a career of photographing the waterfalls, forests, and granite outcrops of Yosemite National Park. You probably can't duplicate his work, but you can enjoy the park's wonders as much as he did.

The great natural scenery alone captivates young ones, and Merced River is the perfect place to float on a hot summer day for kids of all ages. Staying in one of the park's canvas tent cabins is a real kid-pleaser, too.

The park's collection of hiking trails has only one downfall: You're so busy staring at the surrounding landscape that you risk losing your footing.

Park pros

- ✔ Cliffs, domes, and waterfalls make for outstanding scenery.

- ✔ The Ahwahnee Hotel is arguably the park system's most beautiful lodge.

- ✔ Great backcountry trails allow for solitude.

Park cons

- ✔ The Yosemite Valley floor can be crowded during summer months.

- ✔ Summer's end and low rainfall greatly temper the fury of the park's waterfalls.

- ✔ You need to plan far ahead to land a room in the more-popular lodges.

Zion National Park (Utah)

Five national parks are crammed into southern Utah, and Zion is the kingpin of them all. Oh, Canyonlands may be more rugged, Arches more sculpted, Bryce Canyon home to more *hoodoos* (a cool rock outcrop), and Capitol Reef more sprawling, but Zion is the patriarch — and not just because it's the oldest.

The towering canyon walls that surround you as you drive down into and ride through Zion Canyon are simultaneously awesome and humbling. A hike along The Narrows is a trek that you may never forget. Few other parks offer water-filled riverbeds for hiking trails, and I can't think of another park that features a 16-mile-long hike through a slot canyon that in places is 2,000 feet deep. Other hikes, short and long, lead to hanging gardens in secluded grottos or peaks overlooking the valley. Zion has many wonders.

Park pros

- ✔ Redrock scenery dazzles the eye.
- ✔ The mild winters of southwestern Utah make this park a four-season wonder.
- ✔ You can hike amid incredible slot canyons and towering cliffs.

Park cons

- ✔ The park offers limited in-park lodging.
- ✔ Hot, dry summer weather discourages exploration.
- ✔ Navigating the entire park is tough due to its sprawling terrain and relative lack of roads.

When to Go

Most families' hands are tied when it comes to deciding the right time to take a vacation — they usually go in summer because school is out. But I don't want to discourage summer vacations; in fact, most parks are fabulous in the summertime. (Death Valley is an exception. Although the park is truly interesting, you won't appreciate it in mid-August when the temperature is 120 degrees or more.) However, summer does bring the most crowds, the highest lodging rates (except in Death Valley), and the most difficult-to-find accommodations. But I can tell you how to work around these woes.

To get a room at one of the more-popular lodges in summer, reserve at least three to four months in advance of your trip — six months is even better. By booking way ahead of time, you'll usually be able to choose among the best.

In summer, you can avoid the worst crowds by refusing to move with the pack. Many park visitors like to sleep until around 8 a.m. and then enjoy a leisurely breakfast before beginning to explore around 10 a.m. If you rise soon after the sun and take off by 7 a.m., you can enjoy a few hours of solitude. This plan works on the other end of the day, too. Because most people return to their rooms around 5 p.m., if you schedule a late dinner, you can enjoy relatively peaceful visits to the places you didn't see in the morning.

If you can travel any time during the year, seriously consider spring, fall, and even winter excursions.

Spring and fall are spectacular seasons in national parks. Spring is a time of renewal, a time when forests and meadows come colorfully to life. But for most parks, spring is also mud season; melting snows and spring rains make backcountry trails generally mucky and, in some cases, shut them down temporarily. (Exceptions are southwestern parks.) Still, temperatures aren't bad (aside from the occasional fluke snowstorm in some parts of the country) and crowds are minimal. In many parks, high-season rates don't kick in until Memorial Day, so spring trips benefit cost-conscious visitors. Fall is even better than spring: Crowds shrink, forests dip into their Technicolor wardrobe, temperatures are mild, and lodging rates decline.

If you get cold feet shuffling across your bedroom floor, standing outside in 20-below-zero temperatures in February waiting for Old Faithful to erupt may not be for you. But if you enjoy the season, winter can make for a peaceful escape thanks to the lack of crowds (except in Death Valley). Yosemite, best known for its waterfalls and majestic granite domes, is shamefully overlooked as a winter destination; you can find not only great cross-country skiing, but also a small downhill-ski area. Yellowstone is also a magical winter destination, a place where the Northern Lights occasionally dance in the night skies and where winter storms leave bison shrouded in ice and snow.

You don't need a full week to enjoy a national park getaway. You can experience a satisfying trip in just a few days, particularly if you go in the middle of the week when most park traffic is reduced.

Visiting More Than One Park

In some parts of the West, you can hit two or more national parks during one trip. To do this, you need to budget a little more time (and money) and perhaps be a little more punctual than usual. (I once hit four parks in one week, but that was overdoing it.) Some of the trips are obvious and easy, whereas others require the careful planning of a military assault. I give you several options.

Geysers and grands

Even the park service realizes that **Yellowstone** and **Grand Teton** national parks belong in the same trip. Why else would they charge you one fee that allows access to both places? And even though these two parks are next-door neighbors, you get two entirely different experiences. Grand Teton has a relaxed Western style with its rail fences, grazing cattle, and log cabins. Yellowstone contains so many animals that you may feel as if you're on a wildlife safari. (Many people debate whether Yellowstone is more famous for its wildlife or its geysers. After you visit the park, let me know what you think.)

Redrock wonders

Referred to as the Grand Circle, the parks certainly present a wide circle If you visit the **Grand Canyon** and Utah's five national parks — **Arches, Bryce Canyon, Canyonlands, Capitol Reef,** and **Zion** — in one swing. You can visit them all, but not thoroughly in less than two weeks. My suggestion is to cut the trip in half. Visit the Grand Canyon, Zion, Bryce, and Capitol Reef or the Grand Canyon, Canyonlands, and Arches. Whichever combination you choose, you can count on seeing lots of stunning, redrock landscapes.

I include Arches, Grand Canyon, and Zion in this book. For details on Bryce, Capitol Reef, and Canyonlands, you may want to pick up a copy of *Frommer's National Parks of the American West* (Wiley).

California or bust

California boasts more national parks — eight, in fact — than any other state in the Lower 48. But although these parks are contained within the same state border, you can't visit all of them — nor would you want to — in a single vacation. Death Valley may look close to Sequoia on a map, but a good seven-hour drive separates them (no roads cross the eastern ridge of the High Sierra).

On the plus side, **Sequoia** and **Kings Canyon** share a common border, so you can think of them as one park. And because only 200 miles separates Sequoia/Kings Canyon and **Yosemite**, tackling these three parks on one trip is very doable.

Accomplishing this California "three-step" can easily be done by flying into Fresno and renting a car. From there, your toughest decision is whether you want to visit Yosemite first, and then proceed to Sequoia/Kings Canyon, or vice versa. You'll have to backtrack through the Fresno area no matter which park you visit first. If traffic is light, the drive from the Yosemite Valley to Grant Grove in Kings Canyon takes about a half-day.

Washington two-step

A drive of about four hours separates **Olympic** and **Mount Rainier** national parks in Washington state, so you can reasonably hit these two in one trip. The contrast in landscapes — Olympic with its seacoast and rainforests and Mount Rainier with its snow-shrouded volcano — is incredible to see. The crowds provide another contrast; although Mount Rainier's visitors pack the park's main destinations and roads in summer, the crowds at Olympic are wonderfully dispersed.

Part II

Planning Your Trip to the National Parks of the American West

The 5th Wave   By Rich Tennant

THE HARRISONS PREPARE FOR THEIR MOUNTAIN BIKING VACATION IN SEATTLE'S OLYMPIC NATIONAL PARK.

Awesome move, Mom.

In this part . . .

*W*hoever said, "Getting there is half the fun" didn't have to stick to a budget. And because getting there can be expensive, this section not only contains helpful information on how to get to the park of your choice, but also points out ways to save money along the way. You find helpful tips on getting deals on airfares and car rentals, the ins and outs of escorted and packaged tours, and a primer on the types of accommodations you can expect to find. Curious about whether the kids will enjoy the trip? I'll share some insights on particularly "kid-friendly" parks. Travelers with special needs — senior citizens, disabled, gay and lesbian tourists — also will find helpful information in this section. Finally, I toss in odds and ends on everything from what to pack to how to survive (with a smile) your national park experience.

Chapter 4

Managing Your Money

- -

In This Chapter

▶ Traveling with cash
▶ Choosing a cash alternative
▶ What to do if your wallet is lost or stolen

- -

*I*n this chapter, we help you decide how much money — and in what form — you want to take with you. Plus, we go over an action plan in case you lose (or someone steals) your wallet. No one likes to think of such nightmares, but if you're prepared for the worst, you can survive any turn of events.

Planning Your Budget

A national park vacation doesn't have to be a budget-buster. Of course, the cost can climb quickly if you're the adventurous sort, one who wants to climb to the top of the Grand Teton, go on a two-week supported backcountry trek, or float down the Colorado River through the Grand Canyon. But you can go fairly barebones, too, with nights spent in a campground, meals cooked on a propane stove, and adventures limited to those you craft around hikes and browsing through museums.

Transportation

Unlike the East, the West is a wide-open sprawling place, one where it can take you a good bit of time to reach your chosen destination. As a result, unless you live near the national park of your choice, you'll probably find yourself mulling airline tickets and rental cars. I've included some pointers on conquering those aspects of your trip in Chapter 5. Also, within each individual park chapter you'll find specific directions on how to reach the park.

Lodging: Bunking inside or outside

The national parks offer several lodging options ranging from luxury digs to rustic campsites. A stay in **The Ahwahnee Hotel** in Yosemite is like a stay in a European palace, thanks to its cavernous and elegant dining and reading rooms (see Chapter 17). The **Lake Yellowstone Hotel** resembles a page out of the 1920s, with its Sun Room full of wicker furniture overlooking Yellowstone Lake and with the prim, white-shirted waitstaff in the dining room (see Chapter 16). The **El Tovar** in the Grand Canyon is like a hybrid between a Swiss chalet and a Norwegian villa (see Chapter 11). You can expect to pay $100, $200, or even $300 or more per night at these places.

If you're not looking for elegance, you can sleep in **rustic cabins** in Yellowstone and **canvas tent cabins** in Yosemite for $50 to $55 a night. For considerably less (from free up to about $20 a night), you can stay in one of the parks' developed campgrounds. An outstanding facility, Yosemite's **North Pines Campground** is located along the Merced River in an idyllic setting on the valley floor. Another notable spot is Grand Teton's **Jenny Lake Campground,** which boasts a forest setting near Jenny Lake with huge boulders and knockout views of the Tetons (see Chapter 12).

When booking your reservation, do so through the particular concessionaire that handles lodging in the park of your choice. If you simply turn to the Internet and search for lodging options in and around a national park you'll likely encounter some Web sites that charge fees for making a reservation. Call the concessionaire's reservations desk directly — I've provided their phone numbers in the appropriate chapters — and you won't encounter any hidden fees on top of your room rate.

For more details on accommodations, see Chapter 6.

Dining

I've a longstanding tradition that calls for a wonderful meal at the end of a backcountry adventure in a national park. No matter which park I'm in, I make it a point to spend my last night in a nice hotel eating a meal at a great restaurant. Although you may not associate great eats with national parks, they are there. Oh, sure, you can find fast-food grills and cafeterias in all the parks. But come on, you're on vacation, so treat yourself! Now, this can be spendy, particularly if you eat dinner at **The Ahwahnee Hotel** in Yosemite, where entrée prices quickly surpass $30. But land a table at the **Mountain Room** in Yosemite Lodge and you'll find an equally sumptuous meal for a lesser price, more in the mid-$20s.

The same can be said of all the national parks. For instance, while the **Lake Hotel** in Yellowstone offers the best meal at the highest price, meals at the **Old Faithful Inn**, the **Mammoth Hotel,** and the **Old Faithful Snow Lodge** are just as tasty but not as pricey. Visit the South Rim of the Grand Canyon and the steepest meal prices will be found in the **El Tovar** restaurant, although a less expensive, but tastefully filling meal can be found in the **Arizona Room.** When it comes to breakfast, restaurants in most parks offer hot-and-cold buffets, and these are the best deals you'll find when it comes to eating, with prices typically below $10 per adult and under $8 per child.

Saving Money: A Bargain at Twice the Price

My friends claim I think about money too much. If that means saving a buck when I can, I plead guilty. Maybe my thriftiness is why I love national parks. A national park vacation is one of the best entertainment bargains around. Where else can $10 or $20 get you — and everyone else in your car, truck, or motor home — admission to someplace fun not just for one day but an entire week? (Okay, Jersey may be free, but I said *fun*.)

A $20 fee covers the whole family's weeklong admission to **Yellowstone National Park,** where you can see the world's most magnificent collection of hot springs, geysers, and *fumaroles* (holes leaking volcanic vapors), or you can stand in Lamar Valley and watch hundreds of elk and bison mill about trying to protect their newborn calves from grizzlies and packs of wolves (see Chapter 16). The same $20 gets you into **Grand Teton National Park,** 50 miles to the south, where you can explore craggy peaks and the world-famous Oxbow Bend on the Snake River (see Chapter 12).

In **Olympic National Park,** a $10 entrance fee not only provides access to a temperate rainforest but also allows you to gaze at the Pacific Ocean from the park's pristine beaches (see Chapter 14). You can also drive up to Hurricane Ridge and look south at the snow-capped Olympic Mountains or gaze north into the Strait of Juan de Fuca.

For similarly low fees, you can experience **Grand Canyon National Park** ($20 per car), where you can gape at extraordinary views from the rim or floor of the canyon (see Chapter 11); **Death Valley National Park** ($10 per car), where you can stand on the lowest spot in the Western Hemisphere (see Chapter 10); or **Mount Rainier National Park** ($10 per car), which is dominated by a slumbering, snow-capped volcano and ringed with excellent hiking trails (see Chapter 13).

See what I mean about the parks being a bargain? And I haven't even touched on what you and your kids can discover in the parks' museums or on hikes and walks together — just some of the bonuses included in your admission fee.

If you turn into a regular parkie, you can whittle down the cost of admission through the purchase of an annual National Parks Pass for $50. The pass gets you into as many parks as you can jam into a one-year period. See Chapter 8 for more details.

Handling Money

You're the best judge of how much cash you feel comfortable carrying or what alternative form of currency is your favorite. That's not going to change much on your vacation. True, you'll probably be moving around more and incurring more expenses than you generally do (unless you happen to eat out every meal when you're at home), and you may let your mind slip into vacation gear and not be as vigilant about your safety as when you're in work mode. But, those factors aside, the only type of payment that won't be quite as available to you away from home is your personal checkbook.

Using ATMs and carrying cash

The easiest and best way to get cash away from home is from an ATM. The **Cirrus** (☎ 800-424-7787; www.mastercard.com) and **PLUS** (☎ 800-843-7587; www.visa.com) networks span the globe; look at the back of your bank card to see which network you're on, then call, check online, or look in the "Fast Facts" section at the end of each park chapter for ATM locations at your destination. Be sure you know your personal identification number (PIN) before you leave home and be sure to find out your daily withdrawal limit before you depart. Also keep in mind that many banks impose a fee every time your card is used at a different bank's ATM, and that fee can be higher for international transactions (up to $5 or more) than for domestic ones (where they're rarely more than $1.50). On top of this, the bank from which you withdraw cash may charge its own fee. To compare banks' ATM fees within the U.S., use www.bankrate.com. To find international withdrawal fees, ask your bank.

Charging ahead with credit cards

Credit cards are a safe way to carry money: They provide a convenient record of expenses, and generally offer relatively good exchange rates. You can also get cash advances using credit cards at banks or ATMs, provided you know your PIN. If you've forgotten yours, or didn't even know you had one, call the number on the back of your credit card and ask the bank to send it to you. It usually takes five to seven business days, though some banks will provide the number over the phone if you tell them your mother's maiden name or other personal information.

Toting traveler's checks

These days, traveler's checks are less necessary because most cities have 24-hour ATMs. However, since you will likely be charged an ATM withdrawal fee if the bank isn't your own, you may be better off with traveler's checks — provided that you don't mind showing identification every time you want to cash one.

You can get traveler's checks at almost any bank. **American Express** offers denominations of $20, $50, $100, $500, and (for cardholders only) $1,000. You'll pay a service charge ranging from 1 percent to 4 percent. You can also get American Express traveler's checks over the phone, call ☎ 800-221-7282. American Express gold and platinum cardholders who use this number are exempt from the 1 percent fee.

Visa (☎ 800-732-1322) offers traveler's checks at Citibank locations nationwide, and at several other banks. The service charge ranges between 1.5 and 2 percent; checks come in denominations of $20, $50,

$100, $500, and $1,000. AAA members can get Visa checks without a fee at most AAA offices or by calling ☎ **866-339-3378. MasterCard (☎ 800-223-9920**) also has traveler's checks.

If you choose to carry traveler's checks, be sure to keep a record of their serial numbers separate from your checks in the event that they're stolen or lost. You'll get a refund faster if you know the numbers.

Doting on debit cards

You can use a debit card with a major credit card logo anywhere that accepts the credit card. The difference is that the money comes directly out of your checking account. As long as you record all your debit-card purchases, just as you would check purchases, debit cards are a great way to go. You don't have to worry about carrying cash, and the receipts provide a convenient record of all your travel expenses.

Dealing with a Lost or Stolen Wallet

Be sure to contact your credit card companies the minute you discover your wallet has been lost or stolen, and file a report at the nearest police precinct. Your credit card company or insurer may require a police report number or record of the loss. Most credit card companies have an emergency toll-free number to call if your card is lost or stolen; they may be able to wire you a cash advance immediately or deliver an emergency credit card in a day or two. Call the following emergency numbers in the United States:

- ✔ **American Express ☎ 800-221-7282** (for cardholders and traveler's check holders)
- ✔ **MasterCard ☎ 800-307-7309** or 636-722-7111
- ✔ **Visa ☎ 800-847-2911** or 410-581-9994

For other credit cards, call the toll-free number directory at ☎ **800-555-1212.**

Although national parks are in most ways immune from big-city ills, occasionally thieves break into cars. You can save yourself some grief by not leaving any valuables in sight in your rig. If possible, park in a well-lit area close to pedestrian traffic areas, such as in front of visitor centers or lodges.

Finally, federal law restricts your liability for unauthorized charges. If your card is stolen and you immediately report the incident, you generally aren't required to pay more than $50. Fraud protection also includes debit cards. Check with your bank for the specific limits.

Chapter 5

Getting to the Parks and Getting Around

- -

In This Chapter

▶ Getting to a park on your own
▶ Using a travel agent
▶ Considering an organized tour

- -

iguring out how to plan your national park vacation is one of the toughest — and earliest — decisions you need to make about your trip. Only you can decide whether you want to make your own plans, let someone else call the shots, or devise a combination strategy.

You may want to make all your travel arrangements yourself, whether you're an independent soul or you're into spontaneity and don't pre-arrange anything outside of what's absolutely essential (like your flight). Whatever the reason, I've supplied some basic contact information to help you make the necessary arrangements. If you have a computer and any familiarity with the Web, you can arrange your own airline tickets, and car rental with surprisingly little hassle in amazingly short time. If you'd prefer to use the services of a travel agent, see "Consulting a Travel Agent" later in this chapter.

Flying to the Parks

Most parks, by their nature, are off the beaten path. But don't worry: None of them is very difficult to access. Even though Grand Teton National Park resides in sparsely populated Wyoming, it may be the country's most accessible park thanks to the Jackson Hole Airport, which is actually located *inside* the park's borders. Of the 11 parks described in this book, Arches and Death Valley national parks win the prize for being the farthest away from a major airport. Arches is 125 miles from the airport at Grand Junction, Colorado; Death Valley is 140 miles away from the Las Vegas Airport.

For information about which airport is closest to the park that interests you, see the "Getting There" section of each park's chapter.

Getting the best deal on your airfare

Competition among the major U.S. airlines is unlike that of any other industry. Every airline offers virtually the same product (basically, a coach seat is a coach seat is a . . .), yet prices may vary by hundreds of dollars.

Business travelers who need the flexibility to buy their tickets at the last minute and change their itineraries at a moment's notice — and who want to get home before the weekend — pay (or at least their companies pay) the premium rate, known as the *full fare*. But if you can book your ticket far in advance, stay over Saturday night, and are willing to travel midweek (Tuesday, Wednesday, or Thursday), you can qualify for the least expensive price — usually a fraction of the full fare. On most flights, even the shortest hops within the United States, the full fare is close to $1,000 or more, but a 7- or 14-day advance purchase ticket may cost less than half of that amount. Obviously, planning ahead pays.

The airlines also periodically hold sales, in which they lower the prices on their most popular routes. These fares have advance purchase requirements and date-of-travel restrictions, but you can't beat the prices. As you plan your vacation, keep your eyes open for these sales, which tend to take place in seasons of low travel volume. You almost never see a sale around the peak summer vacation months of July and August, or around Thanksgiving or Christmas, when many people fly, regardless of the fare they have to pay.

Consolidators, also known as bucket shops, are great sources for international tickets, although they usually can't beat the Internet on fares within North America. Start by looking in Sunday newspaper travel sections; U.S. travelers should focus on the *New York Times, Los Angeles Times,* and *Miami Herald.* For less-developed destinations, small travel agents who cater to immigrant communities in large cities often have the best deals.

Bucket shop tickets are usually nonrefundable or rigged with stiff cancellation penalties, often as high as 50 to 75 percent of the ticket price, and some put you on charter airlines with questionable safety records.

FlyCheap (☎ **800-FLY-CHEAP;** www.1800flycheap.com) is owned by package-holiday megalith MyTravel and so has especially good access to fares for sunny destinations.

Booking your flight online

The "big three" online travel agencies, **Expedia** (www.expedia.com), **Travelocity** (www.travelocity.com), and **Orbitz** (www.orbitz.com) sell most of the air tickets bought on the Internet. (Canadian travelers should try www.expedia.ca and www.travelocity.ca; U.K. residents can go for expedia.co.uk and opodo.co.uk.) Each has different business deals with the airlines and may offer different fares on the same flights, so shopping around is wise. Expedia and Travelocity will also send you an **e-mail notification** when a cheap fare becomes available to your favorite destination. Of the smaller travel agency Web sites, **SideStep** (www.sidestep.com) receives good reviews from users. It's a browser add-on that purports to "search 140 sites at once," but in reality only beats competitors' fares as often as other sites do.

Great **last-minute deals** are available through free weekly e-mail services provided directly by the airlines. Most of these deals are announced on Tuesday or Wednesday and must be purchased online. Most are only valid for travel that weekend, but some (such as Southwest's) can be booked weeks or months in advance. Sign up for weekly e-mail alerts at airline Web sites or check mega-sites that compile comprehensive lists of last-minute specials, such as **Smarter Living** (smarterliving.com). For last-minute trips, www.site59.com in the U.S. and www.lastminute.com in Europe often have better deals than the major-label sites.

If you're willing to give up some control over your flight details, use an *opaque fare service* like **Priceline** (www.priceline.com) or **Hotwire** (www.hotwire.com). Both offer rock-bottom prices in exchange for travel on a "mystery airline" at a mysterious time of day, often with a mysterious change of planes en route. The mystery airlines are all major, well-known carriers — and the possibility of being sent from Philadelphia to Chicago via Tampa is remote. But your chances of getting a 6 a.m. or 11 p.m. flight are pretty high. Hotwire tells you flight prices before you buy; Priceline usually has better deals than Hotwire, but you have to play their "name our price" game. *Note:* In 2004 Priceline added non-opaque service to its roster. You now have the option to pick exact flights, times, and airlines from a list of offers — or opt to bid on opaque fares as before.

Driving to the Parks

For directions on how to drive to a specific park, please see the "Getting There" section in the individual park chapters.

Renting a car

Unless you drive your own vehicle to the park of your choice, you need to rent a car. What kind of car should you choose? You definitely won't need any high-performance wheels, because park roads aren't conducive to speeds over 45 mph. For years, I've been traveling in trusty Subaru wagons — they're economical, reliable, hold all the gear I need, and come in all-wheel-drive. (That's not an endorsement, mind you, but an example of the type of rig that works.) Outside of winter months, you're not likely to need four-wheel-drive. But I do heartily recommend a rig with decent ground clearance — just in case you decide to venture a bit off the beaten path and down a washboard-weary dirt road. Look for a station wagon or SUV that gets reasonable gas mileage and has enough space to hold your luggage and gear.

Car rental rates vary even more than airline fares. The price depends on the size of the car, the length of time you keep it, where and when you pick it up and drop it off, where you take it, and a host of other factors. Asking a few key questions may save you hundreds of dollars. Here are some things to look into when you're renting a car:

- ✔ Weekend rates may be lower than weekday rates. If you're keeping the car five or more days, a weekly rate may be cheaper than the daily rate. Ask if the rate is the same for pickup Friday morning as it is Thursday night.

- ✔ Some companies may assess a drop-off charge if you don't return the car to the same rental location; others, notably National, don't.

- ✔ Check whether the rate is cheaper if you pick up the car at a location in town rather than at the airport.

- ✔ Find out whether age is an issue. Many car rental companies add on a fee for drivers under 25, and some don't rent to them at all.

- ✔ If you see an advertised price in your local newspaper, be sure to ask for that specific rate; otherwise you may be charged the standard (higher) rate. Don't forget to mention membership in AAA, AARP, and trade unions. These memberships usually entitle you to discounts ranging from 5 to 30 percent.

- ✔ Check your frequent-flier accounts. Not only are your favorite (or at least most-used) airlines likely to have sent you discount coupons, but most car rentals add at least 500 miles to your account.

- ✔ As with other aspects of planning your trip, using the Internet can make comparison shopping for a car rental much easier. You can check rates at most of the major agencies' Web sites. Plus, all the major travel sites — **Travelocity** (www.travelocity.com), **Expedia** (www.expedia.com), **Orbitz** (www.orbitz.com), and **Smarter Living** (www.smarterliving.com), for example — have search engines that can dig up discounted car-rental rates. Just enter the car size you want, the pickup and return dates, and the location and the server returns a price. You can even make the reservation through any of these sites.

In addition to the standard rental prices, other optional charges apply to most car rentals (and some not-so-optional charges, such as taxes). Many credit card companies cover the ***Collision Damage Waiver*** (CDW), which requires you to pay for damage to the car in a collision. Check with your credit card company before you go so you can avoid paying this hefty fee (as much as $20 a day).

The car rental companies also offer additional *liability insurance* (if you harm others in an accident), *personal accident insurance* (if you harm yourself or your passengers), and *personal effects insurance* (if your luggage is stolen from your car). Your insurance policy on your car at home probably covers most of these unlikely occurrences. However, if your own insurance doesn't cover you for rentals or if you don't have auto insurance, definitely consider the additional coverage (ask your car rental agent for more information). Unless you're toting around the Hope diamond (and you don't want to leave that in your car trunk anyway), you can probably skip the personal effects insurance, but driving around without liability or personal accident coverage is never a good idea. Even if you're a good driver, other people may not be, and liability claims can be complicated.

Some companies also offer *refueling packages,* in which you pay for your initial full tank of gas up front, and can return the car with an empty gas tank. The prices can be competitive with local gas prices, but you don't get credit for any gas remaining in the tank. If you reject this option, you pay only for the gas you use, but you have to return the car with a full tank or face charges of $3 to $4 a gallon for any shortfall. If you usually run late and a fueling stop may make you miss your plane, you're a perfect candidate for the fuel-purchase option.

Safe-driving tips

National park roads aren't autobahns. Speed limits don't approach highway speeds, and you often encounter traffic delays as other visitors stop to gaze at the landscape or wildlife. Also, ongoing road projects are common in the parks, so be prepared for delays. Some parks — Sequoia comes to mind — have stretches of tightly woven switchbacks that can't handle recreational vehicles longer than 22 feet (the Ash Mountain Entrance Road is one, the road into Mineral Basin is another). Death Valley, meanwhile, has many miles of washboard-wracked dirt roads that are fun to explore, but not in your average sedan. Winter also can close many roads to automobiles — most of Yellowstone's Grand Loop shuts down when the snow flies, as do the Tioga Road in Yosemite, the Teton Park Road through Grand Teton, California 180 from Grant Grove to Cedar Grove in Kings Canyon, and the entire North Rim of the Grand Canyon.

Using a Travel Agent

You may never have thought about working as a travel agent, but by the time you finish this book, you'll be qualified to arrange most, if not all, of your travel needs. Still, I realize that some of you don't have the time or inclination to arrange every logistical aspect of your trip. You want someone to make the calls, run down the pricing, and even haggle a bit, and then call you back with the itinerary and bottom-line cost. Finding a great travel agent comes in handy.

In many ways, a good travel agent is like a good mechanic or plumber: hard to find, but invaluable after you've located the right one. The best way to find a good travel agent is by word of mouth.

 To get the most out of a travel agent, do a little homework. Read up on your destination (you've already made a sound decision by buying this book) and choose some accommodations and attractions that appeal to you. If you have Internet access, check prices on the Web to get a sense of ballpark figures. Then take this guidebook and Web information to the travel agent and ask him to make the arrangements for you. Because travel agents have access to more resources than even the most complete Web travel sites, they often can obtain better prices than you can get on your own. And agents can issue your tickets and vouchers right on the spot. If they can't get you into the hotel of your choice, they can recommend an alternative, and you can look for an objective review in this guidebook.

 Some travel agents work on commission. The good news is that you don't pay the commission — the airlines, accommodations, and tour companies do. The bad news is that unscrupulous travel agents will try to persuade you to book the vacations that nab them the most money in commissions. But in recent years, more and more airlines and resorts have begun to limit or eliminate these commissions altogether. As a result, some travel agents now charge customers for their services.

 If you opt to place your trip in an agent's hands, ask the agent if she works with a park concessionaire on lodging or focuses on motels or hotels in gateway communities just outside the park. (Some agents prefer to work with nonpark properties because they receive a higher commission.) This information will help you choose an agent that's right for you.

Weighing the Benefits of Organized Tours

You may be one of the many people who loves escorted tours. The tour company takes care of all the details, and tells you what to expect at each leg of your journey. You know your costs up front and, in the case of the tame ones, you don't get many surprises. Escorted tours can take you to the maximum number of sights in the minimum amount of time with the least amount of hassle.

 If you decide to go with an escorted tour, I strongly recommend purchasing travel insurance, especially if the tour operator asks you to pay up front. But don't buy insurance from the tour operator! If the tour operator doesn't fulfill its obligation to provide you with the vacation you paid for, there's no reason to think that it will fulfill insurance obligations. Get travel insurance through an independent agency. (I tell you more about the ins and outs of travel insurance in Chapter 8.)

When choosing an escorted tour, along with finding out whether you have to put down a deposit and when final payment is due, ask a few simple questions before you buy:

- ✔ **What is the cancellation policy?** Can they cancel the trip if they don't get enough people? How late can you cancel if you're unable to go? Do you get a refund if you cancel? If they cancel?

- ✔ **How jam-packed is the schedule?** Does the tour schedule try to fit 25 hours into a 24-hour day, or does it give you ample time to relax by the pool or shop? If getting up at 7 a.m. every day and not returning to your hotel until 6 or 7 p.m. at night sounds like a grind, certain escorted tours may not be for you.

- ✔ **How large is the group?** The smaller the group, the less time you spend waiting for people to get on and off the bus. Tour operators may be evasive about this, because they may not know the exact size of the group until everybody has made reservations, but they should be able to give you a rough estimate.

- ✔ **Is there a minimum group size?** Some tours have a minimum group size, and may cancel the tour if they don't book enough people. If a quota exists, find out what it is and how close they are to reaching it. Again, tour operators may be evasive in their answers, but the information may help you select a tour that's sure to happen.

- ✔ **What exactly is included?** Don't assume anything. You may have to pay to get yourself to and from the airport. A box lunch may be included in an excursion but drinks may be extra. Beer may be included but not wine. How much flexibility do you have? Can you opt out of certain activities, or does the bus leave once a day, with no exceptions? Are all your meals planned in advance? Can you choose your entree at dinner, or does everybody get the same chicken cutlet?

If your recreational passions include vigorous outdoor activity, I recommend one of the following tour companies:

- ✔ **Backroads** (☎ **800-GO-ACTIVE** or 510-527-1555; www.backroads.com), a company that has been leading trips since 1979, is a good choice for travelers who can't decide whether to bike, hike, or combine a variety of activities during a park visit. Among the offerings is a six-day biking, hiking, rafting, and kayaking family tour through Yellowstone and Grand Teton national parks in Wyoming. The price of $2,298 per person includes shuttle support, guides, bikes, kayaks, rafts, food (except for one dinner and one lunch), and accommodations, but not airfare. Prices are based on double occupancy; an extra fee is usually charged for single occupancy.

- ✔ **GORPtravel** (☎ **877-440-GORP**; www.gorp.com) also focuses on adventure travel. One of its trips is a six-day summer tour of Olympic National Park (from $1,982 per person, including transportation from

Seattle, Washington; five nights lodging; and most meals); another is a ten-day backpacking trip through Sequoia National Park to 14,495-foot-tall Mount Whitney (from $1695 per person, including all meals in the backcountry, backpacking gear, park fees, support vehicle, and guides). For both trips, airfare is extra and prices are based on double occupancy.

✔ Also see Chapter 7 for descriptions of field-study packages offered in many of the national parks.

Choosing a Package Tour

For lots of destinations, package tours can be a smart way to go. In many cases, a package tour that includes airfare, hotel, and transportation to and from the airport costs less than the hotel alone on a tour you book yourself. That's because packages are sold in bulk to tour operators, who resell them to the public. Buying a package tour is kind of like buying your vacation at a buy-in-bulk store — except the tour operator is the one who buys the 1,000-count box of garbage bags and resells them 10 at a time at a cost that undercuts the local supermarket.

Package tours can vary as much as those garbage bags, too. Some offer a better class of hotels than others; others provide the same hotels for lower prices. Some book flights on scheduled airlines; others sell charters. In some packages, your choice of accommodations and travel days may be limited. Some let you choose between escorted vacations and independent vacations; others allow you to add on just a few excursions or escorted day trips (also at discounted prices) without booking an entirely escorted tour.

One package tour source is the **American Automobile Association** (AAA). This group occasionally packages tours to destinations around the country. One two-night trip features a ride on a train pulled by a steam locomotive to Grand Canyon National Park; another is a nine-day tour to Mount Rushmore, Yellowstone, and Grand Teton that starts in Denver and ends in Salt Lake City. Call ☎ 407-444-7000 for the phone number of your local club or check online at www.aaa.com.

AAA members can also receive (for free) the association's "Guide To" maps and travel planners for a select number of national parks. These materials feature information on park history, flora, and fauna. Nonmembers can purchase these guides at large chain bookstores. If you're a member, AAA offices will also be more than happy to arrange your lodging, airfare, and car-rental needs if you tell them where you want to go and how long you want to stay. If you're driving, as a bonus they can compile a "Triptik" booklet with succinct directions to the park and the sights you want to see.

Most **park concessionaires** also offer package tours, which isn't much of a surprise in the one-stop shopping world. These packages can be as simple as lodging discounts or as involved as combinations of lodging, cross-country skiing, or hiking, and wildlife viewing treks, such as those tours offered in Yellowstone. Best of all, you often can save money by calling the concessionaire directly rather than going through a third party. Check out their individual Web sites for activity offerings and lodging options. Then call them to lock in your reservations. Throughout the year — usually during the slow shoulder seasons of early spring, early winter, and early in the year — concessionaires offer great lodging discounts, so stay in contact with them, either by regularly visiting their Web sites or by signing up for e-mail alerts. See the Appendix for concessionaire Web sites and telephone numbers.

Other package tours can be found by checking out the travel section of your local Sunday newspaper or the ads in the back of national travel magazines such as *Travel & Leisure, National Geographic Traveler,* and *Condé Nast Traveler.* **Liberty Travel** (call ☎ **888-271-1584** to find the store nearest you; www.libertytravel.com) is one of the biggest packagers in the Northeast, and usually boasts a full-page ad in Sunday papers.

Finally, the airlines themselves are good sources of package deals. Most major airlines offer air/land packages, including **American Airlines Vacations** (☎ 800-321-2121; www.aavacations.com), **Delta Vacations** (☎ 800-221-6666; www.deltavacations.com), **Continental Airlines Vacations** (☎ 800-301-3800; www.covacations.com), and **United Vacations** (☎ 888-854-3899; www.unitedvacations.com). Several big **online travel agencies** — Expedia, Travelocity, Orbitz, Site59, and Lastminute.com — also do a brisk business in packages. If you're unsure about the pedigree of a smaller packager, check with the Better Business Bureau in the city where the company is based, or go online at www.bbb.org. If a packager won't tell you where it's based, don't do business.

Chapter 6

Booking Your Accommodations

- -

In This Chapter

▶ Running down the options

▶ Reserving the bunk of your choice

▶ Strategizing for last-minute lodgings

▶ Roughing it: Campgrounds and the backcountry

- -

*P*lanning a trip to a national park can be a surprisingly daunting task when you consider the logistics of finding a place to bed down for the night. Many of the best accommodations are fully booked several months, even a year, in advance. Although the park chapters get into the specifics of each lodge and campground, this chapter helps you figure out the right accommodation type for your needs and budget.

Finding the Right Room

National parks are scattered from sea to shining sea, in remote places, and along sandy beaches. As you can imagine, the range of quality of rooms in each park is mind-boggling. In Yosemite, for example, the dizzying variety of accommodations ranges from three-sided housekeeping units (which are tossed together with three canvas walls, a double-layer of canvas for the roof, and a slab of cold concrete that greets you in the morning) to the six-story Ahwahnee Hotel that has catered to royalty.

Because the spread of park accommodations is so vast, about the only **standard amenities** that I'll vouch for are beds and lights (which may be candles or electric bulbs). Some rooms include air conditioning, and some provide wood stoves to fight off the frost. Telephones and televisions are not standard amenities.

But if you step outside of a park, you find a world where good beds, air conditioning/heating, phones, and televisions are standard in most hotels and motels. And in some of the fancier spots, you also find hot tubs and fireplaces — some B&Bs have both!

Fit for royalty, presidents, and actors

In-park accommodations are generally modest throughout the national park system, but some places are exceptions. If price is no object, head to **The Ahwahnee Hotel** in Yosemite (see Chapter 17) or **Lake Yellowstone Hotel** in Yellowstone (see Chapter 16). Both have spectacular settings — the Ahwahnee not far from Yosemite Falls and Lake Yellowstone Hotel on the shores of Yellowstone Lake — and both have suites suitable for kings, queens, and presidents (not to mention Hollywood royalty such as Clint Eastwood, who has stayed at the Ahwahnee). In my middle-class opinion, these hotels epitomize "national park stateliness." They're elegant, dignified, and a heck of a way to end a weeklong trek in the backcountry. Compared to the rest of the options in these two parks, these accommodations are very, very nice. I'm talking thick comforters (atop king- or queen-sized beds) to ward off evening chills, plush carpeting, and handsomely tiled bathrooms. Telephones are standard, but televisions aren't. (You didn't come to a national park to watch the soaps, did you?) Both feature well-appointed public spaces, and the Ahwahnee boasts an outdoor pool. Suites at these hotels are priced in the very expensive range ($$$$$), and standard doubles are priced in the expensive category ($$$$).

A new wave of park motels

An accommodations revolution is slowly moving through the park system. Park Service officials, well aware of the need for lodging upgrades, demanded that concessionaires make a bigger investment in the parks' infrastructure than they had in the past. As a result, concessionaires replaced the 1960s-era buildings with several new lodgings that are cleaner, roomier, and more comfortable. **Dunraven Lodge** and the **Snow Lodge** in Yellowstone (see Chapter 16), for example, use rustic pine furniture and artful lamps to lend a woodsy atmosphere to the rooms. Although the rooms at **Wuksachi Lodge** (opened in 1999) in Sequoia (see Chapter 15) are nothing to rave about, the main lodge, with its cedar and stone construction, blends nicely with the surrounding park. Of course, you pay a moderate amount ($$$) for these abodes (and you still may not have a television in your room!).

Motels and other roadside fare

When the World War II generation rebounded from the war and began to pencil vacations into their summers, roadside America responded with **motels.** These places weren't fancy, but they were clean and offered basic amenities such as beds, telephones, and televisions. Best of all, they were economical. These chain-style hotels sprouted up in the national parks in the 1960s, and they're still common today in almost every park. In the moderate to expensive range ($$$ to $$$$), park motels are generally clean and comfortable. Some have televisions and telephones; some have neither.

National park rustic: Do you want that with or without running water?

At some national parks, roughing it doesn't necessarily mean sleeping under the stars or in a tent. Visit Yosemite and Yellowstone, and you can really curb your spending by staying in **tent cabins** — four walls and a roof of canvas over a concrete slab — or in aging (although not always gracefully) cabins where wood stoves provide the heat and where communal bathhouses only a short walk away contain showers and toilets.

Yosemite's tent cabins are long on romance but short on comfort, privacy, and peace and quiet (see Chapter 17). These cabins provide cots and a few heavy wool blankets to defend you from any cold air that the wood stove can't combat. Some of the cabins at Yellowstone's Roosevelt Lodge and Old Faithful could probably qualify as national historic sites, they're so old (see Chapter 16). They're also stark, tiny, and tend to hold dirt better than lodge rooms.

Rates for these types of accommodations range from very inexpensive ($) to moderate ($$$), and although you may not expect it, they tend to be in fairly high demand. You can have your meals, which aren't included in the prices, at lodges, restaurants, or hotels, usually a short walk away.

On the outside: B&Bs and pricier abodes

Some parks have only a few rooms within their borders. Visit any of these parks, and you may have to stay in a tent, motel, hotel, or bed-and-breakfast in one of the gateway communities. These places come in numerous sizes, shapes, styles, and prices; I don't have space enough to describe all the variations. You can find sumptuous B&Bs with fireplaces and hot tubs in their rooms and with manicured gardens where you can enjoy your breakfast. Outside Mount Rainier's Nisqually Entrance, you can even stay in a deluxe tree house with running water (see Chapter 13). Naturally, gateway communities are packed with chain properties (see the Appendix for a list of toll-free telephone numbers). These accommodations offer little in the name of ambience but are usually clean, comfortable enough for a multiday stay, and reasonably priced.

Among the extent of accommodations outside the parks, prices range from inexpensive ($) to very expensive ($$$$$). At any of the bed-and-breakfasts that I recommend in this book, you can expect a full breakfast and, in some cases, an afternoon snack.

Finding the Best Room at the Best Rate

As wide-ranging as the accommodations in and around the parks are, so are their nightly rates, which can range from $60 for a rustic cabin at Roosevelt Lodge in Yellowstone to more than $800 a night for a suite at

Yosemite's Ahwahnee Lodge. Of course, setting affects price as well as amenities. (An Old Faithful Inn room facing the Old Faithful geyser, for example, is more expensive than one not facing the geyser.) To guide you through the maze of pricing options, I give each accommodation in this book a dollar sign rating from $ to $$$$$. The number of dollar signs is based on the *rack rate* — the maximum rate a hotel charges for a room — per night for two people in a double room during high season, which is summer in all parks except Death Valley. The dollar signs represent the following price ranges:

$	Less than $75
$$	$76–$100
$$$	$101–$200
$$$$	$201–$250
$$$$$	More than $250

Now about that rack rate: Although all the hotels in this book charge rack rates, those hotels outside the park are more flexible. These places are happy to charge you the rack rate, but you usually don't have to pay it — hardly anyone does. The best way to avoid paying the rack rate is surprisingly simple: Ask for a cheaper or discounted rate. Make sure to mention membership in AAA, AARP, frequent flyer programs, or any other corporate rewards programs you can think of. You may be pleasantly surprised by the discount you receive. For the in-park hotels, you should ask about off-season deals when you call, and look for Internet specials on the Web. A little bit of research can save you dollars.

Surfing the Web for hotel deals

Shopping online for hotels is generally done one of two ways: by booking through the hotel's own Web site or through an independent booking agency (or a fare-service agency like Priceline). These Internet hotel agencies have multiplied in mind-boggling numbers of late, competing for the business of millions of consumers surfing for accommodations around the world. This competitiveness can be a boon to consumers who have the patience and time to shop and compare the online sites for good deals — but shop they must, for prices can vary considerably from site to site. And keep in mind that hotels at the top of a site's listing may be there for no other reason than that they paid money to get the placement.

Of the "big three" sites, **Expedia** offers a long list of special deals and "virtual tours" or photos of available rooms so you can see what you're paying for (a feature that helps counter the claims that the best rooms are often held back from bargain-booking Web sites). **Travelocity** posts unvarnished customer reviews and ranks its properties according to the AAA rating system. Also reliable are **Hotels.com** and **Quikbook.com**. An excellent free program, **TravelAxe** (www.travelaxe.net), can help you search multiple hotel sites at once, even ones you may never have heard of — and conveniently lists the total price of the room, including the taxes and service charges. Another booking site, **Travelweb** (www.travelweb.com), is partly owned by the hotels it represents (including the Hilton, Hyatt, and Starwood chains) and is therefore plugged directly into the hotels' reservations systems — unlike independent online agencies, which have to fax or e-mail reservation requests to the hotel, a good portion of which get misplaced in the shuffle. More than once, travelers have arrived at the hotel only to be told that they have no reservation. To be fair, many of the major sites are undergoing improvements in service and ease of use, and Expedia will soon be able to plug directly into the reservations systems of many hotel chains — none of which can be bad news for consumers. In the meantime, **get a confirmation number** and **make a printout** of any online booking transaction.

In the opaque Web site category, **Priceline** and **Hotwire** are even better for hotels than for airfares; with both, you're allowed to pick the neighborhood and quality level of your hotel before offering up your money. Priceline's hotel product even covers Europe and Asia, though it's much better at getting five-star lodging for three-star prices than at finding anything at the bottom of the scale. On the down side, many hotels stick Priceline guests in their least desirable rooms. Be sure to go to the **BiddingforTravel** Web site (www.biddingfortravel.com) before bidding on a hotel room on Priceline; it features a fairly up-to-date list of hotels that Priceline uses in major cities. For both Priceline and Hotwire, you pay up front, and the fee is nonrefundable. *Note:* Some hotels don't provide loyalty program credits or points or other frequent-stay amenities when you book a room through opaque online services.

Checking out park lodgings online

Curious about the lodging possibilities in each park? In addition to using this book, you can find out more about the national park lodgings on the **National Park Service** Web site at www.nps.gov. Links to individual parks let you know which concessionaires to call for in-park reservations, which towns offer out-of-park lodgings, and, in some cases, an online reservations page. Some national park concessionaires provide their own Web sites (see the Appendix for these), where you can get a rundown on rooms, find out about availability and pricing, and occasionally stumble upon Internet specials that can save you money.

Nabbing Bunks at Popular Lodgings

Even though national parks don't advertise on television, people know that they exist. Park lodgings are usually in high demand because of limited offerings and, in the case of the northern parks, short seasons. If you want to stay within the park, you need to plan ahead. For summer vacations, reserve at least three to four months before your trip — six months is even better. For the most popular lodges — Yosemite's Ahwahnee Hotel (Chapter 17), Yellowstone's Old Faithful Inn (Chapter 16), and the

Grand Canyon's El Tovar (Chapter 11) — you need to call earlier than six months ahead. In fact, in Yosemite, you should start dialing a year in advance. In the individual park chapters, I give you the lowdown (and share a few tricks) on how to get the room of your dreams.

Also keep in mind that not all parks experience the same busy seasons; look for reservation guidelines in each park chapter. Although December and January are very slow in Sequoia, these months are bustling in Death Valley.

Private companies also run lodges inside national parks. Some of these concessionaires operate in more than one park. **Xanterra Parks & Resorts,** for instance, oversees lodges in Yellowstone, Grand Canyon, Death Valley, and Zion national parks. Big companies such as this one (and even some of the smaller ones) provide their own Web sites where you can check out the accommodations, inquire about availability and pricing, and even lock in a room. See the Appendix for a list of these concessionaires and their Web site addresses.

Making Reservations at the Last Minute

I'm a procrastinator — a darn good one, too (just ask my editor). So I understand how you can forget about making a room reservation until a month before your scheduled vacation. Frankly, the odds aren't good that you can land a room in Yosemite in August if you wait until July to call. But hey, it can happen.

How, you wonder? Well, every now and again tour *wholesalers* — commercial folks who book tours (see Chapter 5) — fail to sell out trips and are forced to cancel large blocks of their reserved rooms. These releases typically occur 21 to 30 days in advance of their bookings, so try calling the park's reservation desk during this time frame to find out if they've received any cancellations. Sometimes, you can find a vacancy even if a wholesaler hasn't relinquished any of its rooms. Astute folks (such as the ones reading this book) who make reservations months in advance sometimes need to cancel at the last minute — and voilà! — a room opens up.

Another way to find a vacancy — either when you're booking in advance or at the last minute — is to inquire about Tuesday and Wednesday night possibilities because most folks stretch their weekends by booking the more popular Thursday and Friday nights.

Pitching Your Tent or Parking Your RV

At last count, 25,700 campsites at 548 campgrounds are located in 77 areas of the national park system. If you're after one of these campsites, you can chase it down via telephone, by mail, in person at the park, or

over the Internet. The **National Park Reservation Service** (NPRS)
maintains the reservation system and operates a Web site (http://
reservations.nps.gov) where you can find campground listings and
make a reservation.

You can also make park reservations over the phone by calling NPRS at
☎ **800-365-2267** (800-530-9796 TTY and 301-722-1257 for international
calls). Yosemite, due to its popularity, has its own phone number (☎ **800-
436-7275**). You can pay for your reservation with Visa, MasterCard, or
Discover, or by check or money order. However, if you want to make a
phone reservation and pay by check or money order, you need to call at
least 21 days in advance of your arrival, and NPRS must receive your
check within 7 days of making your reservation. Don't dally!

If you want to mail in your payment or make a campsite reservation by
mail, the address is NPRS, P.O. Box 1600, Cumberland, MD 21501. If
you're sending a letter by a service that requires a signature and can't
be delivered to a PO Box (such as UPS, FedEx, and other expedited services), the address is 12501 Willowbrook Road, Cumberland, MD 21502.
On your mail-in application, which must be received 21 days before your
arrival, be sure to list the following information:

✔ Your name, address, and telephone number.

✔ The name of the park and specific campground.

✔ Your arrival and departure dates.

✔ The number of persons in your party.

✔ Whether you're hauling an RV or plan to pitch a tent.

✔ Your method of payment (Visa, MC, Discover, personal check, or
money order). If paying by credit card, include the card number
and expiration date; checks should be made out to the National
Park Service.

✔ Any pass holder discounts you can claim (Golden Age or Golden
Access).

✔ Whether you're bringing a pet.

Thanks to the park reservation system, you can now book a campsite up
to five months before you actually arrive in the park. For example, for all
parks except Yosemite, if you call on January 5, you can make a reservation for dates as late as June 4; if you call on February 5, you can make a
reservation for dates as late as July 4; and so on.

For Yosemite, beginning on the 15th of each month, you can make a
reservation for up to five months in advance. So if you call on January 15,
you can schedule an arrival for June 14; on February 15, you can schedule an arrival for July 14, and so on.

When you call to book your campsite, make sure to ask your reservation agent for park-specific restrictions, such as the one that places a maximum of two reservations per customer for the same dates in the same park. A good idea is to make several choices before you call (or list alternatives on the mail-in application) in case your first choice is booked solid. Also, if you need a wheelchair-accessible site, mention that when making a reservation.

Keep in mind that not all campgrounds are open year-round. Also, not all campgrounds charge a fee. Some provide running water, some don't. In the individual park chapters, I detail the specifics of each campground. A final word of caution: Some parks periodically change which campgrounds are open seasonally and which ones are open year-round. If in doubt, double check.

Gambling for Backcountry Permits

Even though all parks require you to pick up a permit before you head off into the backcountry, some places are so popular that you have to enter a lottery or go through a permit process to win a chance to visit them. Why? Because officials allow only a specific number of campers into the backcountry at any given time to protect the backcountry from overuse. Yellowstone and the Grand Canyon are among the parks that use this system. Yellowstone's Shoshone Lake is the most sought after backcountry attraction, and on April 1 of each year park officials conduct a lottery to see who wins a campsite reservation. After this date, any available campsite reservations are issued on a first-come, first-served basis.

Yellowstone is a pretty big place, though. If you can't obtain a permit for a specific piece of backcountry, chances are, you can head someplace else in the park.

The demand for the High Sierra backcountry tent camps in Yosemite and Sequoia national parks, which are available from late June to Labor Day, is ridiculously high. Applications for the camps are accepted between October 15 and December 15, and winners are notified by the end of the following February. See the Sequoia and Yosemite chapters (Chapters 15 and 17, respectively) for information on how to obtain an application.

Chapter 7

Catering to Special Travel Needs or Interests

. . . .

In This Chapter

▶ Traveling with tots and teens
▶ Making age work (and pay) for you
▶ Rising above disabilities
▶ Going it alone
▶ Traveling with gay (and lesbian) abandon
▶ Exploring special interests in field courses

. . . .

*I*f you have special needs, interests, or concerns that affect your travel plans — and almost everyone does — this chapter is for you. I may not be able to address all your questions on a particular topic, but I can direct you to some additional information sources.

Bringing the Brood: Advice for Families

The prospect of visiting a national park excites most kids. With a little advance planning and by taking advantage of the parks' many kid-friendly activities, you can hold onto their attention after you arrive. In this section, I let you know which parks offer activities and attractions that appeal to children, and I suggest resources to check out for additional information. I also share tips to make the most of your family time together.

Just for kids

You find top-notch children's activities at almost all the national parks. One of my favorites (for kids of all ages) is the **National Parks Passport Book.** This pocket-sized booklet available in national parks breaks down the national parks system by region, contains interesting narrative, and provides space for "cancellation stamps" that show which parks you've visited and when you visited them.

Yosemite National Park offers a wide variety of kid-friendly stuff, such as floating down the Merced River in a raft or swimming in one of the valley's pools. At **Olympic National Park,** kids can explore the Hoh Rain Forest and, in early summer, have a snowball fight atop Hurricane Ridge. At **Sequoia National Park,** kids like to walk among the towering trees, which make them feel like they've entered the Land of the Giants. **Grand Teton National Park** offers boating opportunities, and you can go for a stagecoach ride in **Yellowstone National Park.**

Throughout this book, I use the Kid Friendly icon to point out these recreations and other kid-pleasing activities.

All parks offer special programs for children. One of the most popular is the **Junior Ranger Program,** which uses puzzles and games to teach kids about their surroundings. As a part of the program, kids occasionally perform some public service — such as collecting trash — for which they receive a Junior Ranger badge. Park rangers also conduct kid-friendly campfire programs addressing such topics as wildlife or geology.

Are your kids older? Are you looking for ways to restore family bonds with a world-weary teenager? Consider a joint climb of the **Grand Teton** or **Mount Rainier,** a backcountry adventure into **Kings Canyon,** a rim-to-rim backpack trip in **Grand Canyon National Park,** a day hike to the top of Half Dome in **Yosemite,** or a Discovery Tour in **Sequoia National Park's** Crystal Cave.

Where to find information

You can find information about kids' programs in each **national park newspaper,** which is available at the entrance station, at the visitor center, and often in advance by mail. (See the "Fast Facts" section of each chapter for contact information.) You can also find information online at the **National Park Service Web site,** www.nps.gov.

John Bigley and Paris Permenter mix kids and national parks in *National Parks With Kids* (Open Road Publishing, 2000), available at most major bookstores or via the Internet at Amazon.com. This book covers park service properties in every state and focuses on kid-friendly activities and programs. Frommer's *Family Vacations in the National Parks* (Wiley) is another good resource.

You can find good family-oriented vacation advice on the Internet from sites like the www.familytravelforum.com, a comprehensive site that offers customized trip planning. Also try the **Family Travel Network** (www.familytravelnetwork.com), an award-winning site that offers travel features, deals, and tips; **Traveling Internationally with Your Kids** (www.travelwithyourkids.com), a comprehensive site that offers customized trip planning; and **Family Travel Files** (www.thefamily travelfiles.com), which offers an online magazine and a directory of off-the-beaten-path tours and tour operators for families.

Some quick travel-with-kids tips

About to explore a national park with a car full of kids? Here are some tips to increase their enjoyment and comfort while on the road.

Before you go:

- ✔ **Pack "security blankets."** Take along some of your youngest kids' favorite books and toys, even if they add bulk to your luggage. Going to new places can be hard on even the can will help ease transitions.

- ✔ **Read up on the park.** Take your children to the library to study up on the national park you're about to visit. They can become experts on wildlife and natural attractions before you leave home. Internet-literate kids can dial up www.nps.gov/learn to delve into the natural and cultural resources of the park system.

- ✔ **Prepare for the sun.** Take steps to ward off the hot sun that beams down on most parks — pack sunscreen or sun block, hats, and sunglasses.

- ✔ **Get car safety seats.** If your kids are small, be sure to arrange with the car rental companies for child safety seats.

After you arrive at the park:

- ✔ **Pick up Junior Ranger Program materials.** You can get these materials from a visitor center. They usually include crossword puzzles and other games pertaining to the park.

- ✔ **Buy snacks.** Don't forget to stock up on snacks to combat energy lows and car sickness.

- ✔ **Watch your children.** Keep a tight rein on young children near overlooks; around rivers, lakes, and beaches; on snowfields; along steep trails with precipitous drops; in Yellowstone's geothermal basins; and near wild animals. (No matter how cuddly bison look, they are *definitely* not tame.)

- ✔ **Don't push your kids to have fun.** Realize the energy limits of your children — don't try to hit every attraction in one day or go too far on hikes. Gear activities to your child's age, physical condition, and attention span.

Making Age Work for You: Tips for Seniors

National parks aren't just for the young. Or middle-aged. Or even the old. They're for everyone. Parks don't go out of their way any more for seniors than they do for youngsters; tourists of all ages are welcomed pretty much equally. One exception is entrance fees. The **Golden Age Passport** serves as a lifetime entrance pass for holders 62 and older. The pass is available for a one-time fee of $10. You can buy this pass only at a National Park Service entrance area. Be sure to bring proof of age and U.S. citizenship or permanent residency. Like the National Park Pass (see Chapter 8), this pass admits the pass holder and any accompanying passengers in a personal vehicle free of charge. What's more, the Golden Age Passport provides a 50 percent discount on federal use fees charged for facilities and services, such as camping, swimming, parking, boat launching, and tours. This doesn't include park lodging or fees charged by concessionaires. For more information, go online to www.nps.gov/fees_passes.htm or call ☎ 888-467-2757.

Mention the fact that you're a senior citizen when you make your **travel reservations.** Although all of the major U.S. airlines except America West have cancelled their senior discount and coupon book programs, many hotels still offer discounts for seniors. In most cities, people over the age of 60 qualify for reduced admission to theaters, museums, and other attractions, as well as discounted fares on public transportation.

Members of **AARP** (formerly known as the American Association of Retired Persons), 601 E Street NW, Washington, DC 20049 (☎ **888-687-2277** or 202-434-2277; www.aarp.org), get discounts on hotels, airfares, and car rentals. AARP offers members a wide range of benefits, including *AARP: The Magazine* and a monthly newsletter. Anyone over 50 can join.

Recommended publications offering travel resources and discounts for seniors include: the quarterly magazine *Travel 50 & Beyond* (www.travel50andbeyond.com); *Travel Unlimited: Uncommon Adventures for the Mature Traveler* (Avalon); *101 Tips for Mature Travelers,* available from Grand Circle Travel (☎ **800-221-2610** or 617-350-7500; www.gct.com); *The 50+ Traveler's Guidebook* (St. Martin's Press); and *Unbelievably Good Deals and Great Adventures That You Absolutely Can't Get Unless You're Over 50* (McGraw-Hill), by Joann Rattner Heilman.

Accessing the Parks: Resources for Travelers with Disabilities

A disability shouldn't stop anybody from traveling. Although people with disabilities won't be able to travel everywhere in a national park, more options and resources are available than ever before.

Even though national parks, by their very nature, feature wide expanses of forests, meadows, mountains, and canyons, they're still accessible to the handicapped. Visit a park's Web site (see the "Fast Facts" section of each park chapter for the address), and you find a rundown on its accessibility. In **Yellowstone,** for instance, wheelchair-accessible boardwalks wind through most of the geyser basins, and the park even offers accessible campsites. At **Grand Canyon National Park,** wheelchairs are available for temporary day use at no charge, and several of the interpretive ranger programs are wheelchair accessible.

The National Park Service offers a **Golden Access Passport** that gives free lifetime entrance to all properties administered by the National Park Service — national parks, monuments, historic sites, recreation areas, and national wildlife refuges — for persons who are visually impaired or permanently disabled, regardless of age. You may pick up a Golden Access Passport at any NPS entrance fee area by showing proof of medically determined disability and eligibility for receiving benefits under federal law. Besides free entry, the Golden Access Passport also offers a 50 percent discount on federal-use fees charged for such facilities as camping, swimming, parking, boat launching, and tours. For more information, go online to www.nps.gov/fees_passes.htm or call ☎ 888-467-2757.

Nationwide resources

Many travel agencies offer customized tours and itineraries for travelers with disabilities. **Flying Wheels Travel** (☎ 507-451-5005; www.flyingwheelstravel.com) offers escorted tours and cruises that emphasize sports and private tours in minivans with lifts. **Access-Able Travel Source** (☎ 303-232-2979; www.access-able.com) offers extensive access information and advice for traveling around the world with disabilities. **Accessible Journeys** (☎ 800-846-4537 or 610-521-0339) has resources for wheelchair travelers and their families and friends.

Avis Rent a Car has an "Avis Access" program that offers such services as a dedicated 24-hour toll-free number (☎ 888-879-4273) for customers with special travel needs; special car features such as swivel seats, spinner knobs, and hand controls; and accessible bus service.

Organizations that offer assistance to disabled travelers include the **MossRehab** (www.mossresourcenet.org), which provides a library of accessible-travel resources online; **SATH (Society for Accessible Travel and Hospitality)** (☎ 212-447-7284; www.sath.org; annual membership fees: $45 adults, $30 seniors and students), which offers a wealth of travel resources for all types of disabilities and informed recommendations on destinations, access guides, travel agents, tour operators, vehicle rentals, and companion services; and the **American Foundation for the Blind** (AFB) (☎ 800-232-5463; www.afb.org), a referral resource for the blind or visually impaired that includes that includes information on traveling with seeing eye dogs.

For more information specifically targeted to travelers with disabilities, the community Web site **iCan** (www.icanonline.net/channels/travel/index.cfm) has destination guides and several regular columns on accessible travel. Also check out the quarterly magazine **Emerging Horizons** ($14.95 per year, $19.95 outside the U.S.; www.emerginghorizons.com); **Twin Peaks Press** (☎ 360-694-2462; http://disabilitybookshop.virtualave.net/blist84.htm), offering travel-related books for travelers with special needs; and *Open World Magazine,* published by SATH (subscription: $13 per year, $21 outside the U.S.).

National park resources

If you're curious about accessibility in a particular park, call the park directly or go to its Web site. (See the "Fast Facts" section of each park chapter for its telephone number and Web-site address.) Every national park Web site, which is linked to the National Park Service site at www. nps.gov, provides a section on accessibility.

Following the Rainbow: Advice for Gay and Lesbian Travelers

National parks are melting pots. You encounter many tourists from all over the United States and the world with many divergent beliefs and practices. Being gay or lesbian isn't an issue.

The International Gay and Lesbian Travel Association (IGLTA) (☎ 800-448-8550 or 954-776-2626; www.iglta.org) is the trade association for the gay and lesbian travel industry, and offers an online directory of gay- and lesbian-friendly travel businesses; go to their Web site and click on **Members.**

Many agencies offer tours and travel itineraries specifically for gay and lesbian travelers. **Above and Beyond Tours** (☎ 800-397-2681; www.abovebeyondtours.com) is the exclusive gay and lesbian tour operator for United Airlines. **Now, Voyager** (☎ 800-255-6951; www.nowvoyager.com) is a well-known San Francisco–based gay-owned-and-operated travel service. **Olivia Cruises & Resorts** (☎ 800-631-6277 or 510-655-0364; www.olivia.com) charters entire resorts and ships for exclusive lesbian vacations and offers smaller group experiences for both gay and lesbian travelers.

The following travel guides are available at most travel bookstores and gay and lesbian bookstores, or you can order them from **Giovanni's Room** bookstore, 1145 Pine Street, Philadelphia, PA 19107 (☎ 215-923-2960; www.giovannisroom.com): *Frommer's Gay & Lesbian Europe,* an excellent travel resource (www.frommers.com); *Out and About* (☎ 800-929-2268 or 415-644-8044; www.outandabout.com), which offers guidebooks and a newsletter ($20/yr; 10 issues) packed with solid information on the global gay and lesbian scene; *Spartacus International Gay Guide* (Bruno Gmünder Verlag; www.spartacusworld.com/gayguide/) and *Odysseus,* both good, annual English-language guidebooks focused on gay men; the *Damron* guides (www.damron.com), with separate, annual books for gay men and lesbians; and *Gay Travel A to Z: The World of Gay & Lesbian Travel Options at Your Fingertips* by Marianne Ferrari (Ferrari International; Box 35575, Phoenix, AZ 85069), a very good gay and lesbian guidebook series.

Learning Outside the Classroom: Educational Programs

Psst! Want to know how to visit just about any national park at any time of year and not only avoid crowds but also gain insights unavailable to other visitors? Take part in a **field course** or **research program.** These activities are organized by the parks themselves or by private groups. Participation takes you off the beaten path into the park's backcountry, where you can study landscape or wildlife or even work on perfecting your brush strokes or paddle strokes. I spent three days one summer in Yellowstone attending a symposium on the park's burgeoning wolf population. Not only did we hear from the wildlife biologists and rangers who oversaw the wolf recovery program, but we also went into the field with hopes of spotting some of the packs. (We didn't spot any, by the way. But now, following the reintroduction effort, the wolf population is thriving and highly visible.)

Most parks offer some kind of educational programming. Go to the parks' Web sites (www.nps.gov) to find out about specific courses and schedules. You can also track down private organizations that invite travelers — for a price — to help with research. Although these options aren't always publicized, you may find information about them on the parks' Web sites or through visitor centers. Still, some programs are advertised in national magazines, such as *National Geographic Traveler* and *Outside.*

The educational programs can get pricey, running more than $300 per person depending on length. But they offer a wealth of knowledge, get you away from the crowds and into some beautiful locations, and introduce you to new friends. They're also very popular, so if you're interested, January is a good time to check with the associations for a catalog of their upcoming summer programs.

The following information gives you an idea of their diversity:

- ✔ The list of programs offered by the **Yellowstone Association Institute** (P.O. Box 117, Yellowstone National Park, WY 82190; ☎ 307-344-2293; http://yellowstoneassociation.org) is incredibly broad, ranging from courses on wildlife and geology to courses on photography, nature writing, and wilderness first aid. In about a third of these courses, you can earn college credits. You can also line up lodging in one of the log cabins at the institute's headquarters at the historic **Buffalo Ranch** in the Lamar Valley.

- ✔ The **Grand Canyon Field Institute** (P.O. Box 399, Grand Canyon, AZ 86023; ☎ 866-471-4435; www.grandcanyon.org/fieldinstitute) runs a similar program, with classes in human history, wilderness studies, natural history, photography, and the arts. In the **Advanced**

Wilderness Studies Workshops, you get a chance to move through the park's backcountry without the benefit of a human trail under your feet. You find out how to follow wash beds and game trails, tossed in with a little scrambling up and over geologic impediments.

✔ The **Yosemite Association** (P.O. Box 230, El Portal, CA 95318; ☎ 209-379-2646; www.yosemite.org) operates in the same fashion as the previous program, offering backpacking treks, birding hikes, art programs, family day hikes, and natural history and photography courses in the park.

One of the best ways to brush up on your national park trivia is to spend some time with a ranger (but not because you're illegally parked or guilty of feeding bears). For years, rangers have offered campfire programs and hikes that explore an aspect of their parks' wildlife or geology or history, and these programs continue in full swing today.

Visit **Yellowstone,** and you're sure to find a program on geysers and hot springs (see Chapter 16). Travel to **Death Valley,** and you see rangers, dressed in period costume at Scotty's Castle, recounting a bit of the park's intriguing human history (see Chapter 10). At **Mount Rainier National Park,** you shouldn't have to look too far to find a program that delves into the park's volcanology (see Chapter 13). In **Grand Canyon National Park,** rangers will fill you in on the incredible geology of that huge canyon (see Chapter 11). Best of all, these programs are all covered by the cost of your admission to the park.

Unfortunately, most parks offer ranger programs only during the high season, which, in all but Death Valley, occurs during the summer months.

Chapter 8

Taking Care of the Remaining Details

*O*kay, so you've made the big decisions about your national park vacation; you've figured out when, where, and how you want to go. In this chapter, you get to consider the last picky details and important safety measures that can make or break your trip.

Packing for the Parks

If you're like me, packing for a national park visit involves taking an inventory of your toys — cross-country skis or snowshoes for the winter excursion to Grand Teton or Mount Rainier, the canoe for the journey to Yellowstone, and the hiking stick for just about every park. What you haul depends on what activities you plan to do.

If you're not spending time in the higher elevations, your **summer** packing list for most parks should include a couple pairs of comfortable hiking shorts, T-shirts (preferably some synthetic ones, not cotton tees that leave you shivering when they're soaked with sweat), a good rain jacket or a water-resistant shell parka, hiking boots, socks, a wide-brimmed hat, a fanny pack, and water bottles. You may also want some nice jeans or a pair or two of slacks and casual shirts for dining out, as well as a light sweater or sweatshirt for cool evenings.

When devising your packing list, remember that dealing with temperature changes is easier if you dress in layers. You can fend off the coldest summer weather with shirt layers, a fleece jacket, a water-resistant shell, and a hat. Layers can usually combat the chilly nights in the Rockies or High Sierra, too. If you plan to backpack, a good summer sleeping bag works in the Southwest, although you may want a three-season bag for the Rockies and High Sierra.

What do you take for a **winter** trip? Again, you want to dress in layers so you can handle Arctic blasts as well as unseasonable warm spells. Polypropylene underwear is a must for dealing with snow and cold because the material dries quickly and, unlike cotton, doesn't hold moisture next to your skin. Wool shirts, sweaters, and pants are good, and so is fleece outerwear. Your final layer should be water-repellent or waterproof. Don't forget a good warm hat and gloves or mittens. A nice pair of warm, weather-resistant boots will ensure your feet don't suffer.

For a variety of reasons, I recommend a hiking stick for almost every park. The best sticks ease the burden on your knees during downhill stretches. If you find yourself fording a stream, a walking stick will go a long way to keep you upright. In some parks, you may encounter a copperhead snake or a rattlesnake. I don't recommend prodding these fellas, but if one is in the middle of the trail and won't scoot, a nice long walking stick is great for shooing 'em on.

Summer gear checklist

❏ Hiking T-shirts	❏ Walking stick	❏ Backpack
❏ Hiking boots	❏ Sunglasses	❏ Topographical maps
❏ Hiking shorts	❏ Fanny pack/day pack	❏ Compass
❏ Dress shirts	❏ Sunscreen or block	❏ Sleeping bag*
❏ Dress slacks	❏ First-aid kit	❏ Sleeping pad*
❏ Dress shoes	❏ Binoculars	❏ Cooking gear*
❏ Light sweater/ sweatshirt	❏ Camera/film	❏ Tent*
❏ Jeans	❏ Water bottles/ hydration system	❏ Water filter*
❏ Sneakers	❏ Insect repellent	❏ Bear spray**
❏ Broad-brimmed hat	❏ Guidebooks	❏ Rain gear
❏ Bird book		

*for camping   **for parks with black and/or grizzly bears

Winter gear checklist

❑ Shell parka	❑ Walking stick	❑ Backpack
❑ Down/synthetic vest	❑ Sunglasses	❑ Topographical maps
❑ Gloves	❑ Fanny pack/day pack	❑ Compass
❑ Hiking boots	❑ Sunscreen or block	❑ Gaiters
❑ Thermal underwear	❑ First-aid kit	❑ Tent^x
❑ Sweater	❑ Binoculars	❑ Cooking gear^x
❑ Fleece pants	❑ Camera/film	❑ Sleeping pad*
❑ Shell pants	❑ Water bottles/ hydration system	❑ Water filter*
❑ Snowshoes	❑ Guidebooks	❑ Sleeping bag*
❑ Extra shoes	❑ Bird book	❑ Broad-brimmed hat
❑ Cross-country skis/poles		

*for camping

First-aid kits are must-haves, even if you don't plan to go far into the great outdoors. You never know whether you'll pick up a splinter, cut a finger, or gash a knee. A good first-aid kit contains tweezers, butterfly and other adhesive bandages, sterile gauze pads, adhesive tape, an antibiotic ointment, children and adult pain relievers, alcohol pads, a knife, and scissors. And don't forget wrapping bandages in case someone turns an ankle, as well as different medicines to combat upset stomachs, motion sickness, minor allergic reactions, and skin rashes. Tossing a whistle into the kit is a good idea, too, so you have something to signal searchers if you wind up lost in the backcountry.

You can buy decent prepackaged first-aid kits at your local outdoor goods store for around $40. They carry all the things you need — some even contain instruction manuals for treating injuries and wounds.

When packing for your trip, use the summer and winter gear checklists in this chapter.

Traveling with Spot or Fluffy

National parks allow pets, but if you really love your pet, leave him or her at home. Park regulations require that they be restrained at all times, and many parks prohibit them from going on trails or entering the backcountry. So while you're out on a half-day hike, Spot sits panting in your car as the heat slowly rises.

In parks with predators, such as Yellowstone where wolves, grizzly bears, and mountain lions roam, if your faithful friend somehow escapes his leash and darts into the woods, he can quickly become some critter's appetizer.

If leaving your pet at home isn't an option, consider boarding him or her at a kennel in your own town or in one of the parks' gateway communities, which usually offer boarding. To find out about an individual park's pet policy, call ahead (see the Appendix for the individual park numbers) or check the park's Web site at www.nps.gov.

Paying Fees and Getting Permits

The national parks are an incredible bargain when you consider what you get for your **entrance fee,** which ranges from $10 to $20 per car in most cases. If you want to visit several parks in a year, you can stretch your buck even farther by purchasing a **National Park Pass.** This $50 pass covers admission to any national park that charges an entry fee. The pass is good for one year, and you can use it as many times as you like. All the folks riding in your car when you arrive at the entrance station get in free as well. The pass even works if you're traveling in some other manner, say by bicycle or on foot. You can buy it at any National Park Service entry station or by sending a check for $53.95 to the National Parks Foundation, Attn: Parks Pass, P.O. Box 34108, Washington, D.C., 20043-4108. You also can purchase the pass, or renew your existing one, through the National Park Foundation's Web site, www.national parks.org. Got questions? Call 1-888-GO-PARKS.

The national parks also offer passes that include **discounts** for travelers over 62 and for the disabled. See Chapter 7 for information on the **Golden Age Passport** or **Golden Access Passport.**

Although the entrance fees cover most of the national parks' attractions, you do need a **permit** for some activities. For instance, if you plan to canoe in Yellowstone, you need to buy a $5 permit. If you want to fish in any of the parks, you need a park permit or a state fishing license. See the individual park chapters for details on required permits.

All the parks require you to pick up a **backcountry permit** for overnight backcountry travel. (Unless noted otherwise in this book, you don't need a permit for day hikes.) In almost all cases, you must buy the permit. The fees, which are nominal, go toward mitigating any impact that travel has on these areas. To determine the cost of a backcountry permit at the park you're going to visit, call ahead (see the Appendix for the individual park numbers) or check the National Park Service Web site at www.nps.gov. For more information on obtaining backcountry permits, see Chapter 6 and the individual park chapters.

Playing It Safe with Travel and Medical Insurance

Three kinds of travel insurance are available: trip-cancellation insurance, medical insurance, and lost luggage insurance. The cost of travel insurance varies widely, but expect to pay between 5 percent and 8 percent of the vacation itself. Here is my advice concerning all three:

✔ **Trip-cancellation insurance** helps you get your money back if you have to back out of a trip, if you have to go home early, or if your travel supplier goes bankrupt. Allowed reasons for cancellation can range from sickness to natural disasters to the State Department declaring your destination unsafe for travel.

A good resource is **Travel Guard Alerts,** a list of companies considered high-risk by Travel Guard International (www.travelinsured. com). Protect yourself further by paying for the insurance with a credit card — by law, consumers can get their money back on goods and services not received if they report the loss within 60 days after the charge appears on their credit card statement.

Note: Many tour operators include insurance in the cost of the trip or can arrange insurance policies through a partnering provider, a convenient and often cost-effective way for the traveler to obtain insurance. Make sure the tour company is a reputable one, however: Some experts suggest you avoid buying insurance from the tour or cruise company you're traveling with, saying it's better to buy from a "third party" insurer than to put all your money in one place.

✔ For domestic travel, buying **medical insurance** for your trip doesn't make sense for most travelers. Most existing health policies cover you if you get sick away from home — but check before you go, particularly if you're insured by an HMO.

✔ **Lost luggage insurance** isn't necessary for most travelers. On domestic flights, checked baggage is covered up to $2,500 per ticketed passenger. If you plan to check items more valuable than the standard liability, see if your valuables are covered by your homeowner's policy, get baggage insurance as part of your comprehensive travel-insurance package, or buy Travel Guard's "BagTrak" product. Don't buy insurance at the airport, because it's usually overpriced. Take any valuables or irreplaceable items with you in your carry-on luggage, because many valuables (including books, money, and electronics) aren't covered by airline policies.

If your luggage is lost, immediately file a lost-luggage claim at the airport, detailing the luggage contents. For most airlines, you must report delayed, damaged, or lost baggage within 4 hours of arrival. The airlines are required to deliver luggage, when they find it, directly to your house or destination, free of charge.

For more information, contact one of the following: **Access America** (☎ 866-807-3982; www.accessamerica.com); **Travel Guard International** (☎ 800-826-4919; www.travelguard.com); **Travel Insured International** (☎ 800-243-3174; www.travelinsured.com); and **Travelex Insurance Services** (☎ 888-457-4602; www.travelex-insurance.com).

Finding Medical Care in the Parks

Getting sick will ruin your vacation, so I *strongly* advise against it (of course, last time I checked, the bugs weren't listening to me any more than they probably listen to you).

Talk to your doctor before leaving on a trip if you have a serious and/or chronic illness. For conditions such as epilepsy, diabetes, or heart problems, wear a **MedicAlert identification tag** (☎ 888-633-4298; www.medicalert.org), which immediately alerts doctors to your condition and gives them access to your records through Medic Alert's 24-hour hotline. Contact the **International Association for Medical Assistance to Travelers (IAMAT)** (☎ 716-754-4883 or, in Canada, 416-652-0137; www.iamat.org) for tips on travel and health concerns. The United States **Centers for Disease Control and Prevention** (☎ 800-311-3435; www.cdc.gov) provides up-to-date information on health hazards by region and offers tips on food safety.

Within the national parks, you find gift shops and general stores stocked with over-the-counter medicines and first-aid items. For more serious injuries, some parks provide clinics within their borders, or you can find hospitals in nearby towns. The "Fast Facts" section at the end of each park chapter lists locations of the nearest pharmacies and hospitals.

Staying Healthy When You Travel

National parks are gorgeous places, but they're also wild places. Surprisingly, many folks swarm into them with the bizarre notion that the wild animals are cuddly and the landscape is safe. Although much of the landscape is safe, certain areas require caution. Despite the best efforts by park officials and guidebooks like this one to convince park visitors that they have to be careful, a surprising number of people wind up in predicaments that require rangers to come to their rescue (lost in the woods, stuck on a mountainside, fallen into a canyon, and so on). In 2001, more than 4,400 people were the subject of search-and-rescue operations carried out throughout the park system. Even though rangers are ready, skilled, and equipped to rescue you, everyone is better off if they don't have to. And about those animals? Well, they may be cute, but they're definitely not tame.

In the following sections, I outline some simple measures you can take to ensure that you joyfully survive your national park trip.

Walking with care

No one plans to get hurt on vacation, but accidents happen. Release a
bunch of people into the woods on a daylong hike, and I'll lay you odds
that someone will return with a twisted ankle or muscle strain. You can
take the following precautions to make sure that you're not the injured
person:

- ✔ **Properly prepare for your hike.** Do you own good, sturdy, comfortable hiking boots that are adequately broken in? Are you carrying enough water to sate your thirst from start to finish? What
  about rain gear? Sure, the weather may look great when you hit the
  trailhead at 8 a.m., but in the Rockies, thunderheads can form
  quickly, and they can drench you by 2 p.m. In case the clouds do
  stay away, pack a good hat, sunscreen, and sunglasses. The hot sun
  can inflict a world of pain on your body unless you ward it off.

- ✔ **Pack some munchies.** Put fruit, granola bars, or candy into your
  fanny pack or backpack for a burst of energy on the trail.

- ✔ **Know your limitations.** Everything is relative when it comes to
  hiking trails. A moderate trail to one person may be strenuous to
  another and easy to a third. A hike that takes the average person
  four hours can take another person two hours or even six.
  Distances can be incredibly deceiving, too. Although the map indi-
  cates 6 miles, the ups and downs of the landscape can make the
  distance feel twice as long. If you feel the trail is getting the better
  of you, don't be embarrassed to turn around and head back to your
  car with plans for tackling the route again some other day.

Filtering your drinking water

Sadly, you probably won't find a stream during your travels that isn't
contaminated with a parasite from feces called *giardia lablia,* which
causes chronic diarrhea. Giardia can remain in your system for years if
untreated. Symptoms usually arise a week to ten days after exposure
and last one to three weeks, but they can return repeatedly.

You contract this nasty bug by drinking from contaminated streams and
lakes without first treating, filtering, or boiling the water. You can treat
the water with tablets, but these leave an aftertaste that some (including
this guy) don't care for. Boiling is effective, but the method leaves you
with hot water and isn't always practical, especially on a hot summer
day. The best option is to use a filter. Reliable filters, which range from
$70 to $140 at an outdoor goods store, may seem costly at first, but consider the alternative.

Also, be sure that your children know not to swallow water while swimming. If someone does come down with diarrhea a month or so after
your outdoor trip, ask your doctor for a giardiasis stool test. Several pre-
scription medicines are available to treat the symptoms.

Getting too hot, too cold, or too high

Spending any amount of time in a national park involves exposure to the elements — rain, sleet, snow, or simply sunshine. If you're not prepared, you can quickly fall victim to one of five serious conditions:

- **Heat exhaustion:** A threat in parks like Death Valley, Arches, Grand Canyon, and Zion (places where the summer temperatures routinely surpass the century mark), this condition strikes if you sweat too much in a short period of time and wind up dehydrating. Under severe conditions, you can lose 1 to 2 liters of water per hour. Your body normally runs through 2 or 3 quarts of water a day, and in the desert, you need to drink four times that amount to ensure proper hydration. If you lose just 2 percent of the water in your body, you can suffer weakness, headaches, and nausea. You may stop thinking clearly or may become irritable.

  How can you identify heat exhaustion? A pale face, nausea, cool and moist skin, a headache, and cramps are all symptoms. If your urine is dark yellow, you're becoming dehydrated. Avoid heat exhaustion by drinking lots of water and by pacing yourself during the hottest parts of the day. Wear a wide-brimmed hat in the Southwest and even in mountainous areas where the atmosphere is thin. If you fall victim to heat exhaustion, drink water, eat high-energy foods, and find a place in the shade to rest and cool down.

  (If you think you're immune to heat exhaustion, the next time you visit the Phantom Ranch or Indian Garden in the Grand Canyon, ask the rangers about their experiences. They treat up to 20 cases of heat exhaustion a day during the summer.)

- **Heatstroke:** This condition is another heat-related one that can be life-threatening. Heatstroke short-circuits your body's ability to regulate its temperature. Symptoms include a flushed face, hot but dry skin, high temperature, and confusion. In extreme cases, you can lose consciousness, and if untreated, you can die. If you see someone with these symptoms, immediately take him to a shady place and cool him down with water while someone goes for help.

- **Hyponatremia:** This little-known condition can arise if you drink too much water. The high water volume drastically reduces the sodium level in your bloodstream through sweating. Symptoms range from nausea and vomiting to frequent urination and mental confusion. The obvious treatment is to eat salty foods and, in extreme cases when the victim loses alertness, seek medical attention.

- **Hypothermia:** Your body may cool too much, usually from swimming in a frigid alpine lake or being soaked to the skin in cold weather. Many people no doubt have faced mild cases of hypothermia. Symptoms include starting to shiver uncontrollably or losing some muscle control. Treat this condition by getting the victim out of the cold elements and having them put on warm clothing, drink warm liquids, and, in severe cases, share a sleeping bag with someone.

 ✔ **Altitude sickness:** If you go from sea level to 8,000 feet or higher, you
   may experience altitude sickness. This problem is most common at
   elevations above 10,000 feet, where the body needs to gradually
   adjust to getting less oxygen in each breath. However, even if you
   don't plan to climb the Grand Teton, which tops out at 13,770 feet, I
   recommend that you take a day or two to get acclimated to a higher
   elevation park before launching into a 10-mile hike.

   How do you know if you're experiencing trouble with the altitude?
   Headaches, insomnia, general sluggishness, and nosebleeds are all
   signs that your body is struggling with the elevation. Usually, these
   symptoms disappear after a couple of days. If they don't, consider
   seeing a doctor.

Minding furry beasts and creepy crawlies

Upon arriving in Yellowstone, you're almost immediately greeted by
bison, grazing contentedly in a meadow. You think, "What a great picture!" So you park your car and hop out, armed with your 35mm, digital,
or video camera. Unfortunately, you don't have a telephoto or zoom
lens. "Heck," you say, looking at these seemingly docile creatures, "I can
get a little closer." So you do. Then a little more. And a bit more. And
then, this big, shaggy, 2,000-pound bison is fed up with your advances
and charges. Not only do you miss the picture, but you're whisked to the
park hospital to have your leg stitched up where the bison gored you.
(True, that makes for an interesting memento of your trip, but probably
not what you had in mind.)

Animals injure people every year in Yellowstone, despite warnings to
keep tourists away from bison, elk, and other park inhabitants. The odds
of you encountering one of the more deadly critters diminish in propor-
tion to their nastiness. In other words, you may see a black bear before
you see a grizzly, and a grizzly before you see a mountain lion. And you
probably won't see a mountain lion.

Legally, you're prohibited from getting within 100 yards of bears or
25 yards of other wildlife or nesting birds. Logically, you should keep at
least the required distance from the animals if you want to ensure that
the memories you take away from your trip are positive ones. Be especially careful when a young animal is around because its momma will be
eager to protect it from you.

In the following sections, I give you my general advice on how to avoid
or handle run-ins with the parks' animal kingdom.

Black bears

These animals are common in Sequoia, Yosemite, and Grand Teton. The
bears that live out West tend to be bigger, stronger, and generally more
obnoxious than their eastern kin. When you enter Sequoia and Yosemite,
rangers tell you how many parked cars have been torn open like sardine
cans by hungry black bears that sniffed an empty potato chip bag from

50 yards. At Sequoia's Lodgepole Campground, the rangers keep a running total of attacks on parked cars, and display some impressive pictures showing the damage.

For the most part, bears are driven by food. So if you're camping out, be sure to clean every chip bag, apple core, and even gum wrapper from your rig or tent before you call it a night. Also, make sure to change your clothes after cooking dinner (and put the clothes somewhere other than in your tent) so you don't go to bed smelling like a hot dog or hamburger. Take advantage of the parks' bear-proof boxes for storing food. One night when I pulled into Tuolumne Meadows Campground in Yosemite, a black bear came trotting out of the woods and inspected each and every bear box in sight, only to pad away in disappointment because he couldn't get into them.

 In the highly unlikely event that a black bear pops into your tent while you're sleeping or approaches you on the trail, reach for a weapon (sticks, stones, flashlights, and pepper spray all work), not your camera. Don't play dead, because black bears approach humans when they're hungry. If you curl up in a ball, the bear may think that you're tossing in the towel and view you as the main course.

Deer ticks

The deer tick, a very small cousin to the wood tick, causes Lyme disease, a disturbing malady named after a town in Connecticut, the site of its discovery. The early symptoms of this disease resemble the signs of the flu, but you also get a rash in the shape of a bull's-eye. If overlooked, Lyme disease can attack the nervous system and cause heart abnormalities.

Keeping Lyme disease at arm's length is pretty easy. For starters, you need to be on the lookout for deer ticks especially in California and the Pacific Northwest. What should you do if you find yourself in these parts of the country? Try to avoid hiking through tall grasses or brushy areas. If you do plan on going into the outback, use a good insect repellent with DEET, and apply it to your arms and legs. After your hike, inspect yourself meticulously; if necessary, ask a friend to search your scalp and the other parts of your body that elude your own eyes. A Lyme disease vaccine does exist, but the vaccination process requires several injections over a year to create immunity. Don't go this route unless you expect to frequently spend time in tick habitat.

If you find a tick, remove it with tweezers by pulling directly outward without squeezing the parasite's body, an action that can inject more bacteria into your bloodstream. Dab the bite with alcohol to help disinfect the wound, and save the tick in a jar to determine later if it is a deer tick. If you're close to a medical facility, see a doctor to handle the extraction; if not, remove the tick yourself and go for testing and treatment as soon as possible, taking the tick with you.

Grizzly bears

The only parks in this book where you may encounter a grizzly bear are Grand Teton and Yellowstone — and I visited Yellowstone for a dozen years before I saw one about 2 miles away from me. Although grizzlies routinely begged from cars and fed from Yellowstone's garbage pits in the 1940s and 1950s, stringent bear management policies in the 1960s returned the park's grizzlies to their wilder nature by convincing them that the backcountry (not the campgrounds) was their territory. Today, you can go into the Lamar Valley or the Hayden Valley and, with a good spotting scope or binoculars, safely see grizzlies in their native landscape doing what grizzlies do in the wild.

Be particularly careful when you go for a hike in the spring or early summer. In Yellowstone in springtime, carcasses of elk and bison that failed to survive the winter litter the park. These remains are magnets for grizzlies famished after a long winter's snooze. After finding a carcass, they often munch on it for days. If you come upon a carcass during a hike, you may not only disturb a bear dining on it, but you may also be perceived as competition for the meat and find yourself in a fight.

In the backcountry, the odds of confronting a grizzly increases, but they're not as high as you may think. Keeping a clean camp (by storing all food on the bear poles that the park service has erected at many designated backcountry campsites) and hiking loudly in groups of two or more further reduces the odds. If you do come upon a bear while hiking, stop, speak softly to it, and slowly back away. If the bear charges, drop to the ground, fold your knees into your stomach, and wrap your arms around your head. Although the bear may swat you with its paws or bite your back, most grizzly attacks occur because they feel threatened. Subtract the threat — playing dead takes guts, but it usually does the trick — and the bear skedaddles off into the woods.

Bear repellent, also known as pepper spray, is gaining more popularity these days as a great way for getting a charging grizzly bear to reverse its course. I carry some myself, although I hope that I never have to use it. The thought of standing my ground in the face of a charging grizzly, waiting for it to come within 5 to 6 yards so I can direct the spray into its face, is not a pleasant one.

Mountain lions

Mountain lions (also known as pumas and cougars) live in Arches, Death Valley, Grand Canyon, Grand Teton, Mount Rainier, Olympic, Sequoia/Kings Canyon, Yellowstone, Yosemite, and Zion national parks. Confronting one of these big cats is scary, but, fortunately, you'll probably never see one. If you come upon one and it doesn't bolt in the opposite direction, stand your ground and throw rocks, sticks, backpacks, or whatever you can heft in its direction. Also try to make yourself seem as big as possible by holding your arms, or even your pack, over your head. If the cat still attacks, fight it as tenaciously as you can. When hiking on remote trails, stay in groups, make noise, and don't let young children lag behind or dart ahead of the group.

Snakes, spiders, and scorpions

Other nasties are poisonous snakes and spiders and, in the Southwest, scorpions. Your best defense is to keep your eyes open, and never to put your hand someplace that you can't see (such as when climbing).

If bitten by a snake, remain calm. Symptoms quickly follow, starting with a funny taste in your mouth. Snakebite kits (the ones that include a razor and a suction cup) are no longer recommended. You can often inflict more damage trying to get the venom out with one of these kits than by seeking medical attention. If you or someone in your party is bitten on the hand or arm, keep the limb below the heart while heading to the doctor. Carry anyone who has been bitten on the leg or foot.

Spider bites can be nasty, depending on which spider does the biting. Bites from black widows and brown recluse spiders need medical attention. Although not typically fatal, they can cause damage to the skin surrounding the bite, and may cause infection. Chances are, though, that you won't see the culprit that bit you. In these cases, play it safe and visit the nearest clinic for precautionary treatment.

Scorpion bites can be painful, but rarely deadly. To help ease the pain, apply an ice pack to the bite. Do seek medical attention in the off chance that your bite came from one of the more harmful species.

Being wary of national wonders

Pounding surf, rugged cliffs, or glistening glaciers — the landscape of the national parks is spectacular but potentially hazardous. Keep safety in mind when exploring the wonders of your chosen park:

- ✔ **Cliffs:** In Yellowstone, trails that lead to observation points of the Grand Canyon of the Yellowstone River leave little room for error, and in early spring, fall, and winter storms can leave the cliffs slippery with ice and snow. In the Grand Canyon, five people fell to their deaths in 1998. Use caution whenever you approach the rim. Don't think you can dart beyond a guardrail for a quick picture and then safely return. Propping yourself atop that guardrail for a picture is never a good idea.

- ✔ **Glaciers:** You may encounter glaciers on the higher elevations of Mount Rainier, Grand Teton, or Olympic national parks. You don't face any risk of being run over by these slow-moving rivers of ice, but if you find yourself in the wrong place — specifically, below the snout (front section) of the glacier — you can be bopped on the head by a chunk of ice, a boulder, or other debris.

✔ **Ocean beaches:** In the Pacific Northwest, rivers running to the sea often carry logs that work their way down the coast before coming ashore with the waves. They will make short work of you if a wave crashes one into your body. In Olympic National Park, you'll see warning signs on your way down to the beaches but no lifeguards caution you at the water's edge, so be extremely careful if you venture into the surf.

When on the coast, also beware of tricky undercurrents known as *rip tides.* These currents can be incredibly powerful, particularly around the full moon, and they can yank you out to sea. Also, in Olympic National Park, rocky shorelines and outcrops of rocks pose dangers, as does the incredibly cold water. Even though rock scrambling is great fun, a misplaced step can send you into the ocean or onto more rocks. Also, if you decide to leapfrog into the water on rock formations, keep an eye on the tide, which can quickly change and leave you marooned far from shore.

✔ **Ocean waves:** Don't an unnecessary bout of seasickness ruin your trip to Olympic, takemotion-sickness tablets. A downside is that these tablets may make you sleepy. If you feel seasickness coming on head for an open deck for fresh air and keep your eyes on the horizon until the feeling passes.

✔ **Snowfields:** At Mount Rainier, you and your kids may be drawn to sliding across the snow and waging war with snowballs, in the name of good cold fun. But if you're out for a hike, pay particular attention to your footing when crossing snowfields, especially if the slope is steep. Stopping a downhill slide can be difficult in these conditions, and you don't want to slide headfirst into a rock.

✔ **Thermal features:** Yellowstone's thermal features never cease to amaze me. Year after year, I return to the park in large part to stare into these steaming aquamarine pools. Every now and then, I see the bleached bones of some unfortunate animal that slipped into a spring and was quickly poached. When you and your kids are touring the geyser basins, keep in mind that these unforgiving waters are near boiling point or even hotter. Over the years, many people and pets have fallen in with fatal results. Don't join the list. Stay on the boardwalks that wind through the geyser basins, keep your children under control, and your pets on their leashes.

The backcountry doesn't have boardwalks to keep you a safe distance from the thermal features. Use common sense and stay twice as far away as you think you should.

✔ **Waterfalls:** Water can pose a problem even when you're hundreds of miles from the coast. In many parks, waterfalls are gorgeous to look at and tantalizing to climb. Some folks even stand on the brink of a fall. But the routes up waterfalls are always steep and often slippery. Yosemite has a long history of people tumbling off the top of Nevada Falls.

Part III

Exploring the National Parks of the American West

SID'S
TARANTULA, SCORPION,
AND RATTLESNAKE
PETTING ZOO

Welcome to
Death Valley

In this part . . .

One of the beauties of the national park system is its diversity. Most folks can find one park that fits them like a glove in terms of things to do, places to stay, and sights to see. After you read this part, I bet you'll have at least one, and maybe a half dozen, parks that you can't wait to visit. In the following chapters, you find out everything you need to know about 11 of the country's best national parks, from what to see and what to do to where to eat and sleep. I even give you the blueprint for a great day in the park of your choice, with some extra ideas tossed in if you have more than one day to visit.

Chapter 9

Arches National Park

. . . .

In This Chapter

▶ Introducing a redrock wonder
▶ Planning your visit to the park
▶ Enjoying the natural highlights
▶ Heading to Moab for the best sleeps and eats

. . . .

*A*mong Utah's five national parks (a total that only California and Alaska can surpass), Arches National Park is often lost in the shuffle. In fact, fewer than one million people visit each year. Why? Well, this park lacks the towering cliffs and slot canyons of Zion, isn't chockfull of the whimsical rock formations found in Bryce Canyon, can't match the mountainous formations of Capitol Reef, and doesn't feature the swallow-the-world canyons of Canyonlands.

What Arches does have is something you can't find anywhere else in the world — within the park's 76,519 dry and dusty acres in southeastern Utah rises an otherworldly landscape of rock arches, windows, spires, pinnacles, and keenly balanced rocks that somehow manage to thumb their collective noses at gravity's constant pull. According to last count, the park features more than 2,000 officially recognized stone arches. But with gravity and erosion of the park's rock walls at work, a new arch can fall into place at any time. Conversely, an existing arch, weary from standing against time, can simply crumble away.

But Arches is more than an art gallery of rocks. If you look past the arches, windows, and balanced rocks, you see a wild and pure desertscape. At first glance, the land seems inhospitable, but if you look more closely you might spot lizards, snakes, ravens, mule deer, foxes, and — in season — gorgeous blooms of wild flowers. And with all the open countryside and sandstone, the sun paints Arches more than parks that are heavily forested. Early morning and late afternoon sun glistens on the sandstone cliffs and arches and even on the sandy earth. When the rays change their angle, the red, yellow, and orange hues of the landscape change, too.

Arches' nearest town, Moab, has drawn tourists for a long time. First they came to see the colorful redrock landscape, and then they discovered the nearby white-water rafting, and more recently, they went nuts over mountain biking opportunities.

Finding fins in the landscape

Rock *fins* (humpback rock formations) that jut up from the landscape are just as imposing as the arches, but not quite as obvious. The results of erosion, fins are the precursors to arches. Over the centuries, erosion has carved archways and windows into these upright sheets of rock. Wherever you see an arch, a fin previously stood.

Must-See Attractions

In a park that boasts the world's largest collection of rock arches, you don't have to hunt far to find them. In this sandstone playground, arches of all sizes and curious shapes abound. You also find intriguing rock mazes and short but worthwhile trails. So where do you head after entering the park? I suggest checking out the following sites:

- ✔ **Delicate Arch:** The image of this arch decorates Utah's license plates, but the real thing is much more impressive. Although you can drive to a viewpoint to glimpse Delicate Arch, the hiking trail provides a more dramatic perspective. Plus, a photograph of you or your family posing under the arch is a classic.

- ✔ **Devils Garden:** Located on the north end of the park, this area features an easy trail that leads to Landscape Arch. Along the trail, you encounter six more arches and Fin Canyon, a sprawling maze of sandstone fins.

- ✔ **Fiery Furnace:** This labyrinth of sandstone fins features so many colorful twists and turns in which past hikers have gotten lost, that park officials require you to get a day pass or enter with a ranger.

- ✔ **Park Avenue Trail:** This easy hike takes you past incredible stone monoliths. Talk about being overpowered by your surroundings!

- ✔ **The Windows:** No need to expend a lot of sweat to see a great collection of arches and windows (see "Name that rock" sidebar for details on these structures). Short walks from a parking lot lead to the various attractions in The Windows, including North and South Windows, Turret Arch, Double Arch, and Cove of Caves.

Planning Ahead

For general information about the park, write Superintendent, Arches National Park, P.O. Box 907, Moab, UT 84532-0907; call ☎ **435-719-2299** or 435-719-2319 (TTY); or check the Internet at www.nps.gov/arch.

When to go and how long to stay

A spring or fall visit is best. No crowds are in evidence, and the weather is absolutely wonderful, not blistering hot. By mid-October, the crowds have waned, and the weather is cooler — daily highs average 77 degrees. Winter can also be great. Even though the mercury drops below freezing at night, daytime highs are routinely in the 40s and 50s, great temperatures for hiking — the best way to explore the park.

Although you can easily navigate the park's major attractions in one day, allow two or three to really get to know Arches. Photographers may need two days in order to capture the late afternoon lighting in two particularly photogenic spots: Delicate Arch and Fiery Furnace. You can take some great hikes when you're not rushed. Plus, **Canyonlands National Park** is right next door, and a half-day's side trip to that park's Island in the Sky District is well worth it.

Advance reservations

Summer is the park's busiest season and the hottest — temperatures frequently surpass 100 degrees in June, July, and August. If you come during the busy summer and early fall months, be sure to book a motel room at least three months in advance. Moab's motels fill up quickly and the *No Vacancy* signs have been known to burn out. Sorrel River Ranch and Sunflower Hill Bed & Breakfast are two noteworthy places in high demand. Although winter is less crowded, many restaurants in Moab close from December through February.

What to pack

Bring layers of lightweight clothing that you can put on and take off. Mornings during the spring and fall can be cool, so bring a light fleece jacket. Summer mornings are gorgeous — warm and typically sunny. But as the days wear on, so does the heat, so come prepared with shorts, T-shirts, large-brimmed hats, sunglasses, and sunscreen.

A good, lightweight pair of hiking boots should also be part of your wardrobe. Although sneakers will generally suffice, if you're going to scramble on the rockscape you'll feel much more comfortable wearing boots with "sticky" rubber soles that grip the rock.

Name that rock

Arches National Park features arches, windows, and natural bridges. What's the difference? Arches are created when erosion, usually without the aid of rushing water, cuts holes in large rock spans (called *fins*). Natural bridges are the result of stream erosion in rock faces. Windows are just small arches. You usually find these gaps, which may resemble the windows in your house, high off the ground.

Don't forget rain gear! Spring, summer, and fall can all bring the occasional rainstorm. For more tips on what to pack, see Chapter 8.

Getting There

Arches is a park that requires a little extra effort to reach, but the visit is worth the inconvenience.

Driving in

If you're driving, U.S. 191 runs north and south past Arches. From the north, take Interstate 70 across central Utah to Crescent Junction and then head south on U.S. 191 to the park entrance. From the south, U.S. 191 connects with U.S. 160 in northeastern Arizona. After you cross the border into Utah, you're 128 miles south of the park.

Flying in

Moab's air service seems to change annually. At last check, **Salmon Air** (☎ 800-448-3413 or 435-259-0566; www.salmonair.com) was using twin-engine aircraft to fly to Canyonlands Field near Moab (which is just 5 miles south of the park on U.S. 191) from Salt Lake City. From the airport, you need to rent a car to drive to the park. **Thrifty** and **Budget** have offices in Moab and will deliver a car to the airport. To reach the park, head 11 miles south on U.S. 191.

The nearest major commercial airport to Arches is **Walker Field** (☎ 970-244-9100) in Grand Junction, Colorado — 125 miles from the park. **America West Express, Delta/Skywest, Frontier, Great Lakes Aviation,** and **United Express** all fly to Walker Field. After you arrive, you must rent a car and drive to the park. **Alamo, Avis, Enterprise, Hertz,** and **National** all rent cars at the airport, whereas **Budget** and **Thrifty** operate nearby and provide a shuttle to/from the airport. To reach the park, take Interstate 70 west 93 miles to U.S. 191 and then head south for 32 miles.

See the Appendix for the toll-free numbers of car-rental agencies and airlines mentioned in this section.

Busing or training in

Greyhound (☎ 800-229-9424; www.greyhound.com) can drop you off at Green River, which is north of Moab and almost 50 miles from the park. Then you can arrange to take a regional shuttle, **Bighorn Express** (☎ 888-655-7433; www.bighornexpress.com), to Moab for $26 one-way, but you must call ahead for reservations. You can also catch the Bighorn Express in Salt Lake City; the bus makes one trip per day to Moab at a cost of $54 one-way and $108 round-trip. From Moab, you need to rent a car to visit the park. (See the preceding "Flying in" section for information on rental car agencies in Moab.)

Arches National Park

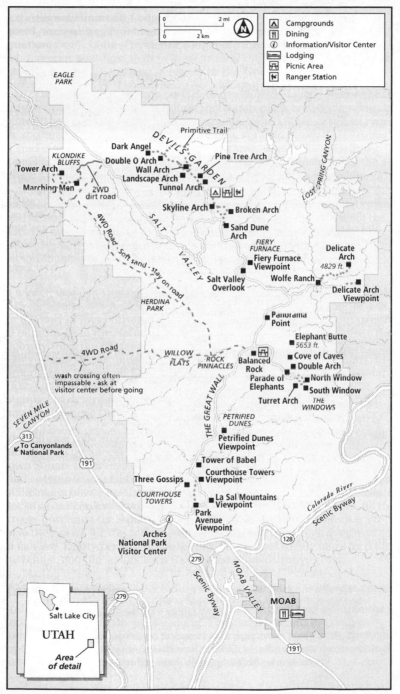

Legend:
- △ Campgrounds
- ⊤⊤ Dining
- ⓘ Information/Visitor Center
- 🛏 Lodging
- 🎪 Picnic Area
- 🚩 Ranger Station

EAGLE PARK

DEVIL'S GARDEN

Primitive Trail

KLONDIKE BLUFFS

Dark Angel
Double O Arch
Tower Arch
Wall Arch
Landscape Arch
Marching Men
2WD dirt road
Pine Tree Arch
Tunnel Arch

LOST SPRING CANYON

SALT VALLEY

4WD Road - Soft sand - stay on road

Skyline Arch
Broken Arch

Sand Dune Arch

FIERY FURNACE

Fiery Furnace Viewpoint

Delicate Arch
4829 ft.

Salt Valley Overlook
Wolfe Ranch

HERDINA PARK

Delicate Arch Viewpoint

Panorama Point

4WD Road
WILLOW FLATS
ROCK PINNACLES

wash crossing often impassable - ask at visitor center before going

Elephant Butte
5653 ft.

Cove of Caves
Balanced Rock
Double Arch
Parade of Elephants
Turret Arch
North Window
South Window
THE WINDOWS

SEVEN MILE CANYON

313
To Canyonlands National Park

191

THE GREAT WALL

PETRIFIED DUNES

Petrified Dunes Viewpoint

Tower of Babel

Three Gossips
Courthouse Towers Viewpoint

COURTHOUSE TOWERS

La Sal Mountains Viewpoint

Park Avenue Viewpoint

Colorado River

Scenic Byway

128

Arches National Park Visitor Center

279

Scenic Byway

MOAB VALLEY

MOAB

191

Salt Lake City

UTAH

Area of detail

279

The closest **Amtrak** station (☎ **800-USA-RAIL;** www.amtrak.com) is at Grand Junction, Colorado. If you choose this route, you need to rent a car to visit the park. (See the preceding "Flying in" section for information on rental car agencies in Grand Junction.)

Orienting Yourself in Arches

Covering 76,519 acres, Arches National Park is laid out in a rather straightforward fashion thanks to a natural clustering of the major arches and windows. The park has one visitor center.

Arches' main road, which runs from the visitor center to the Devils Garden Trailhead (the location of the park's only campground), is just under 18 miles long. Off this main artery run three major spurs: the 2½-mile-long leg to The Windows, a 2¼-mile-long branch to the Delicate Arch Trailhead and the Delicate Arch Viewpoint, and the 7¾-mile-long Salt Valley road to the relatively remote Klondike Bluffs area. All the roads, except for the Salt Valley road, are paved and in good shape. The Salt Valley road is unpaved and, therefore, slower going than the other roads.

A road for four-wheel-drive vehicles runs 9 miles northwest from near Balanced Rock to Klondike Bluffs, but park officials recommend that this route be traversed only from north to the south because of steep, sandy pitches that can mire rigs going the other way. The park's other four-wheel-drive route scampers west from Balanced Rock to U.S. 191, but this road can be impassable when wet. For more information on four-wheeling in the park, see "Keeping active," later in this chapter.

 Even if you're driving your favorite SUV, you may want to think twice and check with a ranger before heading down one of the backcountry roads. SUVs don't always provide the ground clearance needed in the rocky desert, and some tricky stretches may require off-road experience. You don't need to go four-wheeling in Arches anyway, because all the main attractions are along the paved roads.

Finding information after you arrive

Thanks to its compact size and simple road network, Arches is easy to navigate. From the visitor center just off U.S. 191 to the campground at Devils Garden, crisscrossing the park won't take more than 30 minutes.

The Arches National Park Visitor Center (☎ 435-719-2299), which is just inside the entrance gate off U.S. 191 and 5 miles north of Moab, provides maps, brochures, and other information. The center is open year-round from 8 a.m. to 4:30 p.m. A museum tells you everything you need to know about arch formation and other features of the park, and you can go to a short orientation program in the auditorium.

Paying fees

Entry for up to seven days costs $10 per private vehicle or $5 per person on foot or bicycle. See Chapter 8 for information on the National Park Pass and Chapter 7 for Golden Age and Golden Access Passports.

Getting Around Arches

Basically, you need a car in Arches, because the park doesn't provide its own transportation system. You can also get around by bicycle, but bikes are allowed only on the main road and not in the backcountry. (See "Keeping active" for more information on biking in the park.)

You can see many of the park's most famous rock formations through your car's windshield, but by all means, get out of the car and walk around. You can walk short distances to a number of viewpoints or stretch your legs on longer hikes (see "Taking a hike," later in this chapter). The main road is easy to navigate, even for RVs, but parking at some viewpoints is limited. Please be considerate and leave trailers at the visitor center parking lot or in the campground.

Remembering Safety

For your safety, keep the following in mind. Additional tips can be found in Chapter 8.

- ✔ **Use your senses — all of them.** When hiking around arches, keep your ears open for any popping or cracking sounds — noises that signal a rock fall. If you hear such sounds, get out from under the arch immediately and then check to see if anything is falling. Don't stop to look up while you're under the arch, because a falling rock is one natural phenomenon that you want to see from a distance.

- ✔ **Keep an eye on the weather.** Thunderstorms can build quickly in the spring and summer months. Because of the miles of open space and the lack of trees, you make a pretty good impression of a lightning rod. Sudden storms can also generate flash floods, so if you're in the backcountry, never camp in a *dry wash* (a dry stream bed) and never try to cross one during flood conditions.

- ✔ **Drink plenty of water.** In the hotter months (such as July when daytime temperature usually reach 100 degrees), drink plenty of water. With the intense sunlight, high temperatures, low humidity, and lack of shade, the park can be like an oven. If you're not drinking enough water, you can quickly succumb to heat exhaustion or heatstroke. During a summer visit, try to drink at least a gallon of water per day in the park, and do your friends a favor by making sure they drink frequently, too.

> ✔ **Know your limits.** Don't climb higher than your level of skill allows. Park rangers rescue many climbers who have worked their way up rock faces only to realize that they can't get back down. A few unfortunate ones have fallen and suffered broken bones.

Exploring Arches

With its lack of vegetation and fairly flat landscape, Arches National Park is an extremely user-friendly place to see the sights. Although hiking is the best way to get perspective on the size of the park's arches and other formations, you don't need to hike to see many of the major attractions, which are visible from the park's roadways.

Exploring the top attractions

For information on hikes to these attractions, see "Taking a hike" section later in this chapter.

Courthouse Towers

Minutes past the entrance in the southwestern corner of the park, lies a towering collection of pillars. As you walk among them, they impart the same sense of claustrophobia you get from a narrow street lined by tall buildings. Instead of glass and steel, however, these skyscrapers are made of rock. One rock formation clearly visible from the Park Avenue Trailhead bears a striking resemblance to Queen Nefertiti. Use your imagination while strolling the mile-long trail from the Park Avenue Trailhead to the Courthouse Towers Viewpoint. Although you may come up with some noteworthy descriptions of your own, the park calls some of these formations Three Gossips, Organ Rock, and Courthouse Towers.

See map p. 85. The viewpoints and trailheads for Courthouse Towers are just north of the visitor center on the main road.

Delicate Arch

Whether you think Delicate Arch looks like a pair of bloomers or a cowboy's chaps doesn't matter; what matters is that you see it up close. Hiking the 1½-mile trail that winds across slick rock and along a narrow shelf of rock is worth the effort. When you slip around the last corner — stepping onto the sandstone rim of an ancient sinkhole — and see Delicate Arch, you'll understand what I mean. Make sure to pack water, wear a hat, and avoid this hike at midday in the middle of summer. For a truly unique experience, schedule your visit when there's a full moon and make the hike at night.

See map p. 85. The turnoff for Delicate Arch is 11¾ miles north of the visitor center.

Devils Garden

This rumpled area of canyons, fins, and arches anchors the northern end of the park's main road. At Devils Garden, you find the only campground in the park as well as eight major arches, including Landscape and Double O. Make sure you have plenty of time to explore this area. You can spend a couple of hours just on the hike to and from Landscape Arch, Wall Arch, Pine Tree Arch, and Tunnel Arch. If you're not in a rush, toss in longer walks to Double O Arch or the Primitive Trail, unless you're afraid of heights — a stretch of trail runs across the spine of a fin.

See map p. 85. You can find the trail through Devils Garden at the end of the park's main road.

Fiery Furnace

The name of this twisting maze of rock comes not from the heat, but from the glowing reds, oranges, and pinks that flare across the sandstone fins in the rays of the setting sun. On hot days, the fins actually provide shade, which makes this furnace feel cooler than the rest of the park. See "Ranger programs," later in this chapter, for information on the afternoon guided tour — the best way to see the area.

See map p. 85. The Fiery Furnace Viewpoint, accessible by car, is located off the main park road.

The Windows

The easiest and quickest way to appreciate the park's features is to head to The Windows. This attraction is worth a visit for the size of the windows, the rock scrambling you can do, and the closeness of several unusual formations. You can easily see the North and South Windows from the parking lot; however, you should definitely hike through the area to gain a better perspective on their size. Both windows, as well as Turret Arch and Double Arch, are less than a quarter-mile from the parking lot. You can easily spend a half day in this area if you leave the well-trodden trail. Don't miss the Parade of Elephants formation and its associated arch. A primitive trail also winds behind and below the North and South Windows and features placards describing the nearby plants and cacti.

See map p. 85. The turnoff to The Windows is 9¼ miles north of the visitors center on the main road.

Taking a hike

In light of Arches' high temperatures, most hikes are short. The longest, Devils Garden Trail (which includes the Primitive Trail), is only 7¼ miles from start to finish; the rest are 4 miles or less. With film-gobbling redrock scenery scattered throughout the park, who cares about racking up trail miles? You don't need to go far to be impressed.

Capturing Arches on film

Two of Arches' most photogenic attractions, **Fiery Furnace** and **Delicate Arch,** are best photographed in the late afternoon because the low angle of the sun's rays seems to add depth to the formations, igniting their redrock features. In late spring and early summer, if your timing is right and the weather cooperates, you can get a great picture of Delicate Arch with the snow-capped La Sal Mountains in the background.

You can view Fiery Furnace by signing up for the afternoon guided tour (the best way to see it), but you likely won't be finished in time to make the hike to Delicate Arch before the sun sets. I recommend taking the Fiery Furnace tour, which winds through incredible passages and is more of a hands-on experience than standing in front of Delicate Arch.

Early morning light is the best for photographing many of the park's other formations.

Before you set foot on the trail, please heed some words of wisdom: Pack at least a quart of water (preferably two) per person, wear a hat with a wide brim, and slather on the sun block before.

Broken Arch Trail

Passing through sand dunes and across slick rock, the Broken Arch Trail is a good place to look for Western gopher snakes. These yellow snakes with black patches aren't poisonous, but they coil and shake their tails like rattlesnakes to scare off predators.

Distance: 2-mile loop trail from the campground in Devils Garden to the arch. Level: Easy to moderate. Access: Across from campsite 40.

Delicate Arch Trail

The hike to Delicate Arch seems intimidating when you first leave the parking lot. During the busy season, the folks hiking up the trail resemble a line of ants plodding across the redrock. Don't worry, just get in line and follow the path to the top. The first ½ mile takes you across a wide slab of rock with a well-defined trail. If you think that you may not be going the right way, look for the *cairns* (piles of rocks that indicate the trail's direction). Just before you get to the arch, you wander through a rock outcrop and scoot along a ledge for about 200 yards. (Don't worry, the ledge is wide enough to soothe your nerves.) At the end of the ledge, you stroll out onto a sprawling rock basin to face Delicate Arch.

Even though this hike is fairly short, it can be brutal if the temperature is in the 90s or higher. Most of the trail is fully exposed on a sandstone ridge, so don't hike to Delicate Arch in the middle of the day. Setting out at 5 p.m. or even 6 p.m. in summer or early fall is perfect. Plus, around this time of day, the sun gets into position for some great photographs.

On your way to the arch, after you cross the footbridge that spans Salt Wash just beyond Wolfe Ranch, look for a path that leads north about 100 to 200 yards to the nearby cliffs, where you can find a panel of horse **petroglyphs** painted by Ute Indians.

Distance: 3 miles round-trip. Level: Moderate to strenuous in the heat. Access: Wolfe Ranch parking area.

Fiery Furnace Area

This tall maze of red- and salmon-colored sandstone fins is the park's most colorful hike. However, the area doesn't feature marked trails. As a result, some hikers have gotten lost in the mazelike terrain or trampled fragile soils and rare plants. Now, if you want to lead your own hike into the Fiery Furnace, you must obtain a $2 permit at the visitor center and watch a video about minimum impact. These permits are limited to 75 a day, which sounds like a lot, but in the past, hundreds of people have headed into the Fiery Furnace. I recommend that you join one of the excellent ranger-led hikes — you don't need a permit, but you do need to pay a small fee (see "Ranger programs," later in this chapter). The best time for this hike is sunset, when the rays seem to set the rocks on fire.

Distance: 2 miles round-trip. Level: Moderate to difficult. Access: Fiery Furnace parking area.

Landscape Arch Trail

Although the trail to this arch is crowded in high season, this spindly rim of rock is one of the park's classics. With its 306-foot span, Landscape Arch may be the world's largest freestanding arch. A mostly flat gravel trail winds through rock canyons to the arch. For the best photo ops, stop at the viewpoint in front of and just below the arch. This angle allows you to get the entire arch in your viewfinder plus a slice of blue sky.

Distance: 2 miles round-trip. Level: Easy. Access: Devils Garden parking area.

Park Avenue Trail

Although you won't get close to any arches on Park Avenue Trail, you will pass towering walls of sandstone. You can see the notable formations — Courthouse Towers, Tower of Babel, Three Gossips, and Organ Rock — from your car while driving in or out of the park, but on Park Avenue Trail, you can get down to the bases of these giants. The trail winds through groves of juniper, single-leaf ash, blackbrush, and, in spring, wildflowers. The one problem is that you have to backtrack to return to your car, unless you travel in a group and can arrange a shuttle with cars at either end. If not, try starting out at Courthouse Towers so you get the steep part out of the way first and end the walk going downhill.

Distance: 1 mile one way. Level: Easy. Access: Park Avenue or Courthouse Towers parking areas.

Primitive Trail from Double O to Landscape Arch

Don't let the word *primitive* scare you away from this hike, the park's best in my opinion. This 2¼-mile-long loop passes and climbs towering rock fins while weaving through some of the park's heavier vegetation and in and out of sandy washes. To reach the loop, hike past Landscape Arch to Double O Arch on the trail from the Devils Garden Trailhead. Beyond Landscape Arch, the trail narrows substantially and, at times, can be located only by following *cairns,* little stacks of rocks that denote the trail's direction. Shortly before you reach Double O, the trail climbs onto the spine of one of the fins — it's fun, the views are great, but the drop is dangerous, so be careful. When you climb down, before heading on to Double O, take a minute to stroll to your right to see Black Arch below in Fin Canyon. The view is worth the five-minute side trip.

At Double O Arch, you come to the northern end of the Primitive Trail and a spur that leads to Dark Angel, a dark sandstone spire. Unfortunately, Dark Angel isn't as impressive as its name. Skip it and take the loop trail, which circles back to the south and connects with the main trail near Landscape Arch. Along the way, you see stunted and gnarled pinion and juniper trees, yuccas that more than double their height in May and June when they sprout tall shafts of cream-colored flowers, springtime displays of scarlet gilia, spike-laden blackbrush, and scores of sagebrush that, after rains, lend their pungent, aromatic scent to the air.

I don't recommend the Primitive Trail for novice hikers or ones with trepidations about heights. Plus, the trail is rugged in places and following the fins can be difficult. However, this path is the one to take if you like adventure and want to escape the crowds.

Distance: 7¼ miles round-trip from the parking lot at the Devils Garden Trailhead to Double O Arch and back via the Primitive Trail. Level: Difficult. Access: Devils Garden parking area.

Sand Dune Arch Trail

The hike to Sand Dune Arch is great for kids. The trail is easy, and kids enjoy the giant sandbox beneath the arch. Surrounding the arch are fins of rock where you can flee the sun and relax while the kids play.

Distance: Just under ½ mile. Level: Easy. Access: Broken Arch/Sand Dune Arch parking area.

The Windows Trail

Kids enjoy this trail because they can scurry up onto rocks and into windows. Just don't let them get too carried away — the trail doesn't include any protective railings. This hike connects three arches: the North and South Windows and the Turret Arch. A gentle path leads to your first stop, which is in front of North Window; the South Window is just around the corner. To the west (behind you) is Turret Arch. A primitive, 1¼-mile trail begins on the south side of South Window and winds down onto the desert floor for a short distance before circling back up to the parking lot. (This route is interesting for the variety of high desert vegetation you can spot, but isn't a must.) After you visit the Windows and the Turret Arch, head to the north side of the parking area to find the short, less-than-½-mile trail to Double Arch.

Distance: 1 mile round-trip. Distance: Easy. Access: Windows parking area.

One-day wonder

Because of the size and layout of Arches National Park, you can easily see the highlights in one day. For more information on the attractions in the following itinerary, see "Exploring the top attractions" and "Taking a hike" earlier in this chapter.

Start your day around 8 a.m. Pack a picnic lunch and a cooler full of drinks. To ensure that you drink enough water throughout the day, buy a case of bottled water when you're in Moab and stash it in the trunk of your car. Then gauge your intake by the number of empty bottles.

First, stop at the park's **visitor center,** which isn't the most elaborate in the park system but does offer a decent interpretation of the park's geology. You can pick up a hiking guide, make any last-minute restroom stops, and top off your water bottles or buy water. I recommend that you sign up for the afternoon tour of Fiery Furnace at this time (see "Ranger programs," later in this chapter, for information).

Just north of the visitor center, stop at **Park Avenue.** You don't need to hike the trail, but from the viewpoint, get a good look at the rock outcrop on the left rim that resembles Queen Nefertiti. Get back in your car and continue up the road to **Balanced Rock,** which sits precariously on its slowly eroding pedestal. Don't hike this trail, either; the sight of this balancing act is impressive even from the viewpoint.

Back on the road, head north from Balanced Rock and take the first right. Drive 2½ miles to **The Windows.** Follow The Windows Trail mentioned in the "Taking a hike" section. Climbing up into the windows and gazing across the rockscape no doubt duplicates an age-old ritual and also makes for an interesting photo opportunity.

Return to your rig and head back to the main road. If you didn't sign up for the afternoon tour of the Fiery Furnace, head north along the main road to **Devils Garden.** If you did sign up for the tour, make a quick stop at the **Delicate Arch** viewpoint to admire this upright loop of rock before proceeding to Devils Garden. (Those who didn't sign up for the tour will have plenty of time to return here in the late afternoon.)

By this point, you're no doubt ready for lunch. Look for picnic tables, running water, and restrooms in Devils Garden.

After quenching your thirst and eating lunch, top off your water bottles using the water fountain at the trailhead and then start down the **Devils Garden Trail** heading toward **Landscape Arch,** about ¾ miles down the trail. If you're not running too late, are a strong hiker, and aren't traveling with anyone who will slow you down, push on past Landscape Arch to **Double O Arch,** another 1¼ miles down the trail. If heights bother you, you may want to skip this section as part of the trail runs along the top of a rock fin. While retracing your steps back to the parking lot, the short (less than a ½ mile) side trails to **Pine Tree** and **Tunnel Arches** are easy and worthwhile.

After you're back in your car, head back south on the main road toward Fiery Furnace. If you're traveling with kids (or simply want to see as many of the park's arches as possible), stop at **Sand Dune Arch,** found just over 1 mile south of the Devils Garden parking lot.

If you signed up, the **Fiery Furnace** tour is your next stop. If you decided to pass on the tour, hike to Delicate Arch if the weather isn't too hot. In either case, make sure that your water bottles are full before you leave the trailhead.

Following your final hike through Fiery Furnace or to Delicate Arch, call it a day — return to your lodging and enjoy a relaxing dinner.

If you have more time

Klondike Bluffs, in the park's northwestern corner, is worth exploring if you're here more than a day. Come here to flee the crowds — and to test the stability of your vehicle. To get to Klondike Bluffs, take the washboard-weary dirt road off the main road near Sand Dune Arch. The dirt road runs 7¾ miles through the Salt Valley to the Klondike Bluffs Road turnoff. Check the road conditions before traveling because runoff from thunderstorms can create problems. Also be careful not to drive off the road — soft sand along the shoulders can strand your rig. And finally, don't take the left turn just before the Klondike Bluffs Road unless you're in a four-wheel-drive vehicle (see "Keeping active," later in this chapter, for information on this road).

From the Klondike Bluffs parking area, you can take a round-trip hike just under 2½ miles past two notable formations. The first is **Marching Men** — a collection of stone spires that to some creative minds resembles soldiers. The second, visible from the top of a sand dune, is **Tower Arch,** a gigantic opening in the rock wall. Near its bottom on the right side is an inscription left in 1922 by Alex Ringhoffer, a gentleman who explored this area and who is credited with lobbying to designate Arches as a national park.

With **Canyonlands National Park** (☎ **435-719-2313;** www.nps.gov/cany) just 33 miles away, it'd be a shame if you traveled all the way to Arches without sampling this other outstanding park. Via U.S. 191 and Utah 313, you can make a nice half-day trip to Canyonlands' Island in the Sky

District, where you'll find a wonderful collection of hikes that reveal an arch on the edge of a cliff, granaries left behind by Native Americans who lived in this region hundreds of years ago, a whale masquerading as a rock, and breathtaking views. One of the most rugged national parks in the Lower 48, Canyonlands is for adventurous souls who truly enjoy rock climbing, white water paddling, and disappearing into the landscape.

Ranger programs

This relatively small park, with its small staff, offers only a few ranger programs. One that I heartily recommend is the ranger-led tour of **Fiery Furnace** (see "Exploring the top attractions," earlier in this chapter). Rangers offer insights into natural history, vegetation, and geology; for example, they point out the difference between an arch and a bridge. The 2-mile hike takes 2½ to 3 hours and occurs twice a day between March and October. You must sign up for this tour in advance at the visitor center and pay a fee ($8 adults, $4 ages 6–12 and ages 62 or more). *Tip:* These hikes often fill quickly during the high season, so advance

---

Spotting local wildlife

You may be surprised by the number of animals that live in the park's seemingly harsh environment. Bird-watchers have spied 273 bird species, including seasonal and year-round residents as well as migrants, in the park. Closer to ground level, 65 types of mammals, 22 reptile species, 9 types of amphibians, and 8 fish species make Arches their home. Where are they? Well, they're smart. The mammals and most reptiles lie low during the heat of the day and reserve their travels for the evenings and early mornings.

The largest animals you're likely to see are the big-eared **mule deer,** which are highly visible in the Devils Garden area. Not so obvious are the **mountain lions** and **coyotes** that consider the park home (and consider mule deer, **black-tailed jackrabbits,** and **desert cottontails** dinner). You probably won't see either lions or coyotes, but if you camp out in the park and have a little luck, you may hear coyotes yipping and howling in the night.

Desert bighorn sheep also live in this arid corner of Utah. The best place to look for them is on the cliffs created by the Moab Fault to the west of the visitor center.

Lizards are fairly usual in the park. The **western whiptail,** which totes a tail twice the length of its body, is the most common. Photographers prefer to spot the **western collared lizard,** which has a bright-green body with a black collar.

The park also houses a few poisonous critters — **rattlesnakes, scorpions,** and **black widow spiders.** So keep a close eye on your kids and tell them not to put their hands into nooks and crannies or on top of ledges they can't see.

Although you may see wildlife in most areas of the park around dawn and before sundown, the Devils Garden Trail and its Primitive Trail offer the best odds for sighting wildlife thanks to their distance from roads and traffic. Of course, anywhere in the park, you may spot a **golden eagle** or **redtail hawk** circling overhead in search of a meal.

reservations are a good idea. You can make a reservation in person up to seven days in advance.

Between early April and late October, rangers lead daily, one-hour hikes at various locations in the park, so check at the visitor center for times and locations. During this same period, rangers also give nightly talks at the amphitheater at Devils Garden. Although topics vary from season to season, one of the more interesting talks delves into the geology that produced Arches; another good one touches on the mysteries of canyon country.

 For kids, make sure that you pick up information on the **Junior Ranger Program** (see Chapter 7) at the visitor center.

Keeping active

If you want to work up a sweat while taking in the scenery, consider one of the following activities. (Unless indicated otherwise, all outfitters are located in Moab, zip code 84532.)

✔ **Biking:** You can bike the scenic drive through the park, but keep in mind that this almost 18-mile dead end is narrow and winding in spots and can be crowded with motor vehicles in summer. Mountain bikers can also tackle one of several four-wheel-drive roads (see "Four-wheeling," later in this section). However, remember that bikes are prohibited on all trails and off-road in the backcountry. Cyclists can get information as well as rent or repair bikes at **Rim Cyclery,** 94 W. 100 North (☎ **800-304-8219** or 435-259-5333; www.rimcyclery. com), and **Poison Spider Bicycle Shop,** 497 Main St. (☎ **800-635-1792** or 435-259-7882; www.poisonspiderbicycles.com). Bike rentals start at around $32 to $34 per day.

✔ **Canoeing/kayaking/rafting:** Although Arches doesn't encompass any bodies of water, the Colorado River follows the park's boundary along its southeast edge, and river-running is a wonderful change of pace from hiking over the park's dry, rocky terrain. You can rent a canoe, kayak, or raft from **Canyon Voyages,** 211 N. Main St., Box 416 (☎ **800-733-6007** or 435-259-6007; www.canyonvoyages.com). Rentals begin at $30 for a half day. Canyon Voyages also offers guided river trips.

✔ **Four-wheeling:** For an antidote to your daily car commute, drive one of the park's two four-wheel-drive roads — but check with rangers first for road closures and conditions that make roads impassable. The more interesting of the two routes is the one from Klondike Bluffs to Willow Flats, which is best driven from north to south because of soft sand on steep grades. To access the road, turn west off the main park road 1 mile south of Devils Garden Trailhead; follow the road up through the Salt Valley 7¾ miles to the turnoff for Klondike Bluffs. The next 10¾ miles, which head into high desert terrain, are strictly for four-wheelers. The route passes drifting sand dunes, the redrock Marching Men formation, and the Eye of the

Whale Arch. The road ends at the Balanced Rock parking area. Four-wheel-drive vehicles are available for rent from **Slickrock 4X4 Rentals,** 900 South Hwy. 191 (☎ **888-238-5337,** or 435-259-5678; www.moab-utah.com/jeep/jeep.html), beginning at $135 per day, and from **Farabee Adventures,** 397 North Main (☎ **435-259-7494;** www.moab-utah.com/farabee).

✔ **Rock climbing:** Unless you plan an overnight expedition, you can climb in Arches without a permit; however, you must follow a few rules. You can't use a motorized drill to set an anchor and you can't climb on any arch identified on current U.S. Geological Survey topographical maps. If you use chalk, the color must blend in with the rock, which is mostly buff or reddish. Climbers are encouraged to use dull-colored webbing if they plan to leave any behind, and they should access climbing routes via established trails, across slickrock, or by sandy washes. You can get climbing guides at the visitor center (see "Finding information after you arrive," earlier in this chapter) for a leg up on where to climb.

Where to Stay

Arches doesn't offer any lodging within the park unless you're toting a tent. But Moab, just 5 miles south on U.S. 191, overflows with lodging possibilities, ranging from roadside motels to quaint B&Bs. For more information on finding a place to stay, see Chapter 6.

Top lodgings

Aarchway Inn
$$ Moab

You can find this motel on the south side of the Colorado River when you cross the bridge on the way to Moab. Although the place isn't particularly unique, most of the large rooms feature two queen-size beds. All the rooms come with small refrigerators and microwave ovens, so you can store and warm up snacks in your room. You will find barbecue grills in the courtyard and an outdoor pool great for dips after a long day in the park. If you're toting bikes, you can keep them in the inn's storage room.

1551 North U.S. 191. ☎ *800-341-9359 or 435-259-2599. Fax: 435-259-2270.* http://moab-utah.com/aarchway/inn.html. *90 rooms, 7 suites. A/C TV TEL. Rack rates: March–Oct $95 double, $120–$150 suite; Nov–April rates lower. Rates include Continental breakfast. AE, DISC, MC, V.*

Cali Cochitta Bed & Breakfast
$–$$$ Moab

Although this quaint B&B is relatively new, the adobe brick house isn't. In this historic building dating to the 1870s, guests can choose from three doubles, a suite, and a cottage. Each comes with its own bathroom, queen-size beds, and cable TV. On the property you'll also find a hot tub, bike storage, and, if you absolutely can't live without the Internet, modem hookups. As for the B&B's name, it means "House of Dreams" in Aztec.

110 South 200 East. ☎ *888-429-8112 or 435-259-4961. Fax 435-259-4964.* www.moab dreaminn.com. *5 units. A/C TV. Rack rates: March–Oct $89–$110 double, $125 suite, and $150 cottage; Nov–April $69–$90 double, $115 suite, and $130 cottage. DISC, MC, V.*

Sorrel River Ranch
$$$$$ Moab

Sorrel River Ranch places you in the middle of some of southeastern Utah's famous redrock countryside. The inn also offers what is probably the best lodging in the area — but at a price. The Colorado River flows on the north side of the ranch, and towering buttes and canyon cliffs dominate the other directions. The large guest rooms feature plush furniture, a small kitchen area with microwave and mini-refrigerator, and Southwestern-influenced decor. From the covered porches outside, you can watch herons in the Colorado River or see the sun cast fiery rays on the redrock landscape in the evenings. The River Grill provides day-long meal service, and the 4,300-square-foot lodge offers a place to retreat for a cool drink and a chat in front of a roaring fire. The ranch also features a swimming pool and hot tub, and you can even board your horse!

Highway 128 (17 miles northeast of Moab). ☎ *877-359-2715 or 435-259-4642.* www. sorrelriver.com. *57 units. A/C TV TEL. Rack rates: $209–$379 double. Ask about summer specials. AE, DISC, MC, V.*

Sunflower Hill Bed & Breakfast Inn
$$$–$$$$ Moab

This picturesque spot is the nicest place to stay in town. The most colorful flower gardens in Moab grace the lawns surrounding this B&B, located just three blocks off Main Street on a quiet dead-end street. The rooms are elegant and include use of an outdoor hot tub. Richly restored antique furnishings highlight the rooms, all of which feature private baths. The rooms are split between two buildings. Land a room in the Garden Cottage and you can enjoy the Great Room's fireplace and library.

A picnic table and grill are at your disposal, so you don't have to eat out every night. Prepare for a day in the park with a breakfast of homemade breads and granola, fresh fruits, and hot entrees like Belgian waffles.

185 North 300 East. ☎ *800-MOAB-SUN or 435-259-2974. Fax: 435-259-3065.* http:// sunflowerhill.com. *12 units. A/C TV. Rack rates: March–Oct and holidays $125–$195 double; Nov–Feb $85–$155 double, $20 each additional person (up to 2). Rates include full breakfast. DISC, MC, V*

Runner-up lodgings

Comfort Suites

$$–$$$ **Moab** Near the heart of downtown, this chain motel is dutifully reliable, if unremarkable, with large suites, a refreshing pool, and a suitable exercise room if you didn't get enough of a workout in the park. *800 South Main St.* ☎ *800-228-5150 or 435-259-5252.* www.moab-utah.com/comfort suites.

The Gonzo Inn

$$$–$$$$$ **Moab** Hunter S. Thompson would feel at home at this bright, eclectically colored inn with 43 rooms and suites. Just off Main Street, the inn offers rooms with fireplaces, vaulted ceilings, and jet tubs. *100 West 200 South.* ☎ *800-791-4044.* www.gonzoinn.com.

Moab Best Western Greenwell Inn

$$ **Moab** In the heart of downtown, this 72-room inn comes complete with a restaurant, pool, and fitness center. *105 South Main St.* ☎ *800-528-1234 or 435-259-6151.* www.moab-utah.com/bestwesternmoab.

Redstone Inn

$ **Moab** Five miles south of Arches on the northern edge of Moab, the Redstone is not only inexpensive but also puts together packages involving white-water rafting, four-wheeling, or horseback riding. *535 South Main St.* ☎ *800-772-1972 or 435-259-3500.* www.moabredstone.com.

Campgrounds

The **Devils Garden Campground,** located just past Fiery Furnace, is the only campground in Arches. Facilities are limited to restrooms within walking distance. The campground offers 52 sites at $10 a night. Thirty of the sites can be reserved through the National Park Reservation Service (☎ 877-444-6777; http://reservations.nps.gov) for visits between March 1 and October 31. You can make reservations up to 240 days in advance, but they must be placed at least four days in advance. The remaining 22 sites are available on a first-come, first-served basis each day. You can try to claim one at the visitor center.

Sites fill early during late spring and fall. If you're traveling in a group of 11 or more, you can reserve one of the two group sites through NRRS up to 360 days before your visit. Group fees are $3 per person per night, with a $33 minimum charge.

Bring your own wood if you want a campfire, because wood gathering in the park is prohibited. You must also carry out all trash, even cigarette butts.

Although you can backpack anywhere in the park, trails and campsites aren't marked, so you should know how to read a topographical map and a compass before you head out. Streams are nonexistent, so you need to tote all your water, too. Plus, backcountry overnight hikers must get a free permit from the visitor center.

Where to Eat

You won't find any restaurants in the park, so head to Moab for your meals. Don't be discouraged by the many restaurants that call themselves cafes. This eclectic town offers a variety of possibilities, ranging from brewpubs with pizza and burgers to multicourse spreads comparable to those found in ritzy New York City eateries. And although many Moab restaurants shut down during the winter, you still won't have a problem finding a place to eat.

Center Café and Market
$$$$ Moab   CONTEMPORARY AMERICAN

This eatery consistently ranks among Utah's top restaurants, and serves innovative game, vegetarian, seafood, and pasta dishes. You'll find such offerings as grilled venison rack with huckleberry demiglace and hazelnut wild rice, Maine lump crab meat cakes with fresh tomato coulis and citrus crème fraîche, and cedar planked salmon with applewood bacon-shallot crust and roasted garlic white beans. The cafe features an adobe-walled patio out back that's great on warm summer evenings, as well as a deli with a wide array of cheeses, house-smoked salmon, and other picnic goodies.

60 North 100 West. ☎ *435-259-4295. Reservations recommended. Main courses: $14–$32. DISC, MC, V. Open: Daily 5:30–10 p.m. Closed Dec–Jan.*

Desert Bistro
$$$$ Moab   CONTEMPORARY AMERICAN

Karl and Michelle Kelley have carved a unique niche in Moab with a menu crafted around fresh seafood flown in regularly, top-of-the-line beef, wild game, and creative combinations that please the palate. Examples range from a tequila-cured salmon, smoked sea scallop, and avocado timbale appetizer to a filet of beef tenderloin with gorgonzola crust, served with roasted tomato demiglace, garlic mashed potato, and fresh vegetables. Nightly specials are also available.

92 East Center Street. ☎ *435-259-0756 Reservations recommended. Main courses: $16–$30. AE, DC, MC, V, AE. Open: Daily 5:30–10 p.m.. Closed Dec–Feb.*

Eddie McStiff's Restaurant and Microbrewery
$–$$ Moab   AMERICAN/ITALIAN

You'll find a baker's dozen of brews to wash down the pizzas, burgers, ribs, and steaks that keep the locals happy at Utah's oldest legal brewery. There are specials every night, but do you really need one with a menu that offers 22 pizza toppings, ten different pasta entrees, and smoked dinners ranging from Jack Daniels Beef Short Ribs to a hickory smoked salmon dish? A special kids menu makes little ones feel right at home.

57 South Main St. ☎ 435-259-2337. Main courses: $7–$15. AE, DISC, MC, V. Open: Daily 5 p.m. to midnight.

Jailhouse Café
$–$$ Moab   BREAKFAST

The best breakfast in Moab is served in this renovated jailhouse or on its covered patio. From the Jailhouse Chorizo Scramble (three eggs scrambled with seasoned potatoes and chorizo sausage and topped with sour cream and fresh salsa) to the Old-fashioned Ginger Pancakes with Dutch apple butter, this place serves an overwhelming breakfast. You certainly won't leave hungry — and you may even skip lunch.

101 North Main St. ☎ 435-259-3900. Main courses: $ 4.75–$7.95. MC, V. Open: Daily 7 a.m. to noon. Closed Nov to early March.

Slickrock Café
$–$$$ Moab   AMERICAN/SOUTHWESTERN

Innovative courses, great atmosphere, central location, and cold drinks — what else do you need? This reliable restaurant features some of Utah's best microbrews on tap, and the menu is diverse and tasty, although it doesn't epitomize fine dining. Lunches features the usual burgers, wraps, and sandwiches, but you can also enjoy Penne Puerto Angel, a pasta dish made with shrimp, roasted red peppers, mushrooms, and onions in a spicy tomato sauce with tequila over chili penne. For dinner, try the grilled steak brushed with a teriyaki and ginger marinade and served with a side of Gallo pinto rice (rice and beans with cilantro and onion).

5 North Main St. ☎ 435-259-8004. Main courses: $4.75–$7.50 breakfast; $7.25–$16.25 lunch; $7.25–$17.50 dinner. AE, MC, V. Open: Daily 7 a.m.–10 p.m. Closed Dec–Feb.

Fast Facts: Arches

Area Code
The area code is **435**.

ATM
ATMs are located in most banks and at City Market, 425 South Main St., Moab.

Emergency
In case of an emergency, dial **911**.

Fees
Entrance fees are $10 per vehicle per week and $5 per person on foot or bicycle.

Hospitals/Clinics
For medical attention, head to Allen Memorial Hospital, 719 West 400 North, Moab (☎ 435-259-7191).

Information

To more information, write to the Superintendent, Arches National Park, P.O. Box 907, Moab, UT 84532-0907, call ☎ 435-719-2299 or 435-719-2319 (TTY), or check the Web at www.nps.gov/arch.

Pharmacies

Two area drug stores are Walker Drug at 290 South Main St., Moab (☎ 435-259-5959), and City Market at 425 South Main St., Moab.

Post Office

The post office is at 50 East 100 North, Moab.

Road Conditions and Weather

Call ☎ 800-492-2400 for information on the weather.

Time Zone

Arches is on mountain time.

Chapter 10

Death Valley National Park

. . . .

In This Chapter

▶ Introducing a hot winter getaway
▶ Planning your vacation
▶ Making your way to the valley's highlights
▶ Finding the best meals and beds

. . . .

1 want to get it out of the way right from the start: Death Valley
National Park is hot in the summer. True, it is a "dry" heat, but just
the same, this place broils in July and August. Death Valley boasts the
highest mean temperature readings on Earth. Average highs in the
summer top 110 degrees. (On July 10, 1913, the temperature boiled to a
record 134 degrees.) What else would you expect from the lowest spot in
the Western Hemisphere?

Badwater, a roadside stop in the valley, is a mind-boggling 282 feet *below*
sea level. Framed by the Panamint Range to the west and the Amargosa
Range to the east, Death Valley in the summer is a frying pan that challenges the existence of anyone or anything that crawls into it.

This park is hot even in the shade — and visitors definitely need some
shade, not to mention a gallon or two of water. Automakers actually seek
out this heat during the dead of summer to see whether their latest
models can function when the road tar flows like maple syrup. And
because park officials know that not everyone's car, truck, or RV can
handle the park's intense baking, they kindly locate tanks of radiator
water near the top of the park's few hills so you can cool off your rig
when you arrive.

You can avoid this ovenlike experience by traveling to Death Valley in
December and January, when the daily highs struggle to reach 65
degrees and wildflowers color the landscape. But if you skip the park
during the summer months, you miss the essence of Death Valley. Ask
any Europeans you meet in the park (and you meet plenty of them in
June, July, and August) why they come during the summer. They'll probably tell you they came for the challenge of surviving Death Valley at its
worst. Think of a summer trek into the valley as a badge of courage.

A work in progress

Death Valley has been slowly dropping for thousands of years, and the valley is still falling at a rate of roughly 6 inches a century. At the same time, wind and water erosion are chiseling away at the surrounding mountains. As a result, rubble in the form of sand dunes and sprawling *alluvial fans* (spreading beds of rock, gravel, and dirt washed down-hill and deposited at the mouth of canyons) spill onto the valley floor. The dunes near Stovepipe Wells Village are a great example of how powerful erosion can be.

But don't go solely for the dry heat (which supposedly has some thera-peutic effects for people with asthma). Although Death Valley looks inhospitable, the park is rich in geology, human history, and — believe it or not — wildlife.

Stand in the middle of this 3.4-million-acre park, and you're surrounded by a surreal landscape painted in varying shades of gray, buff, yellow, and red. You find towering sand dunes constantly rearranged by the winds, fractured plates of salt pan baked a blinding white by the bright sun, and mile after mile of gently rolling sagebrush flats. Beyond the valley's sunken floor, mostly barren and angular mountain ranges riddled by ero-sion tower over the valley on all sides like the walls of a convection oven. Near the park's northern border, a 500-foot-deep crater, Ubehebe, serves as a bowl-shaped calling card of Death Valley's volcanic past.

Death Valley's name is certainly intimidating, but it tells a great story. While you travel the park, take time to soak up the intriguing human sagas that left their marks on the landscape. The most dramatic story is the tale of the '49ers — groups of pioneers who struggled to cross the valley floor on their way to California's gold fields in the mid-1800s. One of these groups gave the valley its harsh name, even though only one of its members died during the trek. These pioneers actually crossed the valley in the winter, when the temperatures are relatively mild.

Over the years, other miners drifted in and out of the valley searching futilely for gold and silver. In the crumbling ghost towns that dot the park, you hear sordid tales of hardscrabble miners who hoped to redeem their lives by finding the mother lode. A man named Death Valley Scotty struck it rich, but not with pick and shovel. A slick-talking eccentric, he mined the pockets of Easterners blinded by tales of the golden mother lode that he promised to share with them.

Must-See Attractions

All of Death Valley seems to lie before your eyes when you top the Panamint or Amargosa Ranges on your way to the park. Of course, that's only a mirage. In its 3.4 million acres, the park hides more than a few surprises for visitors. While you're poking into its nooks and crannies, be sure to visit these highlights:

- ✔ **Badwater:** This stop is a can't-miss photo op, thanks to the "Badwater, Elevation -282 FT" sign, the brackish spring waters, and the crusty and fractured salt beds in the background.

- ✔ **Dantes View:** Telescope Peak, the highest point in Death Valley, may offer a more stunning view, but Dantes View is the best vantage point you can reach by car. At 5,475 feet above sea level, the air makes this spot cooler than the valley floor, too.

- ✔ **Furnace Creek Inn:** This historic inn, which dates to 1927 when it opened as a private corporate retreat, is planted on a hillside and nurtured by a spring that also sustains the groves of 1,800 imported date palm trees. Don't overlook the swimming pool.

- ✔ **Sand Dunes:** The park features several dune fields. The most accessible field is near Stovepipe Wells Village in the center of Death Valley. A moonlight stroll across these dunes is something to talk about.

- ✔ **Scotty's Castle:** Located near the park's northeastern corner, this elaborate "castle" was built by a Chicago millionaire who came to Death Valley to invest in a gold mine and wound up building an opulent "winter" home in his friend's name.

- ✔ **Zabriskie Point:** This outlook, 4½ miles southeast of the Furnace Creek Visitor Center, offers not only a view of present-day Death Valley but also a glimpse into its past. The erosion-riddled mounds were laid down millions of years ago as volcanic deposits.

Planning Ahead

For general information before you go, write Death Valley National Park, P.O. Box 579, Death Valley, CA 92328-0579; call ☎ **760-786-3200;** or check the park's Web site: www.nps.gov/deva.

When to go and how long to stay

You kinda need to think in reverse when planning a visit to Death Valley National Park. This park is crowded when most other parks are empty. Death Valley's busy season runs from February through mid-April when daytime temperatures are relatively cool. November can also be busy. Although December and January (outside of the holidays) are the slowest months, and therefore the easiest for making lodging reservations, the hot months of June, July, and August are also fairly slow.

To get the most out of your visit to Death Valley, plan to stay at least two days.

Advance reservations

If you want to stay at **Furnace Creek Inn** during high season, make reservations at least three months in advance. During the heat of summer, though, a week's leeway is usually enough time to get a room at the **Ranch.** See "Where to Stay" later in the chapter for descriptions of this hotel and others mentioned in this section.

In recent years, as traffic wanes between late May and early October, the **Furnace Creek Inn** has closed its doors for those months and redirected all lodging and dining traffic across the street to its sister property, the **Furnace Creek Ranch.** This practice is evaluated at the beginning of each year so if you're planning a summer visit, by all means check on the inn's status. Not only is it a great place to stay but, when open, it offers summer discounts. See "Where to Stay" below for details.

If you plan a trip to the park between mid-October and mid-April and want to stay at one of the campgrounds, you can make a reservation for a spot at the **Furnace Creek Campground** and group sites at **Texas Springs Campground** up to five months in advance of your trip by calling ☎ **800-365-2267.** The rest of the campgrounds fill on a first-come, first-served basis.

What to pack

Any visit to Death Valley, no matter what time of year, requires a good supply of sunscreen, a wide-brimmed hat, good shades, and sturdy footwear. A fanny pack with holsters for two water bottles is a great asset if you plan on hiking. For winter visits, toss a midweight jacket, a sweater, and some slacks into your suitcase for those cool nights. For more information on what to pack, see Chapter 8.

Getting There

Not surprisingly for such an inhospitable place, Death Valley isn't easy to reach. You'll find no direct flights to the park, unless you fly your own plane or hire a charter to one of the private runways at Furnace Creek or Stovepipe Wells Village. Short of that, plan on a long drive.

Driving in

Coming from the West, U.S. Route 395 connects with Route 178 (near Ridgecrest) and Highway 190 (near Olancha). Both Route 178 and Highway 190 lead into the park. On the east side, U.S. Route 95 intersects with Route 267 at Scotty's Junction, Route 374 at Beatty, and Route 373 at Lathrop Wells. Furnace Creek, the heart of the park, is five hours and 310 miles from Los Angeles via Baker or Lone Pine and 285 miles via Trona. Bakersfield is 236 miles away.

Death Valley National Park

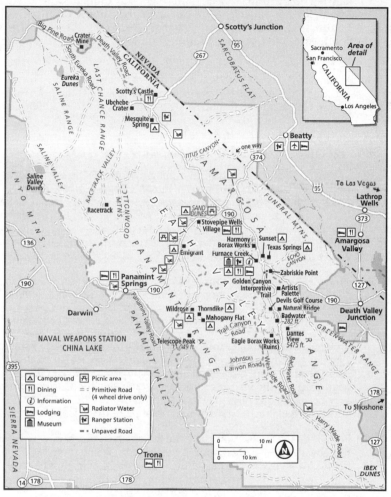

From Las Vegas, Death Valley is about two hours, and 140 miles, away via Death Valley Junction. The distance isn't great, but the ride can get monotonous. Don't fall prey to the tedium. Watching for jets from the Indian Springs or Nellis Air Force bases as they head out to their practice bombing ranges just north of U.S. Route 95 is one way to stay alert.

Flying in

The nearest commercial airport is **McCarran International Airport** in Las Vegas, 140 miles away. The following airlines have regularly scheduled flights into Las Vegas; some of these are regional carriers, so they may not all fly from your point of origin: **Air Canada, Alaska Airlines, America West, American/American Eagle, American Trans Air, Continental, Delta/Skywest, Frontier, Midwest Express, Northwest, Southwest, Sun Country, United,** and **US Airways.** See the Appendix for their toll-free numbers.

At the Las Vegas airport, you need to rent a car to travel to the park. Some of the car-rental agencies represented at the airport include: **Avis, Budget, Dollar, Hertz,** and **National.** See the Appendix for their toll-free numbers.

Orienting Yourself in Death Valley

In a place with such a colorful mining history, it's fitting that Death Valley's paved roads — Highway 190 and Routes 267, 374, and 178 — resemble a treasure map: They slash across the park much like a gigantic X, coming together just east of Stovepipe Wells Village. Unfortunately, you won't find a pot of gold at this intersection — or a handy circular route connecting all the highlights. If you want to see all of the park's main attractions, you have to backtrack at least once or twice.

Route 267 runs north from the intersection to the Titus Canyon road, the Mesquite Spring Campground, Scotty's Castle, and Ubehebe Crater. **Route 374** juts off to the northeast up Mud Canyon and past Hell's Gate and Daylight Pass before leaving the park and running to Beatty, Nevada.

Running south from the intersection is **Highway 190,** which snakes 19 miles to **Furnace Creek,** the best place to base a visit to Death Valley because of its central location and accommodations. You find the park headquarters, the visitor center, a museum, gift shops, restaurants, a service station, a convenience store, and even a golf course. The lavish Furnace Creek Inn, nestled in a grove of palm trees, is across the highway.

From Furnace Creek, you can head south on **Route 178,** which runs down to Badwater (the lowest spot in the Western Hemisphere at 282 feet below sea level) before beginning a slow rise to the ghost site of Ashford Mill. Then the road swings east and up into the Black Mountains, through 3,315-foot Salsberry Pass, and out of the park.

Running parallel to 178 for 40 miles through the middle of Death Valley and along the foot of the Panamint Range is the unpaved **West Side Road,** which leads past the ruins of the Eagle Borax Works, one of the valley's old mining operations. Several four-wheel-drive roads head west into the mountains from this road. (See "If you have more time," later in this chapter, for information on off-road routes.)

Meanwhile, **Highway 190** cuts east from Furnace Creek and passes Zabriskie Point after 4½ miles. After another 5½ miles, 190 divides. At this intersection, you can continue east and leave the park via 190, or turn south and head down a spur road 13 miles back up into the Black Mountains and Dantes View.

Going west from the junction of the four roads, Highway 190 passes a parking area for Death Valley Sand Dunes (22 miles from Furnace Creek), Stovepipe Wells Village (24 miles), and Panamint Springs (60 miles) before leaving the park.

Besides Furnace Creek, **Stovepipe Wells Village** is the other major "community" in Death Valley. Although its accommodations aren't as nice as the ones at Furnace Creek, Stovepipe Wells Village is nevertheless an adequate way station with a lodge, restaurant, gas station, convenience store, campground, and ranger station.

Panamint Springs is near the park's western border on Highway 190. Although not as fancy as Furnace Creek, Panamint Springs does offer a comfortable motel, a restaurant, a service station, a campground and RV park, and showers.

Between Panamint Springs and Stovepipe Wells Village is a spur road that darts to the south from Highway 190. This road leads 21 miles to the Wildrose Campground and the trailhead for a hike up Telescope Peak.

Finding information after you arrive

Located in the center of the park on Highway 190, the **Furnace Creek Visitor Center** offers museum exhibits, an information desk, and a bookstore. The center is open daily from 8 a.m. to 6 p.m.

Paying fees

Entry for up to seven days costs $10 per private vehicle. A $20 Death Valley Park Pass is good for one year's entrance to the park. See Chapter 8 for information on the National Park Pass and Chapter 7 for the lowdown on Golden Age and Golden Access passports.

Getting Around Death Valley

How do you tour this sprawling park? In an air-conditioned vehicle with plenty of water to stave off dehydration, with a map pinpointing the tanks of emergency radiator water, and by returning to a room reserved near a swimming pool at day's end. The park doesn't offer public transportation and given the heat (and risk of dehydration), I advise against touring by bike.

Remembering Safety

In summer, protect yourself and your car from Death Valley's intense heat. For yourself, pack a **case of bottled water** so you can easily grab a drink when you need one. For your car, tote a **gallon or two of water** so you can top off your rig's radiator when you need to if you're not in the general vicinity of one of the park service's water tanks.

Also, invest in some good **sunscreen** or **sunblock.** Death Valley is a hot place, and the brilliant salt pan on the valley floor reflects a lot of sunshine.

 Besides the drive to Dantes View, you really won't encounter any steep grades. But when the temperature is above 100 degrees, you don't need much of a hill to overwork your **engine's radiator.** If you do notice your temperature gauge heading for the red zone, shut off your air conditioner. True, you'll miss the blasts of cool air, but living with the windows open for 10 to 15 minutes while your radiator simmers down is a lot better than sitting on the side of the road trying to fix a busted radiator hose. If turning off the air-conditioner doesn't do the trick, try pulling over and turning the heater on full blast. If that doesn't work, turn off your rig for a while and admire the landscape.

Death Valley's **abandoned mines** are mysterious and intriguing, but stay out of them. Their roof supports could collapse at any time, and their shafts may be filled with poisonous air.

Before you head out on that four-wheel-drive adventure into the back-country, make sure you have a map of the park and check at the visitor center or a ranger station for the park's *Morning Report.* These reports provide the day's weather forecast and alert you to impassable roads. Even though Death Valley's scenery is certainly captivating, your eyes shouldn't wander too far from the road while you're driving. The number one cause of death in the park is single-vehicle accidents that occur because motorists drift off the road onto soft, sandy shoulders. (When drivers whip the wheel around to steer their rigs back onto the road, the vehicles can roll.)

For additional tips on how to ensure a safe park visit, see Chapter 8.

Exploring Death Valley

 Is Death Valley truly inhospitable? On the surface, perhaps. But if you take the time to explore the park, you come to appreciate its many nuances. The key to enjoying a summer visit is to lie low during the heat of the day and explore the park during the early morning and evening hours.

Exploring the top attractions

Badwater

At the roadside turnoff at Badwater is one of the park's best photo ops — the "Badwater, Elevation -282 FT" sign. However, in the years ahead, the sign may read -283 FT. The valley floor is a victim of fault-block geology, in which the surrounding mountains rise as the valley floor sinks — in this case, at a rate of roughly 6 inches per century.

From the turnoff, you can walk due west past the sign and onto salt flats. The way the surface of these flats is fractured into plates by the brutal heat is an interesting sight — and a warning that you shouldn't dally too long. But before leaving the turnoff, look high up on the rock cliff across the road for the sign denoting sea level.

 If you're thirsty enough to sample the water in Badwater, you'll find out how the place got its name. Saltier than the ocean, the water won't kill you, but it won't slake your thirst, either.

See map p. 107. Badwater is south of Furnace Creek about 18 miles on Route 178.

Dantes View

You gain a lot of elevation heading to this 5,475-foot summit, and one of the park service's trusty radiator water tanks waits near the top in case your rig wasn't ready for the climb. From the overlook on top, you can clearly see how Death Valley's rimming mountain ranges prevent any stream outlet to the sea. That's why any minerals and salts washed into the valley by storms stay in the area and accumulate. On the valley floor, the greatest accumulations stand out clearly as a snow-white layering of salt pan.

From the overlook, you can look up more than a mile to see 11,049-foot Telescope Peak atop the Panamint Range directly to the west. You can look down more than a mile to see the lowest point in the Western Hemisphere. And you can see the Grapevine Mountains to the north, the Funeral Mountains to the east, and the Greenwater Range to the south.

You may be tempted to spend all day at Dantes View because the temperature typically is 25 degrees cooler than the temperatures below at Badwater.

 If you're driving a motorhome longer than 25 feet or hauling a trailer that extends your rig by 25 feet or more, the spur road's tight curves will prevent you from traveling to the top. You can drop off your trailer at a parking lot about halfway to the top.

See map p. 107. To reach Dantes View, head east on Highway 190 from Furnace Creek for 16 miles; turn right onto the spur road to the viewpoint and go another 13 miles.

Sand Dunes

One of five dune complexes in the park, the Sand Dunes is the easiest site to reach, with access available along Highway 190 just 2 miles east of Stovepipe Wells Village. Standing 120 feet tall in places, these dunes roam back and forth as the winds blow. Interesting patterns are swirled into the sand by vegetation that is pushed back and forth by the breezes, which makes for intriguing photos. Kids love climbing up the dunes and sliding back down. (For a walk in this area, see Sand Dunes under "Taking a hike," later in this chapter.)

See map p. 107. Access to the Sand Dunes can be found 2 miles east of Stovepipe Wells Village on Highway 190.

Scotty's Castle

"Summer home" isn't an accurate description of this palatial mansion, but that's what it was to Chicago owner Albert Johnson, who built the opulent estate in 1922. The castle contains a tiled courtyard, a streaming indoor waterfall opposite a fireplace in the living room, and a music conservatory with a massive pipe organ taking up one wall. Walter Scott, a schemer adept at convincing gullible investors to give him money, boasted that he built the castle for himself with gold mined from shafts beneath the structure. Johnson contributed to the story by telling inquiring reporters who trekked to the castle that he was merely Scotty's banker. (For more information on Scotty and Johnson, see the sidebar "The tale of Death Valley Scotty.")

You easily can spend two or three hours at Scotty's Castle. Before or after the 50-minute castle tour, which I recommend that you take, roam the grounds to inspect the sprawling (but unfinished) swimming pool, stand before the clock tower, visit the stables, and pay your respects at Scotty's grave. The grounds are free to roam; during high season, rangers give tours of them. You also find a gift shop and snack bar, as well as a gas station nearby.

See map p. 107. From the junction of Highway 190 and Route 374 just east of Stovepipe Wells Village, head north for 33 miles to the intersection with Route 267. Turn right onto 267 and drive 3 miles up Grapevine Canyon to Scotty's Castle. ☎ *760-786-2392. Open: Castle grounds and picnic areas open free to the public 7 a.m.–6 p.m. Tours: Daily 9 a.m.–5 p.m. on the hour (last tour starts at 5 p.m.). Tour admission: $9.*

Ubehebe Crater

Nine miles west of Scotty's Castle is a 500-foot-deep hole in the ground known as Ubehebe Crater. The recession was blasted into existence during a volcanic period about 1,000 years ago when eruptions fueled by ground water mixing with molten rock tossed rocks and cinders across a 6-square-mile area. You won't find any steam venting from the ½-mile-wide crater today, but you can walk to its lip and stare down into its rocky maw. Although the main crater is right next to the parking area, you can take a ½-mile walk to the right (around the rim) to inspect two other, smaller craters.

See map p. 107. From the junction of Highway 190 and Route 374 just east of Stovepipe Wells Village, head north for 33 miles to the intersection with Route 267. Turn left and drive 5 miles.

Zabriskie Point

Zabriskie Point, just east of Furnace Creek, is a snapshot of the West's renowned painted deserts. The colorful, fingered landscape at this spot was at one time a mishmash of sediments on a lake floor: sand, mud, and a little volcanic ash. Over millions of years, the sediments were compressed into rock, the waters evaporated, and seismic activity buckled and tilted the landscape. Winds and rains then took over the task of carving

The tale of Death Valley Scotty

Walter Scott is Death Valley's most intriguing character. Raised in the comparatively cool bluegrass state of Kentucky, Scott fled home and headed to Nevada to join his brother who worked on a ranch there. The cowboy life suited Scott. He became good enough that, in 1890, he joined the *Buffalo Bill Cody Wild West Show* and toured the world for 12 years. Near the end of his *Wild West Show* career Scott began to swindle wealthy businessmen with tales of a secret gold mine in Death Valley that could make them rich beyond their wildest dreams.

With that pitch, and their money, Scott transformed himself into Death Valley Scotty, an eccentric desert rat who never actually struck it rich by digging in the ground, but who always had money to spend, thanks to his gullible investors.

Scotty met his match in the early 1900s when one of his marks, Albert Johnson, followed up his investment in Scotty's "mine" with a personal visit to Death Valley to inspect the diggings. After several days of leading Johnson around the valley on horseback and hoping that the Chicago insurance tycoon would grow weary under the unrelenting sun and heat and return home, Scotty realized his scheme had been uncovered.

Surprisingly, Johnson, whose health and strength improved in the dry heat and from the horseback rides, didn't turn his back on Scotty. Instead, he returned each winter over the next decade to explore the valley with Scotty. Then, in the 1920s, Johnson dipped into his personal holdings to build a lavish winter retreat in Grapevine Canyon near the northern end of Death Valley. Here, with a reliable and plentiful spring, Johnson spent $2 million (an extravagent sum in 1922 dollars) to erect what is known as "Scotty's Castle."

the landscape, which makes a great early morning photograph. Walking out along the fingers makes you part of the landscape.

See map p. 107. The roadside turnoff for Zabriskie Point is 4¾ miles east of the Furnace Creek Visitors Center on Highway 190.

Taking a hike

Most people are daunted by the thought of hiking in Death Valley. But if you schedule your visit for one of the cooler times of year or if you start early in the morning and concentrate on shorter treks, the valley rewards you with hidden vistas. Few truly long-range hikes are available, but dozens of shorter hikes are well worth the effort — and sweat.

Before heading out, remember to carry plenty of water and to keep an eye out for storm clouds that could produce flash floods.

Golden Canyon Interpretive Trail

You can choose from two ways to explore this colorful canyon that sprawls beneath Zabriskie Point: Into or out of the canyon. I encourage you to take the route into the canyon — it's the more dramatic direction and the one that corresponds with an interpretive trail map that you can pick up at the Furnace Creek Visitor Center. The path, which used to have a paved road until a winter storm in 1976 washed it out, passes through spectacularly colorful scenery. The Red Cathedral — a formation named for the iron oxides that stain its hillsides — is located to your left about a ½ mile beyond the last numbered trail marker along the interpretive trail. For a longer hike, stay on the main trail for another 2 miles, and you find yourself at Zabriskie Point.

Distance: 2 miles round-trip (without the extra hike to Red Cathedral). Level: Easy. Access: Trailhead is at the Golden Canyon parking area 2 miles south of the Furnace Creek Inn on Badwater Road.

Mosaic Canyon

This interesting trail leads through a twisting canyon of buff and tan marble and a conglomerate of black and grey stream gravels — all highly polished over time by runoff waters that punish the canyon walls with their rocky slurry. Although the first mile of the trail is easy, the higher you go, the more difficult the hike becomes. You have to scramble across some slickrock, and take special care when climbing up dry waterfalls, because they're easier to go up than down. You can occasionally see bighorn sheep in this area.

Distance: 4 miles round-trip. Level: Easy. Access: Mosaic Canyon parking area, 2 miles from Stovepipe Wells Village.

Natural Bridge Canyon

Rock arches and natural bridges are common in southern Utah and northern Arizona, but you'll also find one here near the head of a narrow canyon through which this trail passes. The natural bridge, about 50 feet high, spans the canyon three-tenths of a mile from the trailhead. Just beyond the bridge, the trail ends at the bottom of a dry waterfall. Although not as interesting as the Golden Canyon Interpretive Trail, this is a good short walk.

Distance: 1 mile round-trip. Level: Moderate. Access: Natural Bridge parking area, 1½ miles off Badwater Road, 13¾ miles south of Furnace Creek.

Sand Dunes

Plenty of beach and not a wave in sight! This area is a great place to spend a few hours. Although this sprawling dunefield doesn't have a defined trail, it has dunes and more dunes to scamper up and glide down. Kids love sliding on the sand and searching for animal tracks. For an unusual and somewhat cooler trek, visit the dunes under a full moon. If you head out in the middle of the day, be sure to carry plenty of water.

Distance: 4 miles round-trip. Level: Easy. Access: Sand Dunes parking area, 2 miles east of Stovepipe Wells Village off Highway 190.

Telescope Peak Trail

The highest point in Death Valley (at 11,049 feet) isn't easy to reach, and this trek is not for inexperienced hikers. That said, if you do make the summit in the summer months, you'll enjoy the much cooler air. When winter arrives, however, *crampons* (iron spikes for your shoes) and ice axes are recommended. From the trailhead, you gain 3,000 feet in elevation on the way to the summit. You encounter bristlecone pine trees, some of the oldest living organisms on earth, near the 10,000-foot level. From the summit, you can see the lowest point in the Lower 48 — Badwater — as well as the highest point, Mount Whitney, at 14,494 feet.

Distance: 14 miles round-trip. Level: Strenuous. Access: Mahogany Flat Campground, which is at the end of the upper Wildrose Canyon Road. High-clearance four-wheel-drive vehicles are necessary to negotiate the last 1½ miles of road.

One-day wonder

Scotty's Castle, Death Valley Sand Dunes, Zabriskie Point, Dantes View, Badwater, and Ubehebe Crater — they're the must-see highlights of a Death Valley trip. Despite the nearly 200 miles of asphalt between you and these attractions (assuming you stay at Furnace Creek), you can see them all in one long, but not intolerable, day if you follow the itinerary outlined here. Unless otherwise noted, see "Enjoying the park," earlier in this chapter, for description of attractions in this section.

The key to getting the most out of Death Valley is to get an early start. If possible, eat breakfast at **Furnace Creek** and get on the road by 7 a.m. At this hour, the sun is still low enough to coax the most color out of the landscape, you may be able to see wildlife on the move, and you won't find many other people on the roads. Plus, the stillness at this time of day is intoxicating.

Capturing Death Valley on film

Death Valley's surreal landscape is a photographer's dream. Head out with a camera during the morning or late afternoon and you'll have a hard time not taking a good picture. Some of the best spots for sunrise photos are the sand dunes, Zabriskie Point, Dantes View, and Badwater. Sunset shots pick up a lot of the desert's color; good spots to aim your camera at this time of day include Artists Palette, Zabriskie Point, and the Furnace Creek campgrounds. No matter what the time of day, a shot of the "Badwater, Elevation -282 FT" sign with the salt flats in the background is a classic. Much of Death Valley's landscape looks so otherworldly that you can have fun experimenting with your camera and the lighting conditions. When the famed landscape photographer Ansel Adams visited Death Valley, he often parked his rig near Stovepipe Wells Village and slept on its roof, where he had a camera platform measuring 5 feet by 9 feet.

From the junction just below the Furnace Creek Inn, begin by heading 3½ miles down Highway 190 to **Zabriskie Point.** The early morning light on this colorful landscape makes for a great photograph.

Continue along 190 in the same direction; Dantes View is 19½ miles from Zabriskie Point. (When you come to a fork in the road, be sure to bear right rather than following 190 out of the park.) In addition to the great vista from **Dantes View,** you can enjoy the cooler temperatures here, often 25 degrees cooler than on the valley floor. In the middle of the summer, that alone is enough of a reason to drive to this mountaintop.

You need to backtrack to Furnace Creek to reach **Badwater,** which you can see from Dantes View. From Furnace Creek, head south 17 miles on Route 178. If you make this trip in the middle of summer, you will feel the heat in Badwater. But braving the heat is worth the cool experience of being 282 feet *below* sea level and walking across Death Valley's fractured salt-pan floor.

After exploring the area and taking the requisite pictures to document your visit, turn back north for the 71-mile drive to **Scotty's Castle,** which takes about 90 minutes. In Furnace Creek, take 190 north to Route 267 north. Sure, it's a long drive. But although Scotty's Castle is somewhat out of the way, you don't want to miss it.

Depending on the time, you may want to stop for lunch in Furnace Creek. If you do, I recommend that you go to **Furnace Creek Ranch** (see "Where to Eat" later in this chapter). Or you can head up to Scotty's Castle, buy your tickets for the tour, and eat lunch at the snack bar while waiting for your tour to come up.

On the way to Scotty's Castle, just north of Stovepipe Wells Village on 267, look for the roadside sign that notes how long the wait is for a tour. If you're visiting in the winter months and don't have to wait, stop at **Death Valley Sand Dunes** and **Ubehebe Crater** so you can see them before the daylight wanes. (In winter, if you do have to wait, go directly to the castle to pick up your tickets; otherwise, you may not get on a tour.) In the summer months, when the sun rises early and it stays light as late as 8:30 p.m., take the castle tour first and stop at the crater and the Sand Dunes on your way back.

During the hot summer months, you may want to spread this trip over 1½ or even 2 days. I'd spend one day traveling to Scotty's Castle, Ubehebe Crater, and the Sand Dunes, and set out the next morning to Zabriskie Point, Dantes View, and Badwater. Depending on how fast you're moving, on one of the two days squeeze in a stop at the **Furnace Creek Visitor Center** to cool off and to visit the museum. The visitor center does a great job of chronicling the valley's fascinating mining background, as well as touching on the cultural highlights.

The 2-mile hike along the **Golden Canyon Interpretive Trail,** which is just 2 miles south of the Furnace Creek Inn, is another good addition to your second day. Try to fit this hike into your schedule late in the afternoon, when the setting sun's rays coax the most color out of the canyon.

If you have more time

The **Harmony Borax Works,** just 2 miles north of Furnace Creek, gives you a glimpse of the valley's hardworking past. This mining operation proved more profitable than efforts to bore gold and silver out of the surrounding mountains. The raw borax, known as ulexite cottonball borax, was collected in the alkali flats west of Harmony by Chinese laborers who hauled it to Harmony for processing. The borax was loaded onto wagons, each pulled by 18 mules and two horses, and taken 165 miles west to a train station at Mojave, California.

Today, all that remains are the alkali flats, the ruins of the processing mill, and a haul wagon. But standing before the ruins and realizing the conditions that the laborers endured will give you a new appreciation for hard work.

Artists Palette can be a colorful addition to the photographic record of your Death Valley trip if you can catch the late-afternoon sun igniting this hillside. Located on Artist Drive, which is 9½ miles south of Furnace Creek, a rumpled hillside midway along the drive constitutes the palette. Infused with volcanic sediments containing iron salts, mica, and manganese, the hillside shimmers under the setting sun with hues of reds, grays, blues, pinks, and yellows.

If you have a good four-wheel-drive rig and enjoy bone-rattling rides, head to the park's northwest corner and the **Racetrack.** Riddling Death Valley are old dirt roads leading to and from abandoned mining communities and into the mountains. You must take one of these roads to reach this attraction — no doubt, one of the oddest in Death Valley. The Racetrack is a *playa* — a dry lake bed — across which rocks mysteriously slide. Unless you're incredibly patient for weeks on end, you never actually see them move. Instead, you're left to ponder the tracks that zigzag across the ground. (Scientists believe the rocks are pushed about when the playa takes on water from storms and runoff and strong winds howl across its surface.) To reach the Racetrack, head north on Route 267 to Ubehebe Crater (38 miles from the 190/374 junction near Stovepipe Wells Village), and then drive 27 miles south on a dirt road.

Another four-wheel-drive destination is **Echo Canyon,** site of Needles Eye, a natural arch. For directions and current road conditions, track down a ranger at the Furnace Creek Visitor Center or another ranger station. If you plan to stay overnight in the backcountry, pick up a backcountry camping permit, too.

Finding local wildlife and vegetation

Imagining that much of anything lives in Death Valley is hard. At first glance, your eyes won't detect any living thing when they pan across this apparent wasteland, because you're likely searching in the middle of the day when critters are hiding in some relatively cool place. But as you become more discerning, you begin to see things. Come out before the sun rises or in the waning evening, and you're likely to spot one of the valley's critters.

If you're determined you can spot **desert bighorn sheep.** These recluses prefer rocky hillsides — look for them near Mosaic Canyon — and their dull grey coats provide the perfect camouflage.

The park also has **coyotes,** the consummate beggars. You're likely to run into them near a developed area, such as Furnace Creek or Stovepipe Wells Village. They stand in the middle of the road with hopes that you'll stop and toss them a bite to eat. Don't feed them, but slow down because a number of coyotes have been hit by cars.

If you're patient, you can even find life around the park's sand dunes. **Kangaroo rats, lizards, sidewinder rattlesnakes, coyotes,** and the **kit fox** are among the animals that call the dunes home. If you're quiet and crafty, you may spot one of these guys in the dunes at night. Bring a flashlight to help you find your way, but cover its lens with red cellophane so the light won't spook the animals.

The valley's most unusual residents are **desert pupfish** that live in salty marshes along Salt Creek just 10 miles south of Stovepipe Wells Village on Highway 190. Ancestors of these fish lived in the sprawling freshwater lake that once filled the bottom of Death Valley. As the lake slowly evaporated, the waters became saltier and saltier, and the pupfish managed to adapt quickly enough to stay alive. As the lake eventually separated into smaller, distinct pools, pupfish in each pool evolved to tolerate their respective environments. The Salt Creek pupfish endure water temperatures that fluctuate from more than 100 degrees in the summer to near freezing in the winter.

Death Valley's wildflowers have learned to cope with minimal water. It's hard to believe, but more than 1,000 plant species grow in the valley. Most flowers remain dormant until quenching rainstorms tell them that it's time to awaken, blossom, and go to seed. The alluvial fans that spill out of the mountains are perfect seedbeds for the park's flowers, and after a wet winter or spring, you see scores of **sunflowers** creep across the fans.

Other species that grow in the valley include **evening primrose, orange globemallow,** and 13 varieties of **cacti.** A species that appears dead even when it's alive is **desert holly,** which has evolved to be able to pull nourishment from salt water. The salt forms crystals on the holly leaves, and the result is a shimmering, crusty leaf.

Ranger programs

Because summers are the hottest time of the year in Death Valley, and mostly non–English speaking Europeans come to visit, ranger programs go on a siesta this time of year. But from mid-October into April, there's quite a bit going on, such as nightly ranger sessions in the Furnace Creek

Visitor Center on everything from Death Valley's geology to human history. Pick up a weekly schedule of programs at the visitor center to find out what's happening during your visit. And if you have little ones, don't forget to pick up information on the Junior Ranger Program (see Chapter 7 for information).

The best show — and one that's offered year-round — is at **Scotty's Castle,** an attraction that's one part museum and one part theater. The theatrics come to life through Park Service employees who dress in 1920s garb and infiltrate tour groups to inquire about Death Valley Scotty. Be ready for these interruptions, because the actors may question your opinion on whether a gold mine is deep beneath the castle's floors. For information on visiting Scotty's Castle, see "Exploring the top attractions," earlier in this chapter.

Escaping the heat

What do you do if the heat begins to bake your brain? Head indoors. **Scotty's Castle** is a great place to hide from the sun. (See "Exploring the top attractions," earlier in this chapter.) The castle is not air-conditioned, but its interior is cooler than the air outside. Plus, the castle is set in something like an oasis in Grapevine Canyon, and after your tour you can relax with ice cream under the palm trees. Another place to avoid the sun is the **Borax Museum** at the Furnace Creek Visitor Center (see "Orienting Yourself in Death Valley," earlier in this chapter). Inside, you find exhibits that trace the valley's checkered mining history plus a steam locomotive, antique stagecoaches, and mining tools. If you stay at the **Furnace Creek Inn,** escape the sun for a few minutes by venturing from the lower parking lot through a passageway in the inn's basement that leads to elevators that haul guests to the upper floors. Several illuminated "windows" in this passageway display interesting mining artifacts. Of course, the best way to deal with the heat is to go swimming, which is possible if you stay at the Furnace Creek Ranch, the Furnace Creek Inn, or Stovepipe Wells Village.

Where to Stay

If you're not going to camp out, you have four lodging choices in the park. If price is no object, get a room at the Furnace Creek Inn, which is located in the heart of Death Valley. A less expensive option that shares the inn's central location is the Furnace Creek Ranch. Your third option is Stovepipe Wells Village to the northwest of Furnace Creek. All three are run by **Xanterra Parks & Resorts** (☎ **303-297-2757;** www.xanterra.com). Your fourth option is Panamint Springs Resort, although its location near the park's western border is far removed from Death Valley's heart. For more information on finding a place to stay, see Chapter 6.

Lodging in the park

Furnace Creek Inn
$$$$–$$$$$ Furnace Creek

Think of a desert oasis, and you'll get a sense of the setting here. This Mission-style inn is surrounded by groves of date palm trees. Springs not only help the trees and surrounding gardens thrive, but a warm spring fills the swimming pool. Although swimming in 85-degree water may seem ridiculous in a place as hot as Death Valley, the pool feels refreshing when the air temperature is around 100 or more. If you're not exhausted by the day's heat, you can take to the inn's four lighted tennis courts when things cool down a bit at night.

The rooms are on the small side when you consider today's newest accommodations. But they're comfortable and have a warm atmosphere (no pun intended) thanks to the Mission design. Ceiling fans aid air-conditioners that can struggle during the summer. Are the rooms worth several hundred dollars a night? Probably not. But your options aren't the greatest, either, and this inn offers the best ambience in the park. If you decide to stay here, request a room facing the gardens. The view from the small balcony outside your room is tropical, and the paths that wind down to the pool are perfect for an evening stroll.

Note: At one time open year-round, this inn in recent years has closed from mid-May until mid-October due to the park's drop in visitors. However, this status is evaluated annually, so check early in the year if you're determined to visit Death Valley in the summer.

See map p. 107. Highway 190. ☎ ***888-297-2757*** *or 760-786-2345;* www.furnace creekresort.com *for reservations. 66 rooms, including 2 suites. A/C TV TEL. Rack rates: Mid-Oct to mid-May $240–$375 double. AE, DC, MC, V.*

Furnace Creek Ranch
$$–$$$ Furnace Creek

The pace here is more laid back than at the Furnace Creek Inn across the highway. Rooms have more of a motel feel, and with a general store, three restaurants, a saloon, and a museum on the property, you get the sense that you're staying in a small village. For the budget-minded, this is the place to stay. Kids love cooling off in the pool, and if you brought your clubs, the 18-hole golf course will torment you as its setting at 214 feet below sea level takes some zing out of your Pings. The cabins are single-story duplex units; they're efficient — two double beds, a shower — but that's about it. Realizing the hot weather scares off most tourists, the ranch reduces its prices by $10 to $20 per night during the hot months.

See map p. 107. Highway 190. ☎ ***760-786-2345.*** www.furnacecreekresort.com. *224 rooms. A/C TV TEL. Rack rates: early Oct to Dec 23 $105–$159; Nov 28–30 and Dec 24–31 $120–$174; late May– early Oct, $84–$149 double. AE, DC, DISC, MC, V.*

Panamint Springs Resort
$$–$$$ Panamint Springs

If you come to Death Valley from points west, this is a good place to stop. The resort is near the western border of the park, 48 miles east of Lone Pine, California, and 31 miles west of Stovepipe Wells Village. You won't find many frills, but you do find a gorgeous, laid-back setting; decent food; and ready access to nearby ghost towns, abandoned mines, and even a waterfall. The views aren't too shabby, either — you can see sand dunes off in the Panamint Valley and the Panamint Range. The place is even pet friendly ($5 per night extra). The rooms are clean but plain. The one cottage may not look like much, with its tin roof and walls, but inside are two bedrooms, a full bath, and a living room with the only color TV in a hotel on this side of Death Valley.

See map p. 107. Highway 190. ☎ *775-482-7680. Fax: 775-482-7682.* www.death valley.com. *14 rooms, 1 cottage, 26 tent sites, 42 RV sites. A/C. Rack rates: $65–$79 double; $139 cottage; $12 tent sites; $25 RV sites with full hookups (12 available); $15 RV sites with water only (30 available). DISC, MC, V.*

Stovepipe Wells Village
$$ Stovepipe Wells Village

If the best deal, not location or atmosphere, determines where you stay in Death Valley, this is the place, 23 miles northwest of Furnace Creek. The plain rooms are uninspiring and look like the ones in a run-of-the-mill, roadside motel, but the price is right. You find a general store, restaurant, and saloon, and the Death Valley Dunes are a 10-minute walk away.

See map p. 107. Highway 190. ☎ *760-786-2387. 83 rooms. TV and TEL in some rooms; A/C in all rooms. Rack rates: $79–$99 double. AE, DC, DISC, MC, V.*

Lodging outside the park

Death Valley has few nearby accommodations to which you can retreat and save money. At Beatty, Nevada, 41 miles northeast of Furnace Creek, you find a small handful of uninspiring motels. Las Vegas, with its countless options, is about two hours away.

Looking west, the closest "big" little towns are Lone Pine (104 miles) and Ridgecrest (123 miles); the pickings are a bit better, but the ride is much longer.

Campgrounds

If you really want to experience Death Valley 24 hours a day, camp out. During the summer months, in which hot breezes offer little relief, you may wish that you'd sprung for an air-conditioned room. Still, camping is an inexpensive way to stay in the park, and some campgrounds are at relatively high elevations where the temperature cools off at night.

Although ten campgrounds are scattered throughout Death Valley, only half (**Furnace Creek, Emigrant, Mesquite Spring, Wildrose,** and the privately owned **Panamint Springs**) are open year-round. The seasonal closures are the Park Service's way of telling you that camping out in the open is really too hot at certain times of the year.

The **Furnace Creek, Texas Spring,** and **Sunset campgrounds** are the park's most popular. You can make advance reservations for Furnace Creek and two group sites at Texas Springs, but only for dates between October 15 and April 15 (see the following listings for telephone numbers). Besides these dates, the campsites are first-come, first-served. The busiest periods are in early November and in spring, although after Easter has passed, business dips.

Here's a rundown of your camping options (prices are per night):

- ✔ **Emigrant Campground:** Nine miles south of Stovepipe Wells Village along Highway 190, this year-round campground is free and has 10 tent sites as well as drinking water, picnic tables, and flush toilets. Fires are prohibited.

- ✔ **Furnace Creek Campground:** This most picturesque campground is also the lowest, at 196 feet below sea level. 136 campsites ($16; $10 mid-April through mid-Oct) are adjacent to the ranch's palm groves. The year-round facility has flush toilets and drinking water, but you need to walk to the ranch for a shower, which costs a small fee. With a pool and restaurants nearby, this is my favorite campground. Reserve up to six months in advance by calling ☎ 800-365-2267.

- ✔ **Mesquite Spring Campground:** This campground, 1,800 feet above sea level and 3 miles south of Scotty's Castle off Route 267, is the farthest one north in Death Valley. Open year-round, the facility offers 30 sites ($10), flush toilets, fire rings, an RV dump station, and drinking water.

- ✔ **Panamint Springs Resort:.** Thirty-one miles west of Stovepipe Wells Village on Highway 190, this campground has 26 tent sites ($12). Twelve RV sites ($25) provide full utility hookups for recreational vehicles while 30 other RV sites ($15) just have water hookups. Resort amenities include flush toilets, showers, and drinking water. The campground is open year-round. For more information, call ☎ 775-482-7680.

- ✔ **Stovepipe Wells Village:** If you don't mind camping in a crowd, try this 190-site campground ($10). This campground provides flush toilets and drinking water, and for a fee, you can use shower facilities. Due to the summertime heat, the campground is open only from October to April. Fires aren't allowed.

- ✔ **Sunset Campground:** If you want crowds, come to this campground ¼ mile east of the Furnace Creek Ranch. With 1,000 sites, Sunset is the park's biggest campground. Your $10 per night camping fee gets you a space and access to flush toilets and drinking water, but showers are extra and fires are prohibited. This campground is open October to April.

- **Texas Spring Campground:** This campground is in the same area as Sunset Campground. Its 92 sites ($12) and two group areas, which run $40 a night, are available from October to April. (Call ☎ 760-786-3247 for group reservations.) You get flush toilets, picnic tables, and drinking water, but showers cost extra.

- **Wildrose Campground:** Thirty miles south of Stovepipe Wells Village on the Trona-Wildrose Road is this campground and its 23 free sites. Open year-round, the campground provides water, picnic tables, fire rings, and pit toilets.

- **Primitive Campgrounds:** Two campgrounds offer the coolest nights in Death Valley thanks to their location at above 7,400 feet, but you need a four-wheel-drive vehicle to access them. Located 37 miles and 38 miles south of Stovepipe Wells Village, respectively, are **Thorndike Campground** (six primitive sites, free, open March through November) and **Mahogany Flat Campground** (ten primitive sites, free, open March through November). Both provide pit toilets, picnic tables, and fire rings, but no water.

Where to Eat

While the dining's not on a par with Yosemite's or Olympic's, the food is pretty good and only woefully pricey if you dine at the Furnace Creek Inn.

Forty Niner Café
$–$$$ Furnace Creek AMERICAN

Down the hill from the Furnace Creek Inn, this hole-in-the-wall cafe with ever-present pitchers of ice water offers a varied menu with a wide range of prices. Breakfasts are simple but filling, as you find out if you try the Denver omelet, which comes with a large side of hash browns and toast. Try the taco salad at lunch or dinner, or if you want something heartier in the evening, order the 8-ounce New York steak accompanied by veggies and fries. Chicken, trout, and pasta dishes are also available.

See map p. 107. Highway 190. ☎ 760-786-2345. Main courses: $6–$9.75 breakfast; $8–$13.75 lunch; $8.50–$18.95 dinner. AE, DC, DISC, MC. V. Open: Daily 7 a.m.–9 p.m.

Furnace Creek Inn Dining Room
$$$–$$$$ Furnace Creek AMERICAN

If you feel like dressing up and spending big bucks on a meal, this is the only place to do it in the park. In fact, during the high season, men are encouraged to wear jackets during dinner. The view out the windows is fantastic, but although the dinner entrees are enticing, the prices may dampen your appetite. The least expensive dinner entrée (at $22) is a vegan dish of egg-free pasta stuffed with tofu and vegetables and served with a tomato and sweet potato sauce. The most expensive ($29) is the center cut filet mignon served with a merlot-mushroom sauce and savory mashed potatoes with roasted garlic. This is not the place to haul a large family, but if you can splurge one night, the experience is memorable, particularly when the sun is going down over the palm grove.

See map p. 107. Highway 190. ☎ *760-786-2345. Reservations recommended. Main courses: $6.50–$12.75 breakfast; $8.75–$14 lunch; $22–$29 dinner. AE, DC, DISC, MC, V. Open: Daily 7–10:30 a.m., 11:30 a.m.–2:30 p.m., and 5:30–9 p.m. (until 9:30 Fri–Sat).*

Panamint Springs
$–$$$ Panamint Springs   AMERICAN

Once upon a time, this sleepy resort on the park's western border was hailed for its burgers and beer, and not much more. More recently, though, the menu has become a bit more diverse, with a variety of barbecued items grilled outside on the porch. Steaks — 16-ounce ribeyes and 10-ounce filets — lead the way, but you can also choose from lasagna, seafood, poultry, chili, spaghetti, and homemade soups.

See map p. 107. Highway 190. ☎ *775-482-7680. Main courses: $6–$11.95 breakfast; $5.50 –$11.95 lunch; $15–$23.75 dinner. DISC, MC, V. Open: 7 a.m.–10 p.m.*

Stovepipe Wells Village
$$–$$$ Stovepipe Wells Village   AMERICAN

Looking like a cross between a camp dining room and a relaxed cafe, this restaurant offers little ambience. Breakfasts are built around a buffet offering cereals, fresh fruit, eggs, bacon, yogurt and pastries. Lunch, available mid-October through mid-May, is built around burgers, sandwiches, and salads. Dinners revolve around steaks, seafood, and chicken.

See map p. 107. Highway 190. ☎ *760-786-2387. Main courses: $7.25 breakfast buffet; $5.95–$10 lunch; $10.25–$20.95 dinner. AE, DC, DISC, MC, V. Open: Daily 7 a.m.–2 p.m., 5:30–9 p.m.*

Wrangler Steakhouse
$$$–$$$$ Furnace Creek   AMERICAN

The main reason to opt for this steakhouse next to the Forty Niner Café is to gorge yourself on one of the all-you-can-eat buffets (offered for breakfast 6–9 a.m. and lunch 11 a.m.–2 p.m.). Dinners feature entrees ranging from $18 for half a roasted chicken to $28 for a 16-ounce Porterhouse steak that will leave very little room for dessert. The sizes of the servings aren't bad, but if you're going to pay this much you might as well put on a jacket, head up to the inn, and shell out a few more dollars for a more enjoyable dining experience. The breakfast buffet features fruit, eggs, bacon, waffles, and French toast. The lunch buffet has three hot entrees, like fried chicken or lasagna, as well as a soup and salad bar.

See map p. 107. Highway 190. ☎ *760-786-2345. Reservations recommended. Main courses: $8.75 breakfast buffet; $10.75 lunch buffet; $18–$28 dinner. AE, DC, DISC, MC, V. Open: 6–10 a.m., 10:45 a.m.–2 p.m.; 6:30–10 p.m. (Early bird special 5 p.m.– 6 p.m.)*

Fast Facts: Death Valley

Area Code

The area code is **760**.

ATM

You can find ATMs inside the Furnace Creek Ranch registration office and the Stovepipe Wells Village motel.

Emergency

In an emergency, dial **760-786-2330** or **911**.

Fees

Entrance fees are $10 per vehicle per week.

Hospitals/Clinics

The nearest hospital is the Beatty (Nevada) Health Clinic, which you can reach at ☎ 775-553-2208.

Information

For information write to Death Valley National Park, P.O. Box 579, Death Valley, CA 92328-0579, call ☎ 760-786-3200, or check www.nps.gov/deva

Post Office

The post office is in the Furnace Creek Ranch complex (☎ 760-786-2223).

Road Conditions

For road conditions in California, call ☎ 800-427-7623; for road conditions in Nevada, call ☎ 776-793-1313.

Time Zone

Death valley is on Pacific time.

Chapter 11

Grand Canyon National Park

. . . .

. . . .

*W*elcome to one of the biggest, deepest, and most interesting showcases of erosion in the world. Yes, this chapter is all about that illustrious hole in the ground — the Grand Canyon.

You can see thousands of spectacular canyons around the United States — Hell's Canyon in Idaho, Kings Canyon in California, and the Grand Canyon of the Yellowstone in Wyoming to name a few. But none is quite as magnificent, colorful, or big as the one near the northern Arizona border. Nothing else exists like the Grand Canyon. When you stand on either the South or North rims, you look out across a mile-deep abyss, 18 miles wide in places. This rocky gorge is stunning, both in its display of the power of erosion and in its intricate, delicately carved layers, ridges, and promontories of rock.

The Grand Canyon is a mesmerizing combination of multihued ridges, cliffs, pinnacles, and side canyons unlike any other. You can sample the park in an afternoon by following one of the many hiking trails, or make a more serious exploration by spending several weeks negotiating the Colorado River as it continues to gnaw at the bedrock on the canyon floor. But this is the one park in the country where it pays to just stand in one place for a while — preferably at Point Sublime or the more accessible Hopi Point — and admire the park's ruggedly beautiful essence. At sunset at Point Sublime, the fiery sky melds with the glowing, red- and gold-colored walls of rock. Witnessing the deep and sprawling canyon aglow from these atmospheric fireworks is a humbling experience.

You can see the South Rim's highlights in one day. If you also want to hike and visit the North Rim, plan to spend at least four days in the park — one at the South Rim, one hiking, one driving to the North Rim, and one touring the North Rim.

What gouged the gorge?

The waters of the Green and Colorado rivers run downhill from west-central Wyoming and central Colorado, respectively, before merging in Utah and continuing into Arizona, where the rivers carved the Grand Canyon. During the last 6 million years, the Colorado River did a masterful job of slicing through the rock landscape that took nearly 2 billion years to form. Along the way, the river laid bare an incredible record of North American geology. While steadily and relentlessly washing bits and pieces of rock, dirt, sand, and silt downstream to the Gulf of California, the river created a 277-mile-long canyon that's chock-full of breathtaking views in all directions. (By the way, this 277-mile length is measured in "river miles," beginning at Lees Ferry near Page, Arizona, and ending at the Grand Wash Cliffs near the Arizona/Nevada border.)

Must-See Attractions

When you arrive at Grand Canyon National Park, the biggest attraction — the canyon itself — couldn't be more obvious. But don't overlook what else the park has to offer. The following cheat sheet can save you some time figuring out where to go and what to see:

- **Canyon View Information Plaza:** Accessed by the park's shuttle bus system, the plaza has exhibits on the park's geology, history, and wildlife, and it has a book store/gift shop with a wide selection of trail guides and maps.

- **Desert View Drive:** Along this drive, you see great canyon panoramas from such overlooks as Grand View and Moran points. Lipan Point offers the best sunset pictures.

- **Tusayan Ruins:** To some people, the low lines of foundation stones that remain at this site near the South Rim are nothing more than rocks. But these rocks are the lasting mark of an ancestral Puebloan community that flourished 800 years ago. The ruins, and a nearby museum, offer the park's best cultural display.

- **Watchtower:** Modern man imitated prehistoric man by building this stone tower, located on the eastern end of Desert View Drive. The tower houses a nice Native American art collection and a great observation deck.

- **North Rim:** A refuge from the crowds, the "other" rim has stunning vistas and thick conifer forests with great hiking trails. The higher elevation translates into cooler summers.

- **Point Imperial:** The highest point on the North Rim, reaching 8,803 feet, Point Imperial offers the best view of the canyon's northeastern corner. This is *the* spot for great sunrise photographs.

Geologic layer cake

Think a canyon is nothing more than a V-shaped gouge in the earth? Think again. The Grand Canyon is a myriad collection of canyons cut by the Colorado River and its tributaries. The mazelike formation is the result of different types of rock layers that erode at different rates in different ways. This geologic wonder has at least 13 different layers of rock. From top to bottom, these layers represent roughly 2 billion years of the Earth's history (give or take a few millennia), or roughly half the world's geologic history. Capping these layers is Kaibab Limestone, a fossil-rich, buff-colored layer of rock that holds the rim in place by resisting erosion. Descending beneath the limestone, in order, are the Toroweap formation, Coconino Sandstone, Hermit Shale, the Supai Group, the Surprise Canyon formation, Redwall Limestone, Temple Butte Limestone, Muav Limestone, Bright Angel Shale, Tapeats Sandstone, Zoraster Grante, and, finally, Vishnu Schist.

Study these layers (or talk to someone who makes a living as a geologist) and you discover that they chronicle a history of rivers, oceans, volcanoes, and mountains possibly as tall as today's Himalayas. You also find out that this layer cake is missing some ingredients. One gap in the chronology, known as the "Great Unconformity," represents an estimated 1 billion years of missing geology. As for the canyon's colorful outer frosting, these hues are the result of a wonderful mix of mineral deposits. One of the more common minerals is iron, which is responsible for the reds, oranges, yellows, and even the greens.

Planning Ahead

For general information before you go, contact **Grand Canyon National Park,** P.O. Box 129, Grand Canyon, AZ, 86023; ☎ **928-638-7888.**

When to go and how long to stay

Spring and fall are my favorite seasons in Grand Canyon National Park. The air is cool, occasionally turning crisp after sundown, and crowds aren't as overwhelming as they are during the busy summer season. Plus, hiking into the canyon is much more pleasurable with this cooler weather: Summer can be hot on the South Rim, and life-threateningly hot within the canyon itself for hikers. On the North Rim, you can escape both the heat and the crowds.

Although winter is the least-crowded time of year for the park's South Rim, snow and ice can make hiking hazardous, if not impossible. Also, roads can be closed by storms, and views obstructed by fog. The North Rim is inaccessible by vehicle between late November and mid-May.

During July and August, the South Rim can seem like Grand Central Station at rush hour. If you can't travel at another time of the year, arrive at the park before 10 a.m. or after 2 p.m. in order to avoid the lines at the entrance gates and the parking problems. You can also leave your car in Tusayan or Williams and take a shuttle or train to the South Rim (see "Getting There," later in this chapter).

 To really appreciate Grand Canyon National Park, I recommend that you stay at least three days and two nights. Stay even longer if you're planning an overnight hike into the canyon.

Advance reservations

 Not surprisingly, with a park of Grand Canyon's stature and popularity, you have to **make plans early.** Make reservations as far in advance as possible — even two years in advance — for each activity you plan to do, including mule rides, backcountry hikes, river trips, and lodging. For help in sorting out your trip, get a Trip Planner by contacting the park (Trip Planner, P.O. Box 129, Grand Canyon, AZ 86023; ☎ **928-638-7888;** www.nps.gov/grca/pphtml/planyourvisit.html). This helpful document answers questions for camping, lodging, weather, and backcountry treks.

One company — **Xanterra Parks & Resorts** (14001 E. Eliff, Aurora, CO 80014; ☎ **303-297-2757;** www.xanterra.com) — oversees all the lodging in the park under the auspices of Grand Canyon National Park Lodges. Through their telephone number or Web site you can make reservations up to 23 months in advance. As a general rule, if you have your heart set on visiting during a holiday period or in fall or spring, you should call 20 to 23 months in advance. However, even at some of the park's most popular hotels, such as the El Tovar, you can sometimes get a reservation within a month's time because of cancellations — good news for those who can't conceive of planning so far in advance.

For me, one of the best places to spend a night in the park is in a tent or under the stars. Camping brings you one step closer to the park's essence. The Grand Canyon has four campgrounds, two of which require reservations during some seasons. You can call ☎ **800-365-CAMP,** or log on to the park's Web site at http://reservations.nps.gov, to make reservations at the Mather and North Rim campgrounds. The Mather Campground is open year-round, and I strongly recommend reservations for visits between mid-March and November 1. If you're serious about planning, you can make these reservations up to five months in advance of your visit. From December to March, however, Mather sites are assigned on a first-come, first-served basis. The North Rim Campground, meanwhile, is open only from mid-May to late October, and again, I recommend reservations, although sometimes you can stumble upon last-minute vacancies. For information on all the campgrounds, see "Where to Stay," later in this chapter.

What to pack

Packing is easy for a Grand Canyon trip (unless you're floating the Colorado). During summer, shorts and T-shirts are standard attire during the day, and a pair of slacks and casual dress shirt perfect for any of the park's dining rooms. You'll want a light jacket to stay warm after the sun goes down, and rain gear is always good to pack. With the bright setting on the canyon's rims, you'll be smart to wear a wide-brimmed hat, use sunscreen, and always have sunglasses handy. Of course, if you plan to venture into the canyon for a day hike, pack a good pair of hiking boots, a hydration system or several water bottles, a hiking staff if you have one, and a good day pack.

Winters can be brutal on the South Rim, with heavy snowstorms and wet weather in general. Plan accordingly with layers of warm clothing, gloves, and a comfortable hat. For more tips on what to pack, see Chapter 8.

Getting There

Reaching the Grand Canyon takes effort, especially if you plan to visit the North Rim. Nonetheless, several modes of transport can get you there.

Driving in

Most people drive to the Grand Canyon from one of the region's airports. Grand Canyon Village on the South Rim is 80 miles north of Flagstaff, Arizona (the region's largest city), via U.S. Route 180, and 60 miles north of Williams, Arizona, via Highway 64. The closest town to the park is Tusayan, Arizona, 1 mile beyond the south entrance on Highway 64.

An alternative to driving all the way to Grand Canyon Village is to leave your car in Williams or Tusayan. From these towns, you can take a train or shuttle bus, respectively, to the village. See the following sections, "Flying in" and "Training in," to find out more about these options. See also the "Transportation travails" sidebar in this chapter to find out about proposed changes that, if implemented, will drastically alter vehicle access on the South Rim.

The North Rim is closest to Kanab, Utah, 78 miles to the northwest via Arizona 67 and U.S. Route 89A.

Flying in

If you plan to fly to the park, the biggest runways in the general vicinity are **Phoenix/Sky Harbor International Airport** (☎ 602-273-3300), which is 220 miles from the South Rim, and **McCarran International Airport** (☎ **702-261-5743**) in Las Vegas, which is 263 miles from the North Rim. **America West Express** (☎ **800-235**-9292) has daily jet service between Phoenix/Sky Harbor International Airport and **Flagstaff Pulliam Airport** (☎ **928-556-1234**), which is 80 miles from the South Rim.

If you don't mind smaller airports, **Scenic Airlines** (☎ **800-634-6801** or 702-638-3200) can fly you from Las Vegas to **Grand Canyon National Airport** (☎ **928-638-2446**) in Tusayan, 1 mile south of Grand Canyon Village, on one of their daily flights. Scenic flies out of **North Las Vegas Airport** (☎ **702-261-3800**) as well as McCarran International.

Most of the major rental car agencies have offices at the Phoenix/Sky Harbor International Airport and McCarran International Airport in Las Vegas; see the Appendix for contact information. **Hertz, Budget, Avis,** and **National** rent cars at Flagstaff Pulliam Airport, and **Enterprise** rents cars at Tusayan during the high season. You can also take a shuttle from Tusayan to the Grand Canyon Village; see "Busing in," later in this chapter, for details.

From the **Phoenix airport**, head 136 miles north to Flagstaff via Interstate 17 and then take U.S. 180 51 miles to Arizona 64, which leads 28 miles to the South Rim. From the **Las Vegas airport**, head 103 miles south via U.S. 95 and 93 to Kingman, Arizona, and then 117 miles east on Interstate 40 to Williams, where Arizona 64 leads 57 miles north to the South Rim. For information on driving from the **Flagstaff and Tusayan airports,** see "Driving in."

Training in

Even rail fans have ways to get to the park. **Amtrak** (☎ **800-872-7245** or 928-774-8679; www.amtrak.com) runs into downtown Flagstaff. **Budget** has a car-rental office two blocks from the station.

You can also ride the historic **Grand Canyon Railway** (☎ **800-843-8724;** www.grandcanyonrailway.com), which makes daily runs linking Williams, Arizona, and Grand Canyon Village. A vintage steam engine or 1950 diesel lugs the train 65 miles, leaving Williams in the morning and returning late in the afternoon.

Taking a taxi in

From Tusayan, you can take a **Grand Canyon Coaches** (☎ **928-638-0821;** www.grandcanyoncoaches.com) taxi to Grand Canyon Village. The taxis link five stops in Tusayan to the village. Using a taxi is a great way to avoid parking problems inside the park. The adult one-way fare is $5; ages 16 and under ride free. There is a $10 minimum.

Grand Canyon National Park

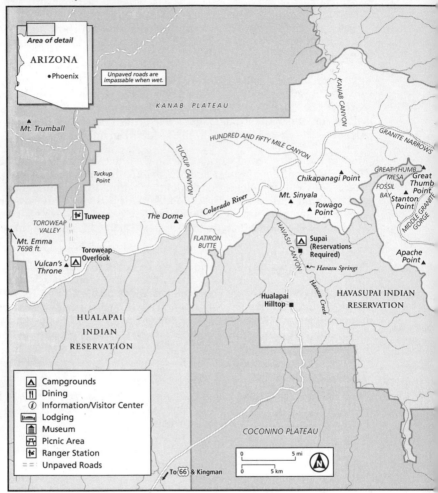

Orienting Yourself in Grand Canyon

Grand Canyon is a fairly straightforward park in terms of layout. Flanking the main attraction — that incredibly large, colorful, and jagged chasm — are two rims that offer fantastic views. The South Rim boasts the most manmade attractions and facilities (and some darn impressive views), but the North Rim offers cooler temperatures, thick forests, and relative solitude (as well as, of course, some darn impressive views).

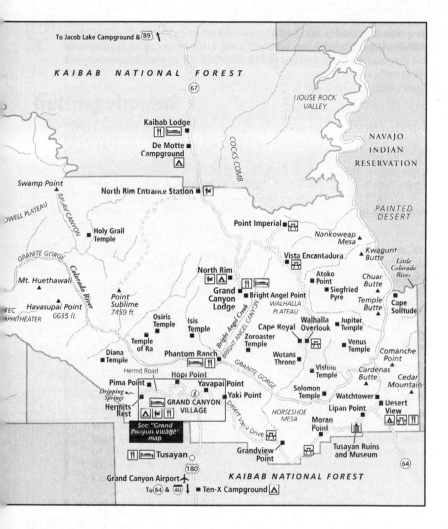

You're probably not going to visit both rims during the same trip. Why not? For starters, an easily traveled route doesn't exist between Point A (the South Rim) and Point B (the North Rim). Going from rim to rim by auto entails a highway odyssey of about 220 miles (one-way) that takes about five hours. Sure, you can hike down into the canyon and up the other side. But doing so is impractical unless you plan to make such a trek the focus of your trip: A hike from one side to the other covers 21 miles via the North and South Kaibab Trails, a trek that usually takes three days each way.

Grand Canyon Village

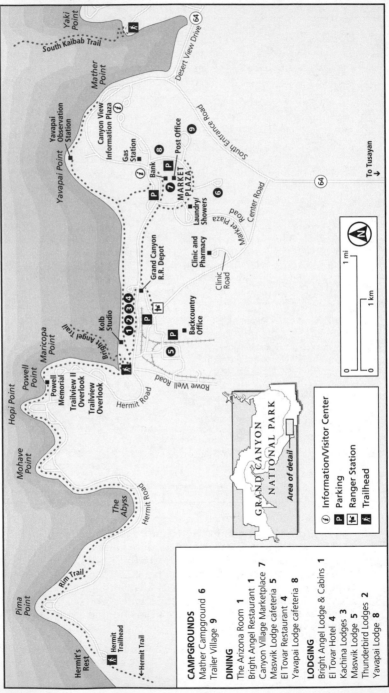

CAMPGROUNDS
Mather Campground **6**
Trailer Village **9**

DINING
The Arizona Room **1**
Bright Angel Restaurant **1**
Canyon Village Marketplace **7**
Maswik Lodge cafeteria **5**
El Tovar Restaurant **4**
Yavapai Lodge cafeteria **8**

LODGING
Bright Angel Lodge & Cabins **1**
El Tovar Hotel **4**
Kachina Lodges **3**
Maswik Lodge **5**
Thunderbird Lodges **2**
Yavapai Lodge **8**

Legend:
(i) Information/Visitor Center
P Parking
Ranger Station
Trailhead

The park covers more than 1.2 million acres, but has relatively few roads and developed areas. The **South Rim** is the main travel corridor for Grand Canyon visitors. The air isn't as cool as on the North Rim, and the trees aren't as tightly packed together, but the views are more numerous and, in some minds, more incredible. Unlike the North Rim overlooks, some of those at the South Rim take in the Colorado River. **Grand Canyon Village** lends a sense of community to this rim, with its lodgings, visitor center, ranger station, restaurants, gift shops, sprawling campgrounds, and picnic grounds (see the Grand Canyon Village map, in this chapter).

You negotiate the South Rim along two roads — Hermit Road and Desert View Drive, both of which have several overlooks. (See "Enjoying the top attractions," later in this chapter, for details on the overlooks.) **Desert View Drive** starts in the village and runs 25 miles to the east, whereas **Hermit Road** starts in the village and travels 8 miles west to the Hermits Rest Overlook. A public highway, Desert View Drive is open year-round to motorists, but private vehicles can't stop at the Yaki Overlook and the South Kaibab Trailhead during high season (March through November), a ban park officials may extend to year-round. Hermit Road is closed to private vehicles during high season but open to them from December through February. During closures, you must take a free park shuttle to visit the outlooks. (See "Getting around," later in this chapter, for information on shuttles.)

Looking for a slower pace than the hustle and bustle of the South Rim? Then head to the **North Rim,** which you can access via U.S. Route 89A and Highway 67. At an average elevation of 8,000 feet — 1,000 feet higher than the South Rim — this rim is incredibly lush (especially in contrast to the South Rim and Inner Gorge). Ponderosa pine, spruce, fir, pockets of aspen, groves of gambel oak, and stands of juniper and pinyon fill the area. Much of the rim is accessible only to the most determined travelers. Roads are few, requiring anyone who wants to go beyond the Cape Royal, Point Imperial, and Point Sublime Overlooks, or the Grand Canyon Lodge (the rim's only hotel), to do so by foot or mule. (See "Keeping active," later in this chapter, for information on mule excursions.)

The only other road into the park is a dirt route that runs to the **Toroweap Valley** on the western edge of the park. Follow this road, and you reach a campground, the Toroweap Overlook, and Vulcans Throne, a volcanic cone. Another dirt route drops south from U.S. Route 89A and bisects **House Rock Valley** near the northeastern tip of the park. This road doesn't go into the park, but it leads to the South Canyon Trail, which heads into the park and toward the Colorado River.

Finding information after you arrive

The **Canyon View Information Plaza** offers one-stop shopping when it comes to getting oriented to the park. Located close to Mather Point, the plaza offers interpretive exhibits and a book/gift store where you can load up on guidebooks, film, postcards and more. There's also an excellent indoor exhibit on the park's geology, as well as seating for daily ranger presentations. If a mass transit system ever replaces the automobile within the park, this plaza will serve as its hub. With that in mind, some day a bicycle rental shop will be located here as well. The park's existing shuttle system is routed through the plaza. Hours are daily from 8 a.m. to 5 p.m.

Transportation travails

If you like traffic jams, make the South Rim your first stop in Grand Canyon. Every year, an estimated 1.5 million private vehicles and another 30,000 tour buses converge on this side of the park. Smog can blur views, and not enough parking lots are available to handle the traffic, so at the height of summer you often encounter lines of rigs parked along the road. Not only are they ugly, but they're also dangerous for visitors and deadly for roadside vegetation.

The National Park Service isn't ignoring the problem. In 1995, officials agreed that they had to change the way people visit the Grand Canyon's South Rim. The park has free shuttle buses available, but that's just a start. One day you won't be able to drive yourself onto the South Rim. Instead, to see the park's beauty from the south side, you'll have to catch a shuttle bus or a light-rail train.

These days, the **Canyon View Information Plaza** (CVIP) near Mather Point is primarily an orientation center. However, when the Park Service implements a mass-transit system, CVIP likely will be the nerve center for tourist traffic on the South Rim. Currently, you can reach CVIP via the park's shuttle bus system or by walking a ¾-mile, paved trail from Market Plaza.

If a light-rail system is built, you'll be kindly asked to park your car at the South Rim gateway community of Tusayan and ride the train into the park. One spur will run to CVIP, where shuttle buses, powered by electricity or natural gas, very likely will haul you to Hermits Rest, Yaki Point, Desert View, and locations within Grand Canyon Village. A second spur likely will run to the Village Transit Center, a second transportation hub near Maswik Lodge. If the light-rail system is deemed unnecessary, a shuttle-bus system likely will haul the bulk of the South Rim's visitors.

If you choose not to ride the rail or shuttle, you'll be able to rent a bike and pedal your heart out along the slowly expanding Greenway trail that is designed to parallel the transit system from Hermits Rest to Desert View and south to Tusayan. The first section of the Greenway opened in the fall of 2001 and runs 2 miles from CVIP to the train depot. Another section, from CVIP to Tusayan, was expected to be under construction by late 2004 or early 2005.

If you have lodging reservations in the park, you'll park at designated parking areas, where you'll take the transit system to reach your accommodations on the South Rim. Campers likely will be able to drive to their campgrounds.

For more details and updates on the transit system, as well as information on the decisions behind it, visit the park's Web site at www.nps.gov/grca/transit.

Paying fees

Admission to Grand Canyon National Park costs $20 per private vehicle and $10 for travelers on foot or bicycle. Your receipt is good for a week and provides access to both rims. See Chapter 8 for information on the National Parks Pass and Chapter 7 for the lowdown on Golden Age and Golden Access passports.

Although you can make day hikes into the canyon without a permit, if you plan to stay overnight in the backcountry, you need to obtain a $10 permit and also pay a $5 per night per person user impact fee. You can obtain a camping permit four months in advance of your planned stay. To find out how to get a permit and request a Trip Planner, see "Planning Ahead," earlier in this chapter.

Getting Around Grand Canyon

As more and more private vehicles pour into the national parks, expect increasing numbers of shuttle systems battling the resulting congestion and air pollution. Grand Canyon Village is a case in point. After you arrive, you don't need a car to enjoy the sights. In fact, during high season, you can't use your car to visit certain viewpoints. From March through November, cars are prohibited on Hermit Road and can't stop at Yaki Point on Desert View Drive.

By shuttle or sightseeing bus

Grand Canyon's **free shuttle buses** move you conveniently around the park's South Rim, stopping at all the key viewpoints, all the lodges, the Canyon View Information Plaza, and many of the trailheads. One bus laps Grand Canyon Village, another traverses Hermit Road, and a third runs along Desert View Drive to Yaki Point and the South Kaibab Trailhead. During high season, shuttles run daily, about every 15 to 30 minutes, beginning an hour before sunrise and running to a seasonal stop time. The Grand Canyon Village shuttle runs from March through May and from September through November until 10 p.m., from June through August until 11 p.m., and from December through February until 9 p.m. (In the off-season, the Desert View shuttle runs until an hour after sunset.) The Hermit Road shuttle doesn't operate during December, January, and February. The Kaibab shuttle runs year-round from an hour before sunrise to an hour after sunset.

You can catch the shuttles in a lodge parking lot; in parking lots A, B, C, D, or E; or at any of the dropoff points along the routes. (You receive directions to the parking lots at the entrance station.) For information and schedules, call **Bright Angel Transportation Desk** (☎ 928-638-3283). Or you can pick up a shuttle map and schedule at the Canyon View Information Plaza.

You can also board one of the sightseeing buses run by the **Fred Harvey Transportation Company** (☎ 928-638-2631 or 888-29-2757 for advance reservations). These tours depart mornings and afternoons from Bright Angel, Maswik, and Yavapai lodges. Rates are $16 per person for a Hermits Rest Tour (two hours), $28 for a Desert View Drive tour (four hours), and $34 for a combination of the two. Children under age 16 are free when traveling with an adult. Tickets are available at the transportation desks at the three departure points. This company also operates a 24-hour taxi service.

Xanterra Parks & Resorts (☎ 928-638-2631) offers year-round sightseeing buses to Sunrise ($12.50), Sunset ($12.50), Desert View Drive ($28.50), and Hermit's Rest ($16.25). For all these tours, kids 16 and under are free when accompanied by a paying adult.

For hikers who travel from one rim to the other, the best way to get back to your car is aboard the **Trans-Canyon Shuttle** (☎ 928-638-2820), which runs a bus each day, in each direction, from mid-May through mid-October. The 220-mile trip takes about 4½ hours each way and costs $65 per person one-way, $110 round-trip. A reservation deposit is required. The shuttle travels between Bright Angel Lodge on the South Rim and Grand Canyon Lodge on the North Rim. You can also arrange to be picked up at a campground or trailhead on the North Rim.

By car

The best way to see the South Rim of the Grand Canyon by car is to park it and board one of the shuttle buses. During the high season, which seems to be constantly expanding, there are just too many vehicles in the park to make travel by auto enjoyable. Parking spaces are hard to find during the busiest times of year, and congestion can arise. There are plenty of shuttle buses negotiating the rim; during the busiest times of day you'll never wait longer than 15 minutes for a bus. Plus, with someone else doing the driving, you can concentrate on enjoying the scenery.

On foot

If you want, you can walk along the South Rim from Hermit's Rest to Pipe Creek Vista via the Rim Trail. Of course, that would be a long walk, spanning nearly 12 miles. Of that total, 3.75 miles are paved. Early morning and evening strolls along portions of this trail are great ways to not only gain great views into the canyon but also avoid the day's heaviest crowds.

Other (mule rides, helicopter flights, and so on)

Mule rides are a unique way to descend into the canyon — and climb back out. Several outfitters offer air tours of the Grand Canyon; for details on both, see the "Keeping active" section later in the chapter.

Remembering Safety

If you stand on one of the canyon overlooks, you'll likely notice that a fall off the ledge would bring a nasty end to your vacation. So no matter how badly you want a slightly different photograph, don't leap over the railings that keep you a safe distance from the canyon's lip. A slip or stumble could be your last. You wouldn't be the first to perish this way, either; over the years a surprising number of tourists have lost their lives in pursuit of that perfect picture.

The park is home to poisonous critters like scorpions and the Grand Canyon rattlesnake, so be careful where you put your hands when scrambling in rocky areas. Think twice about reaching for a spot you can't see.

If you plan to hike, read through the safety tips at the beginning of the "Taking a hike" section, later in this chapter. For additional tips on how to ensure a safe visit to a national park, see Chapter 8.

If, for some reason, you consider yourself immortal and fear nothing in Grand Canyon National Park, I heartily recommend *Over the Edge: Death in the Grand Canyon* by Michael P. Ghiglieri and Thomas M. Myers (Puma). It's an interesting, and sobering, accounting of the park's history of human deaths.

Exploring Grand Canyon National Park

Grand Canyon National Park is divided into four parts: the South Rim, the North Rim, the Inner Canyon, and the river. Only those with unlimited time and ambition can sample each of these realms in a satisfying manner during one visit. As a result, be realistic about your time restraints and physical ability when planning a trip to the Grand Canyon.

How do you want to explore the canyon? Does strapping a 40-pound pack on your back and disappearing below the rim for several days appeal to you? Are you interested in joining one of the mule trips that head down to the Phantom Ranch, a great base from which to investigate the river and the side canyons? Or would joining one of the scenic plane or helicopter flights that jog back and forth over the canyon every day, giving passengers a bird's-eye view of the park, be more appealing?

Don't be afraid to push yourself a bit. Although some trail descriptions may sound daunting, just because you head down a trail doesn't mean you have to drag yourself along its entire length. Walk as much, or as little, as you want. When I came to the top of the South Kaibab Trail late one afternoon, several people asked me how hard the hike was. It can be extremely hard if you attempt to reach the river. But a reasonably paced hike down to Cedar Ridge, 1½ miles from the rim, offers a chance to feel the texture and sense the breadth of the canyon without committing to a major undertaking.

Options, options, and more options. In this section, I introduce the top attractions and tell you how best to enjoy them.

The top attractions

Desert View Drive
South Rim

From Grand Canyon Village, Desert View Drive takes you to six great overlooks. One of the best, **Yaki Point,** offers views of some of the Grand Canyon's more renowned rock monuments — Vishnu Temple, Zoroaster Temple, and Wotan's Throne. Another overlook, **Moran Point,** is named after Thomas Moran, the landscape painter who helped put Yellowstone National Park on the map before journeying to Grand Canyon with Major John Wesley Powell. This overlook offers the best view of the tilting block of rock known as The Sinking Ship. You can spot the "ship" by looking southwest at the rocks level with the South Rim. The ship seems to be submerged in the horizontal layers of Coronado Butte.

If you can't leave the canyon without a killer sunset photo, head to **Lipan Point,** arguably the best spot on the South Rim for watching the setting sun — and for glimpsing the Colorado River. Almost straight below you at this point, the Colorado River makes a long, lazy S-curve. Just downstream of the curve you can see where the river cuts into the Vishnu Schist, one of the oldest rock layers in the canyon, and enters the steep-walled Inner Gorge. **Desert View,** the eastern-most overlook on Desert View Drive, also offers spectacular views into the eastern arm of the canyon.

Near Desert View overlook is the **Watchtower,** an impressive 70-foot stone structure designed by architect Mary Colter in 1932. You can climb a narrow, circular stairway to an enclosed observation deck on the tower's top. Traditional Native American art, including many images seen on rocks in the Southwest, decorate the walls. The most impressive work is by Hopi artist Fred Kabotie, whose depiction of the Snake Legend, the story of the first person to have floated down the Colorado River, graces the Watchtower's Hopi Room. The Watchtower is open from 8 a.m. to sunset during the summer months and 9 a.m. to sunset during the winter.

Just before Lipan Point on the drive is **Tusayan Ruin and Museum,** a must-see if you have any interest in America's ancient cultures. The 14-room, stone-walled structure dates to 1185 and has been traced to ancestors of today's Pueblos. You can take a self-guided walk through the ruins, which are little more than stone foundations. Still, interpretive signs along the way do a good job bringing the place to life. Nearby is the Tusayan Museum, which traces the lives of the region's Native Americans through displays of jewelry, clothing, and tools. This free museum is open from 9 a.m. to 5 p.m.

See map p. 133. Desert View Drive starts at Grand Canyon Village and runs east for 25 miles.

Hermit Road
South Rim

Hop on one of the shuttle buses that ply the 8-mile-long Hermit Road during the summer season (see "Getting around Grand Canyon," earlier in this chapter), and you come upon, among other lookouts, Powell Memorial, Hopi Point, and Mohave Point. **Powell Memorial** is a tribute to Major John Wesley Powell, an explorer who led the first successful navigation of the Colorado River through the canyon in 1869. **Hopi Point** is the best place on the West Rim to take in a sunset. From **Mohave Point,** you can spot some of the Colorado River's best rapids, including Hermit Rapids, Granite Rapids, and Salt Creek Rapids. **Hermits Rest,** a rock shelter designed to look as if some reclusive mountain man had built it, marks the end of the road. Built in 1914 to serve as a resting spot for tourists heading below the rim to Hermit Camp, this building still caters to travelers. You can relax in front of the fireplace or buy a snack to munch on before moving on.

Continuing on with the shuttle to Hermit's Rest is a 45-minute, one-way trek. It grows to 75 minutes with the return ride, which skips several of the stops made on the way to Hermits Rest. Is that worth a 10-minute stroll through Hermits Rest? I didn't think so. Your time can be better spent walking the Rim Trail, or admiring the art on display at the Kolb Studio.

See map p. 134. Hermit Rd. starts at Grand Canyon Village and runs west for 8 miles.

Inner Gorge

In the middle of the Grand Canyon is a relatively narrow, 1,000-foot-deep channel known as the Inner Gorge. At the bottom of this gorge, hidden from most viewpoints on the North and South rims, the Colorado River's often-muddy waters flow. The canyon floor offers you another incredible view: the look up. The towering canyon walls are so impressive — so jagged, fluted, and riddled from erosion — that you risk a sore neck from gazing upwards at them. Springs gush from numerous spots along the river corridor, creating waterfalls that quench wildlife and vegetation. (Before quenching your own thirst, make sure that you treat the water.) **Vasey's Paradise** is one of the more memorable gushers, pouring out of the north canyon wall in Marble Canyon and nourishing a thick bed of vegetation in the otherwise arid landscape.

River-bottom travelers see some of the park's best prehistoric ruins. At Nankoweap, near river mile 52, ruins used for grain storage are tucked under an alcove high on a canyon wall.

The canyon floor has one hotel, **Phantom Ranch**. See "Where to Stay," later in this chapter, for information on this accomodation.

You can access the bottom of the Grand Canyon by foot, raft, or mule. See "Taking a hike" for information on walks and "Keeping active" for raft or mule trips. Both sections appear later in this chapter.

North Rim

The North Rim's lower crowd density — relative to the South Rim, that is — results from the remoteness of this side of the canyon. The rim's major overlooks are at Bright Angel Point, Cape Royal, Point Imperial, and Point Sublime; all offer dazzling views of the Grand Canyon and its many side canyons. Activity at this rim centers on **Grand Canyon Lodge,** a beautiful hotel that practically disappears into the landscape, thanks to its green roof shingles, rugged log beams, and limestone exterior that matches the rim's Kaibab limestone. (See "Where to Stay," later in this chapter, for information on the lodge.) A short walk from the lodge is **Bright Angel Point,** which offers great views of a side canyon and the South Rim. Hardy travelers pause only briefly at this point before heading down the **North Kaibab Trail,** which starts 1½ miles from Grand Canyon Lodge and winds its way through Bright Angel Canyon to the Phantom Ranch nearly 6,000 feet below.

The best view at the North Rim is from the lip of **Cape Royal,** 23 miles from the lodge on Cape Royal Drive off Highway 67. Here the Grand Canyon plunges abruptly away from the rim. Although you can't immediately see the river, a short hike leads to a view through **Angels Window,** an eroded hole in a rock wall, which takes in the lower canyon and a tiny stretch of the Colorado River. Nearby are the **Walhalla Ruins,** once part of an Anasazi community, and **Roosevelt Point,** a small promontory on Cape Royal Drive that offers a view of where the Little Colorado River gorge and the Grand Canyon meet.

Point Imperial, the highest point on the North Rim at 8,803 feet, stands at the end of a 3-mile-long spur road running east from Cape Royal Drive. Although the point can become crowded in summer — when its picnic ground is a magnet — the view is worth it. The overlook faces east, drawing your eyes not only down into the depths of the canyon but also out across to **Mount Hayden,** a spindly spire somehow still standing on the edge of the canyon. Beyond and below Mount Hayden is the **Marble Platform** (a desolate-looking plain that geologists consider to be the top section of the Grand Canyon) and the **Painted Desert.** The hump that appears on the northeastern horizon is southeastern Utah's Navajo Mountain.

After the isolated Toroweap Overlook, the most remote North Rim overlook accessible by vehicle is **Point Sublime,** which lies west of Grand Canyon Lodge and which you reach via a rugged, bouncy road off Highway 67 that sedans should avoid. If you arrive at the point in late afternoon, you find intoxicating sunsets that seem to spray a cascade of colors across the canyon walls. Because the overlook is off the beaten path, this viewpoint (which induces vertigo if you venture to its lip) is not overrun with tourists.

See map p. 133. You can reach the North Rim via U.S. Route 89A and Highway 67

Capturing the Grand Canyon on film

The canyon provides countless good areas to take pictures, but naturally, some spots are better than others. If you're striving for that definitive Grand Canyon sunset, try shooting from the Hopi, Mojave, or Pima points located along Hermit Road on the South Rim. Or focus your camera from Lipan Point and Desert View Overlook on Desert View Drive. If you're an early riser and prefer sunrise shots, try Mather, Yaki, Yavapai, and Lipan points on the South Rim. On the North Rim, Bright Angel Point, Point Sublime, and Cape Royal are good for sunsets and sunrises. To find out how early you need to get up for sunrise or how late in the evening the sun will set, check the park's newspaper, *The Guide*. To get some ideas on specific shots to take, visit the Kolb Studio in Grand Canyon Village. The Kolb brothers, early canyon photographers, used this building as their studio. Inside you find a good bookstore and photography exhibits.

Yavapai Point
South Rim

This point has a neat historic observation station on the canyon rim. Inside, a bank of windows lets you gaze down into the canyon. As a bonus, a long interpretative panel beneath the windows helps you identify many of the landmarks in the central portion of the canyon, including such formations as **Zoroaster Temple, Isis Temple,** and **Buddha Temple.** Also visible from the point is the **Kaibab Suspension Bridge.** A new geology exhibit is tentatively planned for the observation station for the summer of 2005.

See map p. 134. Yavapai Point is about 1 mile east of the visitor center in Grand Canyon Village.

Taking a hike

Grand Canyon National Park offers a great array of hiking trails, from incredibly steep, knee-pounding hikes that plunge deep into the canyon to some relatively level walks through cool, shaded pine forests and along the rims. The bottom line is that you can sweat as much or as little as you want and still see some incredible views of the park.

Remember the following points before you head down the trail:

- ✔ **Gravity is both your friend and your enemy.** If you hike below the rim, gravity works for you and makes the walk down somewhat easy. However, save some strength for the return hike uphill, when gravity is no longer your best buddy.

- ✔ **Timing is everything.** If you plan to hike into the canyon and back out the same day, budget one-third of your time to hike down into the canyon, and two-thirds to climb back out. Do *not* think that you can hike down to the Colorado River and back to one of the rims during one summer day. The terrain and conditions make this trek pretty close to impossible; some past attempts have proven fatal.

✓ **Water is good.** Lots of water is very good. The temperature may not feel that overwhelming while you're walking along the rim or when you first start down into the canyon. But trust me, the lower you go, the more rugged the terrain becomes, and the higher the thermostat climbs. Remember — while you're enjoying 75-degree weather on the top of the North Rim, the temperature way down below at Phantom Ranch can easily be 105 degrees! If you're visiting from either coast, you soon realize how the dry air can suck the moisture out of your body. So after you decide on a hike, but before you set foot down the trail, make sure that you pack at least two quarts of water (preferably more) for every eight hours of hiking.

✓ **Pack some shade.** Wear a wide-brimmed hat and maybe even a neckerchief to shade your neck. Bringing a full tube of sunblock is a good idea, too.

✓ **Energize yourself.** If you plan to go on an overnight hike, you need to give nutrition some serious thought. But even if you're planning on a relatively short hike, say a couple miles, granola bars or some fruit are great to snack on when you reach the halfway point.

Overnight access to the park's backcountry is controlled through a permit system, so if you don't plan ahead, you can arrive ready to head off on a multiday hike only to discover that no permits are available. (See the above sections "Planning Ahead" and "Paying fees," respectively, for information on getting permits in advance and permit costs.) The park does employ a waiting list for this sort of situation, but in spring, summer, and fall you can wind up waiting two or three days for a permit. To get on the list, show up in person at the **Backcountry Office**, where you receive a number. To stay on the waiting list, you have to show up at the office at 8 a.m. every morning until your number is called. Although cancellations don't always happen, the office sometimes sets aside a spot or two at the Bright Angel Campground or Cottonwood Campground for people on the list.

Finally, during the summer months, rangers recommend that overnight backpackers avoid hiking during the middle of the day because of high temperatures. So, begin trips, hike to new campsites within the canyon, or make your return to one of the rims either before 7 a.m. or after 4 p.m.

With these details out of the way, here's a look at some reliable hiking options in the park.

Bright Angel Trail

This trail has existed for quite a while. Both Native Americans and early settlers recognized this path as a good descent into the canyon. Not only do you get to enjoy some shade along the way, but this place is the wettest on the South Rim, so finding water isn't usually a problem.

However, some words of caution to consider: Although this trail is very popular, it's also the scene of many rescues, because folks forget that it's a long, steep way back to the top. The hike to Indian Garden alone drops more than 3,000 feet. Mule trips head down into the canyon via this route and leave deposits along the way, so watch your footing. Also, the trail can be crowded at times. If you're into winter hiking, the upper section of this trail can be very icy, so pack some instep crampons.

If you're just heading out for a day hike, follow the trail as it zigzags below Grand Canyon Village to Mile-and-a-Half House or Three-Mile House. At each location, you find shade, an emergency phone, and water when in season, which is usually from May through mid-October. (Weather can shorten or extend the season.)

If you head below Three-Mile House, you find yourself on a steep descent to a picnic area near the spring at Indian Garden. This setting is almost like an oasis, with lush vegetation and towering cottonwood trees. It's a great place to be, but if you're not experienced with drastic elevation changes, heat, or dry air, don't make this destination your first hike in the park.

See map p. 134. Distance (one-way): Just over 4½ miles to Indian Garden, 7¾ miles to Colorado River, 9¼ miles to Bright Angel Campground. Level: Moderate. Access: Trailhead is just west of Kolb Studio, near Grand Canyon Village.

Grandview Trail

This steep hike to Horseshoe Mesa tests your lungs and your knees, but it rewards you with a visit to a turn-of-the-20th-century mine site, not to mention great views. You definitely need to pack water on this trek, because you won't find any along the way. Also, take care on the steep, cobblestone ramps on the trail, because they become awfully slippery during rain or snow. Depending on your physical condition and the weather, the round-trip hike can take as little as 4 hours or as many as 11 because the trail drops 2,600 feet on the way to Horseshoe Mesa. After you arrive, take time to examine the remains of Pete Barry's copper mine, but don't enter the actual shafts. By the way, this trail dates to the 1890s, when crews used dynamite to blast ledges into the canyon walls for the path.

If you find on your way down into the canyon that you're not as physically prepared for this hike as you thought, a good turnaround point is the Coconino Saddle rock formation, which is just ¾-mile from the trailhead. Atop the saddle, you find some trees for shade, as well as great views of Hance and Grapevine canyons.

This trail connects with the 95-mile-long Tonto Trail, which many use to piece together numerous loop hikes with other South Rim trails.

Distance: 6 miles round-trip. Level: Difficult. Access: Grandview Point, 12 miles east of Grand Canyon Village on Desert View Drive.

North Kaibab Trail

This trail is a great way to get down into the canyon for a variety of reasons. First, you won't encounter as many hikers as you would on the South Kaibab Trail. Second, the trail winds through thick, cool pine forests at the head of Roaring Springs Canyon. Finally, this trail is much kinder to day hikers than the Bright Angel and South Kaibab trails.

However, don't overlook the fact that this trail is much longer and steeper than its South Rim counterpart. From the trailhead, the trail winds down a series of switchbacks into Roaring Springs Canyon. The first major landmark to watch for is **Supai Tunnel,** which is just 2¾ miles from the trailhead. This is a great stopping place for day hikers. You find a seasonal water source, shade, and restrooms. From here, the trail drops in relatively gradual switchbacks through the Supai Group, a 300-million-year-old rock layer about 1,000 feet thick and then crosses a bridge over a creek bed. Past the bridge, the creek plummets. The trail then follows the south wall of Roaring Springs Canyon on ledges above Redwall Cliffs.

A spire of Redwall Limestone known as "The Needle" marks the point where the trail begins its descent of the Redwall. You begin to hear Roaring Springs, the water source for both rims, just above the confluence of Bright Angel and Roaring Springs Canyons. A short (¼ mile) spur trail runs to the springs.

Distance (one-way): 2¾ miles to Supai Tunnel, 4¾ miles to Roaring Springs, 6¾ miles to Cottonwood Campground, 14½ miles to the Colorado River. Level: Moderate to strenuous. Access: On the North Rim entrance road, 2 miles north of Grand Canyon Lodge.

South Kaibab Trail

Steep and shadeless, this trail pretty much dives down into the Grand Canyon. Starting at Yaki Point, the trail drops 3,514 feet along the 7 miles it takes to reach Bright Angel Campground. Thanks to the trail's path along ridgelines, you enjoy spectacular views into the canyon from start to finish. Roughly 4½ miles from the trailhead lies a junction with the Tonto Trail, which runs 95 miles along the lower canyon, tying into many other trails and so giving you many options for crafting your own loop hikes. Because the South Kaibab Trail lacks shade, many hikers follow it to Bright Angel Campground and then return to the South Rim via the Bright Angel Trail. If you don't have all day for a rim-to-river hike, plan on reaching Cedar Ridge, which is just 1½ miles below the South Kaibab Trailhead. The ridge offers a nice setting for a picnic in the shade of cedar trees with a tremendous view.

See map p. 134. Distance (one-way): 1½ miles to Cedar Ridge, 4½ miles to Tonto Trail Junction, 7 miles to Bright Angel Campground. Level: Moderate to strenuous. Access: On the Yaki Point access road, although shuttles run from Backcountry Information Center to the trailhead.

Rim Trails

If you don't have time to head down into the canyon or if you just don't like steep hikes, a walk along the South Rim is a great way to view the canyon. In the village area, the walking (along paved trails) is easy, and you pass some historic buildings. Along Hermit Road, the pavement turns to dirt just west of Maricopa Point. In both areas, the views into the canyon are wonderful.

How far you go is up to you. You can hike for 15 minutes or all day, because the Rim Trail runs from Hermit Rest to the first overlook on Desert View Drive, a distance of nearly a dozen miles. If you hike along the West Rim Trail, you have the option of catching a shuttle bus back to the village at the Abyss, which is about halfway to Hermits Rest.

The drawback for rim trails: In high season, you won't be hiking alone.

See map p. 134. Distance: Varies. Level: Easy. Access: Any viewpoint in Grand Canyon Village or along Hermit Road.

One-day wonder

Seeing the Grand Canyon in one day requires a South Rim visit. After all, some of the best, and most accessible, overlooks are on the south side of the canyon, and most of the accommodations are there, too. Fortunately, the roads on the South Rim don't run on endlessly toward the horizon. Compared to Yellowstone, Olympic, and Mount Rainier, the South Rim is really very condensed. Unless otherwise noted, for information on the attractions in this itinerary, see "The top attractions," earlier in this chapter.

Start your day by stopping at the park's **main visitor center** in the Canyon View Information Plaza (see "Finding information after you arrive," earlier in this chapter). Here you can gorge yourself on park information, including which hiking trails are open and which aren't. You can also buy just about all the maps and guidebooks you need to navigate the park, and pick up some pretty good tips on how to survive your visit.

From Grand Canyon Village, head east to **Desert View Drive** to climb the circular **Watchtower** for a great view of the eastern end of the canyon. The tower has been designed in the image of ancient towers, such as the ones that still stand at Hovenweep National Monument in southeastern Utah. Climb to the observation deck and let the views wash over you. While enjoying the view, make a mental note to stop at **Lipan Point** on your way back to Grand Canyon Village. This overlook is arguably the most impressive in the park.

After leaving Lipan Point, stop at the **Tusayan Ruin and Museum** for some insight into how ancestral Puebloans lived on the rim.

Next, head west to **Yaki Point** and, if the weather isn't too hot, head down the **South Kaibab Trail.** You can follow the trail all the way to the Colorado River, but that's a lot of hiking for one day, unless you have a cabin reserved at Phantom Ranch. Don't overestimate your hiking ability and think you can make it down to the river and back in one day under a hot sun. That could prove to be a fatal error. How far you go depends on how you want to spend the bulk of your day. If you prefer to spend the day hiking, by all means follow the trail to **Cedar Ridge** (see the "Taking a hike" section). This 3-mile round-trip hike offers a beautiful spot for a picnic with great views into the canyon. Depending on your physical condition, this hike takes about 1 hour going down, and 90 minutes or so coming back up. If the weather is cool and you're feeling strong, you can push on to **Skeleton Point.** This 6-mile roundtrip hike offers your first view of the river.

If the weather's too hot, or if you're simply not up for this sort of hike, just take in the view from the point and return to Grand Canyon Village to head over to Yavapai Point. If the timing works, meet in front of the **Yavapai Observation Station** for a short ranger-led walk along the rim, or catch a primer on the canyon's geologic history at the visitor center on the Canyon View Information Plaza. (The ranger schedule changes seasonally; consult your park newspaper.) Another interesting option is to learn about the condors that are recolonizing the canyon. Talks on these big birds are held in front of the **Lookout Studio** near the Bright Angel Lodge.

Ranger programs

Throughout the park's high season — mid-March through October — the rangers can help you keep busy with their daily agendas of interpretive programs. You can always find hikes, walks, and discussions about the park's geology, as well as programs that delve into Grand Canyon's human history. These offerings often change from year to year, so I won't give you a specific rundown of daily programs, because some may be discontinued. To find out what's available, scan the park's newspaper, *The Guide,* or ask for information at one of the visitor centers.

If you have little ones, don't forget to pick up information on the Junior Ranger Program at one of the visitor centers (see Chapter 7 for details).

Keeping active

Want to get another perspective on the canyon? Try one of the popular mule rides or even a rafting trip along the Colorado River. If you prefer a bird's eye view, consider flying over the canyon in a plane or helicopter.

Mule rides

Mule rides into the canyon leave from both the South and the North rims. Those from the North Rim are only day rides — with one option as short as an hour — and those from the South Rim are longer and include day trips and overnight trips with stays at Phantom Ranch.

Spotting the local wildlife

Although you may consider the Grand Canyon a pretty inhospitable place — and you'll likely think so if you stay at the Phantom Ranch in mid-July when the temperature soars above 100 degrees — quite a few animals live here.

Visitors most frequently spot **mule deer.** These fellas can adapt to just about any habitat. To get your mule deer fix, look for them browsing on the bushes and grass around Grand Canyon Village. Harder to spy are the **desert bighorn sheep** that reside inside the canyon, usually on remote slopes. However, from time to time, you may come across one on a trail.

Of course, where prey exists, predators exist, and the Grand Canyon is no exception. Lurking about are **coyotes, bobcats,** and even a few **mountain lions.**

Along the South Rim, a cute, furry mammal called the **Abert squirrel** feasts on seeds. A North Rim cousin is the **Kaibab squirrel,** a funny-looking rodent with tasseled ears that stand up like mule ears. Other small creatures include **ringtails,** which are relatives of the raccoon. Found down along the river, ringtails typically don't show themselves during the day. At night, they head out in search of food, and they have been known to raid campsites.

If you get down into the canyon, either by raft or trail, you're likely to come across lizards and possibly snakes, including the **Grand Canyon pink rattlesnake.** The **chuckwalla** is a lizard that loves to bake under the sun. However, if the chuckwalla feels threatened, it crams its body into a crack in the rock and puffs up its abdomen so it can't be pulled out. A really neat creature is the **collared lizard,** which has a black band around its neck. The canyon also hosts **scorpions,** but you probably won't see one unless you go looking for it.

The canyon cliffs naturally make wonderful nesting areas for birds, and more than 300 species have been spotted in the park. The most visible hawk is the **red-tail hawk,** which you often see turning lazy circles on the air currents. **Golden eagles** also nest in the canyon. You may not see a **canyon wren,** but you'll surely hear its sweet song if you hike down into the canyon.

If you keep your eyes to the sky and are lucky, you may see a **condor.** Beginning in 1996, biologists made several releases of these big birds in an area about 30 miles north of the park. These guys seem to be doing well in the wild, and from time to time, they make a swing down to the park to see whether they can scrounge up a meal. Just remember, though, that they are an endangered species, and park rules prohibit you from getting within 300 feet of a condor that has landed.

The rides can be grueling. Most people's legs aren't used to bending around the wide belly of a mule, and the saddles aren't soft. Along with the pounding, the canyon can be scorching, and breaks are few. Because the rides are strenuous for both riders and mules, the wranglers strictly adhere to the following requirements: You must weigh less than 200 pounds, be at least 4 feet 7 inches tall, speak and understand basic

English, and not be visibly pregnant. If the wranglers think that you weigh too much, they won't hesitate to pull out a scale.

South Rim mule rides begin at 6:45 a.m. (7:15 a.m. in winter) every morning at a corral west of Bright Angel Lodge. You can almost hear the jangling nerves of the riders as they contemplate the prospect of descending narrow trails above steep cliffs on animals hardly famous for their intelligence. Although the mules walk close to the edges and have been rumored to back off the trails, accidents are rare, especially among riders who follow the wrangler's instructions.

You have two options for mule rides from the South Rim:

✔ **A day trip to Plateau Point:** This trip is the more difficult of the two mule rides. It travels down the Bright Angel Trail to Indian Garden and then follows the Plateau Point Trail across the Tonto Platform to an overlook of the Colorado River. Having descended more than 3,000 vertical feet, the riders return on the same trails. This 12-mile round-trip ride, which breaks for lunch at Indian Garden, returns to the rim in the middle or late afternoon. The cost of this trip is $132.88, which includes lunch.

✔ **An overnight trip with lodging at Phantom Ranch:** Going down, riders follow the Bright Angel Trail to the river and then head east on the River Trail before finally crossing the river via the Kaibab Suspension Bridge. Coming back, they use the South Kaibab Trail. The 9½-mile descent takes 5½ hours; the 8-mile climb out is an hour shorter. One- and two-night packages are available at Phantom Ranch (see "Where to Stay," later in this chapter). The one-night package costs $360.54 for one person, $641.57 for two people, and $292.80 for each additional person. The two-night trip, offered only during the winter months, costs $507.05 for one person, $854.92 for two people, and $371.50 for each additional person. Meals are included for all overnight trips.

Despite their arduous natures, these trips are wildly popular and fill up months in advance. For advance reservations, call ☎ 303-297-2757. For reservations in the next four days (in case of last-minute cancellations), call the **Bright Angel Transportation Desk** at ☎ 928-638-2631, ext. 6015. If you arrive without reservations, you can put your name on a waiting list by going to the desk in person.

A small, family-run outfit, Grand Canyon Trail Rides, offers four types of mule rides on the **North Rim.** Open to ages 6 and up, the **easiest ride** goes 1 mile along the rim on the Ken Patrick Trail before returning. This 1-hour ride costs $30 per person. Two **half-day rides,** for those at least 8 years old and costing $55 per person each, are also available. One of these rides stays on the rim, following the Ken Patrick and Uncle Jim Trails to a canyon viewpoint; the other descends 2 miles into the canyon on the North Kaibab Trail, turning back at Supai Tunnel. The **all-day ride,** which includes lunch, travels 5 miles on the North Kaibab Trail to Roaring

Springs before turning back. Cost for the all-day ride is $105; riders must be at least 12 years old. No one over 200 pounds is allowed on the canyon rides; for the rim rides, the weight limit is 220. All riders must speak English.

The mule rides on the North Rim tend to fill up later than the rides on the South Rim. To sign up, visit the Grand Canyon Trail Rides desk (open daily 7 a.m. to 6 p.m.) at Grand Canyon Lodge, or call ☎ **928-638-9875.** The off-season number is ☎ **435-679-8665.**

White-water and smooth-water rafting

The world-class rapids that lure countless numbers of boaters to the Grand Canyon are constantly changing. Simple rises and falls in the river flow can affect the punch of a rapid, and rockfalls or storm debris can create new rapids or wash away existing ones. Crystal Rapid, for example, rose in 1966 as storms sent slurries of rock and mud into the Colorado River near the mouth of Crystal Creek and altered the river bottom.

If you're intrigued by this white water or are looking for a surefire way to cool off in the middle of summer, sign on for a white-water trip. Commercial raft trips inside the park generally last from 3 to 14 days and must be booked about a year in advance. Costs for these commercial trips run about $300 a day. This fee buys you transportation, guides who know which rapids you can run right down the middle and which ones you must "sneak" around, food, portable toilets, much of your camping gear, and access to parts of the Inner Gorge that are hard, if not impossible, to reach any other way. Some of these places, such as Mooney Falls, are among the most beautiful on Earth.

All the companies operating in the Grand Canyon are experienced and run excellent trips, subject to the whims of the Colorado River and the storms that move through the canyon. Most trips begin at Lees Ferry, Arizona, but the endpoints vary. Some companies allow for partial trips by picking up or dropping off passengers at various points in the canyon (most often Phantom Ranch). The companies also differ on what makes a trip special. For example, some allow for plenty of day hiking; others don't. Because the trips vary greatly, consider the following important factors before planning your trip:

  ✔ **Motorized versus nonmotorized trips:** Motorized trips are fastest, often covering the 277 miles from Lees Ferry to Pierce Ferry (Lake Mead) in 6 days, compared to as many as 19 days for nonmotorized trips. The motorized trips use wide pontoon boats that almost never capsize, making them slightly safer than the nonmotorized trips. Also, moving about on these solid-framed boats is easier than on oar or paddle boats, a plus for people who lack mobility. Because of the speed of the trips, however, you have less time for hiking or resting in camp. If motorized trips are for you, consider using the companies **Aramark-Wilderness Adventures** (☎ **800-992-8022** or 928-645-3296) or **Western River Expeditions** (☎ **800-453-7450** or 801-942-6669).

If you enjoy exploring and want to bask in the canyon's beauty, I strongly recommend nonmotorized trips, even if you end up seeing half the canyon rather than all of it. A motorless raft quietly glides close to the water's pace, giving passengers time to observe subtle, enticing patterns — swirls of water in eddies; the play of shadows and light as the sun moves across rock layers; and the opening, unfolding, and gradual closing of each side canyon. Without motors running, the sounds of the water and canyon wrens provide a dreamlike backdrop to the journey.

✔ **Oar boats versus paddle boats:** These are two types of nonmotorized boats. Oar boats are wooden *dories* (flat-bottomed boats with high sides) or rubber rafts, each of which holds six passengers and a guide who does most or all of the rowing. If a guide is highly skilled, the passengers on an oar-powered trip have an excellent chance of floating the entire river without taking a life-threatening swim in the rapids. (Don't let this scenario scare you away from paddle trips. I tell you where to find skilled guides in the next paragraph.)

If an oar-powered trip appeals to you, try the company known as **Oars** (☎ 800-346-6277 or 209-736-2924), which has some of the most experienced guides on the river. During the busiest months, Oars assures quality service by sending six crew members out with each group of 16 passengers — providing one of the best crew-to-client ratios on the river.

In a paddle boat, six passengers paddle, assisted by a guide who instructs them and helps steer. This experience is ideal for fit people who want to be involved at all times. However, because of the inexperience of the participants, these trips can be more risky than others. And paddling can become burdensome during the long, slow-water stretches, especially when a head wind blows. **Canyon Explorations** (☎ 800-654-0723 or 928-774-4559) and **Outdoors Unlimited** (☎ 800-637-7238 or 928-526-4546) both have excellent reputations for paddle trips. **Oars** also offers paddle trips. However, to ensure that each group of paddlers meshes, the company accepts paddle boat reservations only by the boatload (six).

✔ **The season:** Commerical trips run year-round, but the main season is May through September. In April, cacti bloom in the lower canyon, splashing bright colors across the hillsides, and the river is relatively uncrowded. However, cold weather — even snow — can occasionally make an April trip a test of the spirit. In May, the weather is usually splendid, but the river is at its most crowded. June and July can be oppressively hot. In late July and August, monsoons break the heat and generate waterfalls all along the river, but they also soak rafters. From September 16 to December 15, motorized rigs are banned from the river, so the canyon is quiet. Cold weather keeps most people off the river from January through April.

The following partial list of river companies permitted to float through the canyon provides basic tour information. For more vendors, check the park's Trip Planner (see "Planning Ahead" earlier in this chapter for information on where to obtain this booklet).

- ✔ **Aramark-Wilderness River Adventures** (P.O. Box 717, Page, AZ 86040; ☎ 800-992-8022 or 928-645-3296; www.riveradventures. com) offers both motorized and oar-powered excursions. Trip lengths vary from 4 to 14 days.

- ✔ **Arizona Raft Adventures** (4050-F E. Huntington Dr., Flagstaff AZ 86004; ☎ 800-786-7238 or 928-526-8200; www.azraft.com) offers motorized, oar-powered, and paddle trips. Excursions last from 6 to 14 days.

- ✔ **Canyon Explorations** (P.O. Box 310, Flagstaff, AZ 86003; ☎ 800-654-0723 or 928-774-4559; Fax: 928-774-4655; www.canyon explorations.com) offers oar-powered and paddle trips with lengths varying from 6 to 16 days.

- ✔ **Grand Canyon Expeditions Co.** (P.O. Box O, Kanab, UT 84741; ☎ 800-544-2691 or 435-644-2691; www.gcex.com) offers both motorized and oar-powered trips with trip lengths ranging from 8 to 16 days.

- ✔ **Hatch River Expeditions** (P.O. Box 1200, Vernal, UT 84078; ☎ 800-433-8966 or 435-789-3813; www.hatchriverexpeditions.com) offers motorized trips with lengths varying from 4 to 14 days.

- ✔ **O.A.R.S.** (P.O. Box 67, 2687 S. Hwy. 49, Angels Camp CA 95222; ☎ 800-346-6277 or 209-736- 2924; www.oars.com) became the first outfitter to run oar-powered trips through the Grand Canyon in 1969. Today, they offer trips in oar-powered wooden dories as well as paddle-powered rafts.

- ✔ **Outdoors Unlimited** (6900 Townsend Winona Rd., Flagstaff, AZ 86004; ☎ 800-637-7238 or 928-526-4546; www.outdoorsunlimited. com) offers oar-powered and paddle trips with trip lengths ranging from 5 to 13 days.

- ✔ **Western River Expeditions** (7258 Racquet Club Dr., Salt Lake City, UT 84121; ☎ 800-453-7450 or 801-942-6669; www.westernriver. com) offers motorized and oar-powered trips with trip lengths varying from 3 to 12 days.

One- and two-day trips through the westernmost part of Grand Canyon are available through **Hualapai River Runners** (P.O. Box 538, Peach Springs, AZ 86434; ☎ 928-769-2419; www.grandcanyonresort.com). These motorized trips begin with rapids in the lower Granite Gorge of the Grand Canyon and end on Lake Mead. Rates are $265 per person.

Overflights

For a bird's-eye view of the canyon, consider a plane or helicopter tour. Several companies, leaving from Grand Canyon National Park Airport in Tusayan, offer scenic trips over the giant hole.

This type of touring is controversial. With more then 250,000 people flying out of Tusayan alone every year, the flights, which generate a great deal of noise in parts of the park, have become a politically charged issue. Many people claim that the planes and helicopters create noise pollution in what should be a pristine wilderness area. Whether these tours will be discontinued is anyone's guess.

For the time being, though, you can fly over the canyon by plane with **Air Grand Canyon/Sky Eye Tours** (☎ 800-247-4726 or 928-638-2686; www.airgrandcanyon.com), or **Grand Canyon Airlines** (☎ 800-528-2413 or 928-638-2407; www.grandcanyonairlines.com). Prices range from $75 to $90 ($45 to $49 for children under 12) for a 50- to 60-minute flight, including the airspace fee.

You can also whirl through the air in a helicopter with **Kenai Grand Canyon Helicopters** (☎ 800-541-4537 or 928-638-2764), **AirStar Helicopters** (☎ 800-962-3869 or 928-638-2622; www.airstar.com), and **Papillon Grand Canyon Helicopters** (☎ 800-528-2418 or 928-638-2419; www.papillon.com). Tours run from around $100 for a 25- to 30-minute flight and $165 for a 40- to 45-minute flight to $436 for a seven-hour tour; not all tours offer lower children's rates.

Escaping the rain

What do you do when it rains in the park? Well, in the height of summer, you may enjoy the cool drenching. Any other time of year, you no doubt want to head for shelter.

The **Kolb Studio** (☎ 928-638-2481) in Grand Canyon Village is one good option. The Grand Canyon Association sponsors a rotating series of art exhibits in this historic studio. A fun, but somewhat short, time can be spent watching the latest big-screen production at the **Grand Canyon IMAX Theater** (☎ 928-638-2203) located just south of the park's South Rim entrance on Highway 64. A recent 34-minute show, "Grand Canyon — The Hidden Secrets," touched on the park's Native American history, as well as treks into the park by Spanish explorers and by Major John Wesley Powell. The **Yavapai Observation Station**, a great place to seek shelter during a cloudburst, provides a geological primer on the canyon as well as good views. If you're near the east end of Desert View Drive when the rains come, stop at the **Watchtower** (☎ 928-638-2736), where you find Native American artworks on display. Finally, if you haven't gotten your share of souvenirs, head to the **Hopi House** (☎ 928-638-2631, ext. 6383), in Grand Canyon Village, which vends a wealth of Native American arts and crafts.

Where to Stay

Thanks to the logistical marvel that one concessionaire — **Xanterra Parks & Resorts** — oversees all the lodging in the park, one easy phone call enables you to make a room reservation in the Grand Canyon (☎ **888-297-2757** or 303-297-2757; www.grandcanyonlodges.com). You can also check their Web site for discounted rates. AE, MC, DISC, and V are accepted for rooms.

The following listings for the park hotels don't include individual phone numbers or addresses. A single telephone number (☎ **928-638-2631**) is good for all South Rim properties. The Grand Canyon Lodge, the elegant grand dame on the North Rim, has its own telephone number (☎ **928-638-2611**). Don't worry about not being able to find your hotel. When you enter the park, you receive a map pinpointing the location of each one. For more information on finding a place to stay, see Chapter 6.

Lodging at the South Rim

Bright Angel Lodge & Cabins
$–$$$ Grand Canyon Village

This hotel, a National Historic Landmark, is budget central in the Grand Canyon. You find a bed with a roof overhead for as little as $55 a night. Of course, you can pay more than that if you prefer more amenities. For $55, you get a "hiker" room with only a double bed, a desk, and a sink. Two long buildings adjacent to the Bright Angel Lodge house these dormitory-style rooms, the least expensive in the park.

From that base unit, your options escalate as do the prices. Some rooms have double beds and a toilet, but no shower, while others contain a bed, toilet, and tub but no shower. More comfortable, and charming, accommodations are the cabins that stand along the canyon's rim and feature fireplaces, two bedrooms, and a bathroom. Understandably, the cabins often are booked a year in advance. The cabins, which have one or two queen-sized beds, were renovated in 2000 and have new furniture, draperies, and tile floors.

See map p. 134. 39 rooms (6 with sink only, 13 with sink and toilet, 20 with bath); 50 cabin rooms. TVs in cabins. Rack rates: $55–$67 double, some with shared bath; cabins $84–$105.

El Tovar Hotel
$$$–$$$$$ Grand Canyon Village

It's pricy, but the El Tovar, which marks its 100th birthday in 2005, is the most luxurious accommodation in the park. After a hot day of hiking below the rim, most visitors are delighted to return to one of these rooms. The hotel was built from Oregon pine logs in 1905 and was designed to accommodate tourists riding to the canyon on the Santa Fe Railroad. The El Tovar is an architectural cross between a Norwegian villa and a Swiss chalet and bears a strong resemblance to old European hunting lodges. Located just a stone's throw from the canyon's South Rim, the building casts a long shadow across the Grand Canyon Village at sundown. Inside you find moose and elk heads hanging on varnished walls and copper chandeliers casting light. The cool, dark spaces are a dramatic contrast to the warmer, pueblo buildings you find elsewhere in the park. The upstairs offers a nice, private sitting area (reserved for guests) and rooms with classic American furnishings. Turndown service is available and all rooms are nonsmoking.

See map p. 134. 66 rooms, 12 suites. A/C, TV, TEL. Rack rates: $123–$285.

Maswik Lodge
$$–$$$ Grand Canyon Village

Set in a ponderosa pine forest, this lodge offers a cooler perspective than most other Grand Canyon properties. Most of the guest rooms are in the two-story wood-and-stone buildings known as Maswik North and South. The rooms in Maswik North have nice furnishings, queen-size beds, and new carpet; many also have balconies overlooking the pine forest. The rooms in Maswik South are five years older, a bit smaller, and have less pristine views, but they also cost about $40 less per night.

Next to Maswik North are several cabins. Each cabin has two double beds and a shower. Because of their proximity to the road and to festive off-duty employees, these cabins can be noisy. If you stay in one of these, bring a flashlight because the grounds are dark at night.

See map p. 134. 250 rooms, 28 cabins. TV, TEL. Rack rates: $66 cabin; $77 double in Maswik South; $119 double in Maswik North.

Thunderbird and Kachina Lodges
$$$ Grand Canyon Village

These lodges are the newest in the park, but given that they resemble 1960s-era college dormitories, they're not the most attractive. They have flat roofs, decorative concrete panels, and metal staircases on the exterior; inside are concrete steps, tiled floors, and brick walls. Rooms, which were fully renovated during the winter of 2003-2004 with new furniture, carpeting, paint, and bathroom amenities, are pleasant enough. They have Southwestern-style furnishings and windows as wide as the rooms themselves. Although Xanterra (the concessionaire that runs all lodging in the park) refuses to guarantee a canyon view, in both lodges most of the upstairs rooms on the more expensive "canyon side" have at least a partial view of the canyon. Check-in for the Thunderbird is at the Bright Angel Lodge; for the Kachina, it's at the El Tovar.

See map p. 134. 55 rooms at Thunderbird, 49 rooms at Kachina. A/C, TV, TEL. Rack rates: $123 double (park side), $133 double (canyon side).

Yavapai Lodge
$$–$$$ Grand Canyon Village

This lodge is the largest in the canyon. Although it's a mile away from the Grand Canyon Village's historic district, the location is conveniently close to a bank, Canyon Village Marketplace, and the park's visitor center. The A-frame lodge was built in the early 1970s and has a large cafeteria and gift shop. Its rooms are housed in ten single-story buildings known as Yavapai West and six two-story wood buildings known as Yavapai East. Most rooms in Yavapai West have cinder block walls, and all are compact. Yavapai East's rooms are larger and many have good forest views, which make them worth the extra $15 per night. Because the parking lots were built to accommodate tour buses, they are larger than at other lodges. The gravel paths connecting the buildings are dark at night, so don't forget your flashlight.

See map p. 134. 358 rooms. TV, TEL. Rack rates: $91 double (Yavapai West), $105 double (Yavapai East).

Lodging inside the canyon

Phantom Ranch
$–$$ Grand Canyon floor

Staying at the Phantom Ranch takes some effort because no road leads to the front door. You have to hike, ride a mule, or float down the Colorado River to get here. Despite the remote location and so-so rooms, the ranch's rooms often sell out far in advance. To reserve a spot, call as early as possible, as much as 20 to 23 months in advance. If you arrive at the park without a reservation, call the Bright Angel Transportation Desk (☎ **928-638-2631, ext. 6015**) for information about openings in the next four days due to cancellations.

The ranch's nine cabins, which are reserved almost entirely for mule trip riders during the summer months, are a treat. Architect Mary Colter, who also designed Watchtower, designed four of them (the ones with the most stone in the walls) using rocks from the nearby Bright Angel Creek. Connected by dirt footpaths, they stand, natural and elegant, alongside picnic tables and under the shade of cottonwood trees. Inside each cabin, you find a desk, a concrete floor, and four to ten bunk beds, as well as a toilet and sink. A shower house for guests is nearby.

Most of the Phantom Ranch was completed in the 1920s and 1930s; however, four ten-person dorms, each with its own bathing facilities, were added in the early 1980s. Used mostly by hikers, these dorms are ideal for individuals and small groups looking for a place to bed down; larger groups are better served by reserving cabins, which provide both privacy and a lower per-person cost.

For information on mule rides to Phantom Ranch, see the "Keeping active" section, earlier in this chapter.

See map p. 133. ½ mile north of the Colorado River on the North Kaibab Trail. 7 four-person cabins, 2 cabins for up to ten people each, 4 dorms for up to ten people each. Rates: $27 dorm bed; $74 cabin (for 2 people, $10.50 each additional person).

Lodging at the North Rim

Grand Canyon Lodge
$$–$$$ North Rim

Architecture and landscape come together at this lodge, whose Kaibab limestone walls and log beams (similar to the trunks of the nearby pines) blend into the surroundings beautifully. Just past the lobby and into the Sun Room, you see the canyon's grandeur through towering picture windows.

Outside, row after row of cabins surround the lodge. All the cabins have bathrooms, but they're definitely not all alike. The Western Cabins and Rim Cabins are the most luxurious, complete with wicker furniture, bathtubs, and small vanity rooms. The Rim Cabins, which cost $10 more per night than the Western Cabins, perch on the lip of Bright Angel Canyon and are usually booked as much as two years in advance.

Your more rustic choices are the Pioneer and Frontier Cabins on the rim of Transept Canyon. They have walls and ceilings of exposed logs, upright gas heaters, and showers instead of tubs. The Frontier Cabins have one guest room with a double bed and twin bed; the Pioneer Cabins have two guest rooms, one with a double and a twin and the other with two twins. If you stay in a Frontier or Pioneer Cabin, be sure to ask when you check in for one that overlooks Transept Canyon.

The few motel rooms here are nothing to write home about.

See map p. 133. 205 cabin and motel rooms. TEL. Rack rates: $121 double Rim Cabin; $111 Western Cabin; $102 Pioneer Cabin; $92 Frontier Cabin; $91 motel room.

Runner-up lodgings

The following properties cluster together on Highway 64 in Tusayan, Arizona (only 1 mile from the south entrance to the park). They don't have specific addresses.

Best Western Grand Canyon Squire Inn

$–$$$ Tusayan   You won't be lodging in the park, but at least you have two restaurants, a bowling alley, video arcade, billiards inside, and a pool and tennis court outside. *Highway 64, Tusayan.* ☎ *800-622-6966 or 928-638-2681.* www.grandcanyonsquire.com. *$65-$185*

Grand Hotel

$$$–$$$$ Tusayan   This knock-off of a national park lodge takes you to the Old West with its heavy timbers, antler chandeliers, and Native American craftworks. Southwestern cuisine in the restaurant and Western entertainment in the lounge complement the setting. *Highway 64, Tusayan.* ☎ *888-63-GRAND or 928-638-3333.* www.visitgrandcanyon.com. $119-$209

Holiday Inn Express Hotel and Suites

$$–$$$$ **Tusayan** This place offers rooms in two flavors: Generic double or family-friendly suite (with microwaves, fridges, and VCRs). *Highway 64, Tusayan.* ☎ *888-473-2269 or 928-638-3000.* www.gcanyon.com/holiday.htm.

Campgrounds

The park has four developed campgrounds. Each offers its own unique style, from sites surrounded by pinyon and juniper trees or old-growth ponderosa pines to an RV park that you should avoid if all you're hauling is a tent. For my advice on making reservations in the campgrounds, see the "Planning Ahead" section earlier in this chapter.

Camping at the South Rim

Desert View Campground
South Rim

If you agree that there's nothing quite like falling asleep to the sound of yipping coyotes, this is the place for you. Far enough from Grand Canyon Village to be shielded from its noise and lights, this campground is cool and breezy and just a short walk from the Desert View Overlook. The tent sites are set amid pinyon and juniper groves, adding a wonderful dash of fragrance to your dreams. The big problem with this location is that the nearest shower is 26 miles away, in the village. During the high season, this first-come, first-served tent city often fills up by noon.

25 miles east of Grand Canyon Village on Highway 64. No phone, no advance reservations. 50 sites. Rates: $10 per site. Open: Mid-May to mid-Oct.

Mather Campground
South Rim

Given its size and proximity to Grand Canyon Village, you may think this campground would be a loud, crowded tent town, but it's really not that bad thanks to good spacing of the sites and the surrounding pinyon and juniper trees. Of course, for every rule there's an exception, and in this case, you definitely want to avoid sites 150 through 171 on the Juniper Loop because they're way too close to the park's entrance road. Also, although you probably want to be near the showers, which are in the Camper Services Building, you don't want to be so close that you find yourself counting the hundreds of happy campers tramping by.

This campground fills up quickly during high season. You can make a reservation up to 5 months in advance. If you arrive without a reservation, check at the campground entrance for any unclaimed sites.

See map p. 134. Near Grand Canyon Village on the South Rim. ☎ *800-365-2267 advance reservations, 301-722-1257 from outside the U.S. 319 sites, 4 group sites. No hookups. Rates: $15 mid-March to Nov, $10 Dec through March. Open: Year-round.*

Trailer Village
South Rim

If you don't have your own RV to shut out the rest of the campground, you don't want to be at this campground; the sites are very close to each other, and the vegetation is vanishing. If you stay here, take time to scout the campground before settling on a site. At the end of the numbered drives, you find some sites with grass, shade trees, and one neighbor-free side. The showers are roughly ½-mile away from the sites.

See map p. ###. East of Grand Canyon Village, adjacent to the Mather Campground. ☎ *303-297-2757 for advance reservations or 928-638-2631, ext. 6035 for same day reservations and questions. Fax: 928-638-9247. 84 full hookups. Rates: $25 for two people per site, $2 each additional person over 16. Open: Year-round.*

Camping at the North Rim

North Rim Campground
North Rim

The North Rim and the Desert View campgrounds are the two most picturesque in the park. Here at the North Rim, towering old-growth ponderosa pine trees shade the sites set along Transept Canyon. From here you can walk 1½ miles down the Transept Trail to reach Grand Canyon Lodge, and the North Rim General Store is close to the campground. The best sites are those on the rim; they're an extra $5, but the canyon view is worth the cost. Showers are nearby, too. This place fills quickly and stays full. To obtain a site, make a reservation up to five months before your arrival.

44 miles south of Jacob Lake on Highway 67. ☎ *800-365-2267 advance reservations or 928-638-2151. 83 sites, 4 group sites. No hookups. Rates: $15–$20 per site; $4 for tent only (no vehicle). Open: Mid-May –mid-Oct.*

Where to Eat

Grand Canyon offers several restaurant options. You can find meals for the most austere budget, as well as fare suitable for an elegant evening out. In addition to the places listed below, the Maswik and Yavapai lodges have atmospherically challenged cafeterias in the $ to $$ range that serve three meals at day.

Restaurants at the South Rim

The Arizona Room
$$$–$$$$ Grand Canyon Village   AMERICAN

If you dine here, the great canyon views you get through the long windows mean you don't have to miss dinner to watch the sunset. If you want to snag the seats with the best views, you'll have to jockey to be first in line when this restaurant opens at 4:30 p.m. If you decide to watch the sunset and then head here, you may find yourself at the end of an hour-long waiting list. Although the service could be quicker, at least you're not rushed through your meal. You have plenty of time to choose from the wine list or order an appetizer — the fried jalapeno and chipolte chicken poppers are a good, and spicy, choice. Entrees include hand-cut steaks and prime rib, chicken, trout, and a daily vegetarian special.

See map p. 134. At Bright Angel Lodge. ☎ *928-638-2631. Reservations not accepted. Main courses: $13–$23. AE, DC, DISC, MC, V. Open: Daily 4:30–10 p.m.*

Bright Angel Restaurant
$$–$$$ Grand Canyon Village   AMERICAN

If you're looking for a decent family restaurant in the park, this is a good option. The burgers and patty melts are tasty, and so are some of the Southwestern dishes. If you're hauling kids around, you won't have to worry much about their behavior: The games on the kid's menu should distract the small fries until the French fries arrive. Still, the food at the Maswik and Yavapai cafeterias is just as good, and it's cheaper.

See map p. 134. Located in Bright Angel Lodge. ☎ *928-638-2631. Reservations not accepted. Main courses: $2.20–$7.40 breakfast; $5–$9 lunch; $8–$15.20 dinner. AE, DC, DISC, MC, V. Open: Daily 6:30–10:45 a.m. and 11:15 a.m.–10 p.m.*

Canyon Village Marketplace
$ Grand Canyon Village   AMERICAN/MEXICAN

Many Park Service employees dash into this cafeteria for lunch. You can sit in a corner booth, read the paper, and watch the parade of tourists. Order a pizza or a fried chicken basket, or go lighter and healthier with one of the made-to-order salads or sandwiches.

See map p. 134. In Canyon Village Marketplace. ☎ *928-638-2262. Main courses: $4–$6. AE, DC, DISC, MC, V. Open: Memorial Day–Labor Day daily 7:30 a.m.–8:30 p.m., shorter winter hours.*

Desert View Trading Post
$ Desert View   FAST FOOD

This fast-food joint is pretty much what you'd expect. There are no frills, but you can get a sandwich, hot dog, or burger to tide you over until you get back to the village. Breakfast offerings include eggs and French toast.

At Desert View, 25 miles east of Grand Canyon Village on Highway 64. ☎ *928-638-2360. Main courses: $2–$5 breakfast and lunch. No credit cards. Open: Summer 8 a.m.–6 p.m.; rest of the year 9 a.m.–5 p.m.*

El Tovar Restaurant
$$$–$$$$$ Grand Canyon Village   CONTINENTAL

This restaurant has a nearly century-old tradition of fine food and good value that isn't going to change any time soon. The dining room's walls of

Oregon pine are graced with murals depicting the ritual dances of four Indian tribes. Atop the restaurant's fine linen tablecloths, fresh flowers catch light from the windows.

At dinner, a Southwestern influence spices the Continental cuisine. Appetizers include mozzarella roulades of prosciutto and basil pesto and Clesan-Du-Klish, which is Native American Blue Corn Tamales with roasted red pepper coulis and charbroiled corn salsa. For the main course, meat-eaters will enjoy the flame-broiled peppercorn crusted filet mignon with roasted garlic sauce and gorgonzola mashed potatoes. Intriguing seafood and vegetarian dishes, such as broiled portabello Napoleon with a vanilla thyme risotto are also available.

The El Tovar accepts reservations for dinner only, but is also open for breakfast and lunch. If you're on a budget, consider dining here during non-dinner hours, when you can get the same high-quality food for just a few dollars more than you'd spend at the other canyon eateries.

See map p. 134. In the El Tovar Lodge. ☎ 928-638-2631, ext. 6432. Reservations recommended for dinner. Main courses: $4.50–$12.25 breakfast; $8.75–$15 lunch; $17–$25 dinner. AE, DC, DISC, MC, V. Open: Daily 6:30–11 a.m., 11:30 a.m.–2 p.m., and 5–10 p.m.

A restaurant inside the canyon

Phantom Ranch
$$$–$$$$ Inside the canyon   AMERICAN

Even if you don't snag a room at the Phantom Ranch, you can still eat here. And by the time you arrive from your trek down into the canyon, just about anything will taste good. Every evening, the ranch offers two options: a steak dinner at 5 p.m. and a hearty beef stew at 6:30 p.m. The vegetarian plate at the first seating consists of side dishes like vegetables, cornbread, and salad. With any dinner, the dessert is chocolate cake.

Breakfasts April through October are served at 5 a.m. and 6:30 a.m. These family style, all-you-can-eat affairs feature excellent, heaping platters of eggs, bacon, and pancakes that make their way up and down the long blue tables. The only disappointment is the sack lunch, whose simple contents (bagel, summer sausage, juice, apple, peanuts, raisins, and cookies) don't seem worth the price. You may as well stash similar munchies in your pack before heading into the canyon.

Because the ranch can accommodate only a fixed number of diners for each meal, hikers and mule riders must reserve meals ahead of time through Xanterra or at the Bright Angel Transportation Desk. As a last resort, inquire upon arrival at Phantom Ranch to see whether any meals remain. Up until 4 p.m., you can do so in the canteen itself. After 4 p.m., ask at a side window behind the canteen. Between 8 a.m. and 4 p.m. and from 8 p.m. to 10 p.m., anyone is allowed in the canteen, which has snacks, soda, beer, and wine.

See map p. 133. Inside the canyon, ½-mile north of the Colorado River on the North Kaibab Trail. To order meals more than four days in advance, call ☎ 303-297-2757;

to order meals in the next four days, contact the Bright Angel Transportation Desk at 928-638-2631, ext. 6015. Main courses: $15 breakfast; $9 box lunch; $18 stew dinner; $26.60 steak dinner. AE, DC, DISC, MC, V. Open: Breakfast: Two seatings, 5 a.m. and 6:30 a.m. April to Oct. Dinner: Two seatings, 5 p.m. and 6:30 p.m. Canteen: 8 a.m.– 4 p.m. and 8 –10 p.m.

Restaurants at the North Rim

Deli in the Pines
$–$$ North Rim   AMERICAN

This snack bar serves the best pizza on the North Rim — actually, the only pizza on the North Rim. It also churns out calzones, salads, sandwiches, hot dogs, and breakfast. If all you want is a cup of coffee and a muffin, stop by the saloon, where an espresso bar operates daily from 5 a.m. to 9:30 a.m.

See map p. 133. In the east wing of Grand Canyon Lodge. ☎ 928-638-2611. Main courses: $1.75–$4.95 breakfast; $2.95–$7.95 lunch; $5.95–$9.95 dinner; $12–$18 whole pizza. AE, MC, Visa. Open: Mid-May to mid-Oct 7 a.m.–9 p.m.

Grand Canyon Lodge Dining Room
$$–$$$$ North Rim   CONTINENTAL

Long banks of west- and south-facing windows provide views of Transept Canyon and help warm this room, and the high ceiling absorbs the clamor of diners. Although expecting gourmet dining in a place as remote as the North Rim is unreasonable, the food is nearly as satisfying as the surroundings. A long-time favorite is the Pasta Lydia — fresh asparagus and potatoes tossed in pesto sauce with bowtie pasta. Heartier eaters will like the Apple Cider Pork Medallions. You also find interesting preparations of steaks, prime rib, fish, poultry, and excellent desserts. Lunch offerings include a variety of salads, sandwiches, and burgers.

See map p. 133. At Grand Canyon Lodge. ☎ 928-638-2611, ext. 160. Reservations required for dinner, not accepted for breakfast or lunch. Main courses: $2.85–$8.50 breakfast; $5.20–$11 lunch; $13–$21 dinner. AE, DC, DISC, MC, V. Open: Mid-May to mid-Oct daily 6:30–10 a.m., 11:30 a.m.–2:30 p.m., and 4:45–9:30 p.m.

Fast Facts: Grand Canyon

Area Code
The area code is **928**.

ATMs
You can find an ATM on the South Rim at Market Plaza at the bank; in Tusayan at the Imax Theater. The closest ATM to the North Rim is at Jacob Lake, 44 miles north on Arizona 67.

Hospitals/Clinics
The area sports a clinic known as the Grand Canyon Walk-In Clinic on the South Rim. Look for it at 1 Clinic Rd, southeast of Grand Canyon Village (☎ 928-638-2551).

Emergencies
For emergencies, dial **911** or **9-911** from hotel rooms.

Information

For information, write Grand Canyon National Park, P.O. Box 129, Grand Canyon, AZ, 86023, or call ☎ 928-638-7888.

Internet Access & Cybercafes

You will find Internet access at the Grand Canyon Tourist Center, Hwy 180 and 64, Tusyana (☎ 928-638-2626).

Pharmacies

There are no pharmacies in the area but the clinic (see Hospitals/clinics above) has some medicines.

Post Office

The local post office can be found at the Grand Canyon Village at the Market Plaza (☎ 928-638-2512).

Taxis

For a taxi call ☎ 928-638-2822 or 928-638-2631, ext 6563.

Time Zone

The park is on mountain standard time; Arizona doesn't observe daylight savings time.

Transit Info

Shuttle schedules for the South Rim are located in the park's newspaper, *The Guide*.

Weather Updates

For weather updates, call 928-638-9552 or look on the Internet at www.nps.gov/grca.

Chapter 12

Grand Teton National Park

● ●

In This Chapter

▶ Admiring the Grand

▶ Planning your assault on the park

▶ Exploring the mountains and lakes

▶ Finding the best sleeps and eats

● ●

*A*lthough the United States has taller mountains and ranges that are longer and older, I have yet to find anything more rugged and picturesque than Wyoming's Teton Range.

True, the craggy, battleship gray Grand Teton (known simply as the Grand) tops out at *only* 13,770 feet, whereas quite a few other Rocky Mountain peaks surpass 14,000 feet. But to understand the magnificence of this park, you must consider the setting. The Grand ratchets almost 7,000 vertical feet straight up from the Jackson Hole valley floor. Without any foothills to temper the rise, its 13,770 feet are in-your-face impressive. Plus, the peaks and surrounding terrain have been clawed, carved, and sculpted by several periods of glaciation that also left behind some sparkling lakes. This all adds up to a beautiful, remarkable setting that demands attention, encourages recreation, and pays off with great satisfaction.

The Grand offers several world-class climbs. Some climbers tackle the mountain on their own, but others rely on the guidance of Jackson's two resident climbing outfitters: Exum Mountain Guides and Jackson Hole Mountain Guides. (See "Keeping active," later in this chapter, for information on these companies.) But a trip to Grand Teton isn't wasted if you can't climb the Grand. Just looking at these peaks justifies a trip to western Wyoming.

Grand Teton National Park is more than just mountains. You find lakes of all sizes, from the sisterly trio of Jenny, Leigh, and String that graces the front of the Tetons to Jackson Lake — a natural glacial lake, enlarged in 1906 by a dam, where you can rent a motorboat for an afternoon of fishing or a canoe for a leisurely paddle.

The three *what?*

Early 19th-century French-Canadian fur trappers provided the name for Grand Teton National Park. After stumbling too long in the wilderness before arriving in Jackson Hole, they thought the three central peaks bore some semblance to a woman's anatomy and thus named them *le trois tetons* — the three breasts.

East of Jenny, Leigh, and String lakes are rolling sagebrush flats (favorites with pronghorn antelope) that surround U.S. Route 26/89/191 as the highway travels, north to south, the length of the park. Paralleling the road to the west is the trout-filled Snake River, which braids its way from Jackson Lake Dam 27 miles through the park before adding some punch for whitewater enthusiasts in the stretch that runs south of Jackson.

You find swathes of thick evergreen forest in Grand Teton, steep canyons gnawed into the landscape by cascading streams that run flush with melting snow in spring, and lush meadows colored by wildflowers in late June. In 1998, the arrival of wolves from Yellowstone to the north added a dash more wildness to the park, fleshing out a menagerie that already included bison, elk, moose, coyotes, mountain lions, and grizzly bears.

The Old West is kept alive by ranchers who graze cattle inside the park, by the nearby town of Jackson lined with wooden boardwalks, and by the coyote yips and wolf howls in the cool evening air.

With its combination of stunning landscapes and comfortable accommodations, Grand Teton a rugged and a relaxing park, one where you can test your outdoors skills or rest with a book in the afternoon shadow of America's Matterhorn.

Must-See Attractions

With Grand Teton and its sister peaks visible from just about everywhere in the park, you really don't have to work hard to appreciate the gorgeous landscape. Trust me, though; in addition to the mountains you'll definitely want to see some other attractions during your visit. I won't reveal them all, because part of the enjoyment of visiting a national park is discovery and exploring. But here's a good list to get you started:

✔ **Cunningham Cabin Historic Site:** This rustic cabin built by Pierce Cunningham in 1890 is the oldest pioneer cabin still standing in the park. Pierce knew a good view when he saw one. Stopping here really gives you an idea of what roughing it meant to early settlers.

✔ **Grand Teton:** You can't miss this peak: just look for the highest knob on the western skyline. You can climb the mountain if you're in decent shape.

✔ **Jenny Lake:** One of the park's idyllic lakes, this shimmering jewel is perfect for an afternoon paddle or hike. The park's premier lodge, also named Jenny Lake, is nestled in a grove of conifers not far from the shore.

✔ **Oxbow Bend:** This series of bends in the Snake River is a great place to view the Tetons as well as wildlife; swans, geese, and pelicans drift on the waters in the mornings and afternoons. Look for bald eagles and osprey that roost in the trees along the river and moose that browse the marshy meadows.

✔ **Snake River:** Whether you raft it, fish it, or just walk beside it, this river is an American classic.

Planning Ahead

To receive **park maps and information** before your arrival, write to Superintendent, Grand Teton National Park, P.O. Drawer 170, Moose, WY 83012-0170; or call ☎ **307-739-3300** or 307-739-3400 (TTY). You can also check the park Web site at www.nps.gov/grte. For a trip-planning packet, call ☎ **307-739-3600**.

When to go and how long to stay

Grand Teton is a year-round playground, although some seasons are definitely better than others. Summer weather is wonderful, with daily highs roaming between the mid-70s and the high 80s, little humidity, and an occasional thunderstorm followed by cool, clear nights; however, most of the park's 4.1 million yearly visitors show up during this season. The crowds taper off during fall, which is my favorite season in the park. During autumn, aspens flutter in their golden glory, the evenings' crispness is intoxicating, and animals are more visible as they prepare for winter. Although winter can be brutally cold and snowy, the season provides great opportunities for cross-country skiing and snowshoeing. Because of late-season snowfalls and mud, spring is about the worst time for a visit.

Plan to spend at least two to three days in Grand Teton National Park.

Advance reservations

If you want to try climbing the Grand, you need to make a reservation with one of the park's two climbing companies several months in advance. These companies are **Exum Mountain Guides, Inc. (☎ 307-733-2297;** Internet: www.exumguides.com; P.O. Box 56, Moose, WY 83012) and **Jackson Hole Mountain Guides (☎ 800-239-7642,** 307-733-4979; Internet: www.jhmg.com; P.O. Box 7477, Jackson, WY 83002). See "Keeping active," later in this chapter, for more information on climbing.

Even if you don't want to climb, make plans for your summer trip as early as February or March. Starting at this time virtually assures you a room in the park hotel of your choice, including the most popular lodges, Jackson Lake Lodge or Jenny Lake Lodge. Although nearby Jackson has more than 4,200 motel rooms, they fill quickly in summer — and fall, too, if bad weather forces hundreds of elk hunters out of the mountains and into warm, dry rooms. See "Where to stay," later in this chapter for more information on accommodations.

What to pack

Summers in the Rockies generally offer the best weather you can find. As a result, pack a wardrobe that stresses shorts and T-shirts for the daylight hours and jeans with a light jacket or sweater for evenings. A rain jacket is a good thing to have, as well. Winters are another matter. Temperatures can be bitterly cold and snows deep, so be sure to have plenty of warm inner layers that can be topped by waterproof or water-resistant outer layers. Don't forget good boots, your gloves, and a warm hat, too.

If you plan to climb, even in the summer you may discover midwinter snow conditions on the Grand. Although the park's outfitters provide some climbing gear, you may need waterproof shell gloves, water-resistant pants, a shell jacket, and other warmer layers. For more tips on what to pack, see Chapter 8.

Getting There

Getting there is half the fun, right? Located on Wyoming's western border, the park isn't really a short drive from anywhere. Salt Lake City and Billings, Montana, are each about five hours away, and Cheyenne — Wyoming's capital — is a good seven-hour drive. Fortunately, you don't have to drive, because the park has its own airport. But if you do end up taking the trip via automobile, know that you'll pass incredibly beautiful countryside along the way.

Flying in

You could argue that this park is the most accessible in the country thanks to the **Jackson Hole Airport** (☎ **307-733-7682**) that lies within the park's boundaries. **American, Skywest (Delta Connection),** and **United Express** all have flights to and from Jackson Hole Airport. The park doesn't have a public transportation system, so you need a car to get around after you arrive. Most of the major car-rental companies have outlets here. For toll-free numbers, see the Appendix.

Driving in

If you don't fly, getting to Grand Teton takes a bit longer, but the scenic drive is worth the trip. Arriving from the east, U.S. Route 26/287 leads you up and over Togwotee Pass and to the Moran Entrance Station if you're heading to Jackson Lake Lodge. If you're looking for the Moose Entrance Station, drive 18 miles south of Moran Junction to Moose Junction.

If you drive south from Yellowstone to enter the park, you pass through the John D. Rockefeller Jr. Memorial Parkway — a 37-square-mile swath of land between the two parks set aside in 1972 to honor Rockefeller for his formidable land contributions to the national park system. Although no official entrance station to Grand Teton exists along the park's northern border, Flagg Ranch has an information station.

You can also reach the park from the south through Jackson on the main highway, U.S. Route 26/89/191, which leads to Moose, Wyoming, and points north. If you go this way, there's a good chance you'll enter the park before you even realize it, because the highway runs north and south through the park with the entrance stations located off this main road.

No public bus service connects Jackson and the park, and even though Amtrak actually superimposed one of its trains in front of the Tetons for a brochure in the 1980s, no train service exists.

Orienting Yourself in Grand Teton National Park

Unless you visit in the dead of winter, one fact you need to accept on a trip to Grand Teton is that you're not going to be alone. Millions of people flock to this park each year, and just about every one of them is interested in seeing the same handful of attractions that you want to see.

The lack of roads makes avoiding the crowds difficult. **U.S. Route 26/89/191** is the main north-south artery through the park; the more narrow and meandering **Teton Park Road** runs parallel to this highway, sandwiched between it and the Tetons. The U.S. highway remains open year-round, but the Teton Park Road closes to vehicles November 1 and doesn't reopen until May 1.

U.S. Route 26/89/191 is the best route through the park if you're in a rush, whereas Teton Park Road offers a much slower pace with more interesting views and pullouts, plus many trailheads. From its northern end at Jackson Lake Junction to its southern terminus at Moose, the Teton Park Road moseys along, much like the Snake River. The road leads you past the southeastern arm of Jackson Lake, the Signal Mountain Lodge complex, String and Jenny lakes, and Jenny Lake Lodge. Just north of the Moose Visitor Center, the road passes the Menor's Ferry Historic Site, famous for the ferry service used to cross the Snake River.

North of Jackson Lake Junction, **U.S. Route 89/191/287** runs toward Yellowstone, passing Jackson Lake Lodge and Colter Bay Village before entering the John D. Rockefeller Jr. Memorial Parkway.

Grand Teton National Park

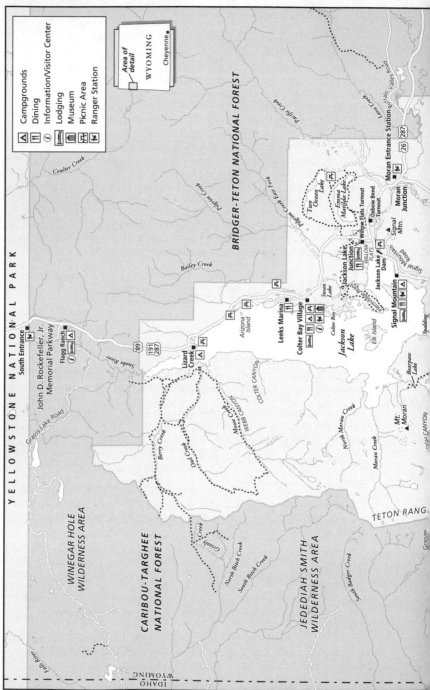

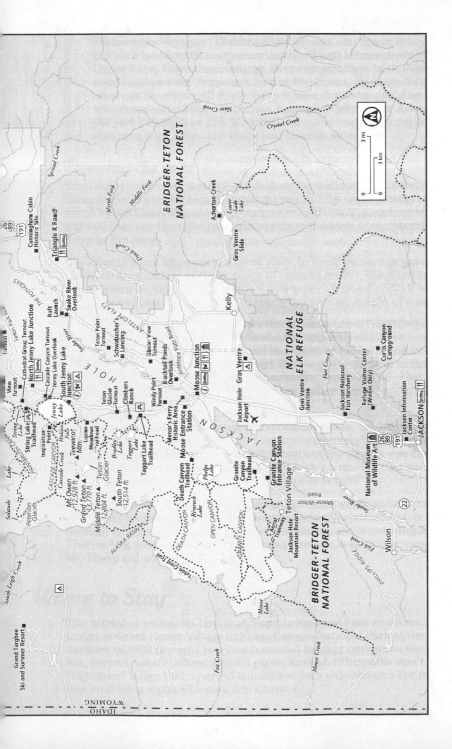

One of the park's scenic back roads is the **Moose-Wilson Road,** which is sort of a shortcut to Moose if you're coming into the park from Idaho or if you want to go from Moose to a restaurant at Teton Village without making the roundabout trek through Jackson. I say "sort of a shortcut" because you shouldn't expect to make up any time on this 9-mile-long route that twists, turns, and bounces its way through the forests. It's sometimes closed by snows and never open to trucks, trailers, or motorhomes. But if you're not in a rush, this scenic route offers opportunities to spot moose and black bears and escape the hordes. If you head into the park this way from Teton Village, you can get park information at the new **Granite Canyon Entrance Station** about 2 miles north of Teton Village.

Another oft-overlooked backroad is the **Antelope Flats-Kelly-Gros Ventre loop.** Travel this road along the "quiet" east side of the park and you stand a good chance of spotting bison, pronghorn antelope, migrating elk in spring and fall, and moose in fall and winter. This route also takes you past historic Mormon Row homesteads and classic rustic barns, and allows you to enjoy the vast, sweeping views of the Teton Range. It's also a great place to bike thanks to minimal auto traffic.

As you move north and south across the park, you come upon three areas chock-full of visitor services. Near the park's southern tip lies **Moose,** home to park headquarters with its sprawling visitor center, museum, and bookstore. Nearby is a small cluster of businesses that includes a liquor store, grocery, restaurant, and outdoor gear shop where you can rent bikes, boats, and climbing gear. Farther north near the park's midsection lies **Jackson Lake Lodge,** where you not only have lodging options but also restaurants, a handful of gift shops, a gas station, and even a medical clinic. A short drive north of the lodge lies **Colter Bay Village** with its lodging, campground, restaurants, grocery, gift shops, picnic area, and marina where you can launch boating excursions or sign on for a scenic lake cruise or an evening dinner cruise. The village also has an engaging museum that features artifacts and artworks of various American Indian tribes.

If you ever find yourself in need of a civilization fix, head south to **Jackson.** This eclectic mountain town has great restaurants, a variety of hotels and motels, gift shops, and boutiques. If you show up during the height of the summer season, head to the Town Square for the nightly Old-West style shoot-outs, complete with damsels in distress, good guys, and bad guys.

Finding information after you arrive

Grand Teton National Park has three visitor centers, so whether you come from the north, south, or east you're never really far from a place where you can get your bearings. The **Moose Visitor Center** (☎ 307-739-3399) is ½ mile west of Moose Junction at the southern end of the park. As the park headquarters, it offers exhibits on geology and natural history, a bookstore, and audiovisual programs. You can check into the schedule of ranger programs and pick up maps and permits for boating and backcountry trips. This center is the only one open year-round. From mid-September to mid-June, hours are 8 a.m. to 5 p.m., and from mid-June through mid-September, hours are 8 a.m. to 7 p.m.

The **Jenny Lake Visitor Center** (☎ 307-739-3392) at South Jenny Lake has maps, publications, and a geology exhibit. The center is open daily from early June to Labor Day, 8 a.m. to 7 p.m. Through the end of September the hours shorten, to 8 a.m. to 5 p.m. The facility is closed October to May.

The **Colter Bay Visitor Center** (☎ 307-739-3594), the northernmost of the park's visitor centers, provides permits, information, audiovisual programs, and a bookstore. You can take part in ranger-led activities here or hike along the lakeshore. You can also explore the on-site **Indian Arts Museum** (hours for both the visitor center and museum: early May to Memorial Day, 8 a.m. to 5 p.m., June to Labor Day, 8 a.m. to 7 p.m., and early September to early October, 8 a.m. to 5 p.m.).

Finally, the **Flagg Ranch Resort** (☎ 307-543-2327) complex has an information station approximately 5 miles north of the park's northern boundary that's open from early June through Labor Day, 9 a.m. to 4 p.m.

Paying fees

U.S. Route 26/89/191 doesn't have park gates, so the views are free as you pass through the park on this route. When you enter park entrance stations near Moose or Moran junctions, you pay the park fee of $20 per vehicle, $10 per hiker or biker, or $15 per motorcycle. All fees are good for a seven-day stay. If you expect to visit Yellowstone, too, the admission fee is good for both parks. Annual permits for Grand Teton and Yellowstone national parks are also available for $40.

See Chapter 8 for information on the National Park Pass and Chapter 7 for the lowdown on Golden Age and Golden Access passports.

Getting Around Grand Teton

The park doesn't have a public transportation system, so you need a car to get around. With the exception of the Antelope Flats-Kelly-Gros Ventre loop, this park isn't great for road bikers because the paved roads have narrow shoulders and are crowded with RVs and other vehicles. That said, bikers flock to the Teton Park Road, so while motoring along keep an eye out for them!

Remembering Safety

While taking in the many sights of Grand Teton National Park, keep the following precautions in mind. For additional tips for a safe national park visit, see Chapter 8.

 ✔ **Prepare for the high elevation.** Even the lowest parts of the park are more than a mile above sea level, which can leave you gasping for breath if you're coming from the lowlands and jump right into cycling, hiking, paddling, skiing, or climbing without acclimating to the park's thinner air. Take at least a day or two to get acclimated to the elevation, and for more information on altitude sickness, see Chapter 9.

 ✔ **Watch out for bears.** Be aware of the park's resident grizzly and black bears. The grizzly bear population is small, but black bears abound in the park. Before you head out on a hike, check with rangers for any reports of recent bear activity. On the trail, I recommend hiking in groups of two to four people and talking or singing loudly so you don't surprise any wildlife lurking just around the next bend. Carrying bear pepper spray in an easily accessible location is also a good idea.

 ✔ **Be wary of other beasts.** The park also has bison, moose, and elk. They may look cuddly, but their horns and antlers are not merely ornamental, so keep your distance. Moose are also highly adept at stomping anything they don't like, and even though they look ungainly, they're surprisingly quick and agile.

 ✔ **Look out for your fellow tourists.** Paying attention to other park visitors while tooling down the roads, particularly the Teton Park Road, is always a good idea. Often people become so caught up with the scenery that they actually forget to look where they're going — a recipe for disaster on this curvy, busy road. Also, if you're driving, watch out for cyclists, and if you're pedaling, keep an eye out for motorists.

 ✔ **Swim with caution.** Do you plan to head to one of the lakes for a dip? It's a great way to cool off during the summer heat, but you won't find any lifeguards in the park, so be careful.

Exploring Grand Teton

No matter why you've come to Grand Teton, you won't have trouble filling your days. After touching on the park's highlights and hikes in this section, I give you a strategy for maneuvering around and a rundown of the park's best programs and activities.

If you come to Grand Teton in the summer, expect the park to be crowded. To negotiate around these crowds, think like a "parkie." Visit prime attractions early or late in the day, head north to Lizard Creek for a campsite instead of joining the masses at Colter Bay, hike into Death Canyon instead of up Cascade or Garnet Canyons, and paddle Leigh Lake instead of Jenny Lake.

Exploring the top attractions

Cunningham Cabin Historic Site

Pierce Cunningham built this well-weathered and slowly slumping cabin in 1890 to hold down his claim to the 160 acres he received from the government for $10 through the Homestead Act of 1862. When you visit, imagine enduring a winter of below-zero overnight temperatures and drifting snows in this shack. A ¾-mile self-guided hike offers some insight into the park's ranching history.

See map p. 171. The cabin is located 5 1/2 miles south of Moran Junction on U.S. Route 26/89/191. Free and open at all times.

Jenny Lake

Grand Teton National Park is a classic piece of America's alpine high-country, with jagged peaks, fragrant pine forests, beautiful lakes, and an elevation of nearly 7,000 feet. Located at the base of the Grand Tetons, Jenny Lake is one of the markers left behind by the glaciers that sculpted the mountains and their valleys. As the ice retreated, the melting water filled in a basin carved by the glaciers.

Jenny Lake is a tourist magnet. But unlike other spots in the park, you have a variety of activities to choose from here. You can take the shuttle boat across the lake and vanish up a trail into the mountains, spend a morning or afternoon hiking around the lake, try your hand at fishing, or rent a canoe or kayak from **Dornans** (☎ **307-733-2415**) in Moose and paddle away from the crowds.

For $5 one-way or $7.50 round-trip adult fares, a shuttle boat operated by **Jenny Lake Boating** (☎ **307-734-9227**) can ferry you from the East Shore Boat Dock to the West Shore Boat Dock. From mid-May through September, weather permitting, the ferry operates daily, departing about every 15 minutes between 8 a.m. and 6 p.m. (May 15–May 31 and Sept 16-Sept 30, 10 a.m.–4 p.m.).

Several hikes, both the easy variety and those that lead deep into the park's backcountry, start and end at Jenny Lake, making it possible for you to spend a few hours or a week or more on the trail. For my recommended hikes, see Cascade Canyon Loop, Hidden Falls/Inspiration Point, and Jenny Lake Loop in the "Taking a hike" section.

You can minimize your contact with crowds by arriving early in the morning to watch the sun's first rays ignite the mountains, or late in the afternoon when most folks are heading out of the park. At either time, press on up the trail past Inspiration Point, and you leave most other tourists behind.

See map p. 171. Jenny Lake is on Teton Park Road 8 miles north of Moose and 12 miles south of Jackson Lake Junction.

Menor's Ferry Historic Area

The Menor's Ferry Historic Area has a self-guided trail that leads you to the site where Bill Menor began his ferry business in 1894. Kids like the free ride across the Snake River on a replica of his ferry.

The nearby **Chapel of the Transfiguration** is a log cabin built in 1925 by settlers who didn't want to make the long ride into Jackson every Sunday for church. Today, the chapel offers Episcopalian services during the summer months.

If walls could talk, **Maud Noble's Cabin** near Menor's Ferry would tell the story of how Grand Teton became a national park. Maud Noble took over the ferry business from Bill Menor in 1918. In 1923, a group of Jackson residents — determined to preserve the land that sprawls beneath the Tetons — gathered at the cabin to talk with Horace Albright, the superintendent of Yellowstone National Park, about creating some sort of federal preserve. The land would be, they said, a "museum on the hoof." Today, the cabin contains some interesting reproductions of photos taken early in the valley's history, including some of the Teton Range taken by William Henry Jackson, a prominent 19th-century explorer and photographer.

See map p. 171. The Menor's Ferry Historic Area is located ¼ mile north of the Moose Entrance Station on Teton Park Road.

Oxbow Bend

A great place to go in search of wildlife (and priceless beauty) is Oxbow Bend just 3 miles west of Moran Junction. On just about any spring, summer, or early fall day you can spot white pelicans, trumpeter swans, geese, ducks, bald eagles, ospreys, and other birds on or around the river. Moose also occasionally appear in the river bottom meadows, and river otters cavort along stretches of the riverbank.

The main road has a pullover for picture taking and gazing, but you can get closer to the river and its wildlife by taking the Cattleman's Bridge Road. This dirt road, found nearly ¼-mile north of the Oxbow Bend Turnout, runs south for 1 mile to a parking area where you can get out and walk along the river or try your luck with a fishing pole.

Even better, rent a canoe to float along the 5-mile stretch of river that runs from below Jackson Lake Dam to Pacific Creek. (See "Keeping active," later in this chapter, for canoe rental information.) The water flows lazily and you can see wildlife up close.

If you do wander along Oxbow Bend during the summer months, be prepared to slather on bug repellent because the mosquitoes are voracious.

Few people head to the trails that wrap Emma Matilda and Two Ocean lakes found due north of Oxbow Bend. (See Two Ocean Lake Trail in "Taking a hike," later in this chapter, for my recommended hike.) As a result, you'll find peace and quiet — as well as wildlife — at these two beautiful lakes. If you head to this area, keep in mind that this is prime grizzly habitat (perhaps explaining why few people hike here). Make lots of noise while hiking (singing is good) so you don't surprise any bears. As a precaution, carry (and know how to use) bear pepper spray. You can drive to the picnic area on the edge of Two Ocean Lake by taking the Pacific Creek Road just north of the Moran Entrance Station.

See map p. 170. Oxbow Bend is 5 miles north of the Moran Entrance Station on U.S. Route 89/191/287.

Taking a hike

With 200 miles of maintained trails, the biggest problem you face in Grand Teton is trying to decide where to hike. When you first glance at the steep mountains, you'll probably guess that most hikes here involve some hills. The park does seem to have more than its share of uphill treks, but other trails are available that won't exhaust you in the first ¼ mile.

Two of the hikes in this section, Cascade Canyon Loop and Hidden Falls/Inspiration Point, begin at the West Shore Boat Dock on Jenny Lake. To reach the boat dock, hike the Jenny Lake Loop Trail or take a shuttle boat from the East Shore Boat Dock. **Jenny Lake Boating (☎ 307-734-9227)** operates the shuttle from mid-May through September, weather permitting; the boat runs daily, departing about every 15 minutes between 8 a.m. and 6 p.m. If you have early dinner reservations, watch your time carefully. Shuttle boats back to the East Shore are in high demand late in the afternoon, and a 45-minute wait is fairly common. Either get in line early or plan time to hike back via the Jenny Lake Loop Trail.

If you plan to head into the backcountry overnight, you must obtain a free permit and reserve a campsite. You also need to fork over a $15 per trip fee that covers everyone in your party. Visit the nearest visitor's center to make these arrangements.

Capturing the park on film

If you consider yourself even the most marginal of photographers, you have to stop at **Oxbow Bend.** This stretch of the Snake River is likely the most photographed setting in the park, thanks to the river's meanders and the background of Mount Moran and the rest of the Tetons. In the early morning hours when the waters are calm, you can get great shots of Mount Moran's reflection in the river.

For tips on how to hike safely, see "Remembering Safety," earlier in this chapter.

Cascade Canyon Loop

This hike is a great way to get away for two to three days. The trail starts out from Jenny Lake's west boat dock with a steep uphill trek that grinds 7¼ miles up Cascade Canyon before reaching Lake Solitude on the way to the Paintbrush Divide and Holly Lake. When you reach Holly Lake, you've traveled 10¼ miles, but at this point, the grade works with you, because you're heading downhill most of the time.

Not only does this overnight hike feature fantastic scenery, but moose and black bears frequent the area, so you may see some wildlife. Keep your eyes open early in the hike, because moose like to browse in the ponds that form along Cascade Creek as it comes down the canyon.

See map p. 171. Distance: 19¼ miles. Level: Moderate to strenuous with an elevation change of 3,845 feet. Access: West Shore Boat Dock on Jenny Lake.

Hidden Falls/Inspiration Point

This trail is probably the busiest hiking corridor in Grand Teton. Not only do shuttle boats haul people to the West Shore Boat Dock, where these trails begin, but climbing schools practice on the rock walls that rim Cascade Canyon. Crowds notwithstanding, Hidden Falls is beautiful, and from Inspiration Point, you get a great view back across Jenny Lake to the eastern side of Jackson Hole and the Gros Ventre Mountains. If you think climbing appeals to you, watching the classes work on rappeling and climbing will either convince you to take a class or dash the thought from your mind.

Hidden Falls is less than ½ mile from the boat dock, and Inspiration Point lies just ½ mile further up the trail. But I do mean *up* — the trail gets pretty steep.

Enough rock slabs and boulders line this trail to keep kids busy; they scramble over them and don't realize how much energy they're expending.

See map p. 171. Distance: 5¾ miles round-trip or 1¾ miles round-trip via shuttle boat access. Level: Moderate. Access: You can take the shuttle boat across Jenny Lake to these trails or follow the Jenny Lake Loop to the West Shore Boat Dock.

Jenny Lake Loop

This mostly level trail, which winds around the lake close to the shoreline, provides a nice hike for families. The setting is great, with the lake wrapped by a thick forest and the Tetons towering over the western shore. The downside is that this is one of the more popular trails in the park. If you have really young children and prefer a shorter hike, you can take a shuttle boat across the lake to the West Shore Boat Dock and then walk back to the east shore. This trail also connects with hikes up into Cascade Canyon (described earlier in this section) and to String and Leigh lakes to the north.

See map p. 171. Distance: Just over 6½ miles round-trip. Level: Easy. Access: The trailhead is at the East Shore Boat Dock.

Two Ocean Lake Trail

This hike on the east side of U.S. Route 89/191/287 gives you a taste of the backcountry without taking a long trek. Because few people stray from the mountains, you're likely to enjoy a little solitude. The trail loops around the lake, so the direction you head from the trailhead doesn't matter. The route passes through conifer forests on the south shore and aspen groves and meadows along the north shore. In the early summer, you can spot swans and ducks in a bay at the lake's north end, or maybe even spy beavers — or at least their handiwork. In June, the meadows blossom with wild geraniums, lupine, and mountain asters.

If you prefer a longer hike, you can make a 13-mile loop around both Two Ocean Lake and nearby Emma Matilda Lake. One bonus is the moderate climb to Grand View Point, which, at 7,327 feet, provides a nice panoramic view of the two lakes as well as Jackson Lake to the west. Another treat is to canoe Two Ocean Lake. (For canoe rental information, see "Keeping active," later in this chapter.) This is bear country, so check with rangers before you head out to find out whether any bruins have been spotted around the lake, and be sure to make noise as you hike.

See map p. 170. Distance: 6½ miles round-trip. Level: Easy. Access: Two Ocean Lake Trailhead on Two Ocean Lake Road.

Willow Flats Trail

This great trail through wildlife habitat often provides glimpses of moose, great blue herons, and other waterfowl or wading birds. Views of Mount Moran and the rest of the Teton Range are priceless. A good daylong adventure is to hike from Jackson Lake Lodge to Colter Bay, where you can stop for lunch, and then backtrack to the lodge for dinner.

See map p. 170. Distance: 8½ miles round-trip. Level: Easy. Access: The trailhead is at Jackson Lake Lodge.

One-day wonder

Just by driving along U.S. Route 26/89/191, you see the focal point of Grand Teton National Park — the Teton Range. But if you don't get off that highway, you cheat yourself and your family by failing to get a feel for this beautiful land, something you can begin to do in just a day with this itinerary. (Unless otherwise noted, for information on the attractions in this section, see "Exploring the top attractions," earlier in this chapter.)

If you're staying at Jackson Lake Lodge or Signal Mountain Lodge, a good place to start a daylong loop tour is at Jackson Lake Junction. (If you're staying in Jackson, start midloop at Moose.) From Jackson Lake Lodge, drive just 1 mile east from the junction on U.S. Route 89/191/287 to the **Oxbow Bend Turnout,** where you can look for moose in the river bottom and then gaze west at Mount Moran with Skillet Glacier seemingly hanging on its flanks.

From Oxbow Bend, continue southeast on the highway to Moran Junction. (In the fall, watch the woods and flats on either side of the highway for wildlife.) At that junction, turn right and head south on U.S. Route 26/89/191 for 5½ miles until you reach the **Cunningham Cabin Historic Site** on your right.

After exploring the cabin, continue about 4 miles south on the highway until you arrive at the **Snake River Overlook,** the spot where renowned landscape photographer Ansel Adams took a dramatic black-and-white photo of the Tetons in 1942. Although not as interesting as the view of the Tetons, the view of the braided Snake River below has its own merits.

As you get back on the highway and head south toward Moose, you pass three more turnouts, but they offer pretty much the same view as the one you saw at the Snake River Overlook.

The **Moose Visitor Center,** located just west of U.S. Route 26/89/191 on Teton Park Road, is a good place to supplement your literature on the park. (My library on national parks grows substantially after each trip, because I have a hard time turning my back on books about wildlife, early settlers, or geology.) Nearby is **Moose Village,** where you find **Dornans (☎ 307-733-2415)** — a jack-of-all-trades family business that offers accommodations, restaurants, a grocery store, a gift shop, sports equipment rentals, a fishing shop, and chuckwagon cookouts, among other things. Some items are pricey (particularly the libations in the package store), so you may want to shop in Jackson instead.

About ¼ mile past the park's Moose Entrance Station, you come upon **Menor's Ferry,** the **Maud Noble Cabin,** and the **Chapel of the Transfiguration.** Unless you're a serious historian, or have children who'd be interested in seeing the ferry cross the river (the ferry operates during the summer months if the river isn't too high), you can skip these attractions and continue north toward Jenny Lake.

Jenny Lake is a great lunch setting, whether you shuttle across the lake, hike around the water to Cascade Canyon, or simply find a spot along the shore not far from the parking area. On the same side of the lake as the visitor center is **Exum Mountain Guides,** so if you're curious about climbing, stop by and inquire about their classes. (See "Keeping active," later in this section, for information on climbing.) If you visit during the height of summer, you're likely to be confronted by crowds along the lakeshore, but just the same, head across or around the lake to Cascade Canyon and take a short hike to Inspiration Point. The view of Jenny Lake below is great. You pass Hidden Falls along the way, and if you're curious about climbing, you can watch classes at work on the canyon's rock faces.

If the crowds are too suffocating, head just north of Jenny Lake to **String** and **Leigh lakes,** two perfect spots for canoeing, swimming, fishing, and simply relaxing. An easy 3½-mile trail curls around String Lake, which has the park's best swimming because its waters are only 10 feet deep and the warmest in the park. Leigh Lake, a 1-mile hike north of String Lake, has the park's best beaches.

From these two lakes, follow Teton Park Road north, arriving after 9 miles at the **Signal Mountain Lodge complex** with its lodgings, restaurants, stores, and marina. From here, you're just 3 miles from Jackson Lake Junction.

If you have more time

Just 2½ miles north of Jackson on U.S. Route 26/89/191 is the **National Elk Refuge** (☎ 307-733-9212). Although thousands of elk crowd the refuge in winter (the best time to visit), spring, summer, and fall are excellent times for spotting birds and waterfowl. The refuge sprawls across 23,754 acres of land covered by various degrees of meadows, sagebrush flats, thin stands of timber, and rocky outcrops. The Gros Ventre River traces the refuge's northern boundary, and Flat Creek slices through its middle.

Elk typically spend the months from November into April on the refuge; the rest of the year, they scoot off into the high country for cooler weather and lush vegetation. When the snows of autumn begin to fall, the elk descend en masse on the refuge, and by midwinter, 7,000 to 8,000 animals live off the feed tossed out by the local U.S. Fish and Wildlife Service.

In winter, you can sign on for a 45- to 60-minute **horse-drawn sleigh ride** ($15 for adults, $11 for kids ages 6 through 12, free for 5 and under, $48 for a family of four) through the refuge. These trips depart about every 20 minutes from the **National Wildlife Art Museum,** which is across the highway from the elk refuge. You also can purchase a combo ticket that gets you into the art museum as well as a sleigh ride ($18 for adults, $14 for kids ages 6 through 12, $60 for a family of four). During early winter trips, you may come across bulls tangling their antlers in battles intended to determine a mating hierarchy and impress the cows. You may also glimpse the wolves that follow the elk to the refuge.

When spring rolls around, Boy Scouts from Jackson scour the refuge for antlers shed by the elk. Then, on the third Saturday in May, Jackson's Town Square takes on a carnival atmosphere when it's overrun by thousands of tourists and antler buyers (who sell the antlers for their reputed medicinal qualities) as the scouts stage their **annual elk antler auction.** Stacks of antlers, collected by the scouts and by private collectors, fill the streets bordering the square. As an auctioneer encourages onlookers to raise their price for the antlers, young scouts heft them high overhead so all can see. Eighty percent of the money raised goes to buy more feed for the refuge, and the scouts keep the rest for administrative costs.

Ranger programs

Grand Teton's rangers always seem to be heading out and about in the park — and inviting the public along. They lead hikes to Inspiration Point above Jenny Lake each summer morning from early June through September. Other ranger-led offerings include talks about Teton geologic history, cultural history, fire ecology, and wildflower walks.

Spotting the local wildlife

Before **wolves** returned to the scene, Grand Teton National Park was best known for its moose, elk, bison, and **pronghorn antelope.** But in 1998, wolves wandered down from Yellowstone and discovered the National Elk Refuge, which thousands of elk call home during the winter months. That was all the wolves needed to know. In recent winters, as many as three wolf packs have been spotted on the refuge in search of a meal. One pack even set up a den in the northeastern corner of the park not far from Moran Junction, but they retain a low profile. Your best bet for spotting wolves is to tour the elk refuge in winter.

Grizzly bears also are showing up with increasing frequency in the park. The area near Lower Slide Lake just east of Kelly has proven popular with the bruins, although backcountry travelers may also see them throughout northern parts of Grand Teton.

Black bears also inhabit the park and are more visible than grizzlies. Unfortunately, some have learned to associate people with food, so make sure to clean up after picnics and keep an eye out while hiking. Black bears occasionally turn up in the Jenny Lake area, and in August, you may catch a glimpse of one in the woods near Signal Mountain where they're drawn to the ripening huckleberries.

Moose are year-round park residents. You can often see them browsing in the ponds along the Moose-Wilson Road. Willow Flats, a big marshy area between Jackson Lake Lodge and Jackson Lake, is a great place to look for moose early in the morning and in the evenings, as is nearby Oxbow Bend. Sometimes, you can find them in the pools formed by Cascade Creek as it falls out of the Tetons on the way to Jenny Lake.

Grand Teton isn't home to as many **bison** as Yellowstone is, but a fair number exist, and they're pretty visible. In June, you can often spot cows and their calves in the grasslands along the Antelope Flats Road north of the town of Kelly and east of Mormon Row. They also graze in the sagebrush meadows between Signal Mountain and North Jenny Lake Junction.

The animal responsible for generating the initial interest in Jackson Hole back in the early 19th century still abounds in the park today. These days, **beavers** continue to ply the park's rivers, creeks, and lakes, building their dams and lodges. If you spend any time along the river and creek bottoms, you'll see their stick-built dams and lodges and the gnawed tree stumps they left behind. Oxbow Bend is a reliable area for seeing beavers, or at least their work.

You can also find **river otters** along the Snake River near Oxbow Bend. These critters like to frolic and will ham it up for you, as long as you don't get too close. On a float through Oxbow Bend, my wife and I came across a family of five otters who posed until we ran out of film.

Oxbow Bend is a great place to spot some of the park's wildlife. In addition to the moose, **elk,** and **mule deer** you may see in the marshy bottom lands along the river, waterfowl usually crowds the river in the mornings and late afternoons. You can see **American white pelicans, Canada Goose, a variety of ducks,** and possibly even **Great Blue Herons** wading along the shore in search of minnows.

If you're lucky during your visit, you may see one of the park's rarer birds — the **trumpeter swan.** These big birds can measure 6 feet long from the tip of their black bills to the end of their white tails. In recent years, a pair of the swans has been nesting in Christian Pond just east of Jackson Lake Lodge. You can't get within 300 feet of the nesting site because the pond is off-limits to give the swans some privacy, but with a good pair of binoculars, you can watch these elegant birds from the Christian Pond Trail. (If you plan to hike along the trail in May or June, check with rangers to see whether any bear activity has been reported in this area. Note, too, that the resident **mosquitoes** are ravenous in summer.)

 A great summer morning's hike with an educational, as well as scenic, payoff is the **Inspiration Point Hike.** This 2-mile-long easy hike into the mountains above Jenny Lake leads to Hidden Falls as well as the beautiful Inspiration Point. Joining a ranger-led hike, you can learn about the geologic upheavals that created this incredible landscape. These 2½-hour hikes start at 8:30 a.m. from the Jenny Lake Visitor Center. There's a 25-person limit to this program, and you have to purchase a ticket for the boat ride across Jenny Lake. For details on any ranger-led activities, consult the park's newspaper, *Teewinot,* or inquire at a visitor center for a schedule.

A more leisurely ranger-led hike roams along the Jackson Lake shores in the Colter Bay area. During the hike, the rangers explain the genesis of this riveting landscape.

In addition to these programs, campfire talks and evening-slide shows take place throughout the park. Check the park's newspaper or bulletin boards in the visitor centers and campgrounds for times and topics.

 Most national parks offer Junior Ranger Programs as a way to get kids interested in parks, but Grand Teton has what's known as the **Young Naturalist Program.** Kids receive a newsletter discussing the park's wildlife, geology, and human history and a related worksheet with questions. After a youngster completes the worksheet (with your help if necessary) and participates in two ranger programs, he or she receives a special patch. You can sign up your kids (ages 8 through 12) at the Moose, Jenny Lake, or Colter Bay visitor centers. The programs are free, but a $1 donation is suggested for the patch.

Keeping active

In Grand Teton National Park, you can pursue a variety of activities, some of which, such as boating, canoeing, and fishing, require permits, licenses, or registration. Special regulations may also apply, so check the park's Web site at www.nps.gov/grte in advance, or stop at one of the visitor centers for complete information.

✔ **Boating:** Many of the park's front-country lakes are perfect for canoeing and kayaking. The Snake River below Jackson is known for its white-water rafting, and the stretch of the river that flows through the park is great for experienced canoeists or rafters. Boat and canoe rentals are available at Colter Bay Village through **Grand Teton Lodging Company** (☎ 800-628-9988) and at Signal Mountain through **Signal Mountain Lodge** (☎ 307-543-2831) for use on Jackson Lake. You can also rent boats for use on park lakes in Moose at **Dornans** (☎ 307-733-2415).

Human-powered vessels are permitted on Phelps, Jackson, Jenny, Emma Matilda, Two Ocean, Taggart, Bradley, Bearpaw, Leigh, and String lakes. Motorized boats are allowed only on Phelps, Jackson, and Jenny lakes, but on Jenny Lake, the motor can't be more than ten horsepower. Only muscle-powered rafts, canoes, dories, and kayaks are allowed on the Snake River within the park. No boats are allowed on Pacific Creek or the Gros Ventre River.

If you bring your own boat, you must register it. For nonmotorized craft, the registration fee is $5 for seven days or $10 for a year; for motorized boats, the fee is $10 for seven days and $20 for an annual permit. You can pay these fees at any visitor center.

✔ **Climbing:** Climbing to the top of Grand Teton isn't as far-fetched as you may think. Each year, thousands of people, many who have never climbed before, set out from Lupine Meadows in a bid to conquer the Grand. I consider the trek more of a long, strenuous hike than a technical climb.

The easiest way to the top is with one of the park's two climbing companies: **Exum Mountain Guides, Inc.** (☎ 307-733-2297; www.exumguides.com; P.O. Box 56, Moose, WY 83012) or **Jackson Hole Mountain Guides** (☎ 800-239-7642, 307-733-4979; www.jhmg.com; P.O. Box 7477, Jackson, WY 83002). They typically require you to enroll in a two-day climbing school conducted in the park before attempting the summit. The cost depends on the route and your experience level. With Exum, figure $600 for one person ($480 per person for two people) to climb the Grand via the Owen-Spalding Route or the Exum Route. On top of that, if you're a rank novice, two days of climbing school cost $250 per person. Jackson Hole Mountain Guides is a tad cheaper; its Grand climb, which includes climbing school, runs $720 per person for two people.

To climb the Grand, you need to make reservations several months in advance. If you have a particular window during the summer for the climb, make sure to call early in the year because reservations fill quickly. Middle to late August usually offers the best climbing weather, whereas in late June and early July, you're likely to encounter snow that can hamper or even cancel a climb.

Speaking of snow, make sure you call the climbing company several days before you arrive to check the weather conditions. I climbed the Grand in mid-July and was confronted by midwinter snow conditions that necessitated not only an ice axe and *crampons* (shoe spikes) but also waterproof shell gloves, water-resistant pants, a shell jacket, and warmer layers that I usually don't pack for a summer vacation.

If you live at a substantially lower elevation, you may want to arrive in the park as much as a week before your scheduled climb so your body can get used to the altitude. Acclimating makes the climb to almost 14,000 feet easier, and quickens the recovery time afterward.

✔ **Fishing:** The lakes and streams of Grand Teton are popular fishing destinations, loaded with lively cutthroat trout, whitefish, and mackinaw (lake) trout in Jackson, Jenny, and Phelps lakes. To angle in the park, you need a Wyoming state fishing license, and you have to check creel limits, which vary from year to year and place to place. Tackle and fishing licenses are available at Colter Bay Village and Signal Mountain.

✔ **Horseback Riding: Grand Teton Lodge Company** (☎ 800-628-9988; www.gtlc.com) offers tours from stables at Colter Bay Village and Jackson Lake Lodge. Choices are one- and two-hour guided trail rides daily aboard well-broken, tame animals. An experienced rider may find these tours too tame; wranglers refer to them as nose-and-tail tours.

✔ **Skiing:** You can ski flat or steep in Grand Teton; the two hazards to watch out for are hypothermia and avalanches. Know your limitations and make sure you're properly equipped. Check with local rangers and guides for trails that match your ability. For downhill skiing, contact **Snow King Resort** (☎ 800-522-7669; www.snowking.com) and **Jackson Hole Ski Resort** (☎ 307-733-2292; www.jacksonhole.com); both have rental facilities on the premises. For cross-country skis and snowshoe rentals, visit outdoor equipment shops in Jackson or stop at Dornans in Moose.

Escaping the rain

A great rainy day spot is the **National Museum of Wildlife Art** (☎ 800-313-9553 or 307-733-5771; www.wildlifeart.org), 2 1/2 miles north of Jackson on Highway 26/89/191 across from the National Elk Refuge. The museum arguably houses the country's best collection of wildlife art, from bronzes to oil paintings to watercolors. You gain a keen appreciation of the West's ruggedness and beauty through the artworks displayed in the museum's 51,000 square feet. Among the 2,000 art pieces are original works by 19th-century masters Albert Bierstadt, Charles M. Russell, and John James Audubon. The museum is open every day of the year, except Christmas, Thanksgiving, Columbus and Veterans days, from 9 a.m. to 5 p.m. in summer and winter (1 p.m. to 5 p.m. Sundays in spring and fall). The cost is $8 for adults, $7 for students and seniors, and $16 for families.

Where to Stay

The park provides a cornucopia of accommodations, ranging from shorefront cottages and rustic log cabins to elegant log lodges and even motel-style rooms. Prices run the gamut, too. The park properties have in-room telephones, but lack televisions and air-conditioning. Nearby Jackson provides options for those who want all the creature comforts.

For more information on finding a place to stay, see Chapter 6.

Lodging in the park

Colter Bay Village Cabins
$–$$$ **Colter Bay Village**

If the park has a central hub of activity, this is it, so don't come here look-ing for seclusion. On the other hand, if you have a troop of kids, this choice is wonderful, both because of the many things to do in the area and because it's easier on your wallet. The 166 cabins have a rustic flavor and are simply furnished and clean. But not all are created equal. Some feature shower stalls, whereas others share baths. The tent cabins have rough log walls, canvas roofs, wood-burning stoves, double-deck bunk beds, and concrete floors. And if that's not rustic enough, you must also use com-munal restroom facilities (showers are available for a fee) and bring your own sleeping bag. The nearby village offers a restaurant, food court, con-venience store, service station, and laundry. You also can sign up for a horseback ride.

See map p. 170. U.S. Route 89/191/287. ☎ *800-628-9988 or 307-543-3100.* www.gtlc.com/CBVLod.htm. *274 units. TEL. Rack rates: $37–$135 cabins; $36 tent cabin; $26–$40 RV spots. AE, DISC, MC, V. Open: Late-May to late Sept.*

Flagg Ranch Resort
$$$ **Flagg Ranch**

This ain't no ranch, so you don't need to worry about stepping around cow patties on your way to your cabin. But the location is a bit remote, so if you plan to spend most of your time below Jackson Lake, you could do better, location-wise. However, if you want to bounce between Grand Teton and Yellowstone, Flagg Ranch is perfect: The location is 5 miles north of Grand Teton and two miles south of Yellowstone in the John D. Rockefeller Memorial Parkway, a parklike middle ground between the two parks.

You won't be roughing it at this resort. In 1992, an old motel was replaced with 92 log cabins that feature king- or queen-size beds, spacious sitting areas, wall-to-wall carpeting, and bathrooms with tubs and showers. The lodge, built in 1995, features a large stone fireplace (perfect for warming yourself after a wintry excursion), restaurant, bar, gift shop, and conven-ience store. The Flagg Ranch is perfect for both summer fly-fishing trips and winter ski adventures. *Note:* The status of the winter season has been affected by the debate over whether to allow snowmobiles into the parks.

See map p. 170. 5 miles north of Grand Teton's Northern Boundary on the John D. Rockefeller Jr. Parkway. ☎ *800-443-2311 or 307-543-2861. Fax: 307-543-2356.* www.flaggranch.com. *92 cabins. TEL. Rack rates: $145–$155 summer. AE, DISC, MC, V. Open: Year-round.*

Jackson Lake Lodge
$$$–$$$$$ Jackson Lake Junction

With such a beautiful location — a bluff overlooking willow flats and Jackson Lake, with the Tetons just beyond the lake — what could the architects have been thinking when they dreamed up this concrete edifice? But this lodge compensates in other ways for what it lacks in design. From the patio off the backside of the lodge, you can often spot moose and waterfowl on spring, summer, and fall mornings and evenings. If the weather is too chilly, you can get the same view in the lobby through 60-foot-tall windows.

If you book one of the lodge's cottages (preferably one with a lakeside view), you can enjoy a bit more atmosphere and feel as if you've escaped most of the crowds. These motel-style units are clean and comfortable, and they sport small patios where you can enjoy a picnic lunch or dinner while watching the clouds swirl about the Tetons and the sun's rays glisten on the lake. Lodge rooms are spacious, and most come with double beds. Suites have one or two bedrooms. You find formal dining in the lodge's Mural Room and soda fountain-style dining in the Pioneer Grill, which seems to have a 1950s' decor hangover. The Blue Heron lounge across from the Mural Room offers great mountain and lake views and occasional live entertainment, but it can be smoky. The lodge also features a number of upscale clothing and jewelry shops, and boasts a heated pool.

See map p. 170. Near junction of US. Route 89/191/287 and Teton Park Road. ☎ *800-628-9988 or 307-543-3100.* www.gtlc.com/JacLLLod.htm. *348 cottages, 37 rooms. TEL. Rack rates: $167–$240 double; $167–$235 cottage; $410–$570 suite. AE, DISC, MC, V. Open: Late May to Oct.*

Jenny Lake Lodge
$$$$$ Jenny Lake

Nestled — no, make that wonderfully hidden — in the woods off a curve along a one-way road between Leigh and Jenny lakes, this elegant lodge epitomizes a romantic Rocky Mountain retreat. This is a place for memorable romantic weekends, not a place to bring the kids. The price alone gets that message across. The lodge, with its crackling fireplace, provides the backdrop for meals and chats, but come bed time, guests retreat to beautiful log cabins topped by pitched shingle roofs and pillared porches. The cabins are comfortably outfitted with log furniture with cowhide upholstery, thick quilts on the beds, generous closet space, and tiled combination baths. The multicourse meals are gourmet, and a classical guitarist often accompanies dinners. (Do pack your jackets, guys, as they're strongly encouraged for dinner.) Oh yeah, the rack rate also covers horse-back rides and the use of the lodge's bicycles. To ensure a reservation, call a year in advance.

See map p. 171. North of Jenny Lake off Teton Park Road. ☎ *800-628-9988 or 307-733-4647.* www.gtlc.com/JenLLLod.htm. *37 cabins. TEL. Rack rates: $348 single; $459 double; $614–$654 suite. Rates include breakfast, dinner, horseback riding, and bicycles. AE, DISC, MC, V. Open: Late May to Oct.*

Signal Mountain Lodge
$$–$$$$ Signal Mountain

You can hear the lapping waters of Jackson Lake from this small resort, which is tucked away in the woods along the southeastern arm of the lake on the main road that runs from Jenny Lake to Moran Junction. Book a room at this lodge and you'll be close to the water and hiking trails. Plus, you have Mount Moran with its glacier fields as a background. The accommodations aren't bad, either. You can choose from cabins and one- and two-bedroom bungalows with beach frontage. The log cabins feature handmade pine fur-niture, electric heat, covered porches, and tiled baths. Some have cobble-stone fireplaces (if you want one, ask when making a reservation) as well as kitchenettes with microwave ovens and refrigerators. Within walking dis-tance is the main lodge with its restaurant, coffee shop, small lounge, and gift shop. As far as the lodge's overall location, you're just 30 miles north of Jackson and 25 miles from Yellowstone National Park's South Entrance.

See map p. 170. Teton Park Road near junction with US. Route 89/191/287. ☎ *307-543-2831. Fax: 307-543-2569.* www.signalmtnlodge.com. *79 units. TEL. Rack rates: $98–$242 double. AE, DISC, MC, V. Open: Mid-May to mid-Oct.*

Top lodging outside of the park

Rusty Parrot Lodge
$$$$–$$$$$ Jackson

Although it's billed as a hotel, this lodge two blocks from Jackson's Town Square operates more like a plush bed-and-breakfast. Breakfasts of fresh fruit, Russian Eggs Benedict with smoked trout, and griddle favorites greet you every morning, and a hot tub waits to welcome you home at night. Dinners are available, but for an additional (and high) charge. In between, the library is a good place to retreat if you're not interested in conversa-tion in front of the river-rock fireplace. Or, you can stop at the lodge's Body Sage spa and get a mud or seaweed wrap or facial. For those cold winter nights or fall's early chill, wool blankets and down comforters top the king-size beds made from logs. To secure particular dates, make a reservation at least three months in advance.

175 North Jackson St. ☎ *800-458-2004 or 307-733-2000.* www.rustyparrot.com. *31 rooms. A/C TV TEL. Rack rates: Late May– early June $199-$500 double; early-June–Sept $284–$500 double; Oct–Dec 23 $164–$525 double; Dec 24–Jan 2 $299–$575 double; Jan 3– late-Feb $245–$550 double; late-Feb– late March $199–$550 double; late March–late May $164–$550 double. AE, DC, DISC, MC, V.*

Spring Creek Ranch
$$$–$$$$$ West of Jackson

If you don't want to stay in Jackson, and if price is not a problem, this resort huddled atop East Gros Ventre Butte just west of town assures a relaxing, off-the-beaten-path stay during any season. You can't beat the views, either. Set atop the butte, 1,000 feet above the Snake River, the resort and its 1,500 acres offer spectacular panoramas of the Tetons. Deer and moose are frequent visitors to the resort's property, and eagles fly by regularly. Hotel rooms and condo units are available. Guest rooms feature wood-burning fireplaces, Native American floor and wall coverings, refrigerators, and coffee makers. The condo units are sized and furnished for people 6 feet and taller. Studio units have kitchenettes. On the grounds, you find a heated outdoor pool, tennis courts, and a small pond. To ensure a reservation, call a year in advance.

1800 Spirit Dance Rd. ☎ ***800-443-6139*** *or 307-733-8833.* www.springcreekranch. com. *125 units. AC TV TEL. Rack rates: $150–$310 double; $160–$1,200 condo per night. AE, MC, V.*

Wort Hotel
$$$$–$$$$$ Jackson

If you stay in Jackson, stay here. It's worth it. The location is in the heart of downtown, less than five minutes from the Town Square. The rooms are spacious and comfortable. Although the building's exterior is Tudor, inside you find Western art and taxidermy. A large fireplace anchors the lobby, and the mezzanine has a small sitting area. All the guest rooms feature "New West" decor — primarily lodgepole furnishings — as well as air conditioning, tub/shower baths, and thick carpeting. The Governor's Suite boasts a traditional parlor. Although you can find better meals a short walk away, the hotel has a restaurant as well as the Silver Dollar Bar, which features a bar top inlaid with 2,032 silver dollars.

50 N. Glenwood. ☎ ***800-322-2727*** *or 307-733-2190. Fax: 307-733-2067.* www.wort hotel.com. *57 rooms, 3 suites. A/C TV TEL. Rack rates: June–Sept $275–$550 double; Oct–Dec $220–$550 double; Jan–March $250–$550 double. Kids 14 and under stay free. AE, DISC, MC, V.*

Runner-up lodgings

Anglers Inn
$–$$$ Jackson Pine-paneled rooms and log furniture give this place a touch of the West. Flat Creek flows nearby, and downtown Jackson is a five-minute walk away. *265 N. Millward St.* ☎ ***800-867-4667*** *or 307-733-3682.* www. anglersinn.net.

Days Inn of Jackson Hole
$$–$$$$ Jackson This property is a good walk from the heart of town, but suites are spacious and equipped with fireplaces. Plus, you get a

Continental breakfast. *350 S. Hwy. 89.* ☎ *800-329-7466 or 307-733-0033.* www. daysinnjacksonhole.com.

Trapper Inn

$–$$$ Jackson   Just two blocks from the Town Square, the Trapper is a short walk from Jackson's best restaurants and a short drive from the park. *235 N. Cache.* ☎ *888-771-2648 or 307-733-2648.* www.trapperinn.com.

Virginian Lodge

$–$$$ Jackson   The Old West thrives here in the form of stuffed and mounted hunting trophies. The rates are reasonable, and you're in the heart of Jackson. *750 W. Broadway.* ☎ *800-262-4999 or 307-733-2792.* www. virginianlodge.com.

Campgrounds

If you want to commune with the great outdoors, you have several camping options within and around the park.

In the park

Grand Teton National Park has five park-operated campgrounds, which charge $12 a night and operate on a first-come, first-served basis. Four of these offer gorgeous lake settings, whereas the fifth — Gros Ventre — is riverside. The park also has one concessionaire-operated RV campground at Colter Bay.

The most popular campground — thanks to its killer views of the Grand, the embracing pine forest, and the nearby lake — is the **Jenny Lake Campground.** If you're not there to check in by 8 a.m., you probably won't be able to snag one of the 49 tent spots during the busy summer months. The sites are sprinkled amid evergreens and boulders left behind by melting glaciers, and the Tetons tower just above the western shore of the lake.

Signal Mountain Campground and its 86 sites just 12 miles north of Jenny Lake is the next campground to fill, which it usually does by 10 a.m. The sites, scattered among spruce and fir trees on the shore of Jackson Lake, provide awesome views. The nearby amenities — a marina, picnic area, camp store, dump station, and the restaurant at Signal Mountain Lodge — are a big bonus.

The **Colter Bay Campground and Trailer Village** just 6 miles north of Jackson Lake Junction has 310 sites, laundry and shower facilities, and a dump station nearby in Colter Bay Village. The sites, not far from the lakeshore, are big and have easy access if you're towing a trailer or using an RV. The proximity to Colter Bay Village with its public showers, laundromat, grocery store, stables, restaurant, and visitor center help make this a high-demand campground. By noon most, if not all, of these sites are claimed.

Grand Teton Lodge Company (☎ 800-628-9988 or 307-543-2855) manages a trailer village with 112 sites at Colter Bay. Summer-season (late May to early September) rates range from $26 to $40 depending on whether you arrive during peak season or on the shoulder.

On a small promontory not far from the northern tip of Jackson Lake is **Lizard Creek Campground.** Although not as developed as the Colter Bay or Signal Mountain campgrounds, Lizard Creek is popular for its quiet, lakeside setting in a spruce and fir forest. The 60 sites often go by 2 p.m.

The **Gros Ventre Campground,** no doubt because of its 360 sites as well as its location away from the lakes and mountains, is the last in the park to fill. Often you can still find space at 6 p.m. The sites are scattered among sagebrush and cottonwoods, and the Gros Ventre River is a short walk away. This campground isn't the most picturesque, but if you're running late, you'll likely find a place here.

Outside the park

Beyond the park boundaries, you find the **Wagon Wheel Campground** (☎ 307-733-4588) close to the heart of downtown Jackson. This campground, with its 45 sites that go for $24 to $45 a night (depending on whether you need to park an RV or simply pop up a tent), is just five blocks north of the town square. Twelve miles northwest of Jackson and not far from Grand Teton's southwestern corner is the **Teton Village KOA** (☎ 307-733-5354). You find 150 sites here; tent sites run about $30 for two people, $5.50 each additional person 5 and older. RV sites run about $45 for two people. A bonus of this location is nearby Teton Village with its shops, saloons, and restaurants, as well as the Jackson Hole Mountain Resort tram that can haul you to the top of Rendezvous Mountain for some hiking or mountain biking.

Back at the **Flagg Ranch Resort** (☎ 800-443-2311) north of Grand Teton are 97 RV sites ($45 for two people, $5 per additional person) and 74 tent sites ($25 for two people, $5 per additional person). The campground has showers, laundry facilities, a restaurant, and a service station.

Finally, the national forests that surround the park have a number of campgrounds where you can pitch your tent. For details on these campgrounds, call the **Bridger-Teton National Forest** in Wyoming (☎ 307-739-5500) or the **Caribou-Targhee National Forest** (☎ 208-524-7500) in Idaho.

Where to Eat

Meals in the park are largely typical national park fare, with steaks, poultry, fish, and pasta dishes presented in American fashion. But head down the road into Jackson and you easily double, or triple, your dining options. You can find wild game, Italian and Mexican meals, even Greek dishes just a short drive from the park. That said, you definitely won't go hungry if you opt to remain within the park's boundaries.

Restaurants in the park

Chuckwagon Steak and Pasta House
$$–$$$ Colter Bay Village   AMERICAN

This restaurant is one of two sit-downs in Colter Bay Village. The Chuckwagon serves three meals a day. Breakfasts revolve around an all-you-can-eat buffet featuring scrambled eggs, French toast, pancakes, bacon, pastries, and hot and cold cereals, although you can also order off the menu. Hot and cold sandwiches and burgers comprise the bulk of the lunch offerings. The dinner menu ranges from turkey breast and fresh rainbow trout to beef, seafood, and Southwestern and Italian dishes.

See map p. 170. Across from the marina and visitor center. No phone. Main courses: $2.85–$9.95 breakfast; $6.75–$8.75 lunch; $10.25–$18.50 dinner. AE, DISC, MC, V. Open: Daily in summer 6 a.m.–10 p.m.

Flagg Ranch Resort
$$–$$$$ Flagg Ranch   AMERICAN

It's not fine dining on silver and china, but the meals are better than what you get at a typical family restaurant. The menu features the American standards — chicken, fish, and beef in their many incarnations. In winter, the setting becomes cozy with a fireplace roaring. The ambience is down-home as well, both in winter and summer. Although you can't see the Snake River from the dining room, its banks are just a short walk away through the forest.

See map p. 170. 5 miles north of Grand Teton's Northern Boundary on the John D. Rockefeller Jr. Parkway. ☎ *800-443-2311 or 307-543-2861. Main courses: $5.75–$9.65 breakfast; $6–$9 lunch; $10.50–$28 dinner. AE, DISC, MC, V. Open: Daily 7 a.m.–9 p.m.*

Jenny Lake Lodge
$$$$$ Jenny Lake   CONTINENTAL

This lodge serves the best meals in the park — both in terms of cuisine and ambience. The chefs have a long history of pleasing not only lodge guests but also U.S. presidents. Dinners are an event, often starting with such mouth-watering creations as prosciutto wrapped prawns, grilled Portabello bruschetta, or roasted Japanese eggplant. Entrees may range from sauteed red trout with chervil-infused succotash and sweet potato chips, to roasted espresso rubbed venison strip loin with vanilla bean potato puree and a juniper-cognac glace, to a shellfish bouillabaisse in a spicy tomato broth. The desserts are decadent, so leave room. If you stay at the Jenny Lake Lodge, the costs of breakfast and dinner are included in your room rate.

See map p. 171. North of Jenny Lake off Teton Park Road. ☎ *307-733-4647. Reservations required. Main courses: $18 fixed-price breakfast; $5.95–$10.95 lunch;*

$55 fixed-price dinners. AE, DISC. MC, V. Open: Summer daily 7:30–9a.m., noon – 1:30 p.m., 6 p.m.–8p.m.

John Colter Café Court
$–$$ Colter Bay Village   AMERICAN

In keeping with Colter Bay Village's bargain nature, quick and easy are the hallmarks of the eateries here. The straightforward meals at this sit-down spot, as well at those as the nearby Chuckwagon Steak and Pasta House, are favorites with kids. You can get three meals a day, but breakfast in the deli is self-serve. The lunch and dinner menu includes sandwiches, chicken, pizzas, salads, and soup.

See map p. 170. Across from the marina and visitor center. No phone. Main courses: $3–$7.75 all-day menu. AE, DISC, MC, V. Open: Summer daily 11 a.m.–10 p.m.

The Mural Room
$$$–$$$$ Jackson Lake Junction   AMERICAN

The view of Willow Flats, Jackson Lake, and the jagged Tetons through this restaurant's floor-to-ceiling windows is particularly intoxicating at sundown. Inside, you'll find rough-hewn oak flooring, comfortable seating, and a menu with a wide array of beef, game, lamb, seafood, and poultry dishes. In Jackson Lake Junction, your only other dining options are to make a 76-mile round-trip to Jackson for one of its fine restaurants or to see whether a last-minute cancellation comes up at Jenny Lake Lodge. Watch for the nightly steak or wild game special, or go vegetarian with the Tower of Grilled Vegetables assembled with the help of chive-whipped potatoes and feta cheese. Breakfasts focus on a buffet of fresh fruits, cereals, egg dishes, and grill items.

See map p. 170. Jackson Lake Lodge (near junction of US. Route 89/191/287 and Teton Park Road). ☎ 307-543-2811. Reservations recommended. Main courses: $4.20–$12 breakfast; $8.75–$11.50 lunch; $17.50–$29 dinner. AE, DISC, MC, V. Open: Summer daily 6 a.m.–10 p.m.

Peaks Restaurant
$$$–$$$$ Signal Mountain   AMERICAN

This full-service dining room has great views of both Signal Mountain and Jackson Lake. The menu isn't bad either, with daily specials based on trout or salmon, and regular offerings ranging from elk medallions to New York strip steaks and shrimp scampi. The bar has one of the few televisions in the park, so this place is packed and noisy during the broadcasts of major sporting events. In addition to the main dining room, a coffee shop — the Trapper Grill — serves breakfast and lunch in an informal setting.

See map p. 170. Signal Mountain Lodge (Teton Park Road near junction with US. Route 89/191/287). ☎ 307-543-2831. Reservations accepted only on Mother's Day. Main courses: $6–$8.25 breakfast; $6.25–$13.50 lunch; $14–$30 dinner. AE, DISC, MC, V. Open: Summer daily 7–11 a.m., 11 a.m.–5:30 p.m., and 5:30–10 p.m.

Pioneer Grill

$$–$$$ Jackson Lake Junction AMERICAN

For a no-frills dinner, the Pioneer Grill in Jackson Lake Lodge is the place to go. The atmosphere is 1950s soda fountain, and the entrees are light and inexpensive when compared to those found at the Mural Room up the hall. The grill is open for three meals a day and keeps kids happy with their own menu. Be careful at breakfast: The "cowboy helping" of huckleberry pancakes could leave you too full to move. The nearby Blue Heron lounge is a great place for a drink, and the only place in the lodge with a television.

See map p. 170. Near junction of US. Route 89/191/287 and Teton Park Road.
☎ *307-543-2811. Main courses: $3.30–$7.95 breakfast; $7.25–$10 lunch; $13–$18 dinner. AE, DISC, MC, V. Open: Summer daily 6 a.m.–10 p.m.*

Restaurants outside the park

Sweetwater Restaurant

$$$$ Jackson NOUVEAU AMERICAN

This turn-of-the-20th-century log home was converted into a restaurant back in 1976, and the locals have never regretted it. Some describe the food as eclectic, others say it's regional with a Greek influence. I just say it's good — very good. The stuffed chicken breast is always reliable, and I can't decide if I prefer the herb-crusted rack of lamb or the garlic mashed potatoes served on the side. Rainbow trout also is on the menu, and the chef decides daily how to prepare it.

85 S. King. ☎ *307-733-3553. Reservations recommended. Main courses: $8–$12 lunch; $16–$24 dinner. AE, DC, DISC, MC, V. Open: 11:30 a.m.– 2:30 p.m.; 6–9:30 p.m.*

Fast Facts: Grand Teton

Area Code

The area code is **307**.

ATM

Banks in Jackson, Jackson Lake Lodge, Colter Bay Village, Dornans at Moose, and Flagg Ranch have ATMs.

Emergency

In emergencies, dial **911** or **307-739-3300**.

Fees

Entrance fees are $20 per car per week (good for entry to both Grand Teton and Yellowstone national parks), $10 per

hiker/biker per week, and $15 per motorcycle per week.

Fishing License

A Wyoming state license is required, which you can purchase at sporting good stores in Jackson or at park marinas.

Hospitals

Grand Teton Medical Clinic at Jackson Lake Lodge is open mid-May to mid-Oct (☎ 307-543-2514). The nearest hospital is St. John's Hospital in Jackson (☎ 307-733-3636).

Information

For information, write to Grand Teton National Park, P.O. Drawer 170, Moose, WY 83012, call ☎ 307-739-3300, or look on the Internet at www.nps.gov/grte.

Pharmacies

You can find pharmacies in most major Jackson grocery and discount stores. Also look in Stone Drug, at 830 W. Broadway, Jackson (☎ 307-733-6222).

Post Office

Branches are located at Moose, Moran, and Kelly, as well as in Jackson.

Road Conditions and Weather

To find out the weather, call ☎ 1-888-996-7623. Call 307-739-3611 in winter.

Time

The park is on mountain time.

Chapter 13

Mount Rainier National Park

● ●

In This Chapter

▶ Discovering a real volcano
▶ Planning your trip
▶ Exploring the mountain and glaciers
▶ Finding the best rooms and meals

● ●

*I*n a state with more than its share of heady alpine vistas and dense evergreen forests, Mount Rainier is the relative new kid on the block. Whereas most of the mountains that comprise the Cascade Range are 12 million years old, Rainier is a geologic youngster at an age of about 1 million years. Rainier certainly has packed a lot into its short life, though, not only standing as Washington's tallest peak but also harboring the greatest concentration of glaciers of any single mountain in the Lower 48.

Gazing at the peak, you wouldn't guess that Mount Rainier is an active volcano. No steam vents are obvious to the naked eye, and you don't see jagged lava beds, like those at Craters of the Moon National Monument in Idaho. What you do see are patches of white that represent 25 major glaciers that are slowly, but steadily, slipping down from the mountain's 14,410-foot summit. Roughly 36 square miles of the mountain's surface consist of glacial ice and perennial snowfields that hide Mount Rainier's lava underpinnings.

Not surprisingly, folks come to Mount Rainier National Park simply to gawk at the mountain and glaciers. But the more adventurous also frolic in snowfields or vanish into the woods along the mountain's hundreds of miles of trails.

No matter where you find yourself in the park, you're never very far from a view of the summit. As an added bonus, the mountain itself provides great views of some of the Cascade Range's other volcanic peaks, all charter members of the Ring of Fire, a lava-spitting fraternity that rims the Pacific Ocean. From an overlook near the Sunrise area on the mountain's northeastern flanks, for example, you can see the Hood,

Baker, and Adams mounts. Not visible, but 165 miles to the south, stand the crumpled remains of Mount St. Helens, a ring member that blew its top in 1980.

To stand on the flanks or in the shadow of beautiful Mount Rainier is an awesome experience. Where the dazzling glaciers and snowfields melt away, towering old-growth forests of Alaska yellow cedar, hemlocks, and red cedar blanket the terrain. In the northwest corner of the park near the Carbon River Valley, you even find a section of temperate rain forest much like that found in nearby Olympic National Park.

Must-See Attractions

Only one main road runs through the park. Here's where you should stop along the way between points A (Longmire) and B (Sunrise):

- **Longmire:** The park's oldest developed area is just 7 miles inside the Nisqually Entrance. You can also find a good park museum, as well as the National Park Inn and Wilderness Information Center for planning backcountry treks.

- **Narada Falls:** These beautiful falls plummet 168 feet through a lush, green forest. The water cascades over a wall of lava left over from one of Rainier's periodic eruptions.

- **Paradise:** The setting surrounding this historic inn, known as Paradise, on the southern flanks of Rainier is gorgeous enough, but the sweeping fields of wildflowers that arise as the snows melt in late June take your breath away. A short hike leads to an overlook of the Nisqually Glacier, the most accessible of the park's glaciers.

- **Reflection Lakes:** On clear days, these lakes, located south of Paradise on the road to Ohanapecosh, offer up mirror images of the mountains and skies above. For the best photo of Rainier and her reflection, head to the east end of the lake parking area.

- **Sunrise:** This is the highest point in the park that you can reach by car. From this 6,400-foot base camp meander more than a dozen hiking trails, including a link to the Wonderland Trail that winds 93 miles around the mountain.

Planning Ahead

For information before you go, write Superintendent, Mount Rainier National Park, Tahoma Woods, Star Route, Ashford, WA 98304-9751; call ☎ **360-569-2211** or 360-569-2177 (TTD); or check the park's Web site at www.nps.gov/mora.

When to go and how long to stay

If you're like me and enjoy crisp nights and cool days that make for great hiking, fall is the best time to visit Rainier. Barring an early season snow-storm, trails are in top-notch condition, the park's few hardwood tree species (red alder, Pacific dogwood, and three species of maple) toss bursts of color into the coniferous forests, crowds are diminished, and rotting huckleberries add an interesting pungent smell to the air. But keep in mind that the likelihood of rain increases in September and October, and heavy snows that can close park roads down can start in October or early November and last through the middle or end of May.

The Pacific Northwest is one of the wetter places in the United States; snow, rain, and clouds come with the territory. July and August can be exceptions. During these two months, rain is infrequent and tempera-tures enjoyable, with highs in the 70s. If you abhor crowds, you may want to avoid the park during the summer months, when the majority of Mount Rainier's 2 million annual visitors show up. If you do come at this time, avoid the full brunt of the summer's crowds by visiting at midweek.

Plan to spend at least two days here. If you're into long hikes or want to visit the Carbon River Valley, set aside at least three days.

Advance reservations

As with a visit to any national park, the key to a successful Rainier trip is to make lodging plans early. If you don't, you may spend most of your trip driving to the park from far away. Paradise Inn and the National Park Inn are the only two hotels in the park, and they're very popular. Call about six months in advance for a room at the Paradise Inn and even earlier for a summer stay at the National Park Inn, which has only 25 rooms.

What to pack

Having rain gear here isn't quite as important as it is in Olympic National Park, but you won't regret having some when the weather turns wet. Spring and fall tend to be wetter than summer. In general, always be pre-pared for inclement weather, because Mount Rainier makes its own.

Paradise is a great place in winter for slipping and sliding on the snow. So if you're heading to the park in winter with kids, **don't forget an inner tube or plastic sled or saucer;** wood toboggans and sleds with metal runners are prohibited to protect sliders during collisions. No need to inflate the tube before you leave; the Jackson Visitor Center has a compressed air hose available on weekends. For more tips on what to pack for your vacation, see Chapter 8.

Getting There

Off the beaten path, but not too far, Mount Rainier is somewhat close to Seattle and Tacoma. Most folks head for the Nisqually Entrance because of its proximity to Longmire and Paradise. Plus, Nisqually is the only

Mount Rainier National Park

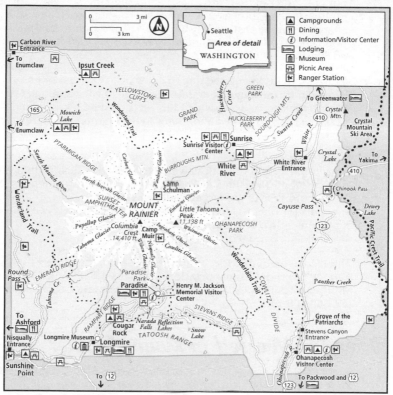

entrance open year-round. As you may imagine, waits can be long here, but you can usually beat the traffic if you enter the park by 10 a.m.

Driving in

The Nisqually Entrance is about 87 miles from Seattle via Interstate 5 and State Routes 7 and 706. Tacoma is about 55 miles from Nisqually via State Routes 7 and 706. The White River Entrance Station, the closest to Sunrise, is 85 miles from Seattle via routes Interstate 5, Interstate 405, Washington 169 south to Enumclaw, and then Washington 410 to the park.

From Portland, Oregon, 136 miles from the Nisqually Entrance, follow Interstate 5 north to Exit 68 and turn right on U.S. Route 12 to Morton, where you head north on Highway 7 to Elbe and then east on State Route 706 past Ashford to the park. You can head for Mount Rainier's northwestern corner and the Carbon River Entrance via Washington 165, but you can't reach Sunrise, Paradise, or Longmire from here because Carbon River Road dead-ends after 6 miles. You can, however, reach a trailhead that leads to the base of Carbon Glacier.

Your only other options are to arrive through the Stevens Canyon Entrance in the southeastern corner via Washington 123 or, during the summer, from the east via Washington 410 and Chinook Pass. This option gives you a choice of heading north to the White River Entrance and Sunrise or south to the Stevens Canyon Entrance.

 Most park roads are closed due to snow from October or early November through middle or late May. The only exception is the Nisqually Entrance Road, which has restricted hours in winter. See "Learning the Lay of the Land," later in the chapter for more details.

Flying in

The closest airport (85 miles away) is the Seattle Tacoma International Airport (☎ 800-544-1965 or 206-431-4444), often referred to as "Sea-Tac." Most of the major airlines and car rental agencies are here; see the Appendix for their toll-free numbers. From the airport, you can link to State Routes 167, 161, and 706, or State Routes 507, 7, and 706 to reach the Nisqually Entrance.

Three companies provide shuttle service from the airport to the park: **Rainier Overland Transportation Company** (☎ 360-569-0851), **Rainier Shuttle** (☎ 360-569-2331), and **Ashford Mountain Center Shuttle** (☎ 360-569-2604).

Orienting Yourself in Mount Rainier

In general, you can get just about anywhere in Mount Rainier National Park, but not always easily. You have to earn your views, either on foot or by persevering down a long and winding road.

State Route 706 runs along the southern edge of the park. Between Nisqually Entrance and Paradise, State Route 706 is known locally as the **Longmire to Paradise Road**; between Paradise and Ohanapecosh, it's known locally as **Stevens Canyon Road;** going north from Ohanapecosh, it's known as **Highway 123** until Cayuse Pass, at which point it becomes **Washington 410** or **Mather Memorial Parkway** until it runs out of the park. Off of Washington 410 is the access road to Sunrise, which passes the White River Entrance station and the White River campground.

A few short roads wind along the park's western side. The **Westside Road** begins a mile inside the Nisqually Entrance. At one time, this road ran 13 miles north, passing several creeks and hiking trails. But floods along Fish Creek forced the closure of the road about 3 miles north of Nisqually. Two other spurs access the park's northwest corner: **Washington 165,** running 27 miles from Enumclaw to Mowich Lake and its campground, and **Carbon River Road,** jogging off 165 just after you cross the Carbon River south of Wilkeson and running into the park through the Carbon River Entrance. All three roads are seasonal.

Rainier has three main visitor areas: **Longmire,** located not far from the Nisqually Entrance; **Paradise,** east of Longmire, on the south flank of the mountain; and **Sunrise,** on the eastern shoulder of the mountain. Although you travel only 7 miles from the Nisqually Entrance to Longmire, the historic heart of the park, you have to go another 12 miles to Paradise and another 50 miles to Sunrise. Visitor centers are in Paradise, Sunrise, and Ohanapecosh (see "Finding information after you arrive," later in this chapter). Longmire, Paradise, and Sunrise all have something to offer tourists (see "Exploring the top attractions," later in this chapter); Ohanapecosh has an interesting name, but not much else in terms of facilities. It does, however, sit amid a beautiful old-growth forest, and several popular trails start here, including the Hot Springs Nature Trail and the Silver Falls Trail.

 Trying to squeeze in stops and walks at the main visitor areas makes for a very long day — not only because of the abundance of things to do but also because heavy traffic can jam the limited road system in summer. Still, if you stay at Paradise and get on the road early in the morning, you can visit Sunrise and Longmire and return to Paradise in time to stroll past the Nisqually Glacier.

 If you enter the park through the Nisqually Entrance late in the morning on a summer day, watch for a sign on the right side of the road indicating that the Paradise parking lot is full. If you see this sign, you'll have to head someplace else or walk at least a mile up the road to the inn. This occurs frequently on weekends and especially on holiday weekends when the weather is nice. Enter the park by 10 a.m., though, and you should be all right.

All is not lost if you do encounter this illuminated sign. You can head through the park to Sunrise and hit Paradise on your way back. Or take a hike around Reflection Lakes and hope the crowds ease by the time you're ready to head over to Paradise.

 Come winter with its heavy snows, getting around is tough. Most park roads are closed due to snow from October or early November through middle or late May. The only exception is the Nisqually Entrance Road, which has restricted hours. When snow falls, plows are out by 6 a.m. to open this road from the Nisqually Entrance to Longmire, and the road from Longmire to Paradise usually is open by 10 a.m.

Arriving in the Park

You'll probably head to the year-round Nisqually Entrance in the southwestern corner. Of all the points of entry, Nisqually is closest to the park's visitor centers and lodgings.

Finding information after your arrive

The park has four visitor centers:

- ✔ **Henry M. Jackson Memorial Visitor Center** (☎ 360-569-6036): This center is a must-stop for anyone heading to Paradise. Inside are exhibits tracing the park's natural and cultural history, as well as telescopes you can use free of charge to search the mountain for climbers heading up or down. This center is open daily from mid-June to early September, 10 a.m. to 6 p.m. and then only on weekends and holidays from October through April.

- ✔ **Ohanapecosh Visitor Center** (☎ 360-569-6046): Located in the southeastern corner of the park, this center is open daily from late June to early September 9 a.m. to 6 p.m.

- ✔ **Sunrise Visitor Center** (☎ 360-569-2211, ext. 2357): This center on the eastern flank of Rainier focuses on Rainier's geologic history and future. As with the Paradise center, you can also use free telescopes here to scan the mountain activity, human or volcanic, although if you see the latter, you're not in a very good place. Open daily from late June to mid September 9 a.m. to 6 p.m.

- ✔ **Longmire Museum** (☎ 360-569-2211, ext. 3314). Inside this museum located at Longmire, you find a visitor center, open daily June to early September from 9 a.m. to 5 p.m. In addition to dispensing park-wide information, the museum's exhibits tell the park's human history, as well as some natural history.

Paying fees

The fees for entering Mount Rainier National Park are $10 per vehicle for seven days or $5 per person (on foot, motorcycle, or bicycle) for seven days. A $30 annual pass covers entrance fees to the park for one year from the month of purchase. Of course, if you have a parks pass, you don't need to pay the entrance fee. See Chapter 8 for information on the National Park Pass and Chapter 7 for the lowdown on Golden Age and Golden Access Passports.

You don't need to pay a fee for backcountry use, but you must pay one to climb the mountain ($30 per person annually) or to stay in one of the backcountry sites ($20 per party of up to 12 individuals for 1 to 14 nights), which require reservations. You can obtain information and permits from the **Longmire Wilderness Information Center** (☎ 360-569-HIKE) or the **White River Wilderness Information Center** (☎ 360-569-6030) located at the White River Entrance. If you plan to climb in the park, you can get a permit at the ranger station in Paradise. Permits also can be obtained at the **Wilkeson Wilderness Information Center** (☎ 360-569-6020) outside the northwest corner of the park in downtown Wilkeson.

Getting Around Mount Rainier

Unless you're walking or can fly, the only way to tour Mount Rainier National Park is to take the roads that skirt the flanks of this magnificent mountain. No road neatly and completely circumnavigates Rainier. The park doesn't have a public transportation system; you need a car to get around.

Remembering Safety

If you visit in winter, be prepared for winter driving conditions. You need snow tires or all-season radials on your rig to manage the snowy and icy roads. State law also requires that you carry chains when traveling in mountainous terrain, and a shovel wouldn't be a bad idea, either, if you're determined to reach Paradise.

Remember that Mount Rainier is a living and breathing volcano. You may not see it exhaling from where you're standing, but on some parts of the mountain, steam vents come through the earth's surface. Chances are that you won't ever see Rainier blow its top during your lifetime. But just the same, you may want to keep the following in mind:

- ✔ **Avalanches:** With so much snow and glacial ice in the park, avalanches happen. They are hard to predict, but you should be okay if you stay off steep slopes following heavy snowstorms.

- ✔ **Glacial outbursts:** If you're walking along a river and see a noticeable rise in the water level or if you hear a roaring sound like a locomotive, head to higher ground immediately. A glacial outburst may have unleashed a wall of water, mud, and rocks that could be heading your way.

- ✔ **Volcanic eruptions:** An earthquake is usually a precursor to a volcanic eruption. Another signal can be jets of steam venting from the mountain's flanks. In either case, seismic monitoring would indicate increased volcanic activity and rangers will provide you with plenty of advance notice if that's the case.

Before you lose any sleep over the possibility of a volcanic eruption, allow me to toss some perspective your way. Although at least two minor eruptions occurred on Mount Rainier in the 1800s, the last significant eruption occurred about 500 years ago. Plus, the volcano likely will give off some early warning signals that a major eruption is on the way. In the case of Mount St. Helens, a sister volcano that erupted in 1980, scientists noted warnings two months before the actual eruption.

For additional tips on how to ensure a safe park visit, see Chapter 8.

Exploring the Top Attractions

Sure, Mount Rainier is an active (albeit soundly sleeping) volcano, but much more than just a volcano awaits you here. The park has incredible glaciers and wonderfully thick forests for hiking and camping. And if you look around, you find some really cool waterfalls (particularly in late spring and early summer during the height of the snowmelt) and historically significant structures.

Carbon Glacier

It's big, it's bad, it's white, and it's right in front of you. No, not Moby Dick. I'm talking about the Carbon Glacier. This river of ice (at 700 feet thick) is accepted as the thickest glacier in the Lower 48, as well as the country's lowest elevation glacier — its snout creeps down to just about 3,600 feet above sea level. Best of all, a relatively short, 4-mile hike from the Ipsut Creek Campground in the park's northwestern corner leads you right to it. (See Carbon Glacier Trail, under "Taking a hike," later in this chapter.)

 For a two- or three-night trip, hike up to the Carbon Glacier, over to Mowich Lake via the Spray Park Trail, and back to your starting point at the Ipsut Creek Campground via the Wonderland Trail.

 Before you set out on the drive to the Carbon River Entrance, check with a ranger to see whether the road beyond the entrance is open, because the river frequently washes it out.

See map p. 199. The Ipsut Creek Campground is 5 miles from the Carbon River Entrance (from Wilkeson on Washington 165 northwest of the park, drive Carbon River Road 13 miles to the entrance).

Longmire

This community was named after James Longmire, who, in 1883, went in search of his horse and stumbled upon the nearby mineral springs. Recognizing a veritable gold mine when he saw one, Longmire built a resort of sorts around the springs. The resort is now gone, but you can follow the Trail of Shadows to the still active, but relatively cool, hot springs. This easy, ½-mile trail features interpretive panels on the Longmire family and the occasional Park Service employee dressed in period garb pretending to be James Longmire.

Here you also find the 25-room National Park Inn, the Wilderness Information Center, and the **Longmire Museum.** Open daily from 9 a.m. to 4 p.m., the museum is free and features exhibits on wildlife, climbers, and Native Americans, as well as fascinating photographs that show the ebb and flow of some of the mountain's glaciers. You can pick up a map for a self-guided tour of the area's Historic Landmark District, designated in 1997; the tour, which isn't long, reveals some interesting tidbits about Longmire's past.

See map p. 199. Longmire is 7 miles east of the Nisqually Entrance on the park's main road.

Narada Falls

The Paradise River falls 168 feet at Narada Falls over hard andesite lava, a substance that provides a glimpse of the mountain's volcanic underpinnings. For a good (and dry) camera angle of the falls, hike down to the base of the falls and go a bit farther along the trail beyond the observation point. The parking lot above the falls has several picnic tables, making this area a good place to stop for lunch.

See map p. 199. Narada Falls is 4 miles west of Paradise on the park's main road.

Paradise

No place in the park packages a Rainier summer vacation quite like Paradise, which has glaciers to gaze at, an active volcano, hundreds of miles of trails, spectacular subalpine wildflower meadows, and a ranger station and visitor center. To explore the area, follow the Nisqually Vista Trail (see the following "Taking a hike" section) to the glacier of the same name or hike to Alta Vista, a 1¾-mile trek that pays off with a great view of the Tatoosh Range to the south. *Note:* It's often late June before melting snows open many of the trails and nourish the wildflowers.

Also on the site is the historic Paradise Inn, dating from 1917 when a group of Tacoma businessmen realized that they could make money off the mountain. This inn is a marvel of rustic woodwork and ingenuity. Alaska yellow cedars that survived a fire in the Silver Forest below Paradise were used for its construction. You may scratch your head looking at the cedar beams and rafters holding up the roof that were put in place without nails; the notched pieces are held in place by weight. (See "Where to Stay," later in the chapter, for information on the inn.)

See map p. 199. Paradise is 18 miles east of the Nisqually Entrance on the park's main road.

Reflection Lakes

If the skies are clear and the winds calm, this area provides a great photo opportunity. A 2½-mile hike wraps around the lakes, leading through lush meadows that explode with wildflowers in the summer. I've also seen black bears near here, so keep your eyes open and camera ready.

See map p. 199. The lakes are 3½ miles east of Paradise on the park's main road, known locally as the Stevens Canyon Road.

Sunrise

At 6,400 feet, Sunrise is the highest point in the park that you can reach by car. Although this piece of trivia may be forgettable, the in-your-face view of the Emmons Glacier, the largest ice flow on the mountain, is not.

Once upon a time, Sunrise was a thriving summer community of rental cabins. Now the spot serves as a kind of environmentally sensitive way station for backcountry travelers and day hikers. You won't find any rooms for rent in the Sunrise lodge, which is reserved for concession employees, and the snack bar is overpriced and struggles to keep up with summer's crowds. But the view of Mount Rainier from Sunrise is stunning, and hiking possibilities abound, with trails suited for both novices and long-distance warriors. You can take a self-guided, 1½-mile walk along Sourdough Ridge that introduces you to the environment and perhaps provides a glimpse of some of the park's mountain goats. Other options include the hike to Frozen Lake and the Mount Fremont Lookout Station; long-distance hikers can jump onto the Wonderland Trail. (See information on the Mount Freemount Lookout Station and the Wonderland Trail in the "Taking a hike" section.)

The road to Sunrise is open only from July to late September.

See map p. 199. Sunrise is 16 miles from the Mather Memorial Parkway (also know as Highway 410) in the northeast corner of the park.

Taking a hike

Mount Rainier National Park has almost 250 miles of maintained trails, including half-day hikes, long-distance treks, and family-friendly walks that will interest, but not exhaust, youngsters. This section includes just a small sampling of the trails that Rainier offers.

Snow still covers many of the trails in June. July and August are the driest and warmest months in the park, although you can see snow on trails as late as mid-July. Late July through early September is the most reliable time of year for hiking, ensuring little snow on trails and decent weather.

A hike in the Carbon River section of the park is cool, literally, because you walk through dense temperate rain forest. The Carbon River Rain Forest Nature Trail, which makes a short loop through the forest, is perfect for younger kids.

Carbon Glacier Trail

You can get so close to the Carbon Glacier along this trail that it's scary. In fact, rangers warn you not to get too near because rock and ice fall off the glacier's snout fairly regularly. But if you want to see a glacier up close, this hike is a must, and one that's relatively short in light of the payoff. From this trail, you also can move on past the glacier and continue deep into Mount Rainier's backcountry.

Distance: 7 miles round-trip. Level: Moderate; the elevation gain to Carbon Glacier is 1,200 feet and to Moraine Park is 3,300 feet. Access: Ipsut Creek Campground, 5 miles inside the park's northeast entrance.

Glacier Basin Trail

This interesting hike mixes natural and cultural attractions. During the early stretch, watch for rusting remains of a mining operation that rooted into the mountain's flanks in the late 1800s. The trail follows an old road up past the headwaters of the White River. After 1 mile, veer to the left onto 1-mile Emmons Moraine Trail that leads to an overlook with beautiful views of the Emmons Glacier. Just past the junction of the main trail with the Buroughs Mountain Trail, you arrive at Glacier Basin Camp. From the camp, it's not far to Camp Schurman in the crook of the Emmons and Winthrop glaciers, where you may be able to spot some climbers heading up Mount Rainier or perhaps some mountain goats.

Distance: 7 miles round-trip. Level: Moderate to difficult. Access: At the far end of the White River Campground in Loop D.

Mount Fremont Lookout Station

Thanks to its southern exposure, this trail is one of the first to lose its snow in the summer. In early to mid-July, you may encounter some small snowfields on the way to Frozen Lake, but past the lake, the trail is usually clear. Mount Rainier is a constant companion over your left shoulder as you head to the lookout tower. Keep your eyes on the slopes above and below you for wildlife; if you're lucky, you may spot some of the park's mountain goats. The lookout tower, which was built in the 1930s, isn't open for entry, but you can climb up onto its deck (although doing so isn't necessary for a beautiful view). To the north, Grand Park sprawls below you, and way off toward the horizon rises the North Cascade Range. Far off to the west are the snow-capped peaks of Olympic National Park.

Distance: 5½ miles round-trip. Level: Moderate. Access: North side of the Sunrise parking lot.

Nisqually Vista Trail

This loop trail delights both young and old with its great views of the snout of the Nisqually Glacier. You may spot pocket gophers rooting through the meadow vegetation. In late summer, you can snack on the blueberry and huckleberry bushes — as long as you can reach the berries without leaving the paved trail. From the trail, you can see the entire length of the glacier, as well as the pile of boulders being pushed downhill by it. Pick up a self-guided brochure for the trail at the Paradise Visitor Center or at the trailhead.

Distance: 1¼ miles round-trip. Level: Easy. Access: Just north of the Henry M. Jackson Memorial Visitor Center at Paradise.

Wonderland Trail

This hike is time-consuming; many trekkers spend 10 to 14 days on this trail, which wraps around the base of Mount Rainier. You need to approach this hike carefully because of the time and logistics it requires. Some hikers even cache food at various points along the trail before they head down the path. On the way to completing the circle this trail creates, you pass through subalpine meadows, ford or cross over glacial streams, funnel through mountain passes, and walk through towering forests. If you don't have two weeks to spare, you can use connecting trails to create a shorter trek. Historically, rangers used this route to patrol the park and some of the original ranger cabins still remain along the trail. If you're determined to make the entire circuit, contact one of the park's Wilderness Information Centers for details on caching food along the way.

Vegetation and soil in subalpine meadows are easily damaged. To protect these fragile resources, hike only on trails and don't take shortcuts.

See map p. 199. Distance: 93 miles round-trip. Level: Strenuous; 7,000-foot elevation gain. Access: Longmire, Paradise, Sunrise, Mowich Lake, or Carbon River.

One-day wonder

Thanks to its gorgeous setting on the flanks of Mount Rainier, the **Paradise Inn** should be your base camp for a park stay (see "Where to Stay" later in this chapter). After you've checked in, though, where do you go? What follows is my recommendation for a one-day itinerary. Unless otherwise mentioned, see "Exploring the top attractions," earlier in the chapter, for information on the various sights.

The concessionaire that operates the Paradise Inn is debating whether to close the inn in 2006, and possibly 2007, to perform electrical and plumbing upgrades. If this closure comes about, seek a room at the National Park Inn or one of the motels outside the Nisqually or Ohanapecosh entrances.

Plan on getting an early start, preferably by starting with the breakfast buffet in the **Paradise Inn** dining room by 7 a.m. (While ordering breakfast, you may want to also order a picnic lunch — a much cheaper alternative

---

Capturing the park on film

Keep a photographic record of your visit to Mount Rainier, and your family and friends may think you visited several different national parks. At Paradise, you can get some great, brilliantly white close-up shots of snow-shrouded Rainier itself. Head a few miles west of Paradise to Narada Falls and capture a wonderful waterfall in action. Head a few miles east of Paradise for a stop at Reflection Lakes, and you can snap a shimmering reflection of Rainier in the water. Journey to the park's northwestern corner along the Carbon River and find a lush example of temperate rain forest, much as you would see in nearby Olympic National Park. At Longmire, you can capture the historic log architecture. Early summer is a particularly good time for photography because the runoff from melting snow nourishes acre after acre of wildflowers and generates cascading waterfalls throughout the park. Thanks to the diversity of the landscape, you need different film speeds — slow to capture the low-light forest settings and fast for the bright snowfields.

Stepping off trails onto fragile wildflower meadows won't get you a better picture, but it could get you a lecture (and possibly a ticket) from a park ranger!

to the lunch counter at Sunrise.) After breakfast, if you're a caffeine addict, snatch one more cup of coffee from the mezzanine coffee table on your way out.

First, head east on the park road to **Reflection Lakes,** with their picture-perfect scenery. If the weather is clear, you can get a great shot of Rainier's reflection in the water. Walk along the lakes' edges to glimpse some wildflowers, but because you have plenty of time for flower gazing down the road, don't dally too long.

Next stop: **Sunrise,** the crossroads of many hiking trails. You can jump onto the Wonderland Trail, take a self-guided walk along Sourdough Ridge, or head off in several other directions. I recommend the trail to the **Mount Fremont Lookout** (see "Taking a hike" earlier in the chapter). If you start your hike by 9 a.m., you can easily return to Sunrise by noon. If you were wise and ordered a picnic lunch back at Paradise, dig into it upon returning. If you didn't, your only option is the overpriced snack bar.

After lunch, head back south in the general direction of Paradise but stop at the **Grove of the Patriarchs** just north of the Stevens Canyon Entrance Station. The flat, 1½-mile round-trip hike through the grove takes no more than an hour and leads you past towering stands of Douglas fir and western red cedar trees nearing 1,000 years in age. You find the park's biggest red cedar tree on an island in the Ohanapecosh River; a trail reaches the island by a suspension bridge. The milder, moister climate in this corner of the park is responsible for the moss-covered forest floor and its sword fern, salmonberry, and oak fern.

From the grove, head south toward the Stevens Canyon Entrance and leave the park on Washington 123. When you reach U.S. 12, 5 miles from the entrance station, turn right and head to Packwood, where, after stopping for some ice cream, you want to head west on Skate Creek Road, which is a 25-mile shortcut back to the Nisqually Entrance. Why do I suggest that you leave the park to return to the park? Because Skate Creek Road offers a much quicker return to Nisqually than staying inside the park and retracing your morning's winding tracks. Skate Creek Road delivers you back to Washington 706, just outside the Nisqually Entrance.

After you reenter the park, head 7 miles to **Longmire** for a quick walk through the historic district. If you think that you may want to come back to Rainier for a backpacking trip, check into the Wilderness Information Center, located in the old administration building, for information and a wilderness trip planner. The museum here is particularly good.

From Longmire, you have a 12-mile drive back to Paradise, where you should arrive in time for a tour of the **Henry M. Jackson Memorial Visitor Center** or a stroll along the **Nisqually Vista Trail,** a relaxing dinner at the inn, and a gorgeous sunset (on a clear day).

Spotting the local wildlife

You can never predict where you'll see Mount Rainier's animals. Heading down the road to Sunrise one morning, just past Reflection Lakes, I saw a **black bear** just off the road munching on vegetation. The bear wasn't in the least bothered by us sitting in our car, not 10 feet away. He contentedly ate as I unpacked my 300mm lens and captured some photos.

Although you, too, may spot one of the park's black bears this way, a more reliable place to look for them in late summer is near Bench and Snow lakes just east of Louise Lake. A 1¼-mile-long trail runs from the road to the lakes.

Nothing quite compares to the sight of a **mountain goat** nimbly hopping along a steep rocky cliff. Unfortunately, you're not likely to see any goats during your visit, at least not up close, because they're highly elusive and shy. If you want to try, Rampart Ridge is a good place to search. You can access the ridge from a trail near the Trail of the Shadows at Longmire. Van Trump Park and Comet Falls, reached via a trail near Christine Falls, are two other good areas to look for goats in late June and early July.

Elk also roam the park. They're not the native Olympic species but, rather, imports from Yellowstone. After hunters killed the region's native elk, a trainload of Yellowstone elk arrived near the park in 1912 for a restocking project. Another batch from Wyoming, taken from an elk refuge near Jackson, arrived in 1933.

Cougars, which rely on the park's elk and mule deer populations for sustenance, are even more secretive than the mountain goats. About the only time you hear of the big cats is when they come down to the lowlands, and the campgrounds are temporarily closed until they leave the area.

No doubt, when you reach the park's subalpine and alpine zones around Paradise and Sunrise, you'll spot the **hoary marmots** that claim the meadows as their own. Somewhat used to people, these critters let you get surprisingly close before lumbering off. Sharing the meadows and rocky slopes with the marmots are **pikas** (a small relative of rabbits) and the ubiquitous **chipmunks** and **squirrels.**

A strange, and usually out-of-sight, park creature is the **sooty grouse** (also called the blue grouse). These birds are cousins to sage grouse found in Grand Teton National Park. Males have a distinctive mating call that they combine with a dance during which they fan their tails and puff up yellow neck sacks to court females.

A fun bird to watch is the **American Dipper,** which forages for food on stream bottoms. You often can spot them perched on rocks in midstream, gazing into the water for a bite to eat. When they spy something, they dive in. Most of the time, they appear to be swimming upstream after a meal, although sometimes they manage to walk on the stream bottoms if the current isn't too swift.

Ranger programs

With the bulk of Mount Rainier's visitors arriving during summer, and with so many hiking trails winding through the park's forests and subalpine and alpine regions, you won't be surprised that most ranger-led activities take place in summer and involve walks. The programs are always changing, so check the park's newspaper for offerings and schedules.

 I recommend the ranger-led walk to Nisqually Vista. This 90-minute hike takes you to a strategic overlook of the glacier — something kids get a kick out of. The ranger discusses the mountain's volcanology and explains the difference between glacial ice and regular ice.

Another glacier-gawking program that I recommend is the two-hour ranger-led hike from the Glacier Basin Trailhead at the White River Campground to the Emmons Glacier, the largest glacier in the Lower 48.

Winter ranger programs are few; however, one good option is the snowshoe walk that originates at the Jackson Memorial Visitor Center. This 1¼-mile walk lasts about two hours and roams the landscape in the Paradise area. Offered twice daily between Christmas and New Year's Day, and then on weekends through mid-April, the walk is limited to 25 people, ages ten and older, and the cost is just $1 for snowshoe rental. Have your own snowshoes? The stroll is free.

Although exceptions exist, you find most nonwalking programs in Paradise. One such example is the video *Perilous Beauty,* which you can view at the Jackson Visitor Center. This interesting, potentially scary video explains how the mountain can unleash a massive mudslide down its flanks without any warning or eruption. I highly recommend this intriguing video if you want to gain an understanding not only of the park, but also of volcanics in general.

If you're not staying in Paradise, either put on your hiking shoes or wait for the weekend when rangers offer programs at the amphitheaters at Ohanapecosh and Cougar Rock and the campfire circle at the White River Campground. During the summer, rangers also present nightly programs at 9 p.m. at Longmire, Paradise, and Ohanapecosh; check the park's newspaper or bulletin boards for topics.

 If you have kids, pick up information on the Junior Ranger Program (see Chapter 7) at the visitor centers.

Keeping active

In addition to hiking, Mount Rainier National Park is a great place for cross-country skiing and mountain climbing.

Cross-country skiing

The park has several cross-country trails. If you're new to the sport, test your balance on Barn Flats, which has a ¾-mile route. Intermediate skiers often head to the Nisqually Vista Loop, which runs 1¼ miles and offers great views of the mountain and Nisqually Glacier. Also marked for intermediates is the 3¾-mile round-trip from Paradise to Narada Falls. Veteran skiers enjoy the Skyline Loop (6 miles) and the Camp Muir Trail (9 miles), although both are unmarked and not suitable for skate-skiing or lightweight classic skis. You can rent skis in Longmire at the **National Park Inn** (☎ 360-569-2411).

Mountain climbing

Think you want to try to summit 14,410-foot Mount Rainier? Call Rainier Mountaineering, one of the country's most respected climbing companies. Just be sure that you're in shape before you pursue this adventure. To attempt a summit climb, you must participate in a one-day climbing school that exposes you to the fundamentals of traveling over snow and using an ice axe to stop yourself from sliding down the mountain, an incredibly helpful skill. If the guides feel that you can handle yourself well on the snow and that you're in good physical shape, you're allowed to join a group aiming for the top. For details and an application form, contact **Rainier Mountaineering**, Post Office Box Q, Ashford, WA 98304 (☎ 888-892-5462 or 360-569-2227). For east side climbs, try **Alpine Ascents International** (☎ 206-378-1927), **American Alpine Institute** (☎ 360-671-1505), **Cascade Alpine Guides** (☎ 800-981-0381), or **Mount Rainier Alpine Guides** (☎ 360-569-2889).

Where to Stay

If a winter visit appeals to you, reserve a room at the National Park Inn at Longmire. This inn is the only in-park lodging available during winter, and from the front doors, you don't have to go far for great cross-country skiing or snowshoeing. Hardier folks can try snow camping, which is allowed throughout most of the park after a thick blanket of snow has accumulated to protect plants. For more information on finding a place to stay, see Chapter 6.

Lodging in the park

National Park Inn
$$–$$$ Longmire

This great little getaway is a good base of operations for winter trips to the park. Located at Longmire, just 7 miles from the Nisqually Entrance, this inn is all that remains of the original 16-cottage, 17-room National Park Inn that burned down in 1929. Fully renovated in 1990, the inn has 25 rooms open year-round. From the inn's front porch, you have a nice view of Mount Rainier. The small guest lounge is a welcoming spot to relax with a book, board game, or refreshment in front of the river rock fireplace. The rooms vary in size, but all come with rustic furniture, wall-to-wall carpeting, and coffeemakers. However, not all have private bathrooms. In the winter, you can rent cross-country skis or snowshoes. The inn's restaurant offers something for everyone.

See map p. 199. Off State Route 706. ☎ **360-569-2275** *reservations only, or 360-569-2211. Fax: 360-569-2770.* www.guestservices.com/rainier. *25 rooms, 18 with bath. Rack rates: $95 double without bath, $129–$177 double with bath. AE, DC, DISC, MC, V.*

Paradise Inn
$$–$$$$ **Paradise**

This rustic lodge, opened with just 33 rooms in 1917 and built from Alaska yellow cedar taken from within the park, offers sweeping views of Mount Rainier and the Nisqually Glacier. Miles of trails and meadows dappled with wildflowers in midsummer makes it a perfect spot to base a Mount Rainier vacation. Cedar-shake siding, huge exposed beams, cathedral ceilings, and oversized rock fireplaces combine to create an idyllic mountain retreat. Age has taken a toll on the structure, sadly. The guest rooms vary in size — some feel barely big enough for packrats, and floors aren't always level — and amenities, so be sure to specify exactly what you want when making reservations. The inn's dining room is anchored by a large fireplace, and the windows with alpine views fill the long walls. For adults, the Glacier Lounge is the perfect spot to relax after a long day on the trail. Kids will probably prefer a seat in front of the fireplace or on the mezzanine playing a game.

See map p. 199. Just east of the Henry M. Jackson Memorial Visitor Center. ☎ **360-569-2275.** *Fax: 360-569-2770. 118 rooms, 98 with bath; 2 suites. Rack rates: $89 double without bath, $134–$188 double with bath; $205 suite. AE, DC, DISC, MC, V. Closed early Oct to mid-May.*

Lodging outside the park

Alexander's Country Inn
$$–$$$$ **Ashford**

This turn-of-the-20th century inn with its signature waterwheel has long welcomed visitors to the park. After a long day of hiking, you can return here for a hearty meal and a dip in the hot tub. Not only does Alexander's have the best accommodations in the area, but also the best dinners. The dining room and a small gift shop consume the first floor, and a large sitting room with a fireplace is on the second. The best guest room is the tower suite, located in a turret with plenty of windows for surveying the surrounding woods. On the grounds are two guest houses that sleep up to eight and feature kitchens.

37515 State Route 706 East. ☎ **800-654-7615** *or 360-569-2300. Fax: 360-569-2323.* www.alexanderscountryinn.com. *TV TEL in guest houses. 7 rooms, 5 suites, 2 guest houses. Rack rates: May–Oct $120 double, $150 suite, $210 guest house; Nov–Apr $99 double, $125 suite, $165 guest house. Rates include full breakfast. MC, V.*

Alta Crystal Resort at Mt. Rainier
$$$$–$$$$$ **Greenwater**

This is the closest lodging to the northeast park entrance and the Sunrise area. Although this condominium resort with wooded grounds is most popular in the winter when skiers flock to nearby Crystal Mountain, you can find plenty to do in the summer, with a heated outdoor pool and nearby hiking trails. A hot tub is set in the woods. Accommodations are in one-bedroom and loft chalets. The former can handle two adults and two young children (under 12), and the latter have bed space for up to six people. All condos feature a full kitchen and fireplace.

68317 Washington 410 East. ☎ *800-277-6475 or 360-663-2500. Fax: 360-663-2556.* www.altacrystalresort.com. *24 units. Nonsmoking. TV TEL. Rack rates: June–Sept $139–$249 (1–4 people). AE, MC, V*

Cedar Creek Treehouse
$$$$ **Ashford**

Swaying 50 feet up amid the limbs of a towering cedar tree, this treehouse offers some of the best views in the area. I mean, how many other lodgings can guarantee you a view of Mount Rainier from your bed? You don't lose track of the tree, either, because the trunk runs up through the kitchen of this treehouse, which features a sleeping loft with two double beds, dining room, observation room, and bathroom. The space isn't sprawling, just 16 feet by 16 feet, but it's incredible and unique. Plus, you get the whole place to yourself; the treehouse isn't staffed.

State Route 706 East (10 miles from the park). ☎ *360-569-2991.* www.cedarcreek treehouse.com. *Sleeps five. Nonsmoking. Rack rates: $250 for two; $25 each additional person. Open: Mar–Oct. Cash, check, MO.*

Storm King Spa at Mount Rainier
$$$ **Ashord**

Nestled in 10 acres of woods, these three cabins, each with its own, distinct personality, offer a charming, secluded retreat after a day in the park. The Raven, a 16-sided yurt design features a gas fireplace, river rock-lined shower, queen bed, and private hot tub. The Eagle boasts a kingsize bed and a "green" shower complete with hanging plants. The Bear is the original circa 1920 homestead that has been gracefully restored to provide three bedrooms, a kitchen and living room with brick fireplace. Each cabin has a private hot tub.

37311 State Route 706 East. ☎ *360-569-2964 or 360-569-2964.* www.stormking spa.com. *3 cabins. Home entertainment system in each. Rack rates: $144–$175. MC, V, Travelers Checks.*

Wellspring Spa and Log Cabins
$$–$$$$$ **Ashford**

Rustic and eclectic sum up this relaxing hideaway in the woods. And the spa does a good job of pampering you, too. The accommodations are a fanciful mix. You have your modern log cabins, which are tucked up against the edge of the forest and feature feather beds, woodstoves, and vaulted ceilings. If you're more adventuresome, request the Nest, where you find a queen-size bed suspended by ropes under a skylight. If that's a bit too much, settle into the Three Bears Cottage, which has rustic log furniture and a full kitchen. Another option is the Treehouse, a wooden structure, about the size of a tent, suspended in a tree with a TV/VCR and fold-out futon. For bigger groups, the Tatoosh Lodge features a large stone fireplace, a whirlpool tub, a waterfall shower, and room for 14. Want to sleep in a greenhouse with a cedar hot tub and wood-fired sauna? You can, but you have to wait until 9 p.m. to have the room to yourself (the hot tub and sauna are available for rental until that hour). Several of the rooms and the cabins come with a breakfast basket. Hot tubs and saunas are an additional $5 per person per hour for guests, $10 per hour for visitors. This New Age retreat isn't for everyone, but it's certainly the most distinctive place to stay in the area.

54922 Kernahan Rd. ☎ *360-569-2514. 4 rooms, 4 log cabins, 3 tent cabins, 1 cottage, 1 treehouse, 1 lodge that sleeps 14. TV in treehouse. Rack rates: $79–$369 double. MC, V.*

Runner-up lodgings

Inn of Packwood

$–$$$ **Packwood**   Just south of the park's Stevens Canyon Entrance, this inn has standard motel rooms as well as kitchen units, plus a heated indoor pool. *13032 U.S. Route 12.* ☎ *877-496-9666 or 360-494-5500.* www.innof packwood.com.

Mountain Meadows Inn

$$$ **Ashford**   This bed-and-breakfast on 11 acres offers 6 rooms and an outdoor spa just 6 miles outside the Nisqually Entrance. You can enjoy evenings on the wraparound porch or in the outdoor hot tub. *28912 State Route 706 East.* ☎ *360-569-2788.* www.mountainmeadowsinn.com.

Mounthaven Resort

$$$–$$$$ **Ashford**   These 10 cabins sleep from three to eight people and offer amenities ranging from kitchenettes to full kitchens and fireplaces. The convenient location is ½ mile from the Nisqually Entrance. *38210 State Route 706 East.* ☎ *800-456-9380 or 360-569-2594.* www.mounthaven.com.

The Nisqually Lodge

$$ Ashford. There's nothing fancy about this chalet-style motel, but its 24 large, clean rooms come with air conditioning, telephones, and TV. You can relax in the hot tub outside or in a small sitting area with a fireplace just off the registration desk. An annex added in the fall of 1999 provides meeting rooms and a laundry. *31609 State Route 706 East.* ☎ *888-674-3554 or 360-569-8804. Fax: 360-569-2435.* www.escapetothemountains.com.

Campgrounds

Mount Rainier has six campgrounds with nearly 600 sites accessible by car. These range from the 18-site Sunshine Point Campground along the Nisqually River in the southwestern corner of the park to the 188-site Ohanapecosh Campground in the southeastern corner.

Reservations (☎ 800-365-CAMP; http://reservations.nps.gov) must be made for the Ohanapecosh and Cougar Rock Campgrounds for stays between the last Monday in June through Labor Day. You can make reservations up to five months in advance. With this one exception, all campgrounds operate on a first-come, first-served basis.

None of the campgrounds offer showers or RV hookups, although you can find showers at Paradise in the basement of the visitor center. All campgrounds except Ipsut Creek and Mowich Lake have potable water.

- ✔ **Cougar Rock Campground:** Just over 2¼ miles northeast of Longmire in the park's southwestern corner, this is one of the more popular campgrounds thanks to its location between Longmire and Paradise. You find 173 sites, including 5 group sites that you can reserve (☎ 360-569-2211, ext. 3301) up to 90 days in advance. Fees are $15 a night in summer, $12 after September 6. Amenities include flush toilets and a dump station for RVs. You can pass evenings by attending ranger talks in the campground's amphitheater. Open from Memorial Day weekend through mid-October.

- ✔ **Ipsut Creek Campground:** Its 30 sites are technically open year-round, but heavy snows and road closures can restrict access to this area 5 miles east of the Carbon River Entrance. The campground has pit toilets only. You find a ranger station and amphitheater here, and weekends feature campfire programs. $8 per site. *Note:* For access, the Park Service recommends high-clearance vehicles.

- ✔ **Mowich Lake Campground:** Near the park's biggest and deepest lake, this campround is located just beyond the end of Washington 165 in the park's northwestern corner. You have to walk about 100 yards from the parking area to reach the camping area, which holds 30 tents. Campsites are free, but amenities are nonexistent, because of a lack of potable water. Only pit toilets are available. However, the lakeside setting and relative isolation is beautiful. You also can jump onto the Wonderland Trail. Open July through mid-October.

✔ **Ohanapecosh Campground:** Eleven miles north of Packwood, this 188-site campground is in a gorgeous stand of old-growth forest. The tall forest canopy mutes the sunlight and the mostly shady atmosphere is refreshing during August's hot weather. Fees are $15 per site during the summer, $12 after September 6. The campground has flush toilets, drinking water, and a dump station for RVs. Open from Memorial Day weekend through mid-October.

✔ **Sunshine Point Campground:** Tucked ¼ mile inside the Nisqually Entrance, this campground is more open than Ohanapecosh, and the melodic gurgling of the nearby Nisqually River is hypnotic when the time comes to call it a night. Each of the 18 sites cost $10 a night. This campground has drinking water, but only pit toilets. Open year-round.

✔ **White River Campground:** This is a great base for hiking. Five miles west of the White River Entrance along the cascading White River, the campground's 112 sites are close to the Wonderland Trail; the trails to Glacier Basin and Emmons Moraine start here. The campground has flush toilets and drinking water. Sites cost $10 a night. Open from late June through mid-September.

Where to Eat

Formal dining in the park is restricted to the National Park Inn at Longmire and the Paradise Inn at Paradise. Expensive snack bars with limited offerings can be found at Sunrise and in the Henry M. Jackson Memorial Visitor Center at Paradise. Outside the park, your options increase extensively.

Restaurants in the park

National Park Inn
$–$$ Longmire AMERICAN

The dining room at this historic inn, just inside the park's Nisqually Entrance, is smaller and cozier than the one at Paradise Inn, even though it seats 90 people. Menus change each year, if not each season, but you usually can order pancakes, French toast, or even biscuits and gravy for breakfast. Lunches are built around burgers and sandwiches. You find New York steaks, trout, salmon, and pasta dishes on the dinner menu.

See map p. 199. Just off State Route 706. ☎ *360-569-2275 reservations only, or 360-569-2411. Reservations suggested for dinner. Main courses: $6–$8 breakfast; $7–$9 lunch; $13–$19 dinner. AE, DISC, DC, MC, V. Open: Daily 7 a.m.–8 p.m. in summer and until 7 p.m. in winter.*

Paradise Inn
$$–$$$$ Paradise AMERICAN

This dining room is the park's most picturesque. The long, rectangular space has windows lining both walls and a massive stone fireplace that dominates the north end of the room. The Paradise buffet — featuring breakfast fare such as fresh fruits, pastries, hot and cold cereals, muffins, and scrambled eggs — is the best deal in the morning at $10.50. If you prefer, you can order omelets made to order, French toast with hazelnuts and blackberry sauce, or oatmeal pancakes. One of the more interesting dinner dishes is Bourbon Buffalo Meatloaf, a hearty main course made from ground sirloin buffalo and served with a sauce made with Jack Daniels' bourbon whiskey and leek mashed potatoes. A buffalo stew also appears on the lunch menu.

Reservations aren't accepted for the 200-seat dining room, so you may end up waiting a bit for a table. If you do, relax in the Glacier Lounge or in front of one of the lobby's fireplaces.

See map p. 199. Located just east of the Henry M. Jackson Memorial Visitor Center. ☎ 360-569-2275. Reservations not accepted. Main courses: $6.50–$10.50 breakfast; $8–$12.50 lunch; $16–$19.50 dinner. AE, DC, DISC, MC, V. Open: 7–9:30 a.m., noon to 2 p.m., 5:30–8 p.m. (until 8:30 p.m. between mid-June through Labor Day).

Restaurants outside the park

Alexander's Country Inn
$$–$$$$ Ashford   AMERICAN

Although this inn's main business comes from overnight guests, the dining room is open to the public and draws crowds with its varied menu that features steak, seafood, and pasta. The trout is as fresh as can be, having come from the trout pond out back, and the rack of lamb coated with a pesto-Dijon sauce, then seared and served over a mushroom-olive ragout and polenta will satisfy any empty stomach. If you like smoked salmon, be sure to try the smoked salmon spread appetizer.

37515 State Rt. 706 E. ☎ 800-654-7615 or 360-569-2300. Reservations suggested. Main courses: $9.25 breakfast; $5.95–$9.95 lunch; $9.95–$23.95 dinner. MC, V. Open: Summer 8 a.m.–9 p.m. In winter open to inn guests during the week; open to the public on weekends.

Copper Creek Inn
$–$$$ Ashford   AMERICAN

Just two miles west of the Nisqually entrance, this historic inn dates to 1915. This low-key, family-friendly restaurant with its cedar plank walls arrived in 1946 and has been feeding visitors ever since. The whiskey still, however, is no longer in use. Steaks, poultry, and fish dominate the dinner menu, burgers and deli sandwiches are offered for lunch, and breakfasts are built around eggs and grill items.

35707 State Route 706 East. ☎ 360-569-2326. Main courses: $6.95–$13.95 breakfast; $6.95–$9.95 lunch; $5.95–$19.95 dinner. DISC, MC, V. Open daily 7 p.m.–9 p.m. summer; Mon-Thurs, noon–7 p.m., Fri, noon–8 p.m., Sat–Sun 7 a.m.–8 p.m. winter months.

Fast Facts: Mount Rainier

Area Code

The area code is **360**.

ATMs

You'll find no ATMs in the park. Look for them in grocery stores in Ashford, Packwood, and Enumclaw.

Emergency

In emergencies, dial **911**.

Fees

Entry fees are $10 per vehicle per week and $5 for walk-ins per week.

Fishing License

Licenses aren't required, although some streams are off-limits. For details, pick up a brochure at a visitor center or check the park's Web site.

Hospitals

The closest hospital is Morton General Hospital, 521 Adams Ave., Morton, WA (☎ 360-496-511.

Information

For information, write to Superintendent, Mount Rainier National Park, Ashford, WA 98304-9751; call ☎ 360-569-2211 or 360-569-2177 (TTY); or look on the Internet at www.nps.gov/mora.

Pharmacies

In Eatonville, the local pharmacy is Kirk's Pharmacy, 104 Mashell Avo N, (☎ 360-832-3121). In Enumclaw the local pharmacy is Rite Aid, 232 Roosevelt Ave (☎ 360-825-2558).

Post Office

A post office is at the National Park Inn at Longmire; from late May to early October you'll also find one at Paradise Inn.

Road Conditions and Weather

For information on road conditions, call ☎ 360-569-2211.

Time Zone

The park is on Pacific time.

Chapter 14

Olympic National Park

● ●

In This Chapter

▶ Introducing three parks in one
▶ Planning your trip
▶ Exploring mountains, beaches, and rain forests
▶ Finding the best hotels and restaurants

● ●

*O*lympic National Park is the perfect park for people who can't decide where to head on vacation. If you're asking yourself whether you should go to the beach or the mountains this year, a trip to Olympic will solve your dilemma. Within its 922,651 acres, the park offers three totally different experiences. The only problem you face is packing for three such different vacations.

Interested in mountains and glaciers? Olympic is capped by a range of sky-scraping, snow-clad mountains that support the lowest-elevation glacier system in the Lower 48. In roughly 40 miles, the park's terrain runs from crashing Pacific Ocean waves to peaks nearly 8,000 feet high. Topped by 7,965-foot-tall Mount Olympus, the park's roof features alpine and sub-alpine communities you can hike through in summer on multiday back-packing treks or kick-and-glide through in winter on cross-country skis.

Love to roam wave-pounded beaches? Olympic boasts 63 miles of some of the most scenic coastline anywhere, thanks to towering *sea stacks* — rock monoliths left behind when the coastline receded under the relentless pounding of the waves — that rise above the foaming surf. Thick conifer-ous forests run up to the edge of the sand-and-cobble beaches, hiding them from the roads and lending some solitude. Although this stretch of Pacific Ocean probably is too cold to enjoy anything but a brief swim on a dare, the water teems with marine life ranging from whales and sea lions to colorful sea stars (starfish). If that's not enough, on clear days you're guaranteed spectacular sunsets thanks to the surf and sea stacks.

Thankfully, you won't find any beachfront homes or seaside burger joints along the park's coast, which is one of the largest sections of wilderness coast in the continental United States.

If neither snow-capped peaks nor surf-swept beaches sound appealing, head into the Northwest's largest remaining undisturbed old-growth and temperate rain forests. The park's muggy forests, soaked by 12 to 14 feet of rain a year and often cloaked in low-lying clouds or drizzle, wrap around you with thick, mossy-green walls of vegetation. You can almost feel the forest growing.

In addition to rugged mountains, wilderness beaches, and lush rain forests, you also find meadows strewn with wildflowers, deep valleys, shimmering lakes, soothing hot springs, and cascading waterfalls tossed in between the coastline and the peaks. Three unique choices — but only one park, one trip.

Must-See Attractions

Where to go, where to go, where to go? That's the dilemma with a park of Olympic's diversity. So let me give you some suggestions for a wonderful sampling of all the different landscapes — and seascapes — that this national park has to offer:

- **Hoh Rain Forest:** This pocket of humidity, with its moss-covered trees, bushy ferns, and slimy banana slugs, is a perfect example of the world's temperate rain forests.

- **Hurricane Ridge:** The highest point in the park you can easily reach by car, its views of the Strait of Juan de Fuca and Mount Olympus and the rest of the Olympic mountains are riveting.

- **Lake Crescent:** Anglers appreciate this glacier-carved lake for its rare Beardslee and Crescenti trout species, whereas romantics are happy just to pull up a lakefront chair at Lake Crescent Lodge.

- **Marymere Falls:** This 90-foot waterfall that cascades out of the forest nourishes a moss community that blankets the cliffside and the boulders at the falls' base.

- **Rialto Beach:** Sea stacks — rocky outposts that are remnants of a coastline long knocked down by Pacific storms — make this nook of the park a favorite with photographers, rock hounds, and kids who enjoy investigating the sea stars, anemones (small, colorful, spineless creatures with tentacles) and other creatures revealed in a tidal pool during low tide.

- **Sol Duc Hot Springs:** Most parks have a commercial side, and this spot is Olympic's. But its pools are kid magnets and wonderful for us older folk to ease into, too, after a long day on the trail.

Planning Ahead

For information before you go, write Superintendent, 600 East Park Avenue, Port Angeles, WA 98362; call ☎ **360-565-3130**; or check the park's Web site at www.nps.gov/olym.

When to go and how long to stay

Frankly, your choice of when to visit boils down to how much you like wet weather. Spring can be on the raw side and wet, but it does have its own magic. For starters, the wetness enhances the emerald color of the rain forests. And you often see gray whales cavorting along the coastline while they migrate north.

Summers can't be beat. July and August are the driest months in the park, and September can be quite nice, too. The threat of the forests growing moldy disappears because rain is relatively minimal this time of year. Fog banks often roll inland from the Pacific in the mornings, but the mist usually burns off by midday to reveal mostly blue skies.

Like spring, fall can also be wet and raw, but even this season has a positive side. The rain forests become extra lush, and in early fall, you can often spot sea lions lounging along the coast.

 Crowds are sparse in Olympic during winter — and no wonder. Winter brings the onset of the rainy season, with the year's heaviest showers falling in December and January. At this time, the park's upper elevations become buried in snow. The park's high country receives an average of about 15 or more feet of snow each winter.

 You need at least three days to explore Olympic National Park.

Advance reservations

A lead-time of several weeks to a month is usually sufficient for reserving a room at many of the motels and hotels found in the Port Angeles area, but several months would be more appropriate for such resort locations as Kalaloch, Lake Crescent, and Quinault Lake.

Due to the park's popularity with backpackers, some backcountry sites — Ozette Coast, Grand and Badger valleys, Royal Basin, Lake Constance, Flapjack Lakes, and the Sol Duc/Seven Lakes Basin — operate under a quota system. You can reserve one of the designated sites in these areas for trips between May 1 and September 30 by calling the **Wilderness Information Center** (☎ **360-565-3100**) up to 30 days before your trip.

What to pack

 Don't forget your rain gear when packing for Olympic National Park. You may be able to sneak in a multiday trip in summer without needing it, but rain gear almost always comes in handy here. If you're going to be camping, make sure that your tent has a good rain fly. For more tips on what to pack for your national park vacation, see Chapter 8.

Getting There

Reaching Olympic National Park is easy, thanks to the international airport near Seattle, which is a relatively short car ride — or shuttle flight — from the park. Heck, you can even reach the park from the sea, thanks to the docks at Port Angeles (the park's nearest town) and the ferries that arrive there from Victoria, British Columbia.

Driving in

Seattle is the major gateway to Olympic National Park, which anchors Washington State's peninsula in the Pacific. From the city, you can reach the park either by taking a ferry across Puget Sound or by heading south on Interstate 5 to Tacoma, and then Washington 16 north to Bremerton and Washington 3 north to U.S. 101 to reach the east side of the park, or drive west from Olympia on Washington 8 to Aberdeen and then north on U.S. 101 along the park's western side.

Traveling up U.S. 101 from Aberdeen, you have the choice of entering the park in the Quinault or Queets valleys, or at Kalaloch Beach, the Hoh Rain Forest, or Mora. You reach Ozette in the northwestern corner via a road off Washington 112. From spur roads off U.S. 101 on the east side of the park, you can reach Staircase and the park's entrance at Dosewallips. You find an entrance to Hurricane Ridge on the southern border of Port Angeles, and you can reach Deer Park via a road that heads south off U.S. 101 just east of Port Angeles.

Some of these entrances may closed in winter, so check with the park visitor center at ☎ 360-565-3130 before setting out for Olympic.

Flying in

If you want to fly to the park, **San Juan Airlines** provides service to **Fairchild International Airport** (☎ 800-874-4434) in Port Angeles from Seattle's **Boeing Field** airport. It runs shuttles to and from Seattle-Tacoma International Airport. **Budget Rent-A-Car** (☎ 360-457-4246) has an outlet at Fairchild. (See the Appendix for the toll-free number for Budget.)

The closest major airport is the **Seattle Tacoma International Airport** (☎ 800-544-1965 or 206-431-4444), known as Sea-Tac, located 15 miles south of Seattle on Interstate 5. Most of the major airlines and car-rental agencies are here; see the Appendix for their toll-free numbers. For bus service from the airport, see the next section, "Busing in."

To drive to the park from either Boeing or Sea-Tac, you can take a ferry across Puget Sound to reach U.S. 101, which circles the park, or drive south on I-5 to Olympic and pick up 101 there.

Olympic National Park

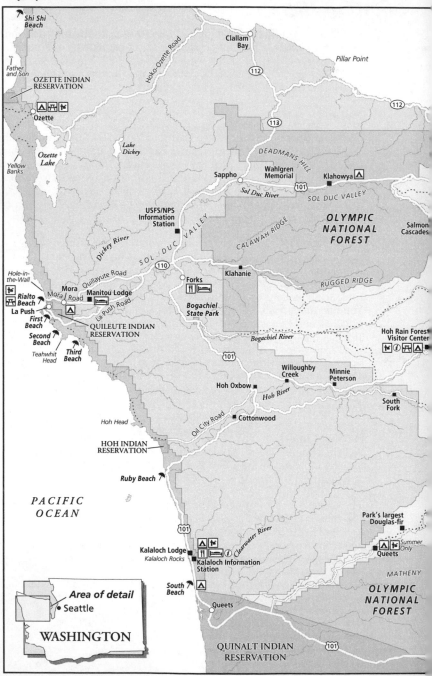

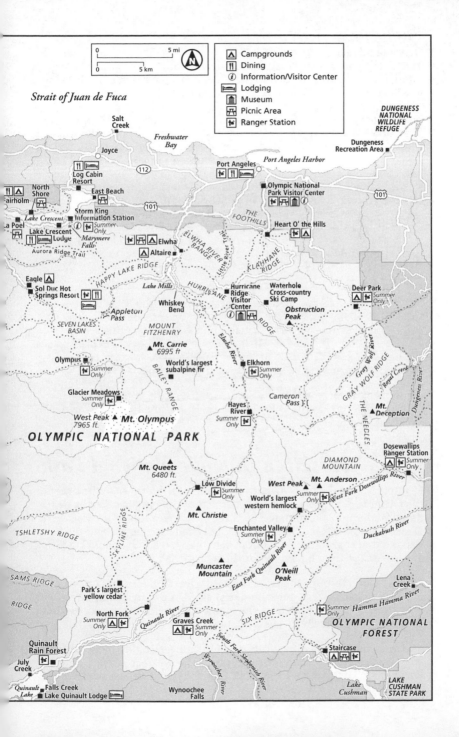

0 ____ 5 mi
0 ____ 5 km

⛺	Campgrounds
🍴	Dining
ⓘ	Information/Visitor Center
🛏	Lodging
🏛	Museum
🛏	Picnic Area
⚑	Ranger Station

Strait of Juan de Fuca

DUNGENESS
NATIONAL
WILDLIFE
REFUGE

Salt
Creek

*Freshwater
Bay*

Dungeness
Recreation Area ▪

Joyce

Log Cabin
Resort

Port Angeles

Port Angeles Harbor

112

North
Shore

Fairholm

East Beach

101

Olympic National
Park Visitor Center

101

Lake Crescent

Storm King
Information Station

*THE
FOOTHILLS*

Heart O' the Hills

La Poel

Lake Crescent
Lodge

*Summer
Only*

*Marymere
Falls*

Elwha

ELWHA RIVER RANGE

Little River

*KLAHHANE
RIDGE*

Aurora Ridge Trail

Altaire

Eagle

Sol Duc Hot
Springs Resort

HAPPY LAKE RIDGE

Lake Mills

HURRICANE RIDGE

Hurricane
Ridge
Visitor
Center

Waterhole
Cross-country
Ski Camp

Deer Park

*Summer
Only*

*Appleton
Pass*

Whiskey
Bend

*Obstruction
Peak*

SEVEN LAKES
BASIN

MOUNT
FITZHENRY

Elwha River

Mt. Carrie
6995 ft

Olympus

*Summer
Only*

BAILEY RANGE

World's largest
subalpine fir

Elkhorn

*Summer
Only*

Gray Wolf Ridge

Royal Creek

Dungeness River

Glacier Meadows
*Summer
Only*

Cameron
Pass

GRAY WOLF RIDGE

THE NEEDLES

Mt.
Deception

West Peak ▲ **Mt. Olympus**
7965 ft.

Hayes
River

*Summer
Only*

OLYMPIC NATIONAL PARK

Mt. Queets
6480 ft.

DIAMOND
MOUNTAIN

Dosewallips
Ranger Station

*Summer
Only*

Low Divide

*Summer
Only*

West Peak ▲ **Mt. Anderson**

*Summer
Only*

West Fork Dosewallips River

World's largest
western hemlock

Mt. Christie

Duckabush River

TSHLETSHY RIDGE

SKYLINE RIDGE

Enchanted Valley

*Summer
Only*

East Fork Quinault River

Muncaster
Mountain

O'Neill
Peak

Lena
Creek

SAMS RIDGE

RIDGE

Park's largest
yellow cedar

Quinault River

Graves Creek

SIX RIDGE

*Summer
Only*

Hamma Hamma River

**OLYMPIC NATIONAL
FOREST**

North Fork
*Summer
Only*

*Summer
Only*

South Fork Skokomish River

Staircase

Quinault
Rain Forest

July
Creek

*Quinault
Lake*

Falls Creek

Lake Quinault Lodge

Wynoochee
Falls

Wynoochee River

*Lake
Cushman*

LAKE
CUSHMAN
STATE PARK

Busing in

Olympic Bus Lines (☎ 800-457-4492 or 360-417-0700; www.olympicbus lines.com) offers twice daily service from Seattle and Seattle Tacoma International Airport to Port Angeles. **Pennco Transportation** (☎ 888-673-6626 or 360-582-3736; www.penncoshuttle.com) makes five round-trips daily to the airport from Port Angeles; it also offers charters. Other bus companies on the peninsula include **Clallam Transit** (☎ 800-858-3747 or 360-452-4511; www.clallamstransit.com), which operates Monday through Saturday within Port Angeles with commuter services to Sequim, Joyce, Forks, Neah Bay, and La Push; **Jefferson Transit** (☎ 360-385-4777; www.jeffersontransit.com), which is based in Port Townsend and serves Brinnon and connects with Clallam Transit in Sequim; **Grays Harbor Transit** (☎ 800-562-9730 or 360-532-2770; www.ghtransit.com), which operates from Olympia and Aberdeen with service to Lake Quinault; and **Mason County Transit** (☎ 800-374-3747 or 360-427-5033; www.masontransit.org), which runs between Shelton, Olympia, Bremerton, and Brinnon.

Ferrying in

For Puget Sound ferry schedules, contact **Washington State Ferries** (☎ 206-464-6400; www.wsdot.wa.gov/ferries/). For ferries arriving in Port Angeles from Victoria, British Columbia, contact **Black Ball Transportation** (☎ 360-457-4491; www.cohoferry.com) in Port Angeles. **Victoria Express** (☎ 800-633-1589 or 360-452-8088; www.victoria express.com), meanwhile, offers seasonal, walk-on ferry service.

If you take the ferry across the sound from Seattle, you will find park entrances along U.S. 101 at Port Angeles, Hurricane Ridge, Elwha, Lake Crescent, and Sol Duc.

Orienting Yourself in Olympic National Park

Olympic National Park is a veritable island of wilderness in the heart of the Olympic Peninsula. In fact, 95 percent of the park is officially desig-nated wilderness. Surrounded on three sides by water — the Pacific Ocean to the west, the Strait of Juan de Fuca to the north, and the Hood Canal to the east — the park offers sanctuary to a rich animal kingdom and an escape from humanity for those who visit.

No roads loop through the park. Instead, **U.S. 101** hooks and crawls around the park's west, north, and east sides. A few roads make relatively short forays into the park from the highway. None of these is longer than 17 miles, which usually means a relatively quick trip to your destination.

The one place that is difficult to reach is **Ozette.** Getting there requires a 40-mile side trip from Sappho, near the park's western border, down Washington **Highways 113** and **112** that lead you through the Olympic National Forest to the coast.

Park headquarters and the biggest (and best) visitor center are both located on the north side of the park in **Port Angeles.** From the visitor center, **Hurricane Ridge** — with its smaller visitor center, picnic area, hiking trails, and panoramic views of the glacier-strewn Olympics, and the Strait of Juan de Fuca — lies 17 miles south via the aptly named **Hurricane Ridge Road.** Branching off this road are hiking trails and a dirt road leading to Obstruction Peak.

Other side roads that dash into the park include the following:

- ✔ **Elwha Valley Road** leads to Altaire Campground, Elwha picnic area, and Lake Mills just below the northern edge of the park.

- ✔ **Sol Duc Road** leads to the Sol Duc campground, Sol Duc Hot Springs Resort, and several popular trailheads in the park's northwestern corner.

- ✔ **Hoh River Rain Forest Road** leads to the Hoh Rain Forest and its visitor center and campground in the west side of the park.

- ✔ **Queets Valley Road** leads to the remote Queets campground near the park's southwestern corner and hiking trails.

- ✔ **North Shore Road** runs along the north side of Quinault Lake to the Quinault Rain Forest and the North Fork and Graves Creek campgrounds on the southern tip.

- ✔ **South Shore Road** runs along the south side of Quinault Lake to the North Fork and Graves Creek campgrounds.

- ✔ **Staircase Road** in the park's southeastern corner runs to the Staircase campground and several trailheads that lead you to breathtaking alpine vistas and thick forests.

- ✔ **Deer Park Road** leads to the Deer Park campground on the northeastern corner.

Although physically separated from the alpine heart of the park by the Olympic National Forest, the 63 miles of **coastline** are indeed part of Olympic. This rugged stretch of sand and rock runs from Kalaloch Beach just above the Quinault Indian Reservation all the way north to Shi Shi Beach, which borders the Makah Indian Reservation. **U.S. 101** runs 10 miles along the coast between South Beach and Ruby Beach, and **Washington 110** runs to Rialto Beach and La Push midway along the coastline. The only other coastal access in the park is via the **Hoko-Ozette Road,** which runs about 20 miles from Washington 112 to Ozette Lake.

 When exploring the park, remember to be patient; Olympic's roads bear no resemblance to freeways. U.S. 101 has a few straight stretches, but for the most part it winds and bends and creeps over and around the mountainous landscape. After you leave this main road for one of the spur roads, the number of bends and turns seems to double and the asphalt may change to gravel and dirt.

Arriving in the Park

When you enter the park, you'll receive a copy of the park's newspaper, *Bugler,* a great resource for discovering what's happening during your visit. For more information, head to one of the visitor centers or ranger stations.

Finding information

The park has three visitor centers that offer exhibits, maps, guides, and information, plus smaller ranger and information stations (open only in summer) located at popular trailheads.

Olympic National Park Visitor Center (☎ 360-565-3130), on the southern edge of Port Angeles, is the park's largest visitor center and offers great exhibits on Olympic's Native American history and wildlife, as well as a good selection of park books, posters, videotapes, and postcards. The center is open daily year-round; hours vary by season.

A 45-minute drive from the main visitor center brings you to one of the most popular spots in the park, the **Hurricane Ridge Visitor Center.** Here you find free telescopes for spying on distant peaks and glaciers, as well as a (pricey) snack bar, interpretive exhibits, and trails. The center is open daily from 10 a.m. to 4:30 p.m.

The **Hoh Rain Forest Visitor Center** (☎ 360-374-6925), on the west side of the main part of the park, is some 15 miles down a turnoff from U.S. 101. This tiny center, open 9 a.m. to 6 p.m., offers a good explanation of rain forests and their climate, as well as a primer on glaciers. You can pick up wilderness trip permits here if you plan to take the Hoh River Trail 18½ miles to Glacier Meadows. The center is open daily; hours vary seasonally.

Smaller information centers include the seasonally open **Storm King Information Station** at Lake Crescent in the northern section of the park, and the **Kalaloch Information Station** (☎ 360-962-2030) at the south end of the beach section of the park. You can get food and some supplies near the **Sol Duc Ranger Station** at the Hot Springs Resort and at Kalaloch.

For maps and updated trail conditions, stop at the nearest ranger station or at the **Wilderness Information Center** (☎ 360-565-3100), located just behind the main visitor center in Port Angeles.

Paying fees

Entrance into the park for up to a week costs $10 per vehicle, or $5 per individual hiking or biking. Annual passes cost $30. If you have a park pass, you don't need to pay the entrance fee; see Chapter 8 for information on the National Park Pass and Chapter 7 for the lowdown on Golden Age and Golden Access passports.

Parking at Ozette costs $5 per day.

All overnight hiking trips require a $5 permit registration fee that is good for two weeks and covers up to a dozen people, as well as an individual nightly fee of $2 per person for every night out. (Hikers 16 and younger are exempt from the nightly fee.) Permits are available at the **Wilderness Information Center** (☎ 360-565-3100) in Port Angeles.

Getting Around

To get around Olympic National Park, you need a car. The park does not have a public transportation system.

Remembering Safety

 If you plan to head off into the park's backcountry, keep these pointers in mind to ensure a safe trip:

- ✓ **Hypothermia:** A real danger with Olympic's generally wet, cool climate. Protect yourself by having rain gear with you and by dressing in layers of synthetic clothing, which dries much more quickly than cotton clothing.

- ✓ **Cougars:** They roam the park's backcountry, and although you most likely won't spot one, if you do, don't turn your back on it or try to run away. These actions can encourage the cougar to attack. If the big cat seems aggressive and begins to stalk you, try to scare it off by waving your arms and shouting or by throwing rocks or sticks at it.

- ✓ **Black bears:** These animals also call the park home and are much more visible than cougars. If you see a bear down the trail, either give it a wide berth or backtrack until it leaves. If a bear comes into your camp, make some noise to scare it off. Also, be sure to hang your food high above the ground from a bear wire, where available, or store the food in an animal-resistant food container, which are available for a $3 per trip donation from the **Wilderness Information Center** (☎ 360-565-3100) and any staffed ranger station.

If you're going to visit the beach, remember the following:

- ✓ **Coastal hiking:** This activity can be dangerous because tides can trap you. Never hike around headlands unless you know how high tides can get and when they come in. Detailed maps, showing safe routes around headlands, as well as tide tables, are available from visitor centers, the Wilderness Information Center (☎ 360-565-3100), and staffed ranger stations.

- ✓ **Swimming:** Along the coast, swimming can be hazardous because of logs in the surf. Felled by storms and washed into the ocean by streams, they can easily knock a swimmer unconscious or worse. Also, the cold water and strong currents make swimming a risky proposition along the coast.

> ✔ **Raccoons:** Believe it or not, these critters can be troublesome for campers on the beach near Ozette. Park officials suggest that you store your food in animal-resistant food containers to thwart these masked marauders.

For additional tips on how to ensure a safe visit to the park, see Chapter 8.

Exploring Olympic National Park

Although the vast majority of Olympic National Park is rugged back-country that you need a horse or a pair of hiking boots to reach, you can get a strong sense of place through visiting a few easily accessible areas.

Beaches

Having grown up in New Jersey, I'm a sucker for beaches. But **Rialto Beach** is nothing like the smooth, sandy beaches of my childhood. Towering stacks of basalt stand out in the surf, and lush forests of Douglas fir and cedar run right down to the beach. The stacks are remnants of cliffs that were slowly, but steadily, pounded into sand by the waves.

This is the most accessible beach in the park, with the Mora Road running to a parking lot just above it. A thick tangle of drift logs separates the parking lot from the beach, creating a kind of maze you have to negotiate in order to reach the water. This beach is a beachcomber's dream, with polished agates, stacks of drift logs, some 6 feet in diameter, and other flotsam tossed up by the waves. "Rock aquariums" — depressions in some of the sea stacks that fill with water — swarm with marine life; spend some time searching in the small pools for green anemones, sea urchins, shellfish, and brightly colored sea stars, also known as starfish. You find a picnic area at the beach and camping nearby at Mora.

Although not as accessible, **La Push,** just below Rialto Beach, has a larger collection of sea stacks.

Enjoy solitude and ample opportunities for beachcombing on the one-and-a-half-mile walk north along the beach to **Hole-in-the-Rock,** a jutting piece of headland through which the surging surf has chiseled a tunnel that you can explore during low tide. This is the best time to visit Rialto Beach, because the dropping water level reveals more water pockets full of marine life and allows you to walk through Hole-in-the-Rock.

If you're determined (and foolhardy enough) to dash into the surf for a dip, watch for rogue logs that were washed out to sea by rivers after being toppled by storms. Waves toss these around like toothpicks, and you can't win a collision with them.

If you're worried about running into crowds at Rialto Beach, try one of the six beaches along the coast between Ruby Beach and South Beach. Known simply as **Beach 1, Beach 2, Beach 3,** and so on, you reach these beaches via footpaths across from small pullouts on U.S. 101. Some of these beaches have tide pools to explore; others are great for beachcombing or clamming during the season. (Clamming season varies depending on the beach and type of clam. For more details, check with the nearest ranger station.)

Before you walk out across the rocks during low tide, be sure to check the tide table for the day and keep an eye on the incoming water or you can quickly find yourself stranded.

The rules of most national parks state that taking anything out of the park is illegal, but in Olympic you're allowed to collect a handful of stones or empty shells from the beaches, so you don't have to look nervously over your shoulder as you pocket a few.

See map p. 224. Rialto Beach is at the end of Mora Road off Washington 110. La Push is at the end of Washington 110. The beaches on the coast between Ruby and South Beach are along U.S. 101.

Hoh Rain Forest

Overload your senses here. Your nose fills with the rich, loamy scent of the earth that nurtures the forest while your eyes try to decipher the varying hues of green that tint this emerald cathedral. Sitka spruce trees 8 feet thick climb skyward for 200 to 300 feet, mossy curtains droop from vines and big-leaf maples, and blankets of Oregon oxalis and waist-high Sword ferns cover the forest floor.

As you walk the forest's trails, be careful not to squish the Banana and European Black slugs, which are oversized snails traveling without their shells. These slimy critters come in various sizes and colors. The Banana Slug is the biggest (up to a foot long) and the most colorful, coming in greens, browns, and yellows. While looking for the slugs, you may spot large tracks left by the elk that live in the forest.

For recommended hikes in the rain forest, see Hall of Mosses Trail and Spruce Nature Trail in "Taking a hike," later in this chapter.

See map p. 224. The rain forest is at the end of Hoh River Rain Forest Road, which is roughly 10 miles south of Forks off U.S. 101.

Hurricane Ridge

If you visit Hurricane Ridge during any season but winter, you won't find yourself alone. The ridge is immensely popular, and the drive there during warm-weather months often is done in convoy. But where else can you stand in one place and see both the ocean and a nearly 8,000-foot-tall peak covered with snow and glaciers?

On the 17-mile drive up to the ridge along Hurricane Ridge Road, you're quickly pulled out of the muggy lowlands, transported past dazzlingly colorful meadows of wildflowers, and deposited near the roof of this corner of the world. On a clear day, you can stand on the trails that scamper across the ridge and gaze north to the Strait of Juan de Fuca and beyond to Canada. (See High Ridge and Alpine Hills, in "Taking a hike," later in this chapter.) To the south, snowy Mount Olympus and her sister peaks, which are home to 60 glaciers, tear at the horizon. If you're standing on Hurricane Ridge under the summer sun, you may find yourself longing for a little shade.

If you abhor crowds, plan either an early-morning or late-afternoon trip to the ridge top. Or, for similar views and fewer people, go to nearby **Deer Park,** located at the end of a serpentine 15-mile-long road that begins outside the park just east of Port Angeles. What's the catch? The steep gravel road is off-limits to recreational vehicles and rigs hauling trailers. Plus, negotiating this road takes a lot longer than the paved Hurricane Ridge Road.

See map p. 224. Hurricane Ridge is 17 miles south of Port Angeles on Hurricane Ridge Road.

Lake Crescent

You may think that you've been transported to New York's Adirondack region when you reach Lake Crescent on the north end of the park. Dense forests surround this glacial lake, and the shorefront Lake Crescent Lodge features the same dark paneling and stone fireplace that you would find in an Adirondack lodge. If you need to take a breather, you can settle into a lawn chair with a view of the lake.

Lake Crescent is a great place to rent a canoe or rowboat to ply the waters in search of the Beardslee or Crescenti trout that lurk far beneath the surface. This is a catch and release fishery, so pack your camera to record your catch. See "Keeping active," later in this chapter, for details on boating.

Near the Lake Crescent Lodge are the Storm King Ranger Station and a 1¼-mile trail that leads to **Marymere Falls,** a beautiful, feathery 90-foot waterfall. Along the trail, mosses, lichens, and ferns clutter the forest floor and climb up into the canopy. Narrow, single-log bridges twice cross Barnes Creek just before the falls. (Unless they're wet and slippery, these bridges aren't difficult to cross.) Just after you begin a steep climb up the hillside toward the top of the falls, a shortcut breaks off to the left and follows a more level, less strenuous path to an overlook opposite the falls. At the most, plan on a 90-minute round-trip, but if you're in a hurry, you can visit the falls and get back to your car in half that time.

See map p. 224. Lake Crescent is roughly 21 miles west of Port Angeles on U.S. 101.

Sol Duc Hot Springs

Although the Sol Duc area has hot, spring-fed swimming pools, the reason to visit is not for the pools — although the watery diversion is a good one if you've got some restless kids in your car. The real reason is for the roughly 1½-mile round-trip hike to **Sol Duc Falls** (see the description under "Taking a hike," later in this chapter). Although less than half as tall as Marymere Falls, these falls offer more water volume and plunge into a rectangular flume that the Sol Duc River has cut through the bedrock. A wooden bridge just below the falls is a great spot for photographs.

The trail to the falls also provides access into the backcountry. From it you can hike to the High Divide for stunning views of the Hoh Valley and Mount Olympus, explore the Seven Lakes Basin, or trek to the headwaters of the Bogachiel River.

See map p. 224. Sol Duc Hot Springs is 40 miles west of Port Angeles via U.S. 101 and the Sol Duc Road.

Taking a hike

With its coastlines, dense rain forests, and alpine terrain, Olympic offers too many hiking opportunities for you to just drive through this park and stay in your room. You have beaches to comb, rain forests to explore, and high country trails to cruise along. In all, more than 600 miles of marked trails and 955 designated campsites exist in the park. Following are just some of the hiking possibilities.

See "Arriving in the park" earlier in this chapter, for information on back-country hiking and fees.

Bogachiel River

Let your energy level determine how far you hike on this trail, which features a rain forest setting similar to that of the Hoh Rain Forest but without the crowds. The trail runs about 21½ miles from the park boundary to the junction of the Mink Lake and Little Divide trails. The first few miles

Capturing Olympic on film

Make sure your camera bag is well-stocked for a trip to Olympic National Park. Along with having a wide range of films — slow-speed films for rain forest settings and fast-speed films for shots of crashing surf and those bright snowfields near Hurricane Ridge — or memory-rich flash cards, you'll definitely appreciate a good tripod.

For the ultimate rainforest shot, spend time in the Hoh Rain Forest. The hike to Marymere Falls provides more opportunities for lush, emerald-green old growth-forest photographs, although the best subject at this end of the park is the beautiful waterfall. If you're a fan of waterfalls, another good one to frame with your lens is Sol Duc Falls, which you find about a mile down the trail from the trailhead at the end of the Sol Duc Road just beyond the Sol Duc Hot Springs Resort.

Timing is a prerequisite for a good shot of the waves smashing into the sea stacks along the park's coastline. I've always found late afternoon to be the best time to photograph here, because the setting sun's rays backlight the crashing waves.

Hurricane Ridge is perhaps the best spot you can reach — without hiking — to capture the park's alpine personality. And if you tire of taking pictures of Mount Olympus and the other snow-shrouded peaks, turn around and take a picture of the Strait of Juan de Fuca to the north.

wind through thick rain forest with towering Douglas firs, Sitka spruce, Western cedar, and big-leaf maples, all sporting mosses. Along the way are several stream crossings. The Bogachiel Shelter, 6 miles from the trailhead, is a good destination for an overnight, round-trip hike. Of course, heartier hikers may want to go further.

Distance: 43¼ miles round-trip. Level: Easy to moderate in the lowlands, steeper as you head inland. Access: 5 miles south of Forks, turn onto Undie Road and drive 5 miles to the trailhead.

Cape Alava/Sand Point Loop

This great three-legged loop trail offers rainforest scenery, ocean views, beach camping, *petroglyphs* (prehistoric rock art), and an easy round-trip back to your car. The trail begins on a cedar-plank boardwalk that winds about 3 miles through coastal marsh and grasslands to the beach and Cape Alava, the westernmost point in the Lower 48. As you make your way 3 miles south on the beach, be sure to look for the petroglyphs on the rocks along the shore next to the high-tide mark. The end of this leg is marked by the Sand Point Trail, another boardwalk stretch that runs 3 miles through grasslands and rain forest back to the ranger station at Ozette. This is one of the most popular backcountry destinations in the park, so if you're set on visiting perhaps you should think about a trip during one of the park's shoulder seasons.

Before you embark on this trek, check the tide charts posted at the trailhead. Take care on the boardwalks, which can be slippery when wet.

Distance: 9¼ miles round-trip. Level: Easy. Access: Ozette Ranger Station.

Glacier Meadows

This is one of the routes taken by climbers heading to Mount Olympus. Early on, the hiking is easy and captivating as you pass through the rain forest with its dense vegetation and towering trees. If you're alert, you may be able to spot the Roosevelt elk that live in the area. The trail's first 12 miles follow the Hoh River Valley and are easy to walk. Beyond the intersection with the Hoh Lake Trail, you enter a deep gorge past Elk Lake and on to Glacier Meadows and the toe of Blue Glacier on Mount Olympus. Plan this hike carefully. Snowmelt from the glaciers picks up in late July and can make travel tricky. A round-trip Glacier Meadows hike can take several days; most people take four.

Distance: 37 miles round-trip. Level: Easy early on, then moderate as you begin to climb into the high country and encounter stream crossings, most over foot logs or bridges. Access: Hoh Rain Forest.

Hall of Mosses Trail

If you have time for only one hike in the Hoh Rain Forest, this 40-minute loop is it. The trail winds through a green kingdom of lush vegetation. It's not steamy, like a tropical rain forest, but you can feel the humidity. Along the trail, *epiphytes* — plants that grow on other plants — in the form of spongy club mosses, mosses, lichens, liverworts, and licorice ferns scramble across tree trunks and limbs and up into the leafy canopy where they manage to block most of the sun's rays. Scattered here and there on the ground are toppled trees and rotting stumps that serve as nurseries for the next generation of trees. Shallow, crystal-clear creeks flow through the forest.

Distance: ¾ miles. Level: Easy. Access: Hoh Rain Forest Visitor Center.

High Ridge and Alpine Hills

The short, paved, 1-mile High Ridge Route is great for kids: It's short enough so it won't tire them out, offers great views of Mount Olympus and other peaks to the south, and contains interpretive exhibits that engage and teach. If you're up for more, follow the unpaved trail to Sunrise Ridge, which, on clear days, serves up sweeping views of the Strait of Juan de Fuca and Port Angeles to the north.

Distance: 1 to 8 miles round-trip. Level: Easy to moderate. Access: Hurricane Ridge Visitor Center.

Sol Duc Falls

This short, picturesque forest hike offers great photo opportunities, a refreshing waterfall, and kid-friendly hiking. Streams jumping through moss-covered boulders, the dense emerald forest, and the cascading waterfall along the Sol Duc River are picture-perfect backdrops. Just below the falls, you find a bridge across the river that provides a great vantage point to see where the river has cut a channel through the bedrock.

Distance: 1½ miles round-trip. Level: Easy. Access: Near Sol Duc Ranger Station.

Spruce Nature Trail

This trail through the Hoh Rain Forest takes about an hour to negotiate. Because this section of forest is younger, the route is not as densely packed with vegetation as the Hall of Mosses Trail. A highlight, however, includes a side trail to the Hoh River where you can see *glacial flour,* finely ground sediment that the Hoh Glacier scraped from the bedrock as it inched its way down below the snowfields beneath Middle and East peaks. The flour gives the Hoh River its milky appearance.

Distance: 1¼ miles. Level: Easy. Access: Hoh Rain Forest Visitor Center.

One-day wonder

The only way to cross Olympic National Park is on foot. Although U.S. 101 does wrap around three sides of the park, its route runs through the Olympic National Forest, not the park. To get into the park, you need to shoot down spur roads that can run up to 17 miles in length. As a result, if you're determined to see as much of the park as possible, you're going to have to drive quite a bit and pack and unpack your bags every day.

Got goats?

Mountain goats arrived on the peninsula in the 1920s when a dozen of them from Alaska and British Columbia were imported to the region. Unfortunately, the goats did tremendously well in the climate, and by the early 1980s, their population had surpassed 1,000. They began to threaten the park's subalpine meadows by heavily browsing the vegetation and creating dusty wallows by rolling on the ground. A live-capture program in the late 1980s managed to trim the population, but it was discontinued out of concern for the safety of the rangers involved who needed helicopters to reach the goats. These days, several hundred goats still live in the park, and officials are debating how best to deal with them.

But don't despair. You can get a surprisingly good feel for the park in one day. It'll be a long day, for sure, but you'll come away having sampled its three main environments. (Unless otherwise mentioned, see "Exploring the top attractions," earlier in this chapter, for information on the attractions mentioned in this itinerary.)

The best place to start this journey is in **Port Angeles.** After rising early and eating a good breakfast, leave for **Hurricane Ridge** (if weather allows) in time to get there by 8 a.m. On a clear day, you'll be rewarded with eye-popping views of Mount Olympus and the Strait of Juan de Fuca.

A good, quick hike on Hurricane Ridge is the High Ridge route. After an initial 1-mile walk along a paved trail that offers interesting interpretive panels, you can continue to Sunrise Ridge, with its killer views of the strait to the north and the glacier-coated peaks to the south.

By 10 a.m., you should be ready to head back down to Port Angeles and the **Olympic National Park Visitor Center.** Here you can load up on any brochures or additional guidebooks that strike your fancy and also get grounded in the region's cultures and natural history.

Your next stop is **Rialto Beach,** 70 miles and roughly 90 minutes away by car, for an enjoyable walk on the beach and some great photographs of the sea stacks. Take a short stroll whether it's a clear day or raining — walking through mists can be just as interesting as walking in sunshine, plus you can get some beautiful photographs of the sea stacks laced with fog.

From the beach, head into to the **Hoh Rain Forest,** 47 miles and about an hour away by car. It'll probably be approaching late afternoon by the time you near the rain forest, so stop at the **Hard Rain Café and Mercantile** for lunch (see "Where to Dine," later in this chapter). The two-beef-patty Mount Olympus Burger and an order of fries will keep you going for the rest of the afternoon.

After lunch, continue to the rain forest, where a hike through **Hall of Mosses** (see the "Taking a hike" section) is mandatory. The hike won't take long, but the route does lead you through some of the park's best rainforest. Following the hike, you can either continue down the nearby Spruce Nature Trail, which leads along the fringe of the rain forest and out to the Hoh River, or spend some time in the visitor center's tiny museum with its solid primer on rain forests.

A great way to end your day is with dinner and a room at the **Lake Quinault Lodge,** which is about 75 miles from the Hoh Rain Forest, just outside the park's southwestern corner (see "Where to Stay," later in this chapter). This gorgeous, lakefront log-lodge was visited by President Franklin Delano Roosevelt in October 1937 during a trip he conducted to determine whether a national park should be established here.

If you have more time

Although not as big as Yellowstone and some other sprawling Western parks, Olympic National Park requires more than a day or two if you're determined to see it all. (Well, seeing it all can take years.)

If you do have a few extra days, consider a trip to **Lake Ozette** on the coast. Although the lake is popular, a visit is well worth your time. The focal point of this area is the 7,787-acre freshwater lake, but you're also close to the coast with its tide pools, old-growth coastal rain forest, and, if you look hard enough, petroglyphs. (Hint: You can find them on Wedding Rocks found halfway between Cape Alava and Sand Point.) The lake's campground has only 14 sites, so if you're lucky enough to get one, you can enjoy relative solitude at night. The area also has back-country lake sites that you reach by boat, and more backcountry sites along the coast.

For a hike in the area, see Cape Alava/Sand Point Loop under "Taking a hike," earlier in this chapter. The 9¾-mile hike from Cape Alava to Shi Shi Beach is another good option, if you don't mind getting wet. The trail crosses the Ozette River, which can be waist deep at times.

Ranger programs

Campfire talks, guided walks through the rainforest or subalpine meadows, and beachcombing are the hallmarks of ranger-led activities in the park.

Definitely plan to accompany one of the rangers on the tide pool beach walks that they lead daily during the summer months from Mora and Kalaloch. Kids and adults alike love these 2½-hour hikes, which investigate the marine life of tide pools. Meeting times vary according to the tides. Check the *Bugler,* the newspaper that you receive upon entering the park, or park bulletin boards, for exact times.

Spotting the local wildlife

With its vast array of wildlife, Olympic National Park offers incredible opportunities for seeing animals in their natural habitats. Where else can you see both whales and black bears on the same day? Even more fascinating is that the glaciations that once isolated the peninsula from the rest of the continent led to the evolution of at least 18 unique types of animals, including the **Olympic snow mole,** the **Olympic short-tailed weasel,** and the **Olympic marmot.**

Tidepools along the coast are the best places to spot a variety of the park's wildlife in one place. In these shallow pools, you usually can find **green anemones** (small, colorful, spineless creatures) with their tentacles floating in the water. If you stick your finger into the middle of them, or if one snares food with its tentacles, the anemone pulls its tentacles inward. You may also spot **sea stars** (starfish) and **hermit crabs** in these pools, as well as a variety of **mussels.**

While you're searching tide pools, from time to time remember to take a look out at the ocean. If you're lucky, you may spot a **California sea lion** or perhaps a **harbor seal.** These furry critters enjoy sunning themselves on off-shore rocks when they're not frolicking in the water. A good time to look for them is in late summer and early fall when they migrate up the coastline toward the Strait of Juan de Fuca and Puget Sound. Harder to spot are **Northern fur seals,** which prefer the waters off Cape Flaherty on the peninsula's northwestern tip.

East Coasters usually need to board a boat to spot whales, but in Olympic National Park all you need to do is be on the right beach at the right time of year. If you visit in the spring or fall, head to the coast to look for waterspouts made by passing **gray whales.** These guys like to feed just off the beaches where the Hoh and Quillayute rivers pour into the Pacific. Another good place to look for them is from the bluffs of Beach 6 along U.S. 101 north of Kalaloch Lodge. Rangers at the **Kalaloch Ranger Station** (☎ 360-962-2283) can provide information on the whale migrations.

Moving inland, you may cross paths with **Roosevelt elk.** The park was almost named after these slightly bigger cousins of the Rocky Mountain elk. They're easiest to spot in the early morning or evening browsing in old clearcuts in the Olympic National Forest that surrounds the park. The Hoh and the Quinault valleys are also good places to look for elk; in early summer, some elk give birth in the Hoh Rain Forest. Just as visible are **Columbia black-tailed deer,** which prefer Hurricane Ridge during the early morning or late afternoon.

Black bears aren't so easily spotted, but they're out there. In early summer along Hurricane Hill, you may see them munching on the lush vegetation.

If you head into the high country, you may spot a **mountain goat** clattering along a rocky ridge. These animals aren't native to the park. (See the "Got goats?" sidebar, earlier in the chapter.)

Harder to spot, but park residents just the same, are **cougars, bobcats, weasels, river and sea otters, beavers, marmots, flying squirrels,** two varieties of **skunk,** and **coyotes.** A former park resident that may one day return is the **gray wolf.** Early settlers wiped out the peninsula's native wolf population in the 1930s. A wildlife survey released in 1999 determined that the park's habitat and prey base can support a population of 56 wolves, although no recovery plan has been prepared.

In the park's rivers and lakes and in the ocean off the coast are five types of **salmon,** four **trout** species (including the Beardslee and Crescenti trout species native to Lake Crescent), three kinds of **char,** as well as **whitefish, shiners, lampreys, bass, suckers, perch, Northern pikeminnow,** and **sculpin.**

If you're lucky, as I was, you may see a **bald eagle** hoisting one of these fish out of the park's waters. Dozens of bird species travel through Olympic at various times of the year, taking advantage of its fisheries and forests for food and shelter. Along with the more common **blackbirds, finches, ravens,** and **sparrows,** you can spot various **shorebirds, woodpeckers, pelicans,** and **loons.**

Perhaps the park's most comical-looking bird is the **tufted puffin.** Their bodies are covered with black feathers, and they have large, bright-orange bills and heads covered with white feathers that sweep back into yellowish tufts. Unfortunately, you probably won't spot any of them because they avoid people and spend most of their time on off-shore islands, although people who have visited Cape Flattery, which is outside the park's boundaries, have seen them.

Another great family outing is stargazing atop Hurricane Ridge. With much of the light pollution left behind in Port Angeles, the inky black skies above the ridge come alive (on clear nights) with flickering stars and planets. Rangers occasionally lead stargazing parties, so consult the park's newspaper for dates.

Although you can guide yourself along the trails through the Hoh Rain Forest, ranger-led hikes held daily provide background on the forest's plant and animal dynamics, as well as on the nearby Hoh River.

For families with small children, the ubiquitous campfire talks are held regularly at various locations around the park; check the *Bugler* for topics, dates, and times. You can also pick up information on the Junior Ranger Program at the main park visitor center in Port Angeles (see Chapter 7 for information on this program).

Keeping active

In addition to hiking, Olympic National Park offers several opportunities for outdoor fun.

Boating, canoeing, kayaking, and white-water rafting

Although large and often windy, glacier-carved **Lake Crescent** is a beautiful place to do a little paddling. Lush, green forests rise straight up from the shores of this 624-foot deep lake. You can find boat ramps on U.S. 101 at Storm King (near the middle of the lake) and at Fairholm (at the west end of the lake). The Log Cabin Resort, on East Beach Road on the lake's northeast shore, has a private boat ramp.

You can rent canoes at **Fairholm General Store and Cafe** (☎ 360-928-3020) at the west end of the lake or at the **Log Cabin Resort,** 3138 E. Beach Rd. (☎ **360-928-3325**), on the lake's northeast shore. Lake Crescent Lodge rents rowboats (☎ **360-928-3211**).

If you're paddling, be careful not to stray too far out from shore because midday winds can quickly whip up the lake.

In and around the park, you can white-water raft, enjoy a scenic float, or go sea kayaking. Guided trips generally last a half day, and canoe and kayak rentals are available. For details, contact **Olympic Raft & Kayak**, 123 Lake Aldwell Rd., Port Angeles (☎ **888-452-1443** or 360-452-1443; www.raftandkayak.com).

Fishing

If you love to fish, you've come to the right park. However, most fish caught in the park's freshwater streams and lakes must be released. Because fishing regulations can change from year to year, pick up a copy of the fishing regulations from any ranger station or visitor center.

You don't need a Washington state fishing license inside the park, but if you plan to go surf fishing in the ocean or clamming, you need to stop by a sporting goods store to get the requisite state licenses.

Snowshoeing and cross-country skiing

You can have a satisfying winter trek on any of the snow-covered roads leading into the mountains. However, if you want great views, head to Hurricane Ridge with the rest of the winter crowd and set out on any of the area's trails. Cross-country and downhill ski rentals and snowshoe rentals are available from the ski shop on the lower level of the **Hurricane Ridge Visitor Center** (no telephone).

Escaping the rain

On a rainy day, a good place to take your kids is the **visitor center** at park headquarters in Port Angeles (see "Finding information," earlier in this chapter). Not only does this center have top-notch displays on Native Americans and wildlife, but younger kids enjoy the **Discovery Room,** where they can play in a miniature log ranger station, learn about ecology, and build a totem pole with felt stick-on pieces. In the main visitor center, older kids can keep busy with a virtual scavenger hunt that requires them to study the exhibits in order to answer questions about the park.

Where to Stay

The park offers only a few options when it comes to putting a roof over your head. Two of these places are at Lake Crescent, the third is just south of there, and the fourth is along the coast.

Winter offers the year's best lodging rates. You can usually find a bargain at Kalaloch Lodge during the winter months. For more tips on finding a place to stay, see Chapter 6.

Lodging in the park

 ### Kalaloch Lodge
$$–$$$ **North of South Beach**

The lure of this lodge and its huddled cabins is the sea-front location. Be sure to request a cabin with a wood-burning stove, because they help to take the night chill out of the air. The cedar-shingled lodge and the cabins perch on a bluff above the mouth of Kalaloch Creek and the sandy coast, allowing you to fall asleep to the crashing waves if you leave a window open. The cabins accommodate between four to seven people. Despite the coastal location, you find more romantic accommodations at Lake Crescent Lodge and Lake Quinault Lodge, the latter just south of the park.

Still, this lodge is the only one on the coast within the park's boundaries. Some cabins feature kitchenettes that come equipped with cookware and utensils — a great way to cut down meal expenses. You'd be wise to make a reservation at least four months ahead of your arrival. The lodge holds three rooms for walk-in business, but these units pale in comparison with the rest on the property.

See map p. 224. 157151 U.S. 101 (North of South Beach). ☎ **360-962-2271**. *Fax: 360-962-3391.* www.visitkalaloch.com. *8 rooms, 2 suites, 44 cabins. Rack rates: $99–$139 double; $159–$259 suites; $119–$269 cabins, some with kitchenettes. Lower rates weekdays Nov–May. AE, MC, V.*

Lake Crescent Lodge
$–$$$$ **Lake Crescent**

With a great, peaceful location on the park's north end, the lodge is just minutes from Marymere Falls and less than an hour from Hurricane Ridge. Although the historic lodge is picturesque, I strongly recommend the fire-place-equipped Roosevelt cabins. Located along the lakeshore, these cabins offer better views than the lodge rooms; have their own bathrooms (the lodge rooms don't); are gorgeous with their log walls, plank flooring, and panel ceilings; and are simply more comfortable. However, because there are only four of these cabins, they book up quickly — some people, determined to have one of these beauties on a specific date, make reservations two years out! Motel-style rooms with their own bathrooms are also available, but only some of them have lake views.

See map p. 224. 416 Lake Crescent Rd. ☎ **360-928-3211**. www.lakecrescentlodge.com. *36 rooms, 20 cottages. Rack rates: $66–$82 double without bath, $101–$138 double with bath; $122–$195 cottage. AE, CB, DC, DISC, MC, V. Open late April to late Oct.*

Log Cabin Resort
$$$ **Lake Crescent**

This turn-of-the-century resort on the north shore of Lake Crescent offers some of the cheapest lodging in the park. The four lodge rooms give you the biggest bang for your buck, featuring lake and mountain views, a private bathroom, and a queen bed and a queen futon. The resort also has A-frame style chalets on the shoreline with lake and mountain views. The chalets have bathrooms and showers and sleep up to six people. You also find an assorment of cabins, ranging from those with kitchenettes and bathrooms to simple cabins without indoor plumbing (a communal bathroom is nearby). If you opt for a no-frills no-plumbing cabin, you need to supply your own bedding, or rent some from the resort.

See map p. 224. 3183 E. Beach Rd. ☎ *360-928-3325. Fax: 360-928-2088.* www.logcabin resort.net. *4 rooms; 12 chalets; 3 kichenette cabins; 5 cabins with bath; 4 cabins without bath. Rack rates: $104 double; $127 chalet; $94 kitchenette cabin; $78 cabin with bath; $53 cabin without bath. DISC, MC, V. Cabins closed early Sept–late June.*

Sol Duc Hot Springs Resort
$$$ **Port Angeles**

These cabins are nothing fancy, but the hot springs are nearby, so if a good soak is all that matters, or if you've got kids who love splashing around, stay here. However, if heavy traffic from campers, day trippers, and other resort guests is likely to spoil your vacation, you'll be more comfortable elsewhere. If you want to handle your own meals, opt for the higher-end cabins, which come with kitchens. You won't find any phones, radios, or televisions in the cabins, but the lodge has pay phones. The lodge also offers a decent restaurant, pool-side deli, espresso bar, and grocery. You can even arrange a massage, but they're pretty pricey, starting at $45 for 30 minutes.

See map p. 224. Sol Duc Road (near Eagle). ☎ *360-327-3583. Fax: 360-327-3593.* www.northolympic.com/solduc. *32 cabins. Rack rates: $112–$132 cabin for two. AE, DISC, MC, V.*

Lodging outside the park

Best Western–Olympic Lodge
$$–$$$$$ **Port Angeles**

This is a great place to base your vacation, with views of both the Olympic Mountains and the Strait of Juan de Fuca. Adults who don't get enough exercise in the park can work out in the fitness room, and kids can splash around in the heated pool. Rooms are spacious with king- or queen-sized beds and are equipped with coffee makers and dataport phones for those who can't leave their work behind. A golf course is next door.

140 Del Guzzi Dr. ☎ *800-600-2993 or 360-452-2993. Fax: 360-452-1497.* www.port angeleshotelmotel.com. *104 rooms, 1 suite. A/C, TV, TEL. Rack rates: $99–$229 double; $199–$350 suite . AE, DC, DISC, MC, V.*

Lake Quinault Lodge
$$$–$$$$ **Quinault**

Just beyond the park's southern boundary, this lakeshore lodge's setting makes it worth a stay. Built in 1926 (after a fire destroyed the original log hotel on this site), Quinault Lodge exudes a backwoods elegance. The lobby boasts a huge fireplace and the grounds include a small beachfront where you can rent a boat to take out on the lake for a paddle. The accommodations range from small rooms in the main lodge to modern rooms in outlying buildings with wicker furniture and little balconies. Some rooms have fireplaces. The annex rooms are the least attractive and have distressingly thin walls and ceilings. For information on the lodge's restaurant, see "Where to Eat" in the next section.

See map p. 224. South Shore Road. ☎ *800-562-6672 or 360-288-2900.* www.visit lakequinault.com. *92 rooms, 1 suites. A/C. Rack rates: June–Sept $117–$183 double, $255 suite; Oct–May $80–$133 double, $199 suite. AE, MC, V.*

The Tudor Inn
$$–$$$ **Port Angeles**

This inn is a charming getaway winter or summer. Thanks to its setting in a residential area 13 blocks from the waterfront, this quaint inn offers a quieter setting than other downtown accommodations in Port Angeles. Pushing a century in age (it was built in 1910), the home was fully restored in 1995 to bring out the most of its Tudor charm. The bedrooms, located upstairs and featuring European antiques, are fairly simple, yet comfortable with private baths and king- or queen-size beds. Several rooms have views of the Olympic Mountains to the south; the best view is from the Tudor Room. The main-floor lounge and library have warming fireplaces. Outside is a large yard with beautiful gardens. The owners arrange cross-country ski or snowshoe tours in winter.

1108 S. Oak St. ☎ *866-286-2224 or 360-452-3138.* www.tudorinn.com. *5 rooms. Rack rates: Mid-May to mid-Oct. $95–$145 double, mid-Oct to mid-May $85–$135. Rates include breakfast. No kids under 12 years old. AE, DISC, MC, V.*

Runner-up lodgings

The Forks Motel

$–$$$ **Forks**   You'll find standard motel rooms as well as two-bedroom units with kitchens at this property on the park's west side. The Pacific Coast is just 20 minutes away, and the Hoh Rain Forest is a 40-minute drive. *351 S. Forks Ave.* ☎ *800-544-3416.* www.forksmotel.com.

Manitou Lodge

$$–$$$ **Near Rialto Beach**   This lodge started its life as a hunting retreat but now offers seven rooms on 10 wooded acres just a few miles from Rialto Beach. Your room rate buys you a full breakfast as well as cookies, tea, coffee, and hot chocolate in the afternoon. *Kilmer Road. (Call for directions.)* ☎ *360-374-6295.* www.manitoulodge.com.

Olympic Suites

$–$$$ Forks Not only can you rent an inexpensive one- or two-bedroom room with a full kitchen here, but the property is surrounded by thick forest and close to the coast, and, if you're an angler, steelhead fishing is available. *800 Olympic Dr.* ☎ *800-262-3433.* www.olympicsuitesinn.com.

Port Angeles Inn

$–$$$ Port Angeles Just a block from the main drag and two blocks from the ferries, this inn's rooms come with views of either the Strait of Juan de Fuca or the Olympic mountains. *111 E. Second St.* ☎ *800-421-0706 or 360-452-9285.* www.portangelesinn.com.

Campgrounds

The camping options in the park are just as varied as the scenery, with both developed campground and primitive backcountry sites available in the rain forests, along the coast, and in the high country. Despite the high capacity — 16 campgrounds and more than 900 sites inside the park — lining up a spot to pitch your tent or park your camper can be tricky. The weather, lack of an all-inclusive reservation system, and restrictions against RVs and trailers can all conspire against you.

 Campground reservations are restricted to **Kalaloch** for dates between mid-June and early September. Everywhere else is first-come, first-served. Lining up your campsite early in the day is wise — essential on nice weekends when the weather lures more people to the park. Nightly rates range from $8 to $16.

If you want to camp in the off-season, your only options are the camp-grounds at **Elwha**, **Heart o' the Hills**, **Hoh**, **Kalaloch**, and **Mora**. Others are open seasonally or closed during low-use periods. Because weather can keep some campgrounds closed longer than you may expect, call **park headquarters** (☎ **360-565-3130**) to see what's open before you make plans.

 So what are the tricks to landing a campsite? Simply put, knowing the territory and the trends. To enhance your odds and improve your selection, arrive early in the day and in midweek, if possible.

Although Olympic's campgrounds are scattered around the park, the crowds aren't. The **Sol Duc** and Kalaloch campgrounds usually fill first, followed by Hoh and Altaire. **Sol Duc Hot Springs,** with its 82 sites, is also popular because of the pools there.

The park offers many options for **backcountry camping.** Reservations are available in a few spots, too. All the sites on the **Ozette Coastal Loop** require advance reservations; other popular wilderness camp areas, including **Grand Valley** and the **Seven Lakes Basin,** also offer reservations. To make reservations and obtain camping permits for the park's backcountry wilderness, contact the park's **Wilderness Information Center** (☎ **360-565-3100**).

None of the following campgrounds has RV sites, laundry facilities, or showers:

- ✔ **Altaire** has 30 sites along the Elwha River not far from the mouth of Lake Mills. It's closed in winter.

- ✔ **Deer Park** is one of the less crowded, but more remote, drive-in campgrounds. Close to Port Angeles, Deer Park has 14 sites accessible only by a narrow gravel road, which switchbacks its way from sea level to 5,400 feet. RVs and trailers are prohibited on the road.

- ✔ **Dosewallips**, became a walk-in only site when the flooding Dosewallips River washed out five miles of road leading here in the spring of 2002.

- ✔ **Elwha** isn't far from the Altaire campground. The 40 sites here are in the Elwha River Valley. The campground is open year-round, although water isn't available in the winter.

- ✔ **Fairholm** has 88 sites along the western shores of Lake Crescent. A boat launch makes this a popular site with anglers. It's closed in winter.

- ✔ **Graves Creek** has 30 sites along the Quinault River. In winter, it may be closed by the weather. Pit toilets and water are available.

- ✔ **Heart O' The Hills** features 105 sites in a beautiful forested setting not far from Port Angeles (if you suddenly find yourself needing a civilization fix). It's open year-round, although winter snow could make it a walk-in campground.

- ✔ **Hoh** has 88 sites within the Hoh Rainforest along the Hoh River. If you don't mind muggy conditions, this is a beautiful setting. Open year-round.

- ✔ **Kalaloch's** 175 sites are open year-round and highly sought after for their views of the Pacific Ocean and the tranquilizing sound of the crashing surf. It's one of the most beautiful settings in the park, in my opinion.

- ✔ **Mora**, along the Quillayute River has 94 sites that are just two miles from Rialto Beach, making it popular with beachcombers. It's open year-round.

- ✔ **North Fork**, with just seven sites along the North Fork of the Quinault River, offers the most solitude of any of the drive-in campgrounds. Water isn't available, though, and the dirt road could be washed out in the winter, forcing closure of the campground. This is a free campground.

- ✔ **Ozette** is remote, but it's a favorite among many and can be crowded. Fifteen campsites are on the lake and accessible by car. More sites are available in the backcountry; you can reserve them by phone (☎ 360-565-3100). The Ericsons Bay site on the lake promises solitude because you can reach it only by boat — it's well worth the effort.

✔ **Queets'** 20 sites along the Queets River have a picturesque setting, but they can get incredibly soggy and muddy in the spring and early summer. May be closed in winter due to weather conditions.

✔ **Sol Duc's** location next to hot spring-fed pools makes its 82 sites popular. Sometimes closed in the winter.

✔ **South Beach** has 50 sites with the same beautiful views of the Pacific Ocean as those sites at the Kalaloch Campground. No drinking water is available. The site is open May through November.

✔ **Staircase**, just inside the park's southeastern corner offers 56 sites. Weather sometimes closes it in winter.

Where to Eat

The park has few dining options, but you visit Olympic for the scenery, not the food, right? The dining rooms at Lake Crescent Lodge and the Log Cabin Resort, both on Lake Crescent, are open seasonally. Dining rooms at Kalaloch Lodge on the coast and in the Lake Quinault Lodge on the eastern shore of Lake Quinault are open year-round. On the northeastern end of the park, Port Angeles has a better variety of eateries.

Restaurants in the park

Kalaloch Lodge
$$$–$$$$ **North of South Beach   SEAFOOD**

With the ocean a stone's throw from the kitchen, it's no surprise that seafood dominates the dinner menu. Delectable choices may include a grilled salmon filet served with lemon-dill butter or a full pound of peel-and-eat shrimp. You also find vegetarian dishes and chops on the menu. Near the front of the lodge is a coffee shop where you can order breakfast or a sandwich for lunch.

See map p. 224. 157151 U.S. 101. ☎ *360-962-2271. Reservations recommended. Main courses: $3.50–$9 breakfasts; $7–$14 lunch; $11–$23 dinner. AE, MC, V. Open: 7 a.m.– 9 p.m.*

Lake Crescent Lodge
$$$–$$$$ **Lake Crescent   AMERICAN**

The picturesque view of the lake through this restaurant's two walls of windows lends great atmosphere to your meals. The dinner menu, the best in the park, blends creative seafood dishes like "Triple Fins," an entree of salmon, mahi, and halibut, with pastas and steaks. Seafood omelets, traditional egg dishes, fresh fruit crepes, and "Candy Apple French Toast" hold down the breakfast menu. A corner lounge in the lobby serves up drinks that you can enjoy in front of the fireplace or on the veranda.

See map p. 224. 416 Lake Crescent Rd. ☎ *360-928-3211. Reservations required for dinner. Main courses: $4.50–$8.95 breakfast; $5.95–$12.95 lunch; $15–$32 dinner. AE, DC, DISC, MC, V. Open: Late April to Oct 7:30–10 a.m., noon to 2:30p.m., 6–9 p.m.*

Log Cabin Resort
$–$$$$ Lake Crescent   AMERICAN

The dinner menu is built around seafood caught locally, although you can get steak and chicken, too. Try the Neah Bay Halibut, which is either grilled with green onions, garlic, and white wine or deep-fried. Also available are a seafood platter with breaded prawns, scallops, and oysters, and a smoked salmon linguini. If you're not a fish lover, you may want to try the chicken breast, the charbroiled top sirloin steak, or the pot roast with mashed potatoes and veggies.

See map p. 224. 3183 E. Beach Rd. ☎ *360-928-3325. Reservations required for dinner. Main courses: $5.95–$7.95 breakfast; $4.95–$8.95 lunch; $7.95–$19 dinner. DISC, MC, V. Open: Mid-May to Sept, 8–11 a.m. and 5–8 p.m.*

Restaurants outside the park

Bella Italia
$$$–$$$$ Port Angeles   ITALIAN

If you're hungry when you pass through Port Angeles, stop here for some of western Washington's best Italian food. This street-level restaurant starts you out with a basket of bread with an olive oil, balsamic vinegar, garlic, and herb dipping sauce. Along with the traditional Italian dishes, the menu includes salmon ravioli, a smoked salmon fettuccine, and steamed clams and mussels. Nightly specialities creatively blend seafood with local vegetables. Brunch is available on Sunday.

118 E. 1st St. ☎ *360-457-5442. Reservations recommended. Main courses: $12–$24. AE, DISC, MC, V. Open: Sun–Thurs 4–9 p.m., Fri–Sat 4–10 p.m.*

Hard Rain Cafe and Mercantile
$ Forks   AMERICAN

You can pick up postcards, local artwork, souvenirs, and a noontime meal at this funky cafe that doubles as a minigrocery. This restaurant is a great place to stop for a bite either on the way to or from the Hoh Rain Forest. The menu centers on burgers, both beef and salmon varieties. The special is the Big Foot Burger, which comes with two beef patties, bacon, ham, and turkey with huckleberry BBQ sauce on a sesame seed bun. Sandwiches are also available, and the French fries are great. You can take your meal with you or sit out on the porch and enjoy the sunshine.

5763 Upper Hoh Rd. ☎ *360-374-9288. Main courses: $6.50–$8.50 lunch. MC, V. Open: Daily summer 8 a.m.–8 p.m., winter 9 a.m. – 7.p.m.*

Hark! What grows there?

From 200-foot-tall **Sitka spruce trees** to hard-to-find **calypso orchids,** Olympic National Park's flora can be just as dazzling as its fauna. The rain forests are heavy with **spruce** and **big-leaf maples** draped in **mosses** and **lichens,** and the somewhat drier lowland forests feature **Douglas fir, Western hemlocks, Western red cedar, red alder,** and, in especially dry areas, **Pacific madrone,** a red-barked tree that peels its outer layers much like a tourist who has spent too much time in the sun.

In the high country of Hurricane Ridge and above are twisted and gnarled subalpine **fir trees** contorted by the winds and heavy snows, as well as dainty **white avalanche and yellow glacier lilies, marigolds, paintbrushes,** and **buttercups** that burst into color when the snows melt.

Throughout the park are a number of plant species unique to the peninsula, including **Olympic Mountain Milkvetch, Piper's Bellflower, Flett's Fleabane, Olympic Mountain Rockmat,** and **Flett's Violet.**

Lake Quinault Lodge
$$$–$$$$ Quinault   AMERICAN

At Kalaoch's sister lodge, the menu is just as inspiring. You can start with a bowl of homemade clam chowder and move on to a seafood pasta dish with halibut, salmon, Chilean shrimp, and clams sauteed with mushrooms and red onions. Or you can satisify your appetite with the Cajun Chicken Pasta. The dining room fronts the lake and offers wonderful sunsets.

See map p. 224. South Shore Rd. ☎ 800-562-6672 or 360-288-2900. Reservations recommended. Main courses: $4–$14 breakfast; $8–$15 lunch; $12–$30 dinner. AE, MC, V. Open: Daily 7 a.m.–9 p.m.

Fast Facts: Olympic

Area Code

The area code is **360.**

ATM

You will find no ATMs in the park, but you can find them in Port Angeles or Forks.

Emergency

In an emergency, dial **911**

Fees

The entrance fees are $10 per vehicle per week and $5 for walk-ins.

Fishing License

A fishing license isn't required within the park, except when fishing in the ocean, but stop by ranger and visitor centers for regulations.

Hospitals

Olympic Memorial Hospital is in Port Angeles at 939 Caroline Street (☎ 360-417-7000) and Forks Community Hospital is in Forks at 530 Bogachiel Way (☎ 360-374-6271).

Information

For information, write to Olympic National Park, Visitor Center, 600 East Park Avenue, Port Angeles, WA 98362, call ☎ 360-565-3130, or look on the Web at www.nps.gov/olym.

Pharmacies

There is a Rite Aid Pharmacy in Port Angeles, located at 110 Plaza St (☎ 360-457-3456); and a Safeway at 110 E. 3rd St. (☎ 360-457-0788).

Post Office

The nearest post offices are at 424 E. 1st St., Port Angeles and on E. Division St., Forks.

Road Conditions and Weather

To find out information about the weather, call ☎ 360-565-3131 (recorded) or ☎ 360-565-3132 (visitor center).

Time Zone

The park is on Pacific time.

Chapter 15

Sequoia and Kings Canyon National Parks

* *

In This Chapter

▶ Discovering tall trees, rugged canyons, and cool caves
▶ Planning your trip
▶ Exploring above ground and below
▶ Finding the best beds and meals

* *

*B*elieve it or not, some claim Congress doesn't always act rationally. As proof, these naysayers can point to Sequoia and Kings Canyon national parks — two parks in central California that exist where one would suffice. They share a common border and management, and encompass much of the same fantastic High Sierra backcountry.

The parks' aesthetic and natural beauty profits from the lesson the National Park Service learned in nearby Yosemite, which is overrun by visitors during the summer months: Easy access and ample amenities threaten a park's very nature. As a result, Kings Canyon and Sequoia have few man-made attractions and are best experienced on foot.

Kings Canyon is far off the beaten path at the end of a long, circuitous, and steep road. The brakes on your car may hate you for venturing down the steep and twisting stretch of California 180 that leads here (as will any passengers who are afraid of heights). But after you reach the cobbled banks of the raging South Fork of the Kings River, you'll know the trip was worth it.

Kings Canyon National Park needs no frills to augment nature's beauty. A day spent watching the river seethe and roil as it plunges wildly downhill through its riverbed of boulders can nurture your soul. The thrill of hooking one of the trout that lurk in the stream's eddies isn't such a bad thing, either. The park has meadows for strolls (as long as you're well-lathered with bug repellent during the height of summer) and short hikes that serve as samplers for longer forays into the high country. Plus, the scenery is incredible — the park is a miniature Yosemite. Surrounding the Cedar Grove area, towering cliffs of granite (similar to those that made Yosemite famous) rise above the meadows. But Kings Canyon feels wilder than Yosemite due to a fortunate lack of crowds and development.

Sequoia, meanwhile, also is relatively off the beaten path and minimally developed. The only in-park accommodations, at Wuksachi Lodge, are subdued and don't overwhelm the wonderful, forested setting. A day's drive takes you past the park's major attraction — magnificent stands of sequoia trees. However, you need to get out into the backcountry to savor the High Sierra with its craggy, snow-swept peaks.

From Ash Mountain at 1,700 feet to the 14,494-foot crown of Mount Whitney, the 865,257 combined acres of Sequoia and Kings Canyon national parks offer the greatest range in elevation of any protected area in the Lower 48.

The limited access to the High Sierra is both a blessing and a curse. Few folks venture into the high country, so the blessing is the solitude you find there. This remoteness becomes a curse, though, if you're short on time and can't embark on a long hike to explore the parks.

For those who do have the time, these parks deliver the unexpected — granite domes (which most people associate with Yosemite), a sparkling crystalline cavern hidden beneath a landscape of big trees, and majestic alpine settings.

Must-See Attractions

The big, bigger, and biggest trees can be found in these parks, but that's not all that merits a trip to Sequoia/Kings Canyon. The highlights include:

- **Crystal Cave:** In Sequoia, a park dedicated to big trees, a trip underground into a cave is an anomaly. You swap towering forests and sunshine for humidity, cool darkness, and crystalline formations. The Discovery Tours are especially fun.

- **Grant Grove:** A stroll through this grove of sequoias leaves you feeling like an ant walking through a cornfield. Here you'll find the General Grant Tree, the third-largest living tree in the world, as well as the Fallen Monarch, a storm-toppled sequoia you can walk through.

- **Giant Forest:** Meandering through the world's best-known stand of sequoias is hard because your head is constantly tilted back. Among the forest's attractions are the General Sherman Tree, which is considered the largest living thing in the world.

- **Moro Rock:** On clear days from the top of this large granite dome, you can see the rocky rampart of the Great Western Divide to the east and the edge of the San Joaquin Valley to the west.

> ✔ **Tunnel Log**: Okay, it's a bit hokey, but when you drive your rig through the hole cut in this downed sequoia, you gain some appreciation for how big these trees really are.

Planning Ahead

For advance information, write Sequoia and Kings Canyon National Parks, 47050 Generals Hwy., Three Rivers, CA 93271-9700, or check the parks' Web site at www.nps.gov/seki. You can also call ☎ 559-565-3341 for 24-hour recorded information on road/weather conditions (updated daily), camping, lodging, and activities or to reach a ranger.

When to go and how long to stay

Whether you visit these parks in spring, summer, or fall depends on your preference for colorful spring wildflowers or fall leaves (as well as your ability to endure bugs, which plague the lower elevations in June and higher elevations in July). Seasonal crowds aren't a factor in choosing when to visit. You can avoid most crowds, even in the most popular areas. (I explain how in the "Exploring Sequoia/Kings Canyon" section.) For all practical purposes, Kings Canyon is closed in winter, specifically from late November to early April. Only the Grant Grove section of Kings Canyon has year-round road access. But Sequoia is wonderful to visit in winter because you can cross-country ski or snowshoe into the forest with only your shadow as your companion.

Plan to spend at least three days: one day in Sequoia, one day in Kings Canyon, and one day to travel and explore between the two.

Advance reservations

Accommodations in these two parks are very limited, so you definitely need to plan far ahead for your vacation if you want to stay inside the parks' borders. Cedar Grove Lodge in the heart of Kings Canyon has just 22 rooms, and the John Muir Lodge at Grant Grove Village has only 30. In addition, 52 tent and wood cabins are available in Grant Grove. In Sequoia, Wuksachi has 102 rooms, and that's it for the park.

What should you do to ensure you have a place to stay? Call early and often. (See "Where to Stay," later in this chapter, for reviews and contact information for each place.) Or you can pack your tent and prepare to jockey for a campsite. Most of the campgrounds in the two parks fill on a first-come, first-served basis. The exceptions are the highly popular **Lodgepole** and **Dorst** campgrounds in Sequoia. Both campgrounds operate on a reservation system, Lodgepole between Memorial Day and mid-October and Dorst between Memorial Day and Labor Day.

Backcountry permits are required for all overnight camping outside designated campgrounds. The permits aren't required for day hikes, with the exception of those in the Mt. Whitney area. You can obtain them from the ranger station closest to your trailhead.

Quotas limit the number of people who can obtain a permit on a single day for a certain trailhead. Some popular trailheads fill during summer. For a $15 fee, you can reserve a backcountry permit for a trip between mid-May and September. The park accepts reservations for the current year no earlier than March 1 and no later than three weeks before the start of your trip. All reservation requests must be sent to the Wilderness Office by fax (☎ 559-565-4239) or mail (Wilderness Permit Reservations, HCR 89 Box 60, Three Rivers, CA 93271). Fax requests must include payment by Visa or MasterCard. Mail requests must include payment by Visa, MasterCard, money order, or check, payable to the National Park Service. For more information, call the **Wilderness Office** (☎ 559-565-3766).

What to pack

A trip to these parks calls for a wardrobe of comfortable outdoor clothing. Layers of fleece are great for spring and fall, and a light fleece jacket is nice to keep the evening chill away during summer visits. I like shorts or a nice pair of noncotton hiking pants and synthetic shirts for hitting the trails, and of course you'll want a good pair of hiking boots. Meals in both parks are definitely relaxed affairs, so no need to pack dress clothes. As always, have a decent rain jacket handy.

Getting There

Sequoia and Kings Canyon are relatively easy to reach — from the west. That said, don't forget that these parks are mountainous, and the roads that wind through them are twisted, hilly, and narrow. As a result, you have to travel a bit more slowly than usual.

Driving in

The High Sierra blocks you from entering these adjoining parks from the east, leaving you no choice but to enter Sequoia from the southwest or west and Kings Canyon from the west via an incredibly long, steep, and winding road.

 One way to reach **Sequoia** is by driving 36 miles along California 198 from Visalia to the **Ash Mountain Entrance** in the park's southwestern corner. From Ash Mountain, it's 16 miles and about 60 minutes to one of the park's main attractions, **Giant Forest**. Along the way are 130 curves and 12 switchbacks. Don't take my word for it — count them. If your rig is more than 22 feet long, spare yourself the bother (the switchbacks are steep and tight) and skip this entrance in favor of the one at Big Stump.

Another option is to come in from the west via Fresno (53 miles away) on California 180 to the **Big Stump Entrance** of Kings Canyon National Park and then head south on the Generals Highway into Sequoia.

Sequoia and Kings Canyon National Parks

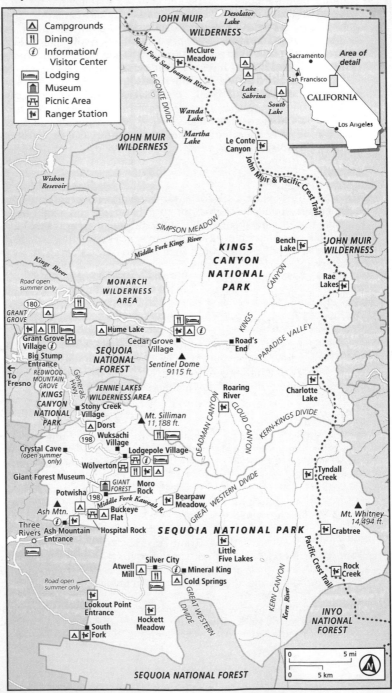

Map legend:
- △ Campgrounds
- ⑪ Dining
- ⓘ Information/Visitor Center
- 🛏 Lodging
- 🏛 Museum
- 🏞 Picnic Area
- 🏠 Ranger Station

JOHN MUIR WILDERNESS

Desolator Lake

McClure Meadow

South Fork San Joaquin River

LE CONTE DIVIDE

Lake Sabrina

South Lake

Sacramento
San Francisco
CALIFORNIA
Los Angeles
Area of detail

Wanda Lake

Martha Lake

Le Conte Canyon

JOHN MUIR WILDERNESS

John Muir & Pacific Crest Trail

Wishon Reservoir

SIMPSON MEADOW

Middle Fork Kings River

Bench Lake

JOHN MUIR WILDERNESS

Kings River

KINGS CANYON NATIONAL PARK

Rae Lakes

MONARCH WILDERNESS AREA

Road open summer only

GRANT GROVE
180

Grant Grove Village ⓘ

Hume Lake

Cedar Grove Village

SEQUOIA NATIONAL FOREST

Road's End

PARADISE VALLEY

KINGS

CANYON

Big Stump Entrance

REDWOOD MOUNTAIN GROVE

← To Fresno

KINGS CANYON NATIONAL PARK

Generals Hwy

JENNIE LAKES WILDERNESS AREA

Stony Creek Village

Crystal Cave (open summer only)

Giant Forest Museum

Potwisha

Ash Mtn.

Three Rivers

Ash Mountain Entrance

Dorst

198

Wuksachi Village

Lodgepole Village

Wolverton

GIANT FOREST

Moro Rock

198

Middle Fork Kaweah R.

Buckeye Flat

Hospital Rock

Sentinel Dome 9115 ft.

Roaring River

DEADMAN CANYON

Mt. Silliman 11,188 ft.

CLOUD CANYON

Charlotte Lake

KERN-KINGS DIVIDE

GREAT WESTERN DIVIDE

Bearpaw Meadow

SEQUOIA NATIONAL PARK

Tyndall Creek

Mt. Whitney 14,494 ft.

Crabtree

Pacific Crest Trail

Atwell Mill

Silver City

Mineral King

Cold Springs

Little Five Lakes

KERN CANYON

Kern River

Rock Creek

INYO NATIONAL FOREST

Road open summer only

Lookout Point Entrance

Hockett Meadow

GREAT WESTERN DIVIDE

South Fork

SEQUOIA NATIONAL FOREST

0   5 mi
0   5 km

N

To enter Sequoia through the **Lookout Point Entrance** that leads to **Mineral King,** turn right off California 198 and onto the Mineral King Road 3 miles west of the Ash Mountain Entrance. Eleven miles later you arrive at the Lookout Point Entrance, and another 14 miles delivers you to Mineral King. However, this steep and winding road (698 curves from start to finish) is only open in the summer, and visitors with trailers and RVs should avoid it.

If you're headed to **Kings Canyon**, unless you're already in Sequoia National Park, your only choice is to travel 53 miles down California 180 from Fresno and enter at the Big Stump Entrance. That's the easy part. After you pass the Grant Grove, go 31 miles down a steep, winding, two-lane highway through the Sequoia National Forest and into the lower stretch of Kings Canyon to reenter the park and arrive at Cedar Grove. Due to the road's gnarly nature, the section between Yucca Point and Cedar Grove is open only from late April to mid-November.

Flying in

The nearest major airport is the **Fresno-Yosemite International Airport** (☎ **559-498-4095**; www.fresno.gov/flyfresno), 53 miles via California 180 from the Big Stump Entrance to Kings Canyon. **American Airlines, American Eagle, Skywest, United Airlines, United Express, Continental,** and **Alaskan Airlines** all fly here. You can connect into Fresno from both San Francisco and Los Angeles. At the airport, you can rent a car from **Avis, Budget, Dollar, Enterprise, Hertz,** or **National.** (See the Appendix for the airlines' and car agencies' toll-free numbers.)

Visalia Municipal Airport (☎ **559-713-4201**), a tiny airstrip 36 miles from the Ash Mountain Entrance via California 198, is served by **United Express** and has an **Enterprise** car-rental agency.

Busing or training in

Bus service is limited, with **Greyhound** (☎ **800-229-9424**; www.greyhound.com) and **Trailways** (☎ **800-343-9999**; www.trailways.com) traveling only as far as Visalia and Fresno. Ditto with train service. **Amtrak** (☎ **800-USA-RAIL**; www.amtrak.com) goes as far as Hanford, where you have to take a bus approximately 30 miles to Visalia or Fresno and then rent a car. For car rentals in both cities, see "Flying in."

Orienting Yourself in Sequoia/Kings Canyon

From lowland foothills to mid-elevation forests and alpine crags, Sequoia and Kings Canyon throw tantalizing possibilities at you in terms of what to do and see. Unfortunately, the lack of easy access limits what you can enjoy on one visit, particularly if it's a short one.

Kings Canyon National Park

Kings Canyon is split in two. The bulk of the park, which contains Cedar Grove, the destination for motorized visitors, rests to the north of Sequoia. A separate, smaller section, called Grant Grove, shares a border with Sequoia National Park and is linked to Kings Canyon only by the rambling umbilical cord of California 180.

As national park developments go, **Cedar Grove** is Spartan. The lodge is old and small, with just 22 rooms, although it does have a well-stocked camp store. You also find four of King's Canyon's seven campgrounds, with a total of 351 sites, here.

In comparison to Cedar Grove, **Grant Grove** is Grand Central Station. You find three sprawling campgrounds with 329 sites, a 30-room lodge, a grocery, visitor center, picnic grounds, and stables. California 180 passes right through the heart of this complex before tying into the Generals Highway that continues into Sequoia.

I can't suggest any shortcuts through Kings Canyon because only one road, **California 180,** goes into the heart of the river canyon that leads to Cedar Grove. (Because this is the only access to the canyon, you encounter fewer people in Kings Canyon than in Sequoia.)

Due to the adventuresome nature of the road to Cedar Grove, plan to stay at least one night there, either at the Cedar Grove Lodge or in a tent. To creep into the park, spend half a day hiking or fishing, and then backtrack out would be much too stressful to qualify as a vacation.

Sequoia National Park

Sequoia also has only one road, **Generals Highway,** which winds into the developed part of the park and passes the gigantic trees that inspired the park's name. From Grant Grove in Kings Canyon National Park, the Generals Highway negotiates a short stretch of the Giant Sequoia National Monument in Sequoia National Forest before entering Sequoia National Park just north of the Dorst Campground. The road continues to **Wuksachi Village,** home of the Wuksachi Lodge, and then on to **Lodgepole Village,** which has a small visitor center, grocery, short-order grill, showers, laundry facilities, and campground.

From Lodgepole, the highway heads south through the **Giant Forest** section, passing spur roads to the Wolverton picnic grounds with its network of trails, the Giant Forest Museum, Moro Rock, and Crystal Cave. Next, the road passes Buckeye Flat and Potwisha campgrounds before reaching the Foothills Visitor Center and the Ash Mountain Entrance.

Just inside Sequoia's southern border lies the primitive **Mineral King.** At one time eyed by ski resort developers, this scenic area is dotted by lakes and laced with trails heading into the high country. In the heart of the basin are two campgrounds — one not far from the Atwell Grove (the highest elevation grove of sequoia trees), the other at Cold Springs — the privately owned Silver City Resort with its rental cabins, restaurant and general store, and the park's Mineral King information station. The dirt road that leads to Lookout Point Entrance and Mineral King is found off California 198 between Three Rivers and the Ash Mountain Entrance; it's open from Memorial Day weekend through October.

Finding information after you arrive

Unless you're hiking or on horseback, you must use one of two main entrances — the Big Stump Entrance on California 180 or the Ash Mountain or Lookout Point entrances on California 198. After you arrive in either park, you're never far from a visitor center.

The parks have four visitor centers. The biggest is the **Lodgepole Visitor Center** (☎ 559-565-4436), north of Giant Forest in Sequoia National Park on Generals Highway. This center features exhibits on geology, wildlife, air quality, and park history. Although hours of operation can fluctuate from year to year, in general the center is open mid-June through Labor Day from 8 a.m. to 6 p.m., September from 9 a.m. to 6 p.m., October through mid-April Friday through Sunday from 9 a.m. to 4:30 p.m., and mid-April until mid-June from 8 a.m. to 5 p.m.

The **Foothills Visitor Center** (☎ 559-565-3135), on California 198 just inside Sequoia's Ash Mountain Entrance, includes exhibits on the region's ecosystem. The center is open daily, mid-April through October from 8 a.m. to 5 p.m., and November through mid-April from 8 a.m. to 4:30 p.m.

The **Giant Forest Museum** (☎ 559-565-4480), on the Generals Highway in Sequoia National Park, includes wonderful exhibits on sequoia ecology. The center is open year-round, daily, with hours of operation similar to the Lodgepole Visitor Center.

The **Grant Grove Visitor Center** (☎ 559-565-4307), on California 180 in Kings Canyon National Park, includes exhibits on logging and the role of fire in the forests. It's open year-round, daily, from approximately 8 a.m. to 5 p.m., except from November until mid-April when the hours are 9 a.m. to 4:30 p.m.

Paying fees

A fee of $10 per vehicle or $5 per individual (on foot, motorcycle, or bicycle) provides access to both parks for seven days. A $20 annual pass covers entrance fees to the parks for one year. If you have a park passport, you don't need to pay the entrance fee; see Chapter 8 for information on the National Park Pass and Chapter 7 for the lowdown on Golden Age and Golden Access passports.

Although backcountry permits are required for all overnight camping outside designated campgrounds, the permits are free . . . but there is a $15 fee to make permit reservations. For reservations on certain trails, see the earlier section, "Planning Ahead."

Getting around Sequoia/Kings Canyon

The parks aren't linked by a public transportation system. Unless you plan a very long hike, you need a car to travel from one park to the next. Although at one time a free shuttle bus system operated between Giant Forest, Lodgepole, and Wuksachi, the service has been discontinued.

Remembering Safety

If you plan to head down California 180 into Kings Canyon, double-check your rig's brake system. Also, because no gas stations operate inside the parks, make sure to top off your tank before you pass through one of the entrance stations. Kings Canyon Lodge on California 180 in Sequoia National Forest has a gas station, but expect prices much higher than you would find in the small communities just west of the parks.

See the "Spotting the local wildlife" sidebar, later in the chapter, for important information about black bears, mountain lions, and rattlesnakes.

For additional tips on how to ensure a safe park visit, see Chapter 8.

Exploring Sequoia/Kings Canyon

Just as you may expect from two connected parks, Sequoia and Kings Canyon offer a lot to see and do. Your biggest problem may be narrowing down your options. To help you make your choices, let me give you a concise rundown of what you should try to pencil into your itinerary.

The only congested spots in these parks are the Giant Forest and Grant Grove areas; however, you can flee these crowds by following the longer, less popular trails.

The top attractions

Crystal Cave
Sequoia National Park

With only 3 miles of explored passages, Crystal Cave can't compare to larger caves like Mammoth Cave or Carlsbad Caverns. But in this land of big trees, going underground for an hour makes for a nice change of scenery. One of an estimated 200 caves in the park, Crystal Cave is the most beautiful with its crystalline formations, *cave bacon* (thin strips of flowstone that look like bacon), *soda straws* (long, thin formations that look like, well, straws), stalactites, and stalagmites. Two park employees out on a fishing expedition discovered the cave in 1918. Initially, the underground space was off-limits to the public because park officials feared that vandals would damage the formations.

Today, you have to pass through a gate in the shape of a spider web to enter the cave. After you get underground, you wind through about ½ mile of paved and lighted trails, stopping in the Dome Room, the Junction Room, the Organ Room, and the Marble Room so your guide can impart some cave history and science. In the Marble Room, the largest room in the cave's explored sections, the guide turns out the lights for a few minutes to let you experience total darkness. The gurgling and dripping water, which continues to carve the cave, can be eerie in the dark, but most visitors get a kick out of it.

If you want to tour the cave, purchase your tickets at the Lodgepole or Foothills visitor centers, because none are sold at the cave itself.

Because the 7-mile road leading to the cave from Generals Highway weaves through the forest and is followed by a 15-minute hike to the cave entrance, head for the cave 1½ or even 2 hours before your scheduled tour.

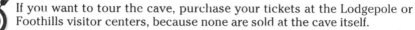

This attraction is open only from mid-May through late September.

See map p. 254. Crystal cave is 7 miles down a paved side road (open seasonally), about 14 miles north of Foothills Visitor Center, off Generals Highway. Admission: $10 adults, $8 seniors, and $5 ages 6 to 12; 5 and under free. Open: Mid-May to late Sept.

Grant Grove
Kings Canyon National Park

Grant Grove started out as a national park of its own, called General Grant National Park. When Kings Canyon was established as a national park in 1940, General Grant National Park was incorporated into it.

The towering sequoias in the Grant Grove annex of Kings Canyon National Park explain why this nook at one time was a national park in its own right. Located in the Grant Tree section of the grove, which is a mile northwest of the visitor center, is the 267.4-foot **General Grant Tree,** recognized as the world's third-largest living tree. It also doubles as the Nation's Christmas Tree, a designation bestowed by President Coolidge in 1926. Every December, a yuletide celebration is held in front of the 2,000-year-old tree. On the second Sunday of that month, a high school choir sings carols in front of it, and rangers place a wreath at its base. The tree also serves as a National Shrine, the only living memorial to Americans who have died at war. President Eisenhower extended that designation in 1956.

A paved, ⅓-mile trail in Grant Grove takes you past the General Grant Tree and to the **Fallen Monarch.** In the untold years since this humongous sequoia was toppled, the tree has served as a homesteader's cabin, a bar, and a stable for the U.S. Cavalry. Take a walk through this big old log and imagine what it must have been like to seek shelter inside it.

To escape some of the crowds that clog the path, head down the North Grove Loop trail, which roams for 1½ miles through a section of sequoias, past meadows, and into a mixed-conifer forest. The trailhead is in the Grant Tree parking area.

See map p. 254. Grant Grove is on California 180 just north of the Big Stump Entrance to the parks.

Giant Forest
Sequoia National Park

Just south of Lodgepole Village is the heart of the Giant Forest, the park's largest collection of sequoias. Four of the world's five largest sequoias grow here. (The fifth is the General Grant Tree in Grant Grove.) Walking among these ancient and towering trees, you feel as if you've entered a wilderness cathedral, a place of reverence. The 2-mile Congress Trail weaves past the **General Sherman Tree,** the largest living tree in the world, as well as the "House" and "Senate" groups of large sequoias. You also come upon the President, Chief Sequoyah, General Lee, and McKinley trees. A short spur off the Congress Trail leads past the "Room Tree," into which youngsters can scramble, and the "Founders Group," which is dedicated to those citizens who worked to see the national park established, to Cattle Cabin, a log structure dating back to the late 1800s when cattle grazed in Giant Forest. Trail access moved in the fall of 2004 to a new parking area along the Wolverton Road. From there, you face a ¼-mile hike to the General Sherman Tree.

Two miles south of Lodgepole Village on Generals Highway, Crescent Meadow Road leads first to **Moro Rock** (see the listing in this section) and then to **Tunnel Log,** a downed sequoia through which a hole that can swallow a car was cut back in 1938. Kids get a kick out of driving through the tree.

A parking lot 1¼ miles beyond Tunnel Log marks the western terminus of the High Sierra Trail. This is where you leave your car if you're heading into the high country along this route. But you don't have to hike the entire 71 miles to Mount Whitney to savor the gorgeous High Sierra countryside. You can just go 200 yards to the southern edge of **Crescent Meadow,** a dazzling place for spring wildflower photos.

You can also hike a mile from the parking lot to **Tharp's Log,** which is on the edge of Log Meadow. Talk about a real log cabin; Hale Tharp lived in this hollowed out sequoia during summers from 1861 to 1890 when he would bring his cows up to graze in Huckleberry, Crescent, and Log meadows. Judging from the wooden bunk inside, I don't think his nights were entirely comfy, but he was no doubt dry when the rains came.

From Tharp's Log, you can head around the northern tip of Log Meadow and hook into the **Trail of the Sequoias,** or you can head west on a path that leads to **Chimney Tree.** This towering tree trunk was gutted by fire; you can crawl into it and look out through the sheared off top. The Crescent/Log Meadow Loop Trail then loops back to Crescent Meadow, passing dozens of sequoia and small forest openings that blaze with color when the flowers bloom.

See map p. 254. Giant Forest is on Generals Highway between Lodgepole Village and Giant Forest Musem.

Mineral King
Sequoia National Park

Unfortunately (because it's time-consuming), or fortunately (because not many people do it), you have to temporarily leave Sequoia National Park to reach Mineral King. Most families intent on seeing the big trees in the park won't make the 90-minute drive to reach this glacially carved valley. As a result, although backpackers use Mineral King as a starting point for the High Sierras, this is a good place to head to avoid crowds.

The valley is breathtaking, with thick stands of conifers and outcrops of red and orange shale offset by white marble and black metamorphic shale and granite. Towering over the basin is Sawtooth Peak, which stands 12,343 feet tall and holds snowfields throughout the year. If you make the drive, spend a night in one of the campgrounds or at the Silver City Resort (see "Where to Stay" later in this chapter) and follow a trail into the mountains.

The basin is accessible by car only during the summer months. More importantly, early in the summer, the area's marmots develop a nasty habit of gnawing on radiator hoses and electrical wiring. Park officials actually suggest you bring enough chicken wire to encircle your vehicle to keep these furry rodents from chewing it up.

See map p. 254. Mineral King is on a mostly unpaved road that leads from the Lookout Point Entrance.

Moro Rock
Sequoia National Park

Moro Rock is a big granite dome jutting into the deep canyon cut by the Middle Fork of the Kaweah River. On days when the air pollution isn't too bad, this bulbous rock offers breathtaking views of the canyon below, the snow-capped peaks that form the Great Western Divide to the east, and the San Joaquin Valley far off to the west. If you keep track of such things, it's 370 steps to the rock's top from its base. Although the trail is steep in places and passes through some slots and keyholes, it's all worth it when you're standing on top, 4,000 feet above the river. If you need some inspiration on the way up, look for lizards scurrying over the rock face.

From the top, look for the serpentine Generals Highway as it snakes up from the Ash Mountain Entrance. You may feel sorry for the road crews that had to hack the road out of the forests and mountainsides.

This place is great for sunrise photos. If you're an early riser, get to the top by 8 a.m. during the week and you may have it to yourself for some peaceful meditation and inspiration. Sadly, air pollution problems in the San Joaquin Valley just west of Sequoia often sully the best views from Moro Rock. Air pollution is most intense during the summer months.

Capturing the parks on film

These two parks offer a wonderfully diverse array of photographic subjects, from the frothy Kings River to the stately sequoia trees and pillars of granite. Roam the Giant Forest and Grants Grove and discover countless subjects standing tall for their pictures to be taken. Just remember, though, that these trees are so big your pictures will benefit from a wide angle lens. I find that young kids perched on gnarled roots of a towering sequoia are particularly photogenic because of the scale they lend. You can obtain another intriguing photo by standing near the foot of a sequoia and pointing your camera up into the forest canopy. If you find yourself passing through the Big Stump Entrance to Kings Canyon National Park, take time to make the short hike down into Big Stump Basin. The huge tree stumps, left behind from the days when this area was logged, are worth a picture or two.

Because of relatively low light in the sequoia forests, your best pictures will be captured with a fast film. If you have slow film, be sure to use a tripod to steady the camera for the relatively long exposures the film will require. In the Cedar Grove section of Kings Canyon, you find soaring towers of granite for worthy pictures. For an interesting shot, try capturing the reflection of North Dome in the South Fork of the Kings River.

A few warnings: If thunderstorms threaten, don't turn yourself into a lightning rod by climbing to the top. Keep a tight grip on little tykes who could easily slip through the railings. Don't kick or toss stones into the great beyond because climbers may be below you. Finally, don't try to scale the rock if ice and snow cover the steps.

Moro Rock is on Crescent Meadow Road (not plowed in winter), which is by the Giant Forest Museum on Generals Highway.

Taking a hike

With so much fantastic backcountry, staying out of the mountains is hard. Even if you don't have enough time for an extended hike, both Kings Canyon and Sequoia have a variety of short- and medium-length hikes that allow you to discover the parks on foot. Of course, they may also convince you to return in order to go farther into the High Sierra. For information on permits for backcountry hikes, see "Planning Ahead," earlier in this chapter.

Alta Peak
Sequoia National Park

Alta Peak tops out at 11,204 feet, so not surprisingly, this hike's steepness and altitude make it one of the most strenuous on the western side of Sequoia. If you're not in good shape or if you're not acclimated to higher elevations, take the hike to Tokopah Falls instead (described later in this section).

You start out on the Lakes Trail for this jaunt, but turn right on the Panther Gap Trail rather than left. After you pass through the 8,400-foot gap, turn left onto the Alta Trail and go past the junction with Seven-Mile Hill Trail. When you hit the junction for the Alta Peak Trail, turn left and get ready to grunt. The final 2 miles include a 2,000-foot increase in elevation. After you reach the peak, though, you find great views in all directions. If the sky is clear, you can see past the Great Western Divide to Mount Whitney.

Distance: 13¾ miles round-trip. Level: Strenuous. Access: The southeastern end of the parking area at Wolverton picnic area, off Generals Highway.

Bubbs Creek Trail
Kings Canyon National Park

This hike treats you to views of Paradise Valley, Cedar Grove, and a large emerald pool filled by a waterfall. The start isn't encouraging, though, because you cross Copper Creek twice early on. This area was at one time an Indian village, and you may spot some shards of *obsidian* (dark volcanic glass) in the area. After the first mile, you enter a swampy area popular with wildlife. Here the trail closes in on the river, where deer and bear often drink. Two miles from the trailhead is a junction; the trail to the left heads to Paradise Valley, whereas the hike to Bubbs Creek veers right and crosses Baily Bridge over the South Fork of the Kings River.

You cross four more bridges back and forth over Bubbs Creek, and then begin climbing on the creek's north side. The switchbacks offer good views up Paradise Canyon and down to Cedar Grove. Three miles from the trailhead, you come upon the emerald pool and its waterfall. Far up on the mountainside is the Sphinx, a rock formation John Muir named for its likeness to the sphinxes in Egypt. One more mile brings you to Sphinx Creek, which is a nice place to spend the day. If you plan to camp, you need to pick up a backcountry permit before leaving the valley.

Distance: 8 miles round-trip. Level: Moderate to strenuous. Access: The east end of the parking area at Road's End.

Lakes Trail
Sequoia National Park

Unless you're a marathon hiker or plan to spend the night in the woods, this trip is best started early in the morning so you're not stumbling your way back in the dark. This hike's payoff is a series of lakes cradled in glacier-scooped basins. Head east from the trailhead, making sure to follow signs that help you stay on the Lakes Trail and avoid the Long Meadow Trail. You soon climb up a ridge and hike above Wolverton Creek, which cuts through a meadow lush with wildflowers in season. When you reach the junction with the Panther Gap Trail, head left toward Heather Lake. At the next junction, choose between going right up the Hump Trail, which is aptly named for its steepness, or head left along the Watchtower Trail, which leads along a granite ledge blasted in the rock with dynamite. If you don't have the constitution of a mountain goat, you may want to forsake this vertigo-inducing section by taking the Hump Trail. Both lead to Heather Lake, and a bit farther down the trail, Emerald and Pear lakes (5¾ miles and 6¾ miles, respectively, from the trailhead).

Distance: 13½ miles round-trip. Level: Moderate to strenuous. Access: The eastern end of the parking area at Wolverton picnic area off Generals Highway.

River Trail
Kings Canyon National Park

This trail hugs the Kings River and offers several hikes of different lengths. From the parking lot, you can make the up-and-back trip to Roaring River Falls for a total of ½ mile, or follow the trail in the other direction to Zumwalt Meadow and back for a total of 3 miles. If you continue to follow the path along the river from Zumwalt Meadow, you come to Zumwalt Bridge. Cross here, and you're ¼ mile from the Zumwalt Meadow parking lot. If you don't cross but continue down the trail, you come to the meadow's edge in another ¼ mile. If you continue, you face another footbridge in about a mile. Cross it and you're a ½ mile from the Road's End parking area.

Distance: 5½ miles round-trip. Level: Easy. Access: From the Cedar Grove Ranger Station, drive 3 miles to the Roaring River Falls Parking area.

Tokopah Falls
Sequoia National Park

This short trail is fairly level. The payoff is Tokopah Falls, which tumble 1,200 feet down smooth granite cliffs. When you get there, you can make your way to the river at the falls' base or pull up a rock and catch some rays.

Distance: 3½ miles round-trip. Level: Easy. Access: Lodgepole Campground on the north side of Log Bridge.

One-day wonder

Sequoia and Kings Canyon don't have many roads that delve into all the parks' various nooks and crannies, so you're fairly restricted as to what you can do and see in a limited amount of time. If you have only one day, you can make the most of your time if you concentrate on the more user-friendly Sequoia.

The following is my recommendation for a one-day itinerary of Sequoia National Park. Unless otherwise indicated, see the "Exploring Sequoia/Kings Canyon" section for information on the attractions.

Most visitors to Sequoia tend to sleep in. As a result, if you start your day early, you almost get the feeling that you're in your very own national park. So spend the night at **Wuksachi Lodge** (see "Where to Stay" later in this chapter) and get an early start in the morning. After breakfast at the lodge, head over to the **Lodgepole Visitor Center** or the **Giant Forest Museum** (see "Finding information" earlier in this chapter) to pick up any self-guiding trail brochures you may be interested in or to buy postcards to document your journey. Then drive down to **Moro Rock** and climb to the top. In summer, watch for the hummingbirds that feast on the nectar from the flowers growing on the granite.

From Moro Rock, continue east on the Crescent Meadow Road, passing through **Tunnel Log** and heading for the parking lot at the end of the road. From there, hike to **Crescent Meadow,** to **Tharp's Log,** and onto either the **Trail of the Sequoias** or the trail that leads to **Chimney Tree** — both are worthwhile.

By now you should be ready for lunch. Just down the road toward Lodgepole, you find **Wolverton** with its pleasant picnic area. (Here you also find marked cross-country ski trails in the winter, so keep it in mind when you're wondering where to go in mid-February.)

After lunch, hike down to the **General Sherman Tree** and venture down the 2-mile-long **Congress Trail.** Afterward, stop at the **Giant Forest Museum.** This museum, located in a historic building that at one time housed a grocery, provides a great primer on the life and times of sequoia trees. Make sure to visit the nearby Big Trees Trail, which goes around Round Meadow.

A great way to spend the rest of the afternoon is to hike, and the trail to **Tokopah Falls** is great for kids and adults (see "Taking a hike" earlier in the chapter). The 1¾-mile trail (3½ miles round-trip) ends at a towering waterfall cascading out of the high country. Afterward, head back to your room and clean up for dinner.

If you have more time

When passing through Grant Grove, check out **Big Stump Basin,** just south of Grant Grove Village along California 180. A 1-mile loop through the basin takes you past the stumps of sequoias that fell to loggers' saws in the 1890s. The forest is steadily coming back, but when you look at the size of the stumps it's clear that it will take 500 to 600 years for the living sequoias to reach that size.

Ranger programs

Your best bet for finding out about ranger programs is to scan the parks' newspaper and keep a close eye on bulletin boards in campgrounds and visitor centers. The parks have a few amphitheaters so you can expect a talk or two during your stay. Most of the programs get under way late in June. For ranger-led snowshoe hikes, see the following section, "Keeping active."

If you have little ones with you, pick up materials for the Junior Ranger Program at any visitor center (see "Finding information" earlier in the chapter). To find out about this program, see Chapter 7.

Spotting the local wildlife

One of the most visible animals in these parks is the **mule deer.** These guys have grown accustomed to having humans around and will usually go about their browsing unless you get too close.

Also around are **black bears,** which humans have managed to spoil with our sloppy ways when it comes to food. When you pull into the Lodgepole Campground, you'll see a sign that tallies up the number of cars bears have broken into during the year. You'll also see the large number of bear-proof storage bins scattered about. Use them. And make sure that you empty your car of all food, including apple cores and chips. The park's bruins can smell these tasty treats and are strong enough to peel your car open like a can of sardines to get to them. The rangers have pictures to show you exactly how much damage bears can exact on your rig.

If you have good eyes and are lucky, you may spot a **gray fox** in a meadow or darting across a road in the evenings. Also present are **coyotes, bobcats, badgers,** and **ring-tail cats.**

Mountain lions also live in the parks — definitely watch out for them. Although coming across one of these big cats is unlikely, if you do, be prepared to face it. Don't flee. Mountain lions view people and their pets as prey. If you try to run, they switch into attack mode. Your best defense is stand up tall and shout at the cat. You can even try pelting the animal with rocks or sticks if it begins to act aggressively.

In the parks' foothills, you're likely to spot **turkey vultures** as well as **red-tailed hawks** overhead. In campgrounds at higher elevations, the raucous and begging **Steller's jays** will find you.

While walking in the foothill areas of the parks, watch out for **rattlesnakes.** They don't seek people out, but if you're not careful where you put your feet and hands, you may inadvertently startle one.

Keeping active

These two parks offer numerous ways to get a workout. In addition to hiking (see the "Taking a hike" section), you have several other options:

- ✔ **Cross-country skiing: Sequoia Ski Touring** (☎ **559-565-3435**) operates at Wuksachi, just north of Giant Forest. They offer rentals, instruction, and trail maps for 35 miles of marked backcountry trails.

- ✔ **Fishing:** Easily accessed waters are limited to Kings and Kaweah rivers, and fishing permits and California state fishing licenses (available at most park grocery stores) are required. High-country lakes have a few nonnative trout.

- ✔ **Snowshoeing:** On winter weekends, rangers lead introductory snowshoe hikes in Grant Grove (☎ **559-565-4307**) and the Lodgepole/Giant Forest area (☎ **559-565-4436**). Showshoes are provided, but a $1 donation is requested.

✔ **White-water rafting:** If you want a thrill, try white-water rafting. **Whitewater Voyages** (☎ 800-400-RAFT; www.whitewatervoyages. com) is a local outfit that runs class III, IV, and V trips down the Upper Kern, Kaweah, and Kings rivers for paddlers both experienced and novice. Trips usually last five hours, although longer ones can be arranged. Availability is from April through August with costs up to $180 per person. **Kaweah White Water Adventures** (☎ 800-229-8658 or 559-561-1000; www.kaweahwhitewater.com) also runs trips down the Kings and Kaweah Rivers.

Escaping the rain

Even though the odds are against daylong rains during a summer visit to these parks, it can happen. So what do you do? Go underground and visit **Crystal Cave.** You won't get rained on while you're underground, but you may see the aftermath of the rain in the form of increased water flows in the cave.

The **Giant Forest Museum** is a great place to avoid rain while gaining a better understanding of the ecology of sequoia groves. Displays inside the museum include one that shows how many elephants (22) it would take, stacked one atop another, to reach the average height of a sequoia.

The setting around the museum is a terrific example of how the park service is working to protect the landscape. Once upon a time a market, cafeteria, gift shop, three motels and hundreds of cabins stood here in the Giant Forest. The restoration work that began in earnest in the late 1990s turned the market into today's museum, removed the other buildings and cabins, as well as nearly 1 million square feet of asphalt parking lot, and replanted the area with native plants.

Standing in front of the museum is the **Sentinel Tree,** a 2,200-year-old sequoia that rises nearly 260 feet. Laid in the pavement between the tree and the museum are tiles that run the length of the tree so you can get a better idea of how tall it is. Every 20 feet there's a marker that shows how thick the tree's trunk is at that point of its height.

Of course, if the rain's not coming down too hard, and you have rain gear, don't let the weather stop you from seeing the parks. A walk through misty sequoia groves can be entrancing, and if you stop at Tharp's Log near Crescent Meadow, you can take in the same view that Mr. Tharp did on rainy days.

Where to Stay

The arrival of Wuksachi Lodge at Sequoia National Park and John Muir Lodge at Grant Grove Village in Kings Canyon National Park in the summer of 1999 brought two much-needed lodging options to the parks, but, overall, your choices are still pretty limited. (The parks don't have a "signature" lodge that's part of a must-see park experience.) For more tips on finding a place to stay, see Chapter 6.

Lodging in the parks

Cedar Grove Lodge
$$$ Kings Canyon National Park

This lodge, situated along the banks of the South Fork of the Kings River, isn't the Grand Hotel, but it's the only place in the heart of the park where you can have a roof over your head and a cafe downstairs. The modest rooms that line a central hallway are comfortable, but you won't find a telephone or TV in them. What you will find are communal decks off the first and second floors, a small picnic area squeezed between the lodge and the river, and a cafe that serves three meals a day. Although the cafe isn't exactly sumptuous, it gets the job done.

See map p. 254. California 180, Cedar Grove. ☎ ***866-K-CANYON,*** *or 559-335-5500;* www.sequoia-kingscanyon.com. *22 rooms. Rack rate: $105–$115 double. AE, DISC, MC, V. Closed in winter.*

John Muir Lodge
$$$ Kings Canyon National Park

This lodge's opening in the summer of 1999 brought a badly needed flourish to accommodations in Grant Grove Village, which previously had been limited to woefully rustic cabins and tent cabins. The rooms offer two queen beds and feature handmade hickory log furniture. You find a large rock fireplace in the lodge's great room; the log mantle over the fireplace was cut in the Giant Forest in the late 1800s. If you plan a summer stay here, book your room at least two months in advance. During the off-season, a week ahead usually is good enough.

See map p. 254. California 180, Grant Grove Village. ☎ ***866-K-CANYON*** *or 559-335-5500;* www.sequoia-kingscanyon.com. *30 rooms. TEL. Rack rates: $109–$149 double. DISC, MC, V.*

Silver City Resort
$–$$$$$ Sequoia National Park

This private resort is popular and books quickly. The 13 cabins are fairly well dispersed across 8 acres. All have kitchens (with dishes, pots, and pans) and decks with barbeque grills; some have wood-burning stoves. Less expensive cabins sleep two to five guests, and some require users to head to centrally located showers and restrooms. The more expensive chalet-style cabins sleep six to eight people and have a living area and private bathrooms. However, you're expected to provide your own bedding, towels, and trash bags. For high-season rentals, folks should call at least six months ahead (reservations are accepted up to a year in advance); for low seasons, a month in advance is usually sufficient.

See map p. 254. Mineral King Road (off California 198; the resort is about halfway between Lookout Point and Mineral King). ☎ ***559-561-3223.*** *In winter, call 805-528-2730.*

www.silvercityresort.com. *13 cabins; 4 with private bath, 3 with shared bath, the rest use a bathhouse. Rack rates: $70–$275 double; 25 percent less from June 1–15 and mid-Sept –mid-Oct. MC, V. Open: Early June to mid-fall.*

The Tent Cabins at Grant Grove
$–$$$ Kings Canyon National Park

A rustic feel pervades these cabins. Only nine have indoor plumbing and private baths. Fourteen have electricity. The rest feature battery-powered lamps for illumination, propane- or wood-burning stoves for heat, and communal bathrooms. Oh yeah, some of the cabins are wooden, and others are canvas. Just make sure you break the news to your family before arriving.

See map p. 254. California 180, Grant Grove Village. ☎ *866-K-CANYON or 559-335-5500; www.sequoia-kingscanyon.com. 52 cabins, 9 with private bath. Rack rates: $45 $117 double. AE, MC, V.*

Wuksachi Lodge
$$–$$$$ Sequoia National Park

Opened in 1999 as the first part of a proposed village with nearly 400 rooms, this lodge has three detached buildings with rooms and a separate lodge holding a great room with wood stove, dining room, small lounge, and meeting rooms. Although the guestrooms are spacious and complete with TVs, phones, and phone dataport (if you just can't leave work at home), they're somewhat motelish and lack the elegance of a top-of-the-line park lodge. They're also hard to get into, literally, because the doors into each building are on the ends and back side and require you to negotiate a paved walkway uphill from the parking lot. That said, these are the best rooms in the park — comfortable and in a gorgeous setting. As to when the rest of the village will be built-out, in 2004 there was no timetable.

See map p. 254. Generals Highway, Wuksachi Village. ☎ *888-252-5757; www.visitsequoia.com. 102 rooms. TV, TEL. $79–$219 double. AE, DISC, DC, MC, V.*

Lodging outside the parks

Stony Creek Lodge
$$$ Giant Sequoia National Monument

Located along the General's Highway between Grant Grove in Kings Canyon National Park and Giant Forest in Sequoia National Park, this river rock and timber lodge is a perfect middleground from which to base your explorations. With just 11 rooms, the lodge operates much like a bed and breakfast. The spacious lobby has a stone fireplace to relax in front of after a day in the parks. Rooms come with televisions and dataport phones, and the lodge has a cyber room if you left your laptop at home.

See map p. 254. Generals Highway (between General Grant Grove and Wuksachi Village. ☎ *866-K-CANYON or 559-565-3909; www.sequoia-kingscanyon.com. 11 rooms. Rack rates: $125–$135 double occupancy. Rates include Cointinental breakfast. AE, DISC, MC, V. Open: Mid-May to Oct.*

Runner-up lodgings

Best Western Holiday Lodge

$$–$$$ **Three Rivers**   This hotel along the banks of the Kaweah River offers standard rooms as well as suites with fireplaces. A pool is on the property, and you can bring your pets. *40105 Sierra Dr.* ☎ **800-528-1234** or *559-561-4119.*

Buckeye Tree Lodge

$–$$$$ **Three Rivers**   Just ¼ mile west of Sequoia National Park, this riverside lodge offers motel rooms and a cottage that sleeps five. A pool and a creek for fishing are on the grounds. *46000 Sierra Dr.* ☎ **559-561-5900.** www.buckeyetree.com.

Montecito-Sequoia Resort

$$–$$$$$ **Sequoia National Forest**   A great family retreat for weeklong summer vacations, this lodge just southeast of Grant Grove occasionally rents rooms by the night on summer weekends and for two nights at a time in winter. *8000 Generals Hwy.* ☎ **800-227-9900** or *559-565-3388.* www.montecito sequoia.com.

Holiday Inn Express-Sequoia

$$–$$$ **Three Rivers**   A few miles west of Sequoia National Park's south entrance, this reliable chain operation includes a pool for cooling off and a Continenal breakfast. *40820 Sierra Dr.* ☎ **559-561-9000.**

Campgrounds

Scattered throughout the parks are 14 campgrounds offering a variety of amenities. They all offer tables, fire grills, garbage cans, and pit or flush toilets. All but South Fork have drinking water. Most also have bear-proof storage bins that you must use. Rates range from $12 to $20 per night. During the summer months, most campgrounds offer ranger programs.

Lodgepole and **Dorst campgrounds** in Sequoia get the most action. They're the only campgrounds that accept reservations (☎ **800-365-2267**), and then only for the busy summer season between Memorial Day and mid-October. You can call five months in advance of your trip. Dorst, which is open from Memorial Day through Labor Day, also has group sites.

To arrange group campsites at **Grant** and **Cedar Groves,** call ☎ **559-565-4341** or write either Sunset Group Sites at Grant Grove or Canyon View Group Sites at Cedar Grove, both at P.O. Box 926, Kings Canyon National Park, CA 93633.

Many of the parks' higher elevation campgrounds close in late fall. There is a limit of one vehicle and six people per campsite. You can get your trailer into 11 of the 14 campgrounds, but none of the campgrounds has hookups.

In Sequoia National Park

For getting away from it all and escaping the crowds, go to **Atwell Mill Campground**. Located along Mineral King Road, 20 miles east of California 198, the campground has just 23 sites ($12 per night) along the East Fork of the Kaweah River. Mineral King Road isn't recommended if you're hauling a trailer or driving an RV.

Much the same description befits **Cold Springs**, closer to Mineral King, 5 miles to the east of Atwell Mill. At 7,500 feet, this campground (which has 40 sites, $12 per night) is the highest you can reach with your car in the park. Popular on summer weekends, the sites often fill up on Friday afternoons and holiday weekends. Come early if you want a spot. During midweek, you shouldn't have any problem finding a site.

If you really want to flee the crowds, head for the **South Fork Campground** in the park's southern tip. To reach this secluded spot and its 13 sites ($12 per night), take the South Fork Road turnoff from California 198 and drive 13 miles. The setting along the South Fork of the Kaweah River is nice. The campground is busy in spring and fall, but in summer, the heat keeps the crowds away. You can self-register here for a backcountry trek, but if you need maps or have questions, go to the Foothills Visitor Center near the Ash Mountain Entrance.

If your idea of camping is pitching your tent next to 214 others ($20 per night), then the **Lodgepole Campground** (☎ 800-365-2267) is for you. Despite the awesome setting in Marble Fork Canyon, I'm not a fan of this place because of the crowds. Still, amenities are plentiful, with a grocery, showers, restaurant, dump station, gift shop, and stables nearby. Plus, ranger talks are held here most evenings in the summer.

Dorst Campground (☎ 800-365-2267) is also an experience in communal camping with its 204 sites ($20 per night). The location isn't bad, just 14 miles northwest of the Giant Forest on the Generals Highway and 8 miles from the Lodgepole marketplace. Like Lodgepole, its selling points are facilities: Grocery, dump station, and laundry.

If it's near sundown as you pass through the Ash Mountain Entrance, the **Potwisha Campground** is just 3 miles up the road. This somewhat small campground has 43 sites ($18 per night). The setting amid oak trees and along the Marble Fork of the Kaweah River is pretty. It can be hot in the summer, but the nearby river has great pools for cooling off in. Also nearby is Hospital Rock, which has a nice collection of Native American pictographs painted on its side.

Buckeye Flat Campground is also close to the Ash Mountain Entrance. About 6 miles inside the park, you see the Hospital Rock Ranger Station. From here, follow the signs to the campground with its 28 sites ($18 per night), which are a few miles further down a narrow, windy road. Like Potwisha, the pretty riverside setting is nice, but it can get awfully hot in the summer.

In Kings Canyon National Park

Kings Canyon has six campgrounds, all of them fairly large.

The best settings, in terms of facilities and atmosphere, are the three campgrounds in Grant Grove. The tall trees are nearby, and all three have evening ranger programs. You also find a grocery, showers, and stables within walking distance. **Crystal Springs Campground** is the park's smallest facility with 63 sites ($18 per night). Nearby is **Sunset Campground** with 200 sites ($18 per night) and **Azalea Campground** with 113 sites ($18 per night). These places don't usually fill during the middle of the week, but they can quickly do so on weekends.

The four other campgrounds are in the vicinity of Cedar Grove, which offers a grocery, laundry, bicycle rentals, stables, and a small cafe at the Cedar Grove Lodge. **Sentinel Campground** fills surprisingly fast even though it has 83 sites ($18 per night). The other nearby choices are **Sheep Creek Campground** with 111 ($18 per night) sites or **Moraine Campground**, which opens its 120 sites ($18 per night) only when the other two campgrounds are full — something that doesn't happen too often. **Canyon View Campground** has 37 sites ($18 per night) for tents only.

Where to Eat

With few lodging options inside the parks, you shouldn't be surprised that dining options are limited, too, outside of the snack bars at Lodgepole, Grant Grove, and Cedar Grove villages. In Sequoia, the only true sit-down dinner is at Wuksachi Lodge; Lodgepole has a fast-food grill. In Kings Canyon, your choices are the Family Dining Restaurant at Grant Grove Village and the Cedar Grove Lodge. The meals aren't terribly creative, but then, this isn't San Francisco. Breakfast options are predictable: Eggs, pancakes, French toast, and cereal. Lunches revolve around burgers and sandwiches, and dinners mainly include beef, pasta, chicken, and fish.

Restaurants in the parks

Cedar Grove Café

$$ **Kings Canyon National Park** SHORT-ORDER GRILL

This place is your only option in the bottom of Kings Canyon National Park. From pasta dishes to nightly specials such as chicken fried steak, the food is basic but affordable. Breakfasts range from eggs and bacon to French toast, and lunch is mostly burgers and sandwiches. You can eat in a small dining area or take your food outside to the deck or even to a picnic area by the river if the bugs aren't biting.

See map p. 254. California 180, Cedar Grove Village. ☎ *559-565-0100. Main courses: $3.50–$6.25 breakfast; $3.95–$7.95 lunch; $3.95–$16.95 dinner. AE, DISC, MC, V. Open: Daily 8 a.m.–8 p.m. Closed Oct–May.*

Family Dining Restaurant
$$–$$$ Kings Canyon National Park   AMERICAN

You won't be dazzled by the ambience — but then, you're here for food, not photo ops. As the name of this place suggests, the menu appeals to all family members. Breakfasts run the gamut from short-order grill items like pancakes and French toast to biscuits and gravy and cheese omelets. A selection of fresh fruit is usually offered, too. Sandwiches and burgers dominate the lunch menu, and dinners reflect the West: Steaks, BBQ ribs, and trout dishes, with a few pasta options.

See map p. 254. California 180, Grant Grove Village. ☎ *559-335-5500. Main courses: $3.95–$6.95 breakfast; $6–$8.95 lunch; $8.95–$18.95 dinner. AE, MC, V. Open: May–Sept 7 a.m.–9 p.m.; Oct–April 7 a.m.–7 p.m; hours may vary.*

Lodgepole Deli and Pizza
$$$ Sequoia National Park   SHORT-ORDER GRILL

There's nothing fancy about this short-order grill, but it's quick and inexpensive. If your're on the run, you can grab a sandwich, wrap, or salad at the adjoining deli or visit the grocery next door.

See map p. 254. Generals Highway, Lodgepole Village. No phone. Main courses: $2–$3 breakfast; $4.75–$5.75 lunch; $3.25–$9.95 dinner. AE, DISC, DC, MC, V. Open: Daily 8 a.m.– 8 p.m.

Silver City Restaurant
$$ Sequoia National Park   AMERICAN

Although it's by no means fancy, you can find home-cooked meals at this restaurant if you can't be bothered to cook for yourself in your cabin. Silver City is open for three meals a day Thursday through Monday; on Tuesdays and Wednesdays the cook heads to town to restock, although you can still get breakfast. When the cook's around, breakfasts come from the grill and include omelets, pancakes, and such. When he's gone, look for a cold breakfast buffet with cereals, baked goods, and instant oatmeal. The lunch menu features grill items such as burgers, hot sandwiches, and French fries. Dinners mirror the lunch menu, with the addition of a nightly special such as lasagna, a lemon chicken dish, or steak. Homemade pies are a speciality here. Try the "Fruits of the Forest" pie, which incorporates five different fruits.

See map p. 254. Mineral King Road, Mineral King (off Hwy. 198; the resort is about halfway between Lookout Point and Mineral King). ☎ *559-561-3223. Main courses: $5–$6 breakfast; $6–$7 lunch; $9–$14 dinner. MC, V. Open: Early June to mid-fall Thurs–Mon 8 a.m.–8 p.m; Tue–Wed breakfast buffet 8 a.m.–3 p.m.*

Wolverton BBQ
$$–$$$ Sequoia National Park   AMERICAN

What better place for a barbecue than on the edge of a beautiful meadow in the heart of the park? Wednesdays through Sundays throughout the summer the grills are fired up at Wolverton for an all-you-can-eat dinner buffet that's followed by a ranger-led hike or talk. Dinners served under the evening sky on a redwood deck are traditional barbecue-style, with finger-sucking ribs and chicken, hot dogs, hamburgers, salads, vegetables, cornbread, iced tea and lemonade, and pie for dessert.

Generals Highway, Wolverton. Tickets can be purchased at the Wuksachi Lodge or Lodgepole Market. $9.49 children 12 and under; $18.99 adults. AE, DISC, DC, MC, V. 6 p.m.–8:30 p.m.

Wuksachi Lodge
$$$–$$$$ Sequoia National Park   AMERICAN

Beams and rock-work lend a rustic elegance to this lodge, which features a small lounge and 130-seat dining room. The views of 11,188-foot Mount Silliman from the dining room are gorgeous, particularly as the sun is setting. Breakfasts are built around a buffet that features hot and cold cereals, fresh fruits, pancakes, and pastries. Lunch offers a nice variety of creative salads and sandwiches, and dinners can get elaborate — and expensive — if you splurge for the prime rib with garlic mashed potatoes, for example.

See map p. 254. Generals Highway, Wuksachi Village. ☎ 888-252-5757. Dinner reservations recommended. Main courses: $6.25–$9.95 breakfast; $7.75–$11.75 lunch; $13.25–$28.95 dinner. AE, DISC, DC, MC, V. Open: 7 a.m.–4:30 p.m., 5:30–9 p.m.

Restaurants outside the parks

Kings Canyon Lodge Bar and Grill
$–$$ Sequoia National Forest   AMERICAN

Found at the bottom of the mountain as you head to Cedar Grove, this waystation is good for a quick bite or a cool drink before you continue to the park. The restaurant offers short-order dishes for breakfast and burgers, soups, and salads for lunch and dinner. The atmosphere is interesting, because meals are served inside a well-aged bar with an Old West feel.

California 180 (between Grant Grove and Cedar Grove Villages). ☎ 559-335-2405. Reservations not needed. Main courses: $2–$7 breakfast; $6–$8 lunch and dinner. MC, V. Open: Daily 8 a.m.–8 p.m. Closed mid-Nov to April.

Fast Facts: Sequoia and Kings Canyon

Area Code

The local area code is **559**.

ATM

You can find ATMs at Grant Grove, Lodgepole Villages, and Stony Creek.

Emergency

In an emergency, dial **911**.

Fees

Entrance fees are $10 per vehicle per week, and $5 for those on foot, bicycle, or motorcycle.

Fishing License

California license are required and are available at most park grocery stores. Get a copy of park fishing regulations at any visitor center.

Hospitals

One local hospital is the Kaweah Delta Hospital, located at 400 W. Mineral in Visalia (☎ 559-624-2000). Another hospital is Community Regional Medical Center, located at 2823 Fresno St. in Fresno (☎ 559-459-6000).

Information

For information, write to Sequoia & Kings Canyon National Parks, 47050 Generals Hwy., Three Rivers, CA 93271-9651, call ☎ 559-565-3341, or look on the Internet at www.nps.gov/seki.

Pharmacies

One local pharmacy is Three Rivers Drug Store, at 40893 Sierra Drive in Three Rivers (☎ 559-561-4217).

Post Office

One local post office is in the Lodgepole Market Center in Sequoia National Park (559-565-3468). Another is in Grant Grove at Kings Canyon National Park (☎ 559-335-2499).

Road Conditions and Weather

For information on road conditions and weather, call ☎ 559-565-3341.

Time Zone

The parks are on Pacific time.

Chapter 16

Yellowstone National Park

● ●

In This Chapter

▶ Introducing my favorite park
▶ Planning your trip
▶ Exploring geysers, hot springs, canyons, and lakes
▶ Finding lodging and restaurants around the park

● ●

*W*hich park in America is my favorite? Yellowstone National Park, hands down. Nowhere else can you find the diversity that distinguishes this park. From the world's greatest collection of geysers and hot springs to sparkling alpine lakes, rugged peaks, and an incredible array of wildlife, Yellowstone packs more into its boundaries than any other American park. Early explorers called it "Wonderland" for good reason.

With more than 10,000 **geothermal features** in all shapes, sizes, temperaments, and temperatures, Yellowstone is geyser central. Old Faithful is just one of roughly 150 geysers in the park's Upper Geyser Basin. In the Midway Geyser Basin simmers Grand Prismatic Spring, the park's largest spring with its 370-foot diameter. Grand Prismatic is an azure-hued hot spring ringed by yellow and orange algae. At Mammoth Hot Springs, centuries of cascading, mineral-laden hot water have stacked brilliantly white terraces one atop another. These and the rest of Yellowstone's thermal features are constantly changing. Some die out, others get feistier, and new ones spit, claw, and fume into existence through rifts in the earth.

Not to be upstaged by these waterworks is Yellowstone's **animal kingdom.** This park has the market cornered when it comes to big furry poster animals suitable for environmental issues. With the reintroduction of wolves in the mid-1990s, the park's wild kingdom has been returned to its original state for the first time since government hunters wiped wolves out of Yellowstone in the 1950s. The more than 150 wolves that now lope about Yellowstone share the park with elk, bison, coyotes, bears, and the occasional moose. The animals give Yellowstone a wild, sometimes scary, edge. On spring and fall nights you may hear the baleful howling of wolves. If your timing is right, you may see grizzly bears and wolves tussling over elk and bison carcasses in the Lamar Valley. In the Hayden Valley, you occasionally have to stop your car to make way for bison, which sometimes weigh nearly a ton and have horn-topped heads.

Yellowstone Lake is also unforgettable. Glassy and serene during the early mornings and evenings on calm summer days, the lake can quickly be whipped into a choppy inland sea with 6-foot waves. Dotted by islands and rimmed by dense lodgepole forests, the lake nurtures rich fisheries that lure anglers from around the world. Draining the lake, the Yellowstone River flows serenely to the **Grand Canyon of the Yellowstone,** where it roars over two towering waterfalls. Standing on the brink of 308-foot-tall Lower Falls, you may feel a passing wave of vertigo, but you'll also understand why 19th-century landscape artists, like Thomas Moran, were so taken by the setting. After crashing to the canyon floor, the river continues to cut the canyon deeper and deeper through yellow- and buff-colored walls.

 If you can visit only one national park, make it Yellowstone. Granted, the park's immense popularity generates stifling summertime masses, but in this chapter, I share secrets for avoiding the throngs. In general, remember that, although the front country can get frustratingly crowded during the height of summer when most of the park's 3 million annual visitors arrive, the backcountry provides solitude, serenity, and the same image of the Rocky Mountain West that confronted 19th-century mountain pioneers.

Must-See Attractions

Should you look for geysers? Bison? Wolves? Glassy lakes? Which direction should you head when you arrive in Yellowstone? These questions are always tough for me, because the park has so many wonderful places to go and things to look for. I'm sure that you'll quickly develop your own favorites, but until then, here's a cheat sheet to get you started:

- ✔ **Old Faithful Inn:** This venerable old inn turned 100 in 2004, yet hardly looks its age. In fact, I consider it the prototypical "stately national park inn." It also is arguably the world's largest log cabin. Sitting in a rocking chair in front of the massive four-sided fireplace after dinner is a great way to end a day in the park.

- ✔ **Artist Point:** One of several overlooks below the Yellowstone River's Lower Falls, this vantage point has inspired artists for more than a century.

- ✔ **Lake Yellowstone Hotel:** This Colonial Revival–style hotel, with an interior that might remind you of *The Great Gatsby,* offers the park's most luxurious accommodations. Its Sun Room, just off the lobby, features 1891 wicker furniture and live music nightly.

- ✔ **The Lamar Valley:** This rolling valley in the park's northeast corner comes to life in late spring when elk, bison, grizzly bears, and wolves all converge for nourishment.

- ✔ **Mammoth Hot Springs:** Located just inside the North Entrance, Mammoth Hot Springs is home to park headquarters and, in the Albright Visitor Center, one of the park's best museums. You also

Yellowstone National Park

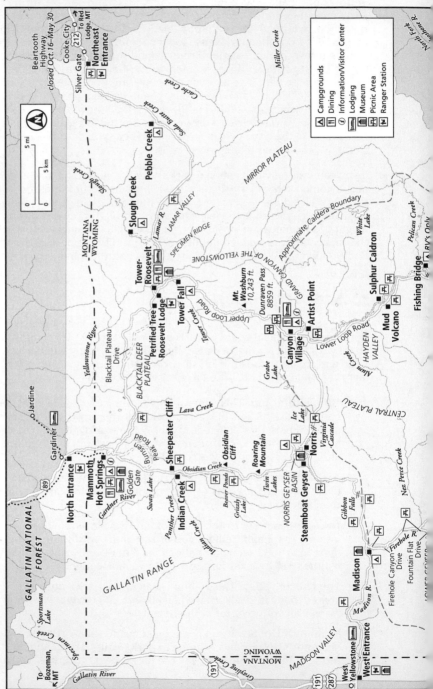

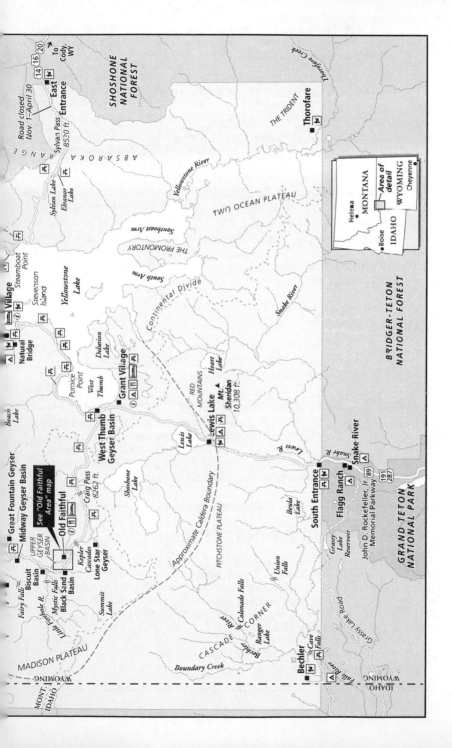

find buildings erected for Fort Yellowstone, which was the military outpost when the cavalry administered the park before the National Park Service took over.

✔ **Mud Volcano:** The sulphurous, sputtering machinations of mud pots and hot springs found at this attraction are amazing. Because the springs are heavy with muds and clays, their fizzling, bubbling, and plopping is different from what you see at the other geyser basins.

✔ **The Norris Geyser Basin:** The park's hottest, and oldest, geyser basin has more than 2 miles of trails that navigate through the geysers and hot springs. The area contains Steamboat, the world's tallest active geyser, which blasts 300 to 400 feet into the sky. Although spectacular, Steamboat is utterly unpredictable. Eruptions often are many years apart; this geyser last erupted in May 2000, and before that in October 1991.

✔ **The Upper Geyser Basin:** One of five basins in the park's front country where thermal features are concentrated, this area is home to Old Faithful, the world's most famous geyser, and the historic Old Faithful Inn.

Planning Ahead

For information before you visit, contact Yellowstone National Park, P.O. Box 168, Yellowstone National Park, WY 82190; ☎ **307-344-7381;** www. nps.gov/yell.

When to go and how long to stay

You should spend at least three days in Yellowstone. When should you visit? Most visitors come in summer and avoid winter, although the weather is unpredictable year-round. Snow can fall any day of the year, and midwinter *chinooks* (warm, dry winds) can spawn springlike days. Fickleness aside, the park has four distinct seasons.

You'll fall for these!

Yellowstone's more than 100 major waterfalls are often overlooked because of the park's geothermal features and wildlife. Among the falls are the well-known Lower Falls in the Grand Canyon of the Yellowstone and the overlooked 30-foot-tall Moose Falls found less than 1 mile inside the park's South Entrance. The extreme southwestern corner of the park has so many waterfalls that it's known as Cascade Corner, where you find Dunanda Falls (150 feet), Ouzel Falls (235 feet), Colonnade Falls (a "double" waterfall that has a 35-foot upper fall and a 67-foot lower fall), and Union Falls (250 feet). But you can only see the falls in Cascade Corner if you plan a multiday backcountry trip; none of them is close to a road.

Spring doesn't really show up in earnest before mid-May. In fact, I find April and early May about the worst times to visit Yellowstone. Sure, you won't encounter many crowds. But the mud, the harsh bite of a late-season snowstorm, and the weather's overall rawness can be trying. But one positive side is that you can good deals on lodging this time of year — a room at Mammoth Hot Springs for $40 a night!

Summer begins to show its hand by mid-June as red, blue, purple, orange, and yellow wildflowers erupt into bloom across the park's lower reaches, a ritual that slowly creeps into the high country throughout July and into August. By late June, the first serious waves of tourists arrive in the park, and their cars, at times choking the roads, begin to crawl along the Grand Loop (the main road). This height of the season is a paradox, capturing the best and the worst of Yellowstone. Comfortable temperatures and long days offer plenty of time for sightseeing. But hotels and lodges are booked, campgrounds fill early in the day, and the narrow roads overflow with cars, trucks, and lumbering motor homes. You'll appreciate having made your room reservations well in advance and heeding my advice for avoiding crowds.

 Fall consists of a handful of weeks of decent weather between Labor Day and the return of winter. If you're not bound by school vacations, early fall — from mid-September to mid-October — is the best time to visit Yellowstone. Crowds are generally tolerable, animals become more visible as they return to the river bottoms to fortify themselves against the onslaught of winter, and the weather is typically reliable. Not to be ignored are the occasional bargain prices — savings of 30 percent and greater! — to be found at the lodges in the fall as closing day approaches.

Winter is Yellowstone's longest season, and although the weather can be harsh, the season can be a magical time to visit the park. Winter can settle in as early as October and stay through April. Heavy snows and freezing temperatures (which can plunge far below zero at night and hover around zero during the day) hamper life for both human and animal. Most park roads are closed to automobile traffic between November and May. Only the route from Mammoth Hot Springs to the Northeast Entrance remains plowed during the winter, so the gateway communities of Silvergate and Cooke City, Montana, aren't detached from the world. But cross-country skis, snow coaches, and snowshoes provide a fun mode of travel else-where in the snowbound park, and heavy snows create a fairy-tale atmos-phere in the forests and around the geyser basins.

Advance reservations

 Fame carries its burdens, and in Yellowstone, the demand for hotel rooms and campsites is high. Fail to plan ahead by at least several months, and you will have a hard time finding any accommodations, even in the fall when crowds drop off. And if you don't start working on reservations at least six months ahead, you won't be able to stay exactly where you want to, or when.

All lodging is managed by **Xanterra Parks & Resorts** (☎ 307-344-7311; www.xanterra.com.) as well as Fishing Bridge RV Park and the Madison, Grant Village, Bridge Bay, and Canyon campgrounds. You can make reservations a year in advance for both hotels and campgrounds through their phone number or Web site. (You also can make dinner reservations months in advance at restaurants inside the park lodges.)

If you're planning to head into the backcountry and want to reserve a campsite in advance, you need to obtain a $20 backcountry permit from the park's **Central Backcountry Office** (P.O. Box 168, Yellowstone National Park, WY 82190; ☎ 307-344-2160). On April 1, the park begins booking reservations for backcountry campsites. All reservation requests received by that date are randomly prioritized by computer and then processed in that order. After April 1, reservations are made as requests are received. If you have specific dates and campsites in mind for your trip, I suggest that you apply before the April 1 date. Otherwise, you chance not getting what you want, although you may still be able to choose from a limited selection. For more information on this process, and for details on backcountry campsites, contact the backcountry office.

What to pack

Summer days in Yellowstone are about the best in the Rockies — sunny skies; warm, but not hot, temperatures; and low humidity. So pack plenty of shorts and T-shirts, as well as a good hat, sunblock, and a rain jacket for those occasional thundershowers. After the sun goes down, though, it really cools off, so be sure to have a light jacket or sweater handy. Although most of the park's dining is informal, you may want to bring something casual but nice to slip into if you're heading to Lake Hotel for dinner.

Getting There

Yellowstone seems terribly far away, because it's located almost entirely in Wyoming's northwestern corner with some spillover into Idaho and Montana. The park is accessible by state and national highways from all three states, as well as by year-round bus service between Bozeman, Montana and West Yellowstone. Unless you live nearby or enjoy long drives, fly into one of the nearby airports, rent a rig, and drive to the park.

Flying in

Commercial air service can get you close to the park, with the nearest airports being in Bozeman, Montana, and West Yellowstone. Bozeman's **Gallatin Field** (☎ 406-388-8321; www.gallatinfield.com) is served daily by **Delta, Northwest,** and **United,** along with regional airlines

Horizon and **Skywest.** Car rentals are available on-site from **Enterprise, Hertz, Budget,** and **National.** Off-site rentals include **Avis, Thrifty, Rentawreck,** and **Dollar.** (See the Appendix for the toll-free numbers of all the airlines and car-rental agencies mentioned throughout this section.)

Skywest, which is affiliated with Delta and United, serves **West Yellowstone Airport** (☎ 406-646-7631) from May through September. **Avis** and **Budget** provide car rentals. The airport closes in winter.

Farther away is Billings, Montana, a 129-mile drive from the park's Northeast Entrance that easily takes more than three hours. Billings' **Logan International** (☎ 406-247-8609; www.flybillings.com) has service from **America West, Big Sky, Delta, Frontier, Horizon, Northwest,** and **United.** Car rentals are available from **Avis, Budget, Hertz, Enterprise,** and **National.**

South of Yellowstone, the **Jackson Hole Airport** (☎ 307-733-7682) lies within Grand Teton National Park. **American, Delta, Northwest, Skywest,** and **United Express** serve this airport, which is 56 miles from Yellowstone's South Entrance. Car rentals are available from **Alamo, Avis, Budget,** and **Hertz.**

In Cody, Wyoming, located 52 miles from the East Entrance, **Yellowstone Regional Airport** (☎ 307-587-5096) offers year-round service via **Skywest** and **United Express** and car rentals from **Hertz, Avis,** and **Thrifty.**

Driving in

If you drive to Yellowstone from Cody, Wyoming, follow U.S. 14/20/16 west to the park's East Entrance. From Jackson, Wyoming, take U.S. 191/89/287 north to the park's South Entrance. From Idaho, U.S. 20 north from Island Park leads 29 miles to West Yellowstone and the West Entrance. In Montana, U.S. 191 leads 91 miles south from Bozeman to West Yellowstone. From Bozeman, U.S. 89 leads 79 miles east to the North Entrance at Gardiner, Montana.

Because winter weather closes most park roads, if you're planning an early spring or late fall trip, check **road conditions** with the park (☎ 307-344-7381) before heading out. Whereas the road from Mammoth Hot Springs to the Northeast Entrance communities of Silvergate and Cooke City is open year-round, weather and road conditions permitting, the West Entrance Road typically closes to automobile traffic from the first Sunday in November through the third Friday in April. The South and East Entrance Roads usually close the first Sunday in November and reopen to auto traffic on the first Friday in May. As soon as snow cover allows — generally the third Wednesday in December — these roads, and the West Entrance Road, reopen to over-the-snow vehicles.

The Beartooth Highway, which climbs through the Absaroka Range on a 69-mile journey from Red Lodge, Montana, to the park's Northeast Entrance, is one of the most scenic routes in America. But its precipitous curves can generate vertigo, and winter weather usually keeps it closed from the day after Columbus Day to Memorial Day weekend. The Chief Joseph Highway from Cody to the Northeast Entrance is also spectacular, with sprawling views of the Sunlight Basin, but the road's many switchbacks aren't designed for speed.

Busing in

During the summer months, you can take **Greyhound Bus Lines** (☎ **800-229-9424** or 406-587-3110; www.greyhound.com) from downtown Bozeman, Montana, to West Yellowstone.

Yellowstone Alpen Guides (☎ **800-858-3502** or 406-646-9591; www.yellowstoneguides.com) operates out of West Yellowstone, Montana, and offers private park tours for families and small groups, as well as winter snow coach tours.

Orienting Yourself in Yellowstone

Yellowstone is bigger than Rhode Island and Delaware combined. Most of the park's 3,472 square miles are rugged wilderness — canyons cut deep by rushing rivers, mountains thrust above 11,000 feet by volcanoes and earthquakes, and alpine lakes gleam under an endless sky. Weaving through the heart and soul of this wilderness is the **Grand Loop,** a lazy, figure-eight, two-lane road that crawls past the major attractions. You won't travel fast on this road (which is broken into the Upper and Lower Loops), because portions of it are continually under repair. Cut from the wilderness as a narrow stagecoach route in the 19th century, the loop road is damaged by ponderous motor homes, largely because underlying thermal heat weakens some spots of the road surface and brutal freeze-thaw episodes buckle the asphalt.

Upper Loop Road

From Mammoth Hot Springs, the 70-mile **Upper Loop Road** runs to the way stations of Norris, Canyon Village, and Tower-Roosevelt before heading back to Mammoth Hot Springs.

Mammoth Hot Springs is home to park headquarters, as well as a museum, hotel, some restaurants, a grocery, a gas station, gift shops, and other facilities. **Norris** has a campground, small visitor center, and ranger museum, but no hotel accommodations or restaurants. **Canyon Village** has lodging, restaurants, a gas station, and a visitor center. **Tower-Roosevelt** has a lodge/restaurant, surrounding cabins, as well as a small grocery and a gas station.

Two miles south of Tower-Roosevelt is the **Tower Fall** complex, which has a convenience store, gift shop, campground, and offers a nice hike to one of the park's most accessible (and most dramatic) waterfalls.

Running to the east of Tower-Roosevelt is the **Lamar Valley Road** that leads through the wildlife-rich Lamar Valley on its way to the park's Northeast Entrance at Silvergate, Montana.

Lower Loop Road

 I haven't seen any studies, but my guess is that the 96-mile **Lower Loop Road,** which ties together Madison, Old Faithful, West Thumb, Bridge Bay, Lake Village, Fishing Bridge, Canyon Village, and Norris, is the busiest strip of road in Yellowstone. The best of Yellowstone's geothermal features are along this road — in the Upper Geyser Basin, West Thumb, Norris, Mud Volcano, and the Lower and Midway Geyser basins.

The **West Entrance Road** ties into Lower Loop Road at **Madison,** which has a campground, museum, and picnic area. Just south of Madison is **Firehole Canyon Drive,** a 2-mile road that follows the Firehole River upstream and passes 800-foot-high lava cliffs. (This stretch of river is popular with swimmers, but diving from the cliffs is prohibited. No lifeguards are present.)

Farther south, Lower Loop Road passes through **Old Faithful,** a great base camp. Here you find three places to stay, plus a few restaurants, a visitor center, gift shops, a grocery, a service station, and a medical center. See the Old Faithful Area map in this chapter for locations.

The **South Entrance Road** meets the Lower Loop Road at **West Thumb,** which has boardwalk trails running through a geyser basin and a small visitor center. From here, moving northeast, Lower Loop Road continues along the western shore of **Yellowstone Lake.** Along this shore, you find a campground and marina at **Bridge Bay** and the gracious **Lake Yellowstone Hotel** and laid-back **Lake Lodge** in Lake Village, which also has a hospital, convenience store, and ranger station.

The **East Entrance Road** winds from Cody, Wyoming, over the 8,530-foot Sylvan Pass and along the northern shore of Yellowstone Lake to connect with the Lower Loop Road near **Fishing Bridge.** Then Lower Loop Road travels northward to **Canyon Village** through the undulating **Hayden Valley** and past short roads leading to lookout points at **Grand Canyon of the Yellowstone.**

Finding information after you arrive

Thanks to its remote location, by the time you reach Yellowstone, you'll be ready to get out, stretch your legs, and gain your bearings. Let me tell you how to do that.

Old Faithful Area

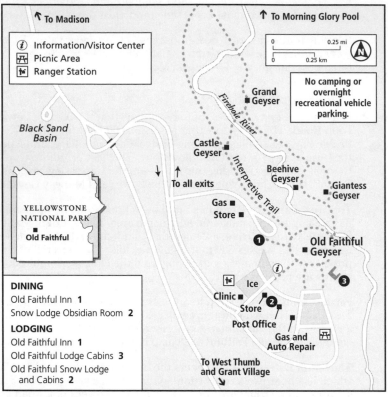

The park has five major visitor and information centers. The **Albright Visitor Center** (☎ 307-344-2263) at Mammoth Hot Springs is the largest. This center provides visitor information and publications about the park, houses a museum and exhibits depicting park history from prehistory through the creation of the National Park Service, and features a wildlife display. A short film explains the role 19th century artist Thomas Moran played in lobbying Congress to create Yellowstone National Park. Hours are 8 a.m. to 7 p.m. late May to September 1; 9 a.m. to 6 p.m. through the rest of September; 9 a.m. to 5 p.m. October through May.

The **Old Faithful Visitor Center** (☎ 307-545-2750) is another large facility. An excellent short film describing the microbial life that survives in hot springs and its value to mankind is shown throughout the day. You can also load up on guidebooks and maps and get a schedule for the day's predicted geyser eruptions. Hours are 9 a.m. to 5 p.m. mid-April to mid-May; 8 a.m. to 7 p.m. late May to September 1; 8 a.m. to 6 p.m. through rest of September. October 1 to early November 9 a.m. to 5 p.m.; and December through mid-March 9 a.m. to 5 p.m.

The **Canyon Visitor Center** (☎ 307-242-2550) in Canyon Village is the place to go for books and an informative display about bison in the park. Hours are 8 a.m. to 7 p.m. late May to September 1 and 9 a.m. to 6 p.m. the rest of September. Hours are reduced in the winter.

The **Fishing Bridge Visitor Center** (☎ 307-242-2450) near Fishing Bridge has an excellent wildlife display. You can get information and publications here as well. Hours are 8 a.m. to 7 p.m. late May to September 1 and 9 a.m. to 6 p.m. the rest of September. Closed through the winter months.

The **Grant Village Visitor Center** (☎ 307-242-2650) has information, publications, a slide program, and a fascinating exhibit that examines the effects of fire in Yellowstone. The open hours are the same as Fishing Bridge, above.

Other sources of park information are at the Madison Information Station; the Museum of the National Park Ranger and the Norris Geyser Basin Museum, both at Norris; and the West Thumb Information Station.

Paying fees

A pass to enter Yellowstone is $20 per vehicle for a seven-day period (no matter the number of occupants), and covers Yellowstone and nearby Grand Teton National Park. Entering on a motorcycle costs $15 for seven days, and if you enter the park on bicycle, skis, or foot, you pay $10. If you expect to visit Yellowstone or Grand Teton more than once in a year, buy an annual pass for $40. With a park pass, you don't have to pay the entrance fee; see Chapter 8 for information on the National Park Pass and Chapter 7 for the lowdown on Golden Age and Golden Access passports.

You must have a backcountry permit for any overnight trip (see "Planning Ahead," earlier in this chapter). For information on boating and fishing fees, see "Keeping active" later in this chapter.

Firestorm central

From Norris, the Upper Loop road runs east passing the tip of a 22-mile-long stretch of flattened forest known simply as the Norris-Canyon Blowdown. The trees here were toppled by a 1984 windstorm and were bone dry when the 1988 wildfires swept the park. As a result, this area burned particularly hot. Today, even though thousands of young pines root in the ash-rich soil, you can see charred reminders of the historic fires. Stopping at the lookout point gives you a sense of how powerfully destructive wind and fire can be — in contrast, the army of young trees demonstrates nature's healing strength.

Getting Around Yellowstone

Inside Yellowstone, you're left to get around by your own means, because the park doesn't offer public transportation.

Concessionaires provide **summer bus tours** and **snow coach tours** in winter, but most of these don't allow for much lingering, and they have a traveling-with-the-pack feel. If that's okay with you, contact **Xanterra Parks & Resorts** (☎ 307-344-7311; www.xanterra.com) about their summer bus tours of the Lower Loop, the Upper Loop, and the Grand Loop. The Upper Loop tour, known as the Washburn Expedition, has been suspended while roadwork continues over Dunraven Pass between Tower and Canyon. If the road reopens in 2005 as scheduled, that bus tour will resume. The Lower Loop tour, known as the Circle of Fire, costs $44 for adults and $21 for kids ages 12 to 16. Children 11 and under are free. The Grand Loop tour, tabbed "Yellowstone in a Day," costs $47 for adults and $23 for those ages 12 to 16; kids 11 and under are free.

In winter, Xanterra's **snow coach tours** travel round-trip from Mammoth Hot Springs to Old Faithful ($105 per person round-trip); West Yellowstone to Old Faithful ($97.50 per person round-trip); Mammoth Hot Springs to Canyon Village ($101 per person round-trip); and Old Faithful to Canyon Village ($106.50 per person round-trip). All trips are half-price for kids 2 to 11 and free under age 2. These all-day trips are expensive if you're taking your family, but a great way to explore the park in winter.

Roadwork in Yellowstone is as common as elk and bison. As a result, you need to expect delays. For instance, construction along the Chittenden-to-Tower road closed the section of the Grand Loop that negotiates Dunraven Pass throughout 2004 and into 2005. Various road projects currently on the books are expected to generate road delays of various lengths into 2008.

Snowmobiles in Grand Teton and Yellowstone

Current proposals call for a limited number of snowmobiles (720 per day) for at least the next three winters while officials once again study the environmental and economic impacts of allowing snowmobiles in the two parks. Past studies have shown that the machines are bad for the parks' environment, wildlife, employees, and visitors. The Clinton administration approved a ban, but once the Bush administration took office, it lifted the ban.

At press time, the current plan was still under review, and the situation could change drastically during the lifetime of this edition. For the latest regulations, your best bet is to check the parks Web site at www.nps.gov.

Remembering Safety

Although relaxing in a hot tub after a long day is great, **Yellowstone's thermal features** are definitely not suited for this activity. They're called *hot* springs for a reason. Temperatures of some springs, stoked by molten rock miles underground, measure well above the boiling point. (Parents should be particularly mindful of their youngsters around these features.) Even if you could survive a dip in a spring, swimming in them can damage their plumbing, so this activity is illegal in the park.

In the backcountry, boardwalks and fencing aren't in place to keep you at a safe distance from thermal features. So be very careful when hiking near these areas. At the **Shoshone Lake Geyser Basin,** for example, you can walk right up to the edge of the hot springs, but fight the urge to do so. The Earth's crust near these features is often very thin and breakable. Sadly, some hikers have fallen in and died as a result of the water's high temperatures.

Yellowstone's **lakes,** although picturesque, can also be quite deadly. Their waters are bitterly cold, and if you capsize a canoe or kayak, you could be overcome by hypothermia in a short time. Quite a few people have drowned in Yellowstone and Shoshone Lakes

Another safety issue to keep in mind when you're in the backcountry is the **wildlife.** Grizzlies and black bears both have a good sense of smell, so you need to keep a clean campsite to keep them away. Also, even though moose may look ungainly, they're amazingly quick and won't hesitate to run you down if you threaten their space.

For more tips on how to ensure a safe visit to the park, see Chapter 8.

Exploring Yellowstone

The park's geographic diversity has led to its division into five districts. **Mammoth Country** covers the northwestern corner, a region of delicate limestone terraces, broad valleys, and dense forests flanking the mountains. In the park's northeastern corner, **Roosevelt Country** embraces the Lamar Valley with its rolling plains that rim the Lamar River. Just to the south is **Canyon Country,** which claims the Grand Canyon of the Yellowstone, with its two towering waterfalls, and the Hayden Valley. **Lake Country** encompasses the park's southeastern corner, including Yellowstone and Heart lakes. The southwestern corner is **Geyser Country,** where you find the bulk of Yellowstone's 10,000-plus geothermal features.

Because these five districts are linked by the Grand Loop, you can split the park in half during visits if you don't have much time. Although you can zoom around the Grand Loop in one day and try to see all the major attractions, I don't recommend it. With unplanned wildlife sightings, the

long list of worthwhile sights, and the inevitable meal breaks, you just can't do it all in 24 hours. However, if one day is all the time you have, see "One-day wonder," later in this chapter, for my suggested itinerary.

Exploring the top attractions

Grand Canyon of the Yellowstone
Canyon Country

This canyon is an eyeful. But don't let that name cause you to confuse it with that other park in Arizona; they're two wonderfully distinct and unique places. Yellowstone's Grand Canyon was colored yellow, tan, red, and buff by thermal water reacting on the park's volcanic underbelly. Spend some time here, and you find numerous overlooks from which to view the canyon and the Yellowstone River. Located on the canyon's south rim, **Artist Point,** which is less crowded than the north-rim overlooks closer to Canyon Village, offers a better view of Lower Falls, and is handicapped-accessible. For a great, off-the-beaten-path view of the canyon, take the Specimen Ridge Trail (see "Taking a hike," later in this chapter).

Watch your step on staircases that lead to canyon overlooks, particularly in spring and fall when snow and ice can make them slippery.

You reach Grand Canyon of the Yellowstone by side roads running east from the Upper and Lower Loop roads as they pass Canyon Village.

Hayden Valley
Canyon Country

The Yellowstone River flows serenely through the valley bottom, luring not only pelicans, osprey, and eagles that seek its fish but also attracting teeming bison herds and grizzly bears that come for a drink while rooting through the hillsides and meadows for meals.

The valley is on Lower Loop Road between Canyon Village and Fishing Bridge.

Lamar Valley
Roosevelt Country

Running through the park's northeastern corner, this valley is one of the most reliable places for seeing wildlife during the spring and fall months. If you have a spotting scope or pair of binoculars, definitely pack them so you can watch grizzlies, bison, and even wolves in this sprawling valley. The area has some nice campgrounds and some great hikes, too.

The Lamar Valley is cut by the Northeast Entrance Road that runs 29 miles from Tower-Roosevelt to Silvergate, Montana.

Mammoth Hot Springs
Mammoth Country

History and geology converge at Mammoth Hot Springs, which in March 2002 was listed on the National Register of Historic Places. In the late 19th century, the U.S. Army set up camp here so soldiers could patrol the park and protect it from poachers and souvenir hunters. Today, this area is the park's headquarters, and many of the Army buildings house park offices. The park's best museum is here, located in the Albright Visitor Center.

You also find **Minerva Terrace,** a natural artwork of cascading pools fueled by hot springs. See the Lower Terrace Interpretive Trail under "Taking a hike," later in this chapter, for a short walk around the area.

Mammoth Hot Springs is at the junction of U.S. 89 and the Upper Loop Road.

Mud Volcano
Canyon Country

What makes the hot springs in the Mud Volcano area different from the hot springs elsewhere in the park? For starters, the soil-laden waters give rise to this area's fuming mud pots. Moreover, the waters are highly acidic, which lends to their pungent smell. At **Dragon's Mouth Spring,** muddy water from an underground cavern is spit forth by escaping steam and sulfurous gases to the surface where the waters color the earth in shades of orange and green. Farther up the path, the actual Mud Volcano spring is a simmering pond of mud, fueled by escaping sulfurous gases and steam.

Although all the park's geyser basins are kid-friendly — kids get a kick out of eruptions — young visitors find Mud Volcano particularly fun because of the plopping and fizzing of the mud pots.

Mud Volcano is on Lower Loop Road between Fishing Bridge and Canyon Village.

Norris Geyser Basin
Mammoth Country

This kid-pleasing attraction is the park's oldest basin with a history of thermal activity that goes back more than 115,000 years. This basin is also the hottest, with a temperature of 459 degrees measured 1,087 feet below the surface. The basin holds 2 miles of trails, which lead to such thermal stalwarts as Steamboat and Echinus geysers. Steamboat is the world's tallest active geyser, with gushers of 300 to 400 feet, but honestly, its eruptions are so infrequent that the odds of witnessing the spectacle are incredibly slim. Echinus, meanwhile, erupts 40 to 60 feet once or twice an hour. (For an orientation of this basin, see the Old Faithful Area map in this chapter.)

Capturing Old Faithful on film

For a memorable shot of Old Faithful, rise early in the morning to capture a sunrise photo without the crowds. The softer light in the early morning makes for a better image and allows you to capture the steam wafting from the basin's geysers and hot springs.

If you have a decent zoom lens, hike the ½-mile to Observation Point just southeast of the geyser. This vantage point 200 feet above the geyser gives you a sweeping view of most of the Upper Geyser Basin. (This spot is good any time of day for escaping the crowds.)

Not an early riser? Then sleep in and get your Old Faithful picture at sundown, when most folks are eating dinner.

Norris is also home to Porcelain Basin, where you can find multihued hot springs. The basin's name comes from the underlying minerals and clays that, depending on the resident minerals, turn the roiling waters pearly with milky or orangish tints.

 At the trailhead to the geyser basin is a small geology-oriented museum, one of the park's original trailside museums. Another larger museum, the nearby **Museum of the National Park Ranger,** showcases the history of rangerdom as well as the birth of the National Park Service. Both museums are free; hours vary depending on season and staffing.

The Norris Basin is at the junction of the Upper and Lower Loop roads.

 ### Upper Geyser Basin
Geyser Country

No geothermal area in the world rivals the Upper Geyser Basin, another kid-friendly attraction, which packs 150 geysers and hot springs into 1 square mile alone. Five of the six geysers whose eruptions are predicted by the park staff are located here: Castle, Grand, Daisy, Riverside, and the famous Old Faithful. (The sixth is Great Fountain in the Lower Geyser Basin.)

The **Old Faithful Geyser** clearly is the park's greatest single drawing card, and its location on a wide gray geyserite mound sets it apart from the rest of the basin and enhances its nobility. Rimmed by a boardwalk that's lined with benches, the geyser performs about every 92 minutes. But frankly, one Old Faithful performance is enough, because its eruptions draw thousands of gawking tourists and turn the performance into something of a sideshow. Other spectacular geysers offer incredible displays without the crowds: Riverside is one, and another is Lone Star (found at the end of the Lone Star Geyser Trail — see "Taking a hike").

Parents, be sure to keep a tight rein on your young children while visiting geyser basins.

Upper Geyser Basin is also the location of the historic Old Faithful Inn. A seat before the fireplace in the log inn's cavernous lobby is almost as awe-inspiring as watching Old Faithful bluster, sputter, and fume into being. (See "Where to Stay" for more on this hotel.)

Upper Geyser Basin is on Lower Loop Road near Old Faithful.

West Thumb Geyser Basin
Geyser Country

Much smaller than the Lower, Midway, and Upper Geyser basins, West Thumb is almost intimate. You don't find towering geysers here, but you do see sputtering, multicolored paint pots and fuming, deep blue hot springs. Off the shore of adjacent Yellowstone Lake is **Fishing Cone,** a hot spring where anglers cooked their fish by dipping them in the cone. (No need to tote your fishing pole, though, as fishing at the geyser basin is prohibited.)

West Thumb is at the junction of Lower Loop Road and South Entrance Road.

Yellowstone Lake
Lake Country

Lower Loop Road has several turnoffs for awesome views of the lake. With a length of 20 miles and a width of 14 miles, Yellowstone is the largest natural freshwater lake situated above 7,000 feet in the United States. (Its elevation is 7,733 feet.) This lake is also home to North America's largest population of cutthroat trout.

The lake drains into Yellowstone River at Fishing Bridge, on the lake's north end. Anglers years ago would crowd the bridge with hopes of hooking one of the river's cutthroat trout, but today, fishing is banned from the span. However, you can still walk across the bridge and, if your timing is right, see osprey, eagles, and pelicans pluck trout from the river. The area also has an excellent museum focusing largely on the lake's aquatic life and a campground specifically for hard-shelled trailers and recreation vehicles.

Lower Loop Road hugs the lake between West Thumb and Fishing Bridge.

Taking a hike

You can't experience the essence of Yellowstone inside a car or bus. Get out and walk through the geyser basins, along the lakeshores, and into the forests. You don't have to stray far from your car if you don't want to. Boardwalks roam through the Upper, Midway, Lower, and Norris Geyser basins, as well as through the Mud Volcano area. Near the start of these boardwalks, you can buy a pamphlet (for a nominal charge) that guides you through the features.

If you go on a day hike, carry water, watch the weather, and pack rain gear. Take extra caution around thermal features, because no fences or boardwalks define a safe distance. Also keep an eye out for wildlife.

Spotting the local wildlife

Because the park boasts the richest, most diverse wildlife community in the Lower 48, you can spend hours debating whether Yellowstone's wildlife takes a backseat to its geological wonders.

Sometimes called America's Serengeti, the park's northern range is where you should focus your search for animals in late spring, early summer, and fall. You can spot most of the animals mentioned here in the Lamar and Hayden valleys. Because the animals — particularly bears and wolves — will be small dots on the far side of the valleys, you'll want binoculars or a spotting scope to bring them into focus.

When park officials reintroduced **wolves** to the park in the 1990s, Yellowstone's wild kingdom became whole, completely representative of the animals that roamed the park a century earlier. Ten packs of wolves have restored balance to the park's animal hierarchy after being absent from Yellowstone for more than 60 years. **Coyote** populations, which erupted after wolf packs were exterminated in the 1920s in the name of predator control (although there were reports of lone wolves in the park in the 1930s), have been reduced by the wolves. **Elk** herds, too, are expected to experience a decline in population, because the wolves came from a region of Canada where they preyed primarily on elk.

The sheer size and generally irascible demeanor of the **bison,** which along with elk are the park's most visible species, make them less vulnerable to the wolves. These shaggy guys prefer nothing more than hanging out in meadows and on the plains to graze on grasses and wildflowers. What too many visitors somehow overlook is that these critters are wild and unpredictable, not hand-fed poster animals for the National Park Service. Although they make great photo ops, every year several people end up becoming too familiar with the sharp horns of an 1,800-pound bison that proved surprisingly quick on its hooves. Watch yourself and your kids closely.

Until the wolves returned, bears were number one on vacationers' want-to-see list. **Grizzly bears** are usually seen from a distance, and that's a good thing. Long gone are the days when Yellowstone's garbage pits were surrounded by bleachers so you could watch grizzlies chow down on whatever you didn't finish for breakfast. Now, grizzlies seldom frequent the front country, preferring to browse distant hillsides and the backcountry for grubs, berries, rodents, and, in the spring, newborn elk and bison calves. You can usually spot grizzlies in the Lamar and Hayden Valleys in the spring, when their mischievous side comes out. Yearlings have been spotted sliding down waning snow fields.

Black bears, on the other hand, don't seem to mind sharing the front country with humans. You may see them browsing hillsides just feet from the Grand Loop as you approach Roosevelt from the south.

In the following section, I list just a handful of day and overnight hikes (remember to get a backcountry permit for all overnight trips). You can find guidebooks that outline the bulk of the park's hiking trails at any of the visitor centers.

 If you prefer not to hike alone, the Yellowstone Association Institute and Yellowstone National Park Lodges (☎ **307-344-5566**; www.yellowstone association.com) offer a wonderful variety of summer and winter **"Lodging and Learning"** packages that mix naturalist-led activities with lodging.

 ## Lone Star Geyser Trail

Great for kids, this easy walk (or cross-country ski or snowshoe in winter) is along a paved trail that follows the Firehole River to a backcountry wonder worth a visit. The geyser, alone in a clearing, rifles a stream of water 20 to 40 feet into the air above its tall geyserite cone. The geyser erupts about every three hours; nearby the park service keeps a written log for observers to note eruption times. Bicycles are permitted on the trail, which is paved almost all the way to the geyser. A bonus of this hike is the view near the trailhead of Kepler Cascades, which plunges 125 feet.

Distance: 5 miles round-trip. Level: Easy. Access: South of the Old Faithful complex, the trailhead is at the parking lot opposite Kepler Cascades.

Lower Terrace Interpretive Trail

This easy, self-guided path winds up through the *travertine* (mineral deposits formed by flowing water) terraces laid down over the centuries. The trail offers up-close views of thermal plumbing and a nice panorama of Mammoth.

Distance: 1½ miles round-trip. Level: Easy. Access: Trailhead is located just south of Mammoth Hot Springs on the road to Norris.

 ## Mount Washburn Trail

If you can only take one hike at Yellowstone, take this one. The rises are fairly gradual, and they're interspersed with long, fairly level stretches. At this elevation, however, you still need to pace yourself. And pacing not only saves energy, but also provides time to appreciate the eastern views of the Absaroka Mountains, the southern views of Yellowstone Lake, and the western views of the Gallatin Range. Odds are good that you'll see mountain sheep, because Mount Washburn is a popular summer grazing area for them. You'll probably also spot yellow-bellied marmots and the wily red fox. The hike to the summit, where you find a fire lookout, is an easy 90-minute walk at a steady pace, or 2 hours with breaks. At this elevation, where weather changes quickly, dress in layers and carry water. Fortunately, a warming hut, complete with viewing scopes and restrooms, is at the base of the lookout.

If road construction continues on Dunraven Pass in 2005 you won't be able to reach this trailhead.

Distance: 6 miles round-trip. Level: Moderate. Access: The trailhead is at the end of the Old Chittenden Road and at Dunraven Pass.

Shoshone Lake Trail

This is my favorite hike in the park. Not only does the trail lead to the country's largest backcountry lake — one you can't reach by car — but it also crosses the Firehole River, moseys into a beautiful lodgepole pine forest, and arrives at a sprawling geyser basin, which appears the same today as it did to explorers in the 1800s. From Lone Star Geyser, the trail traverses the Firehole River before climbing about 300 feet to cross the Continental Divide through Grants Pass and then dropping down to the lake where campsites dot the shoreline. (The campsites must be reserved in advance — see "Planning Ahead," earlier in the chapter.) A spur trail runs to the Shoshone Geyser Basin. Be careful in the basin, though; at least one backcountry traveler has died from a fall into the hot water. Hikers can either retrace their steps back to the trailhead after a multinight stay at the lake, or continue around the lake to the Lewis Lake Trailhead, a one-way trip of about 22 miles from the Lone Star Trailhead.

Distance: 17 miles round-trip via Lone Star Geyser. Level: Moderate. Access: Use the Lone Star Geyser Trailhead.

Specimen Ridge Trail

This kid-friendly trail is another of my favorites. It offers sweeping views of the Lamar Valley, leads you to the world's largest collection of petrified trees, and can be extended to the rim of the Grand Canyon of the Yellowstone depending on how much time you have. Roughly 2 miles from the trailhead, you pass a "grove" of petrifed trees, which also offers excellent samples of petrified leaf impressions, which can be difficult to find. (Keep in mind that taking anything, including fossils, from the park is a federal crime.) Although you can turn back after viewing the fossilized trees, the open country that roams along the ridge invites exploring. When you reach the ridgetop, head west over the open ground to the rim of the Grand Canyon of the Yellowstone for a magnificent view of this abyss.

Distance: 4 miles round-trip. Level: Moderate. Access: Lamar River Bridge east of Tower Junction.

One-day wonder

You want to visit Yellowstone but can only stay for a day. Can you see all the sights? No. But you can see some of the park's most famous features. Just keep moving and be flexible. Yellowstone is a big park and its sights are far-flung. To see as much as possible in one day, you need to get up early and keep going until sundown. For information on the attractions in this section, see "Exploring the top attractions," earlier in this chapter, unless otherwise noted.

Plan to stay in the **Old Faithful** area and concentrate on touring the attractions along Lower Loop Road. Not only do you get to see the park's famous geothermal features, but you can also encounter lots of wildlife, particularly in the Hayden Valley.

Because the **Old Faithful Visitor Center** (see "Finding information," earlier in this chapter) doesn't open until 8 a.m., stop by the night before to see if they've posted a schedule of predicted geyser eruptions for the next day. If you're lucky, Old Faithful will be ready to go right after you finish breakfast, and you can see the show and cross it off your to-do list.

Next, head north on the Lower Loop Road toward Norris, stopping at the **Midway Geyser Basin** to view Grand Prismatic Spring.

Move on to **Norris Geyser Basin,** roughly 30 miles north of Old Faithful. Take the trail leading south from the parking lot to Emerald Spring, Steamboat Geyser, and on to Echinus Geyser. You probably won't see Steamboat erupt, but take the short walk down the trail to Echinus Geyser, whose eruptions occur every one to four hours. A crowd of people surrounding it means an eruption is in the offing. If you don't see a crowd, head down the boardwalk to see Arch Steam Vent and Green Dragon Spring before returning to Echinus, which might now be ready to erupt.

After Echinus's show, instead of making the entire Back Basin loop, backtrack to the Norris Museum and the trail leading down into Porcelain Basin. Follow the boardwalk counterclockwise, passing Ledge Geyser, Whirligig Geyser, Whale's Mouth, and Crackling Lake before ending up back near the start across from the Black Growler Steam Vent.

When you feel that you've seen enough at Norris, head 12 miles east to **Canyon Village** for a quick lunch at the Canyon Glacier Pit Snack Bar or the Canyon Lodge Cafeteria. Afterward, visit the **Grand Canyon of the Yellowstone** by heading along North Rim Drive for a stop at Inspiration Point and then on to the Brink of the Falls Trail to make the 1½-mile round-trip down to the lip of the falls and back.

Back in your car, finish the North Rim Drive, turn left, and head south toward Lake Village, 17 miles away. Along the way, you bisect the **Hayden Valley** with its bison herds before arriving at **Mud Volcano** and **Sulphur Caldron,** which are across the road from one another. You don't need to hike the ⅔-mile, Mud Volcano trail system unless you really want to. Just getting out to peer into Dragon's Mouth Spring gives you an indication of the geothermal activity in this corner of the park.

From Mud Volcano, stop at the **Lake Yellowstone Hotel** (see "Where to Stay") to either relax with a refreshment in the Sun Room or head out to the shore for a short walk along the beach. After this, return to Old Faithful and take a final walk on the boardwalk before or after dinner.

If you have more time

If you visited the Norris and Upper Geyser basins and still haven't had your fill of gurgling and steamy water, head to the Lower and Middle Geyser basins. Both are located on Lower Loop Road between Madison and Old Faithful.

Even though the **Midway Geyser Basin** is minuscule compared to the Upper Geyser Basin, it packs a lot into a small area. An awesome sight is the Excelsior Geyser, a 200- by 300-foot crater that dumps more than 4,000 gallons of water into the Firehole River every minute of every day. Grand Prismatic Spring, the park's largest spring at 370 feet wide and 121 feet deep, is believed to be the third largest in the world, behind two in New Zealand. The yellow-and-orange rimmed pool, with its deep blue waters, is definitely worth some pictures. This area has boardwalks through small sections of hot springs and geysers.

The main attraction of the **Lower Geyser Basin** is the 3-mile Firehole Lake Drive, which leads to terraces fed by the twice-a-day eruptions of Great Fountain. Boardwalks roam through small sections of hot springs and geysers. Check with the rangers at the Old Faithful Visitor Center for estimated eruption times.

Ranger programs

Yellowstone ranger programs typically begin in early June and run through August. Walks, talks, and hikes top the list of ranger-led activities at Mammoth Hot Springs, Norris, Madison, Old Faithful, Grant Village, Lake Village, Canyon Village, and Tower-Roosevelt. The offerings change from season to season and year to year, so check the park newspaper (you receive one upon entering the park) or visitor center bulletin boards for topics and times.

The programs tend to showcase and study nearby features. For example, at Old Faithful, most programs focus on the park's geologic activity. Among the favorites is a **walking tour of Geyser Hill** that gives you a thorough understanding of the geothermal plumbing that fuels Yellowstone's hot springs and geysers.

American history surfaces at Mammoth Hot Springs, which is where the U.S. Army was based (at Fort Yellowstone) when it patrolled the park before the National Park Service was created. Many of the park offices are housed in the fort's buildings, and just walking past them is intriguing because you can imagine soldiers coming and going.

At Grant Village, the programs tend to revolve around **wildlife.** You often can sign on for tours at Canyon Village that lead into the Hayden Valley, and rangers usually offer walks along the rim of the Grand Canyon of the Yellowstone.

You can also enjoy **half-day backcountry hikes** led by rangers. The Ranger Adventure Hiking Series charges a fee, though, to help the Park Service pay for the staff and supplies for these hikes. Still, at $15 for adults and $5 for kids ages 7 to 15, that's a pretty good bargain for 4-to-6 hours of focused interpretation in Yellowstone's backcountry.

 If you have little ones with you, pick up materials for the Junior Ranger Program at any visitor center (see "Finding information" earlier in the chapter). To find out about this program, see Chapter 7.

Keeping active

Yellowstone can keep you on the go year-round. If you want to snow-shoe or cross-country ski in winter, **Xanterra** (☎ 307-344-7311; www.xanterra.com) offers package trips as well as shuttle service to various areas of the park, such as Tower Fall and Indian Creek from Mammoth Hot Springs and Fairy Falls, and to the Continental Divide from Old Faithful. You can also arrange guided tours, year-round, to the Grand Canyon of the Yellowstone and the backcountry around Old Faithful.

Temperatures can be bitterly cold in winter. That's why the park has warming huts at Canyon Village, Fishing Bridge, Indian Creek, Madison, Old Faithful, and West Thumb. With the exception of the Old Faithful hut, which is open only during the day, all huts are open 24 hours.

The following activities are guaranteed to get your heart pumping summer and winter:

✔ **Boating:** The best place to enjoy boating in Yellowstone is on Yellowstone Lake, which has easy access and beautiful, panoramic views. The lake is also one of the few areas where powerboats are allowed. You can rent rowboats and outboard motorboats at **Bridge Bay Marina** (☎ 307-344-7311). You can use motorboats, canoes, and kayaks on Lewis Lake, too. Wherever you float in the park, you're required to have Coast Guard–approved life vests.

If you want to launch your own boat at Bridge Bay, you must obtain a permit. Permit fees are $20 per season or $10 for seven days for a motorized craft; $10 per season or $5 for seven days for a non-motorized craft.

✔ **Cross-country skiing:** Gliding through the park on a bright winter day is a wonderful way to experience Yellowstone's beauty. All the park's trails are open to skiers. The Lamar Valley is a particularly good spot. Another good starting point is Tower Junction, where you can slip past a gate that blocks cars from heading south and ski 2 miles down the road to Tower Fall. Then you can hike a ½-mile trail down to the base of the waterfall, which can be ice-encrusted from around December through February, the park's coldest months. Ski rentals ($11 for a half-day; $16 all day; $38 for three days) are available through **Xanterra** (☎ 307-344-7311) at Mammoth Hot Springs and Old Faithful.

✔ **Fishing:** Yellowstone, Shoshone, and Lewis lakes are good places to drop a line, and many sections of the park's rivers are perfect for fly-fishing. The Madison, Firehole, and Yellowstone rivers are famous for their brown, brook, and cutthroat trout fisheries. If you plan to fish, stop at a ranger station, a visitor center, or Yellowstone General Stores to pick up a **permit** and pamphlet of **regulations**. Some park streams are closed to fishing, some are catch-and-release only, and number and size limits vary by species, so you definitely need a copy of the regulations. You don't need a Wyoming fishing license, but anglers 16 years and older must pay $15 for a three-day park permit, $20 for a seven-day permit, or $35 for a season-long permit. Kids ages 12 to 15 need a no-fee permit, and kids 11 and younger don't need one as long as an adult supervises them.

✔ **Ice skating:** If you stay at Mammoth Hot Springs, take time to skate on the rink behind the hotel. Skates and ice time are free. The rink usually opens December 23, depending on the weather.

✔ **Snowshoeing:** If you seek a slower, quieter pace, snowshoe packages are available through **Xanterra** (☎ 307-344-7311) at Mammoth Hot Springs and Old Faithful ($9 for a half-day; $12 all day). All hiking trails are open to snowshoers, although I recommend those in the Lamar Valley.

Where to Stay

Don't make a last-minute decision to visit Yellowstone. Lining up a place to sleep requires months of planning. With that in mind, your lodging choices run the gamut from rustic cabins at Roosevelt (which have only woodstoves for heat and a communal bathhouse a short walk away) to a presidential suite at the Lake Yellowstone Hotel. As expected, prices vary, too — from $60 for a Spartan cabin to more than $400 for the suite. For a real bargain, try camping. The park has many campground sites where you can pitch your tent ($12 to $17) or park your RV ($31).

The timing of your visit determines your number of lodging options. For example, the Old Faithful Inn is open from early May until mid-October, and the Old Faithful Lodge cabins are available from mid-May to mid-September. The Old Faithful Snow Lodge does business from mid-May to mid-October, then reopens from mid-December through mid-March for the winter season. The Mammoth Hot Springs Hotel and cabins follow this same schedule. Lake Yellowstone Hotel is open from mid-May through September; the Lake Lodge cabins are available from mid-June to mid-September; Grant Village Lodge is open from mid-May to mid-September; and the Canyon Lodge and its cabins, as well as the Roosevelt Lodge cabins, are open from early June through August.

The listings in this section for the park hotels don't include individual phone numbers or addresses. All lodging is managed by **Xanterra Parks & Resorts.** One phone number (☎ **307-344-7311**), Web site (www. xanterra.com), and address (P.O. Box 165, Yellowstone National Park, WY 82190) is good for all properties. Don't worry about not being able to find your hotel. When you enter the park, you'll receive a map pinpointing the location of each one.

Lodging in Lake Village

Removed, yet elegant defines this north-shore community on Yellowstone Lake. Although you're not in the middle of a geyser basin, you're close to Mud Volcano and the West Thumb Geyser Basin. Plus, the sweeping Hayden Valley with its bison herds is fairly close. You can choose from plush accommodations in the elegant Lake Yellowstone Hotel; clean, comfortable, and simple Lake Lodge cabins; or a more rustic experience in aged cabins. Along with a variety of dining options, you'll find a ranger station, gift shops, a small hospital, a grocery, and places to boat and hike.

Lake Yellowstone Hotel and Cabins
$$–$$$$$ Lake Village

Lake Yellowstone Hotel (commonly known as "Lake Hotel") is the Grand Dame of Yellowstone's lodges and features the park's nicest — and priciest — rooms. Erected in 1891 and painstakingly restored in 1989, the hotel is the perfect place for spoiling yourself. You won't have to rough it here, thanks to the Sun Room that fronts the lake, a prim dining room, and 194 carpeted guest rooms. Not five minutes from the lobby is the lakeshore, perfect for an after-dinner stroll.

 You can avoid the hefty $100 plus per night charge and still enjoy the atmosphere by staying in one of the less expensive, and decidedly stark, Lake Hotel Annex rooms or one of the simple Lake Hotel Frontier cabins (with beds, showers, toilets, and sinks) and walking over to the hotel for its ambience and amenities. Neither the annex rooms nor the cabins offer much character, but the walls in the annex are a bit thicker and bathrooms contain shower/tub combinations, while those in the cabins have only showers.

As with Old Faithful Inn, dinner reservations in the hotel are precious, so book early.

See map p. 278. 193 rooms; 102 cabins; 1 presidential suite. TEL. Rack rates: $120–$186 double; $80–$99 cabin; $423 presidential suite. AE, DC, DISC, MC, V. Open: Mid-May to early Oct.

Lake Lodge Cabins
$–$$$ Lake Village

Another option at Lake Village is to check into one of these cabins and walk the ¼-mile to the hotel for meals and atmosphere. These cabins come in two flavors: An older, more economical Pioneer version with one double bed, shower, toilet, and sink; and the motel-style Western cabin, which is a bit more spacious and contains two double beds and a bathroom with tub and shower. The log lodge offers a small lounge and nondescript cafeteria, so any money you save by staying in one of the cabins will likely be spent on food and ambience over at the hotel.

See map p. 278. 186 cabins. Rack rates: $59–$119 double. AE, DC, DISC, MC, V. Open: June–Sept.

Lodging in Mammoth Hot Springs

This community offers it all: fine dining, the park's best visitor center, limestone terraces built up over the millennia, and a range of accommodations from a historic hotel to a campground. The historic Fort Yellowstone, restaurants, gift shops, a convenience store, and a service station complete the package. On the downside, even though the Mammoth Hot Springs Terraces are just a short walk from the hotel, you're far removed from the mainstays of the park's geothermal attractions. In the winter, though, this place is a good base camp, thanks to the hotel, skating rink, and proximity to the Lamar Valley for snowshoeing and wildlife spotting.

Mammoth Hot Springs Hotel and Cabins
$–$$$$$ Mammoth Hot Springs

Somewhere between the highbrow Lake Yellowstone Hotel and the low-rent Roosevelt Lodge cabins is Mammoth Hot Springs Hotel. The hotel is a turn-of-the-20th-century creation 5 miles inside the North Entrance, and its rooms aren't elaborate. Some, however, feature charming claw-footed bathtubs. Most offer comfortable beds and functional bathrooms; if you don't reserve early enough, though, you may need to walk down the hall to the communal bathroom. The hotel has two plush suites. The cottage-style cabins are an economical alternative, and four actually have their own hot tubs. Again, book early because not all cabins come with private bathrooms.

The hotel lobby has a woodstove that you can cozy up to in winter and a wood floor buffed to a high shine. Off the lobby is the sprawling Map Room — a high-ceilinged, rectangular room filled with overstuffed sofas, writing desks, and huge windows through which, in spring, summer, and fall, you can count the dozens of elk lured to the sweet grass lawns surrounding the park headquarters. The room's name stems from a large wooden map (made from 15 different types of woods from nine countries) that hangs on one wall.

If Old Faithful is your destination, pass on staying here; Mammoth Hot Springs Hotel is 51 miles from Upper Geyser Basin along twisting roads.

See map p. 278. 95 rooms; 115 cabins; 2 suites. Rack rate: $73–$96 double; $64 $159 cabin; $291 suite. AE, DC, DISC, MC, V. Open: Early May to early Oct, Dec–March.

Lodging in the Old Faithful area

Sure, this area is crowded, but it's surrounded by the world's greatest collection of geysers and hot springs. Plus, the Old Faithful Inn has the most rustic charm of any of the park's accommodations. And as a bonus, a variety of dining options, from short-order grill to multicourse, sit-down restaurants, are nearby. Come winter, the pace eases a bit and the ambience is heightened, thanks to the snow and cold. The Old Faithful complex includes a convenience store, gift shops, a visitor center, a medical clinic, and a service station. (See the Old Faithful Area map in this chapter.)

Old Faithful Inn
$$–$$$$$ Old Faithful area

Like no other place in the park, this inn and its rooms meld modern comforts and wilderness. If you loved Lincoln Logs as a kid and want the true Yellowstone experience, stay here. Located near the apron of the Old Faithful Geyser, the inn was crafted from trees pulled from the surrounding forests and rock quarried from the nearby Black Sand Basin. Probably the biggest log cabin you'll ever see, this inn oozes rustic charm, from the gnarled lodgepole limbs used as decorative braces to accent the interior, to the Mission-style library desks on the second-floor balcony. The inn also comes with more than a few ghost stories.

When foul weather arrives, squirrel yourself away with a book or a deck of cards in a corner of the second- or third-story balconies. (On clear days, the second-story deck offers nice views of Old Faithful and much of Geyser Hill.)

Reservations fill up quickly for dinner at the inn, so make yours before heading into the park for the day. Also, make sure to visit the Bear Pit Lounge to see the whimsically etched glass panels. Some of the rooms lack baths, so if trudging down the hall in your robe and slippers bothers you, you have even more reason to start making reservations for your trip early.

See map p. 286. Reservations ☎ *307-344-7311. 327 rooms. Rack rates: $78–$185 double; $371 suite. AE, DC, DISC, MC, V. Open: Mid-May to mid-Oct.*

Old Faithful Lodge Cabins
$–$$ Old Faithful area

The lodge houses a cafeteria, a snack bar, and a gift shop. Several cabin options are available depending on how rustic you're willing to go. Although the Frontier cabins come with private bathrooms, the Pioneer units have toilets and sinks but no baths. The bargain-basement Budget units constitute the Upper Geyser Basin's low-rent district. They come with beds, sinks, and a short walk to a communal bathhouse. A tent offers more atmosphere than these claustrophobic and rundown Budget shacks, so definitely call far enough in advance to get a Frontier or Pioneer unit.

See map p. 286. 96 cabins (some without baths). Rack rates: $55–$81 double. AE, DC, DISC, MC, V. Open: May–Oct.

Old Faithful Snow Lodge and Cabins
$$–$$$ Old Faithful area

Dedicated in May 1999, the Snow Lodge is the newest place to stay at Old Faithful. The $20 million rock-and-timber structure replaced an ancient structure originally built as a dormitory for employees. The lodge offers 100 rooms, a restaurant and lounge, a fast-food grill, and a ski-rental shop. The rooms are infused with personality in the form of animal motifs carved into the lamps and the furniture. The lobby with its fireplace is handsome and comfortable, and the inn has a nice lounge and attractive dining room. Because this is the only winter lodging available at Old Faithful, competition is keen for reservations. Thirty-four year-round cabins are also associated with the Snow Lodge. They're motel-like and charmless, but clean and comfortable.

See map p. 286. 100 rooms, 34 1-bedroom cabins. Rack rates: $156 double; $80–$119 cabin. AE, DC, DISC, MC, V. Open: Early May to mid-Oct, mid-Dec to early March.

Lodging in Tower-Roosevelt

The log lodge and its surrounding cabins are near the spot where President Roosevelt camped during a 1903 trip to the park. The cabins aren't luxurious by any stretch of the imagination, but the lodge, although not huge, is rustic and cozy and serves up pretty good meals. Keep in mind that you don't need to be an overnight guest to sample the tasty cornbread or to spend time in one of the front porch's rocking chairs with a view into the Lamar Valley.

The cabins are as close to roughing it in Yellowstone as it gets without having a tent or the open sky overhead at night. Whereas the lodge's Frontier and Economy cabins offer various degrees of plumbing, Roughriders don't even feature sinks. Communal bathhouses are nearby, though, so you don't have to go to bed grimy. If you've come to Yellowstone to look for wildlife, this is the place to be in the late spring and early summer.

Roosevelt Lodge and Cabins

$–$$ Tower-Roosevelt

If it seems as though you don't get much when you reserve the Frontier, Economy, or Roughrider cabins that surround the Roosevelt Lodge, well, you don't. Heated by woodstoves, the few Frontier cabins feature showers, toilets, and sinks — an undistinguished claim to fame until you compare them to the Roughrider units, which have stoves but no running water (the communal bathhouse is a short walk away). The Economy cabins fall in between: They come with toilets and sinks, but no shower facilities. These cabins are very similar to the old models at Old Faithful. Still, I find that this location, with its lodgepole forest, the Lamar Valley falling away to the east, and the log lodge for meals and drinks in front of a roaring fire, displays a decidedly rustic charm absent from the park's other offerings.

See map p. 278. 80 cabins. Rack rates: $56–$91 double. AE, DC, DISC, MC, V. Open: Early June to early Sept.

Runner-up lodgings

Park lodging is also available in Canyon and Grant villages. If you wait too long to book reservations in the park, you don't need to postpone your Yellowstone trip. Just across the park's northern and western borders are a number of motels and lodges in the Gardiner (Chamber of Commerce, ☎ 406-848-7971) and West Yellowstone (Chamber of Commerce, ☎ 406-646-7701) areas. I list the best of these accommodations here.

Absaroka Lodge

$–$$ **Gardiner**   Set high on the banks of the Yellowstone River where you can fish for a trout dinner, the lodge is just a two-block walk from the park's north entrance. *South U.S. 89 (at Yellowstone River Bridge).* ☎ **800-755-7414** or 406-848-7414. www.yellowstonemotel.com.

Canyon Lodge

$–$$$ **Canyon Village**   This national park lodge lacks ambience and has a motel-like feel. However, the location, ½ mile from the Grand Canyon of the Yellowstone, is a plus. Cabins also are available. ☎ *307-344-7311.*

Grant Village Lodge

$$–$$$ **Grant Village**   This national park lodge offers accommodations in six plain buildings, stacked two stories high, along the edge of Yellowstone Lake. Nothing to get excited about, but the location is pretty good. ☎ *307-344-7311.*

Stagecoach Inn

$–$$$ **West Yellowstone**   This hotel, if you can't tell from its name, has a Western flavor. Stuffed animals hang on the lobby's wood-paneled walls, and in the rooms, you find elk-antler lamps and bedspreads and drapes with patterns of elk, bison, moose, and bears. *209 Madison (at Dunraven).* ☎ *800-842-2882 or 406-646-7381.* www.yellowstoneinn.com.

Campgrounds

Yellowstone has a dozen campgrounds: seven overseen by the National Park Service (NPS) and five by **Xanterra.** What's the difference? You can reserve a spot to pitch your tent or park your RV in one of the Xanterra campgrounds months ahead of your arrival, but the NPS sites fill up quickly on a first-come, first-served basis. Nightly rates at both Xanterra and NPS locations range from $12 to $17, except at the Fishing Bridge Campground, where sites are restricted to RVs and hard-shell campers (due to grizzly bears in the area) and cost $31 per night.

None of these campgrounds provides the wilderness experience so readily available with a hike into the backcountry. Instead, you're surrounded by other happy campers — sometimes hundreds of them.

If you don't want to get away from it all, stay at the Tower Fall, Mammoth, Bridge Bay, Fishing Bridge, Canyon Village, or Grant Village locations. These campgrounds are the closest to restaurants and gift shops. But if you're looking for a semblance of peace, some solitude, and the chance to spot animals, the Slough Creek and Pebble Creek campgrounds are the smallest (29 and 32 sites, respectively) and lie within the home ranges of two wolf packs.

Xanterra campgrounds

The Xanterra campgrounds are at **Fishing Bridge, Bridge Bay, Canyon Village, Madison,** and **Grant Village.** Because of grizzly bears drawn to the Yellowstone River and its cutthroat trout, the Fishing Bridge site caters only to hard-sided vehicles. You also can find room for your RV at the other Xanterra campgrounds; although they don't have utility hookups, they do have sanitary dump stations.

To make reservations, call ☎ **307-344-7311,** or write to Xanterra Parks & Resorts, P.O. Box 165, Yellowstone National Park, WY 82190. You can reserve a space, but a specific site isn't assigned until you arrive.

Campgrounds generally are open from early May through October. Weather, however, can force campgrounds to open later or close earlier in the season. If you make an early- or late-season reservation with Xanterra, call shortly before your arrival to find out whether the campground is open.

National Park Service campgrounds

The NPS-operated campgrounds are at **Indian Creek, Lewis Lake, Mammoth Hot Springs, Norris, Pebble Creek, Slough Creek,** and **Tower Fall.**

Camping is allowed only in designated areas and is limited to a maximum stay of 14 days between June 15 and September 15 (30 days the rest of the year). Checkout time for all campgrounds is 10 a.m., and quiet hours (8 p.m. to 8 a.m.) are strictly enforced. No generators, radios, or other loud noises are allowed during these hours.

Backcountry sites

If you want solitude, Yellowstone's backcountry offers more than 1,200 miles of marked trails that enable you to escape the multitudes. I like to flee to **Shoshone Lake,** the park's second largest lake. Located 8½ miles south of Old Faithful via the Lone Star Geyser Trail or 3 miles south of Lower Loop Road via the DeLacy Creek Trail, the lake offers waterfront campsites. Here you can try to land some trout, capture a few great sunset and sunrise photos, or explore the Shoshone Geyser Basin on the lake's west shore. Unfortunately, the lake's popularity over the years has forced officials to ban wood fires to protect the forest, so bring your propane stove.

You must obtain a permit for backcountry hiking. See "Planning Ahead," earlier in this chapter, for information. The park service also makes sure that you learn the do's and don'ts of backcountry hiking before you set out. They give you a handout and require that you watch a short video on hiking in bear country.

Where to Eat

Whether you're in search of linen tablecloths, silverware, and fine china, or a quick burger, you can find what you crave in Yellowstone. All major hotels — Mammoth Hot Springs Hotel, Old Faithful Inn, and Lake Yellowstone Hotel — feature elegant dining rooms with excellent meals. How you dress is up to you. People dining at the Old Faithful Inn come in more comfortable attire, as if they just returned from a hike. However, finding some Lake Yellowstone Hotel diners in semiformal wear isn't unusual. Menus run the gamut, from beef to trout.

Roosevelt Lodge offers a decidedly more relaxed setting, and although the meals aren't as fancy as those at Old Faithful Inn, Lake Yellowstone Hotel, or Mammoth Hot Springs Hotel, the food is hearty.

 A rung down the culinary ladder are less expensive meals available in cafeterias, delis, or fast food grills at Old Faithful, Mammoth Hot Springs, Canyon Village, Grant Village, Lake Village, and Lake Lodge. Assuming that you've worked up a hearty appetite in the park, the chefs don't skimp on the portions.

The dining rooms at Grant Village, Lake Yellowstone Hotel, and the Old Faithful Inn require reservations. You can actually make them when you call to make your lodging reservations. To do so, call the dining rooms directly at the numbers given or try the central reservations office at ☎ 307-344-7311.

Dining in Canyon Village

Canyon Lodge Dining Room
$$–$$$ Canyon **AMERICAN**

A short walk from the Grand Canyon of the Yellowstone River, the lodge offers both sit-down and cafeteria-style dining. Eat early or late to avoid the densest dining room crowds. Breakfasts range from an all-you-can eat buffet to typical short-order-grill fare, lunches revolve around sandwiches and burgers, and dinners get pretty creative with offerings such as Pecan shrimp and Pine Nut Crusted Rocky Mountain Trout sharing the menu with more typical offerings of steaks, chops, and poultry.

See map p. 278. ☎ *307-344-7901. Main courses: $4.50–$8.70 breakfast; $6.75–$7.95 lunch; $9.50–$17.75 dinner. AE, DC, DISC, MC, V. Open: Late May to early Oct. Hours vary.*

Dining in Grant Village

Grant Village Lake House
$$–$$$$ Grant Village **AMERICAN**

The proverbial stone's throw from Yellowstone Lake, this restaurant features buffet breakfasts, hot and cold sandwiches, salads, soup, and burgers; and pizzas and a pasta bar for dinners. The lake view through the restaurant's windows makes this a great place to enjoy a sunset meal.

See map p. 278. ☎ *307-344-3419. Main courses: $4.50–$8.70 breakfast; $6.95–$9.95 lunch; $11.95–$20.95 dinner. AE, DC, DISC, MC, V. Open: Late May to early Oct 7–10:30 a.m., 5:30–9 p.m.*

Dining in Lake Village

Lake Yellowstone Hotel
$$$–$$$$$ Lake Village **AMERICAN**

This restaurant is the best in the park, hands down. The service is highly attentive, the meals creative and well-prepared, and the atmosphere definitely elegant in the high-ceilinged dining room with windows that allow you to gaze out at Yellowstone Lake. Dinner entrees include beef in various forms, pastas, duck breast, quail, salmon, trout dishes, as well as nightly specials such as seafood cioppino, smoked pork chop, or roasted rack of lamb. I recommend the lavish breakfast buffet, although you can also order à la carte from the menu. For lunch, hot sandwiches, burgers, and chicken curry dishes dominate the choices.

See map p. 278. On the north shore of Yellowstone Lake. ☎ *307-242-3899. Dinner reservations required. Main courses: $4–$10.50 breakfast; $6.25–$11.25 lunch; $11.25–$24.95 dinner. AE, DC, DISC, MC, V. Open: Mid-May to early Oct 6:30–10:30 a.m., 11:30 a.m.–2:30 p.m., 5–10 p.m.*

Dining in Mammoth Hot Springs

Mammoth Hot Springs Hotel Dining Room
$$–$$$$ Mammoth Hot Springs   AMERICAN

After the Lake Yellowstone Hotel, this spot probably has the best meals. The setting is elegant, with linen-covered tables, china, and etched-glass windows. Don't pass up the bargain, all-you-can-eat breakfast buffet, featuring scrambled eggs, French toast, bacon, sausage, hot and cold cereals, pastries, fresh fruit, and yogurt for only $8.70 adults, $4.95 kids. Lunch fare focuses on burgers, hot and cold sandwiches, and such specialties as fish and chips or trout. Dinners — beef, fish, chicken, or pasta — aren't gourmet, but they're appetizing and filling. Don't forget to ask about the "Daily Plates," which vary from day to day ranging from porterhouse pork chops to fettucine with mussels.

See map p. 278. ☎ *307-344-5314. Dinner reservations required. Main courses: $4–$8.70 breakfast; $6.25–$9 lunch; $8.95–$20.95 dinner. AE, DC, DISC, MC, V. Open: Early May–early Oct and Dec–March, daily 6:30–10 a.m., 11:30 a.m.–2:30 p.m., 5–10 p.m.*

Terrace Grill
$–$$ Mammoth Hot Springs   FAST FOOD

This hectic, kid-friendly cafeteria always seems crowded. Burgers, hot dogs, soups, and sandwiches are the fare, and if you're in a rush to get on down the road, this is a good place for a quick bite. It's about as close to fast food as you get in the park. Nothing gourmet, that's for sure, but the food will tide you over until your next meal.

See map p. 278. ☎ *307-344-7901. Main courses: $2.50–$4 breakfast; $3–$6.75 lunch and dinner. Open: Early May, 10 a.m.–5:30 p.m.; late May to early Sept, 7–10:30 a.m., 11 a.m.–9 p.m.; mid-Sept to early-Oct, 10 a.m.–9 p.m.; early Oct to mid-Oct, 11 a.m.–5 p.m.*

Dining in the Old Faithful area

Old Faithful Inn
$$$–$$$$ Old Faithful area   AMERICAN

After Lake Yellowstone Hotel, this is my favorite spot to dine, probably because of the setting in the log-walled dining room. Toward the end of summer, the service can be spotty, however, because the college kids are losing their focus and tired of dealing with tourists. The dinner menu features beef, pork, pasta, and poultry dishes, usually with a daily fish special tossed in. The breakfast buffet is king. Lunches include a buffet featuring trout and barbecued chicken, and you can order hot and cold sandwiches, burgers, and salads off the menu.

See map p. 286. Near Old Faithful geyser. ☎ *307-545-4999. Dinner reservations required. Main courses: $4–$8.70 breakfast; $6–$10.80 lunch; $11.95–$20.75 dinner. AE, DC, DISC, MC, V. Open: Mid-May to mid-Oct, 6:30–10 a.m., 11:30 a.m.–2 p.m., 5:30–10 p.m.*

Snow Lodge Obsidian Room
$$–$$$$ Old Faithful area AMERICAN

Featuring large windows and wrought iron trim, this Snow Lodge, which opened for business for the 1999 season, is a vast improvement over its predecessor. The meals aren't bad, either, although your choices for lunch and dinner aren't extensive. Eggs, pancakes, French toast, and hot and cold cereals are the heart of the breakfast menu. The lunch and dinner menus are essentially identical, featuring burgers, sandwiches, chicken, cornish game hen, pasta, and trout. The dinner menu also includes prime rib and nightly specials, such as New Zealand Red Deer Medallions.

See map p. 286. Near Old Faithful geyser. ☎ *307-545-4800, ext. 4010. Dinner reservations required. Main courses: $4–$10.50 breakfast; $5.75–$8.25 lunch; $8.95–$20.75 dinner. AE, DC, DISC, MC, V. Open: Early May to mid-Oct and mid-Dec to early March, 6:30–10 a.m., 11:30 a.m.–10 p.m.*

Dining in Tower-Roosevelt

Roosevelt Lodge
$$–$$$$ Tower-Roosevelt AMERICAN

This is my third favorite place to eat in the park, after Lake Yellowstone Hotel and the Old Faithful Inn. It's not elegant or stately, but cozy, like a backwoods diner that dishes up hearty, heavy meals. You won't find a breakfast buffet, but you can order eggs, pancakes, oatmeal, cereals, and biscuits and gravy off the menu. Lunch focuses on sandwiches, chili, soup and salad, and trout, whereas dinner features delicious barbecued ribs and chicken as well as steak and trout. For a unique experience and a treat for your kids, sign on for one of the chuckwagon dinners. Diners travel by horse-drawn wagon to a nearby meadow for a Western barbecue of steaks, baked beans, potato salad, corn, watermelon, and apple crisp. Your little cowpokes will enjoy the storytelling, music, and horses.

See map p. 278. No phone. Reservations not accepted. Main courses: $4–$7.25 breakfast; $5.75–$8.95 lunch; $9.25–$19.95 dinner. AE, DC, DISC, MC, V. Open: Early June to early Sept, 7–10:30 a.m., 11:30 a.m.–4 p.m., 5–9 p.m.

Fast Facts: Yellowstone

Area Code

The local area code is **307**.

ATM

ATMs are available at Fishing Bridge General Store, Grant Village General Store, Lake Yellowstone Hotel, Mammoth General Store, Mammoth Hot Springs Hotel, Old Faithful Inn, Old Faithful Snow Lodge, Old Faithful Upper Store, Canyon General Store, and Canyon Lodge.

Emergency

In an emergency, dial **911**.

Fees

Entrance costs $20 per vehicle per week and $10 for those on foot, bicycle, or skis.

Fishing License

A park permit is needed for anglers 16 and older: They cost $15 for three days, $20 for seven days, and $35 for the season. People aged 12 to 15 also need a permit, but they're free. Permits and fishing regulations are available at ranger stations, visitor centers, and Yellowstone General Stores.

Hospitals

Three hospitals are available at Yellowstone: Lake Clinic, Pharmacy, and Hospital is open from late May to September 30 (☎ 307-242-7241),

Mammoth Clinic is open year-round (☎ 307-344-7965) and Old Faithful Clinic is open from early May to mid-October (☎ 307-545-7325).

Information

For information, write Yellowstone National Park, P.O. Box 168, Yellowstone National Park, WY 82190, call ☎ 307-344-7381, or look on the Internet at www.nps.gov/yell.

Pharmacies

The Lake Clinic, Pharmacy, and Hospital is open from late May to mid-September (☎ 307-242-7241).

Post Office

You find post offices at Mammoth Hot Springs (open year-round; ☎ 307-344-7764), Old Faithful (open mid-May to early Oct and mid-Dec to mid-March; ☎ 307-545-7252), Grant Village (open mid-May to mid-Sept; ☎ 307-242-7338) and Lake Village (open mid-May to mid-Sept; ☎ 307-242-7383).

Road Conditions and Weather

To find out more about road conditions and weather, call ☎ 307-344-7381.

Time Zone

The park is on mountain time.

Chapter 17

Yosemite National Park

*B*orn of water and ice that cut a fantastic landscape, Yosemite National Park is a storybook fairyland. How else to explain the wispy, 2,425-foot stream of Yosemite Falls that spills into the Yosemite Valley, or the massive granite mound known as Half Dome (which looks like a monument to a loaf of bread). On the valley floor the tranquil, tree-lined Merced River traces lazy oxbow bends, and the palatial Ahwahnee hotel has comforted queens and presidents, actors and athletes.

Take the time to climb up and out of this peaceful notch in California's High Sierra landscape, and you enter a boundless backcountry of granite and pine where you can lose yourself down a trail or savor some solitude on the shore of a lake.

If you're in search of breathtaking scenery, you'll find it at Yosemite, a park overly endowed with natural beauty. Arrive any summer day via California 41 from Fish Camp, a town just south of the park, and you can marvel at the scenery as soon as you pop out of the Wawona Tunnel. To your right is Bridalveil Fall, an impressive 620-foot drop, which serves as a modest opening act for Yosemite Falls just down the road. On your left is El Capitan, one of the world's tallest chunks of exposed rock, which rises 3,593 feet above the valley floor. Dead ahead is the bulging Half Dome.

Meandering through the middle of this paradise is the Merced River, which literally dives into the valley via Nevada and Vernal falls. In spring and summer, showy displays of lilies and columbines and stands of evergreens contrast sharply with the gray granite and the foaming white waterfalls.

What other park offers such a visible feast of water and rock? None. But don't just stay in the valley and ignore the rest of Yosemite. In summer, the ride to Tuolumne Meadows winds first through deep pine forest before breaking into alpine meadows and massive granite outcrops. White Wolf Lodge is a popular base camp for day hikers, and eating family-style at Tuolumne Lodge (a misnomer in that there is no lodge, only tent cabins) is an excellent way to make friends and gain insights into the park.

In the park's southwestern corner, you find not only a sky-scraping forest of giant sequoia trees, but also the stately Wawona Hotel, a National Historic Landmark that dates to the 1850s.

All this beauty naturally generates crowds — big ones, particularly during the height of summer. That's when the Merced River bogs down with convoys of rubber rafts and the Mist Trail to Vernal and Nevada falls swells with the midday masses. But with a little patience, and some careful planning, you can enjoy the park almost as if it were your own.

Must-See Attractions

Wispy waterfalls, granite towers, breathtaking High Sierra landscape, stately national park lodging — Yosemite National Park has much to offer. It takes time to navigate this big park because it has attractions both in the valley and in the high country. Thankfully, appreciating Yosemite doesn't take much time — this park makes an immediate impression. Here's a list of stops to get you started on your explorations:

✓ **The Ahwahnee:** This blue-blood hotel, opened in 1927, is built from granite blocks and concrete stained to resemble redwood beams. A National Historic Landmark, its name means "Place of the Gaping Mouth." You may do some gaping when you stand in the doorway to the cavernous dining room.

✓ **Ansel Adams Gallery:** Yes, this is a retail shop. The gallery pays homage to the renowned landscape photographer whose black-and-white masterpieces from 50 years ago still resonate today. Admire his work, or even buy some. You won't be sorry.

✓ **Curry Village:** Cooled by the afternoon shadow of Glacier Point, this tent camp marked its centennial in 1999. The camp is a bit rustic for some, but others enjoy its simplicity. Even if you don't stay here, the adjoining village is a good place to go for ice cream or pizza. The Yosemite Mountaineering School and mountain shop are located here.

✔ **El Capitan:** The road into Yosemite Valley passes this ridiculously tall chunk of rock — you can't miss it.

✔ **Glacier Point:** You can drive to this overlook, which offers sweeping views of the valley floor, Yosemite Falls, the Merced River, The Ahwahnee, Half Dome, Vernal and Nevada falls, and the peak of Clouds Rest looming far off to the northeast.

✔ **The Mist Trail:** A wonderfully wet hike on a hot day, this trail follows the Merced River upstream from the valley floor to 317-foot Vernal Fall (which provides a drenching with misty spray during spring and early summer months) and 594-foot Nevada Fall.

✔ **Tenaya Lake:** Named after the chief of the last Indian tribe to live in the Yosemite Valley, this high-country lake is rimmed by granite domes and offers picnic grounds on the northeast and southwest ends.

✔ **Tunnel View:** Carrying a camera with you? If so, pull over here, try to squeeze El Capitan, Bridalveil Fall, and Half Dome into your viewfinder, and press the shutter release.

✔ **Tuolumne Meadows:** A short drive from the Yosemite Valley, this pastoral corner of the park features rolling meadows cut by the Tuolumne River and framed by evergreen forests, towering granite outcrops, and a nice selection of hiking options. The Cathedral Range that towers over the meadows just to the south sparkles when the sun goes down.

Planning Ahead

To get information before you go, write Superintendent, P.O. Box 577, Yosemite National Park, CA 95389-0577, or check the park's Web site at www.nps.gov/yose. You can purchase publications about the park by contacting **Yosemite Association,** Box 230, El Portal, CA 95318; ☎ **209-379-2646;** www.yosemite.org.

If you have computer access, you should also check out **Yosemite Area Traveler Information** on the Web at www.yosemite.com. The site has information on the 11,000-square-mile area surrounding the park, with tips on lodging, road conditions, the weather, activities, and just about everything else under the sun. Another good resource is the park's concessionaire, **Yosemite Concession Services** (☎ **559-253-5635;** www.yosemitepark.com).

When to go and how long to stay

Although you can visit Yosemite Valley in one long day, you need at least two days if you also want to head up toward Tuolumne Meadows.

When you visit depends on what you want to see or do. If you want to avoid crowds, summer isn't your season — more people descend on Yosemite between May and September than at any other time of year. But if you follow my advice on how to cope with the masses, summer can be a wonderful time, thanks to warm temperatures and accessibility throughout Yosemite.

If waterfalls are first and foremost on your must-see list, late spring and early summer are the best times for you. If hiking is your passion, fall is your season. In comparison to summer, fall generates fewer crowds, has more comfortable temperatures, and is definitely more striking. If great skiing and solitude are what you seek, visit during winter. Not only are the winter months less crowded — with the exception of the holidays — but lodging rates dip, making a Yosemite trip more affordable.

Advance reservations

 It's late June and you're thinking that spending the Fourth of July weekend at The Ahwahnee would be really cool. And you're right, it would. But if you don't already have reservations, start thinking about next year's Fourth of July weekend, because you certainly won't find a room this summer. In fact, even if you were willing to delay your trip until Labor Day weekend, you probably wouldn't find a room in the lodge.

That's how popular Yosemite is. When it comes to booking lodging in national parks, few parks pose the problems Yosemite does. Even though you can book a room 366 days before your visit, almost within minutes of the opening of the reservation office at **Yosemite Concession Services** (☎ **559-253-5635**), rooms at the Ahwahnee, Yosemite Lodge, and Wawona Hotel sell out for weekends, holiday periods, and every day between May and September.

 So how do you get a room in one of these popular lodges? Trying to book early is one way. A better one is to visit during November, early December, January, February, and March. Not only are you more likely to get the room of your choice, but rates are down 25 percent from the high season. Another angle, if you can leave on a moment's notice, is to call and ask about cancellations. You can also take part in special events — wine appreciation, cooking events, and ski packages — offered during these months. Call **Yosemite Concession Services** (☎ **559-253-5635**) for information and reservations.

 To get into the park during the high season, consider staying in a **canvas tent cabin** at Curry Village, Tuolumne Meadows, or White Wolf Lodge. With wood floors, canvas walls and ceilings, cots, woodstoves, and a communal bathhouse down a short path, these cabins are definitely not plush, but they're far cheaper than lodge rooms and have a rustic flavor. Often, you can snag one of these cabins by calling only two weeks prior to your visit. If you reserve one reluctantly, ask whether cancellations have created an opening in one of the other lodges when you arrive to check in. It's unlikely, but asking is worth five minutes of your time. Even better, check with the reservations desk 30 days before your arrival and again 10 days out and 3 days out — the most likely times when other people will cancel their reservations.

 When trying to make a reservation, you'll have a better chance of getting through if you call on a Sunday, the day fewest calls are made to the reservation desks. You can also try to book online at www.yosemitepark.com.

Going into the backcountry

Heading into Yosemite's backcountry is one of my favorite ways of enjoying the park. Not only do you flee the crowds, but you also see some awesome country. Backcountry wilderness permits are required for all overnight trips, year-round. Reservations are available, and encouraged, for dates from May through September. Reservations can be made as early as 24 weeks in advance and as late as two days before your trip. Permits aren't needed for day hikes. You can obtain your permit by writing to **Wilderness Permits,** P.O. Box 545, Yosemite, CA 95389 or by calling ☎ **209-372-0740.** Although the backcountry permit itself is free, you must pay a $5 per person processing fee for confirmed reservations.

Rangers allow a specific number of backcountry hikers at each trailhead. At least 40 percent of a specific trailhead's hiker quota is available on a first-come, first-served basis on any given day. These last-minute permits are available at the Wilderness Permit Station nearest your departure trailhead.

What to pack

Trips to Yosemite seem to revolve around hiking, both short day hikes and multi-day adventures. If that fits your agenda, be sure to bring shorts, T-shirts, fleece layers, and rain gear. The ever-popular "approach shoes" can handle many of the day hikes, but if you're planning a longer overnight trek you'll want to pack a good pair of broken-in hiking boots. I add hiking sticks to the mix, because they help my knees tolerate the steep downhills that you're bound to encounter if you want to leave the valley floor.

Getting There

Yosemite is easily accessible. If you live outside of California, a morning flight to either Fresno or Merced can be followed by an afternoon in the park. What you need to decide before you head to Yosemite, though, is whether you want to go straight to the high country, visit the park's sequoia groves, or make a beeline for the valley floor. This prioritizing helps you determine which entrance to take into the park.

Driving in

You can get into Yosemite by car in four ways, and all but the Tioga Pass Entrance (10 miles west of Lee Vining, California) are open year-round.

The **South Entrance**, with access to Wawona and the Mariposa Grove of sequoia trees, is 64 miles north of Fresno via California 41. Coming from the west, your options are the 75-mile drive along California 140 from Merced to the **Arch Rock Entrance** and into the valley floor, or the 88-mile drive along California 120 from Manteca to the **Big Oak-Flat Entrance.** The park's northwestern corner is accessed through the **Hetch Hetchy Entrance,** which lies about 9 miles north from the park's Big Oak-Flat Entrance on Evergreen Road.

Tioga Pass Entrance typically closes to all but cross-country ski traffic when the first big snowstorm of the season hits in November and doesn't reopen until late May or early June. The 39-mile-long Tioga Road, which runs between Tuolumne Meadows and Crane Flat, also closes.

Flying in

You can fly into **Fresno-Yosemite International** (☎ 559-621-4500; www.ci.fresno.ca.us/flyfresno/airlines.asp), 90 miles from the South Entrance at Wawona. **Alaska Airlines, American Airlines, American Eagle, America West Express, Delta Connection, Hawaiian, Horizon, Northwest, United Express, US Airlines, and U.S. Airways Express** fly into this airport. Most of the major car rental companies are here. See the Appendix for the toll-free numbers.

The **Merced Airport** (☎ 209-385-6873), 73 miles southwest of the Arch Rock Entrance, is served from Las Vegas by **Scenic Airlines** (☎ 800-634-6801). Two rental car agencies are within 1½ miles of the airport: **Aide Rental Car,** 1530 W. 16th St. (☎ 209-722-8084 or 800-717-8084), and **Enterprise,** 1334 W. Main St. (☎ 209-722-1600).

Orienting Yourself in Yosemite National Park

You can be in one of two places when you visit Yosemite: In the valley or out of it. The two areas are very different.

The **Yosemite Valley** floor is tourist central. At **Yosemite Village,** on the north side of the Merced River, you find shops and restaurants, as well as the valley's only medical clinic and a grocery. The village is also home to park headquarters, Yosemite Concession Services offices, and Yosemite's largest visitor center, the Valley Visitor Center. All are within a short walk of one another.

Yosemite National Park

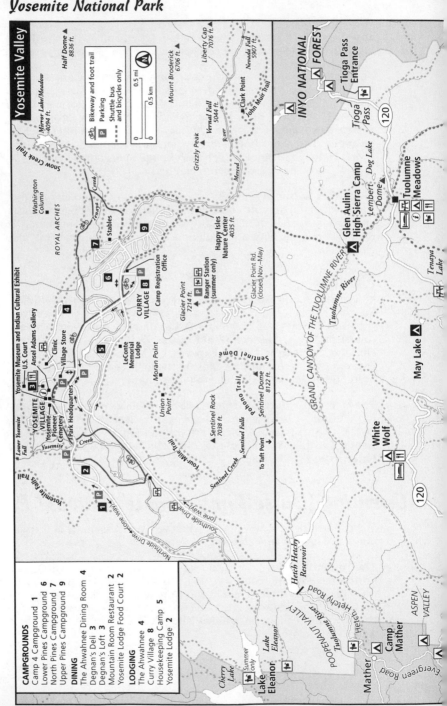

Yosemite Valley

Bikeway and foot trail
P Parking
Shuttle bus and bicycles only

0   0.5 mi
0   0.5 km

Half Dome 8836 ft.

Mirror Lake/Meadow 4094 ft.

Liberty Cap 7076 ft.

Nevada Fall 5907 ft.

Mount Broderick 6706 ft.

Clark Point

John Muir Trail

Vernal Fall 5044 ft.

Grizzly Peak

Merced River

Snow Creek Trail

Washington Column

ROYAL ARCHES

Tenaya Creek

7 Stables

9

6

8 Camp Registration Office

CURRY VILLAGE

Happy Isles Nature Center 4035 ft.

Ranger Station (summer only)

Glacier Point 7214 ft.

Glacier Point Rd. (closed Nov–May)

Yosemite Museum and Indian Cultural Exhibit

U.S. Court

Ansel Adams Gallery

Clinic

Village Store

4

3

5

LeConte Memorial Lodge

Moran Point

Sentinel Dome

YOSEMITE VILLAGE

Yosemite Pioneer Cemetery

Park Headquarters

Lower Yosemite Fall

Union Point

Sentinel Rock 7038 ft.

Sentinel Dome 8122 ft.

Yosemite Creek

Pohono Trail

Sentinel Falls

Sentinel Creek

To Taft Point

Four-Mile Trail

Yosemite Falls Trail

1

2

Southside Drive (one way)

Northside Drive (one way)

INYO NATIONAL FOREST

Tioga Pass Entrance

Tioga Pass

120

Dog Lake

Glen Aulin High Sierra Camp

Lembert Dome

Tuolumne Meadows

Tenaya Lake

GRAND CANYON OF THE TUOLUMNE RIVER

Tuolumne River

May Lake

White Wolf

120

Hetch Hetchy Reservoir

Hetch Hetchy Road

TUOLUMNE VALLEY

POOPENAUT VALLEY

Tuolumne River

Cherry Lake

Summer only

Lake Eleanor

Lake Eleanor

ASPEN VALLEY

Camp Mather

Mather

Evergreen Road

CAMPGROUNDS
Camp 4 Campground 1
Lower Pines Campground 6
North Pines Campground 7
Upper Pines Campground 9

DINING
The Ahwahnee Dining Room 4
Degnan's Deli 3
Degnan's Loft 3
Mountain Room Restaurant 2
Yosemite Lodge Food Court 2

LODGING
The Ahwahnee 4
Curry Village 8
Housekeeping Camp 5
Yosemite Lodge 2

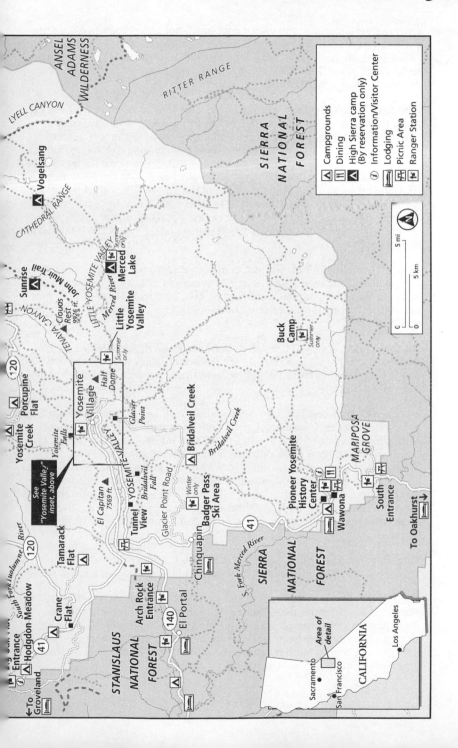

Getting into and out of the valley isn't hard, but travel here takes a little time so you need to be patient. Due to the large amount of backcountry (704,624 of the park's 747,956 acres are official wilderness), Yosemite has few roads. Those that do exist are narrow, wind around mountains, and are often clogged with traffic.

Big Oak-Flat Road (California 120) from Big Oak-Flat Entrance, **El Portal Road** (California 140) from Arch Rock Entrance, and **Wawona Road** (California 41) from South Entrance all converge near the west end of Yosemite Valley, so you won't have a hard time finding the valley floor. After you arrive there, you must take one of two one-way roads: **Southside Drive,** which snakes east to Curry Village, or **Northside Drive,** which runs west from Curry Village back out of the valley. A few bridges cross the Merced River on the valley floor to help you alternate between these one-way ribbons, but if you miss these bridges when you're trying to change your direction of travel, you have to make a lap of the Southside-Northside loop.

Fleeing the valley is easy when it comes to directions, but the actual trip can be harrowing during the height of summer because of traffic. To get down to **Wawona** and **Mariposa Grove,** take Northside Drive to the junction with Wawona Road and then head south for 36 miles. The trip takes about an hour.

Fourteen miles south of the valley, Wawona Road meets **Glacier Point Road,** at Chinquapin junction, which leads to Glacier Point. Although the trip is only 30 miles from the valley floor, the drive takes about an hour depending on traffic.

To reach **Tioga Road** (which runs to White Wolf Lodge and campgrounds at Yosemite Creek, Porcupine Creek, and Tuolumne Meadows), follow Northside Drive out of the valley to Big Oak Flat Road and turn right at the Crane Flat intersection onto the Tioga Road. From Crane Flat, the Tioga Road travels about 14 miles to White Wolf Lodge, 30 miles to Tenaya Lake, and 39 miles to the **Tuolumne Meadows**, a miniature village with a gas station, ranger station, another visitor center, a campground, and the Tuolumne Lodge and tent cabins. From Tuolumne Meadows, the **Tioga Pass Entrance** is another 7½ miles. Tioga Road is open only during the summer months.

Keep in mind when planning a late fall, winter, or early spring trip that Tioga Road usually closes from November to early May because of snow.

The Big Oak-Flat Entrance, accessed via Big Oak-Flat Road (California 120), is just a bit more than 6 miles away from Crane Flat and the Tioga Road junction. You can reach Hetch Hetchy Reservoir, north of the Big Oak-Flat Entrance, by heading 6 miles north from Big Oak-Flat on the **Evergreen Road** to Mather, where you pick up the **Hetch Hetchy Road** that runs 7½ miles to the reservoir.

Finding information after you arrive

When you arrive in Yosemite National Park, you'll want to gawk at the landscape rather than worry about picky details. While checking out the scenery, here are a few tips to keep in mind.

Two park newspapers, the Yosemite Guide and Yosemite Today, are available at entrance stations and visitor centers. They provide up-to-date park information and activity schedules.

The park's best and biggest visitor center is the **Valley Visitor Center** in Yosemite Village (☎ 209-372-0200), which is open daily year-round from 8:30 a.m. to 5 p.m. The center provides information about tours, daily ranger programs, lodging, and restaurants. The rangers are helpful, insightful, and knowledgeable. Inside, information boards update road conditions and campsite availability, and they also serve as message boards. You can buy maps, books, and videos, and check out exhibits on the park, its geologic history, and the surrounding area. Be sure to orient yourself to the park by watching the film, Spirit of Yosemite, in the center's theater.

Also in Yosemite Village is the Yosemite Valley Wilderness Center, a small building with high country maps, information on necessary equipment, and trail information. A ranger at the desk can answer all your questions, issue permits, and offer advice about the high country.

Elsewhere, the **Wawona Information Station** (☎ 209-375-9531) and **Big Oak Flat Information Station** (☎ 209-379-1899) provide general park information spring through fall. In the high country, the **Tuolumne Meadows Visitor Center** (☎ 209-372-0263) is helpful during the summer months. Wasona is open daily 8 a.m. to 4:30 p.m. and Big Oak Flat and Tuolumne Meadows are open daily 9 a.m. to 5 p.m.

Paying fees

The park fee is $20 per car per week, or $10 per person per week if you arrive on bike or foot. If you have a park passport, you don't need to pay the entrance fee; see Chapter 8 for information on the National Park Pass and Chapter 7 for the lowdown on Golden Age and Golden Access passports.

Getting Around

With the park's **free shuttle bus system,** you don't really need your own car to move around the east end of Yosemite Valley, so help reduce congestion and pollution by parking your vehicle. The buses operate year-round, stopping at lodging properties, restaurants, trailheads, and attractions. The park newspaper carries a map of the shuttle routes. Additionally, in summer, free shuttle buses run from Wawona to the Mariposa Grove and from Tioga Pass to Tenaya Lake. Large day-use parking lots are in the east end of the valley near Curry Village and Yosemite Village where you can park your car and board shuttles.

For a fee, **hikers' buses** run daily to Glacier Point from late spring through autumn and to Tuolumne Meadows late June through Labor Day. For fees, schedules, and reservations, call ☎ 209-372-1240 or visit any tour desk.

Yosemite Concession Services offers a variety of **guided tours** for those who want to be led around the park. Choices range from two-hour valley floor tours (which take you past the must-see attractions of El Capitan, The Ahwahnee, Yosemite Falls, and Bridalveil Fall) to six-hour trips to the Mariposa Grove of big trees near the park's southern border. Prices range from $20.50 to $55, depending on the tour. For details and other tour options, call the main tour desk (☎ 209-372-1240) or check with the tour desks at your lodging.

Remembering Safety

 Parts of Yosemite may look like a nicely tended city park, but don't let that impression fool you. This park can be dangerous in places. Waterfalls are beautiful to view, but if you take a hiking trail that passes near one, watch out for slippery footing. And if you climb to the top of Nevada Fall, definitely be careful not to stroll too near the lip of the falls, because it's a long way down if you slip. If you watch climbers scale some of the valley's prominent outcrops, stay a good distance from the cliff base out of the way of falling rocks or dropped climbing gear. Finally, be careful on the roads. Congestion in Yosemite Valley and the steep and twisting high country roads, which are often icy in spring or early fall, make staying alert while driving a must. Plus, wildlife can dart in front of your car at any time.

The park's wildlife is another issue; see the "Yosemite's birds and beasts" sidebar, later in this chapter, for my tips on how to behave respectfully and wisely around these park inhabitants.

For additional tips on how to ensure a safe park visit, see Chapter 8.

Exploring Yosemite

Enjoying Yosemite National Park can be as easy as sitting on a bench watching a cascading waterfall or as involved as backpacking across the park. This section introduces these options, as well as several in between these extremes.

Be prepared to encounter other human beings who share your mission of escaping other human beings. Can you escape the crowds in Yosemite? To a degree. Obviously, in the height of summer your chances of finding solitude in the park are not as good as in the middle of March. But you can minimize your contact with others during summer months by getting out into the park as early as possible and by staying out late in the afternoon. Although your odds of avoiding others on hiking trails that begin on the valley floor aren't as good, you can, literally, walk away from many of them. If you hike the Mist Trail, for example, push on past the top of Vernal Fall to the top of Nevada Fall, because not all folks go the extra mile.

The top attractions

Ansel Adams Gallery
Yosemite Village

If you admire landscape photography (or simply need another roll of film), stop by here. This gallery showcases the life and times of photographer Ansel Adams, America's pre-eminent landscape photographer. You find books and videotapes on him as well as copies of his works — ranging in size from postcards to wall posters — for sale. Contemporary artists' works also are displayed, and revolving exhibitions come through each year.

Near the Valley Visitor Center. Admission: Free. Open: Daily 9 a.m.–9 p.m.

 ### *High Sierra*

North of, and above, the Yosemite Valley is a wonderfully picturesque stretch of rock, forest, and water that is the most accessible piece of backcountry in the park. The Tioga Road slices through this part of the park and offers access to numerous hiking trails (such as the one to Clouds Rest, described in "Taking a hike," later in this chapter) as well as to **Tenaya, May,** and **Dog lakes.** As with the valley floor, you really don't need to get out of your car to admire the High Sierra scenery this road travels through, but why miss an opportunity to hike across some of the granitic mounds or to picnic along one of the lakeshores?

 Before you leave the Yosemite Valley for the High Sierra, stop at the visitor center and snag a copy of *The Yosemite Road Guide*, which notes points of interest along the Tioga Road. If you need munchies, try the Yosemite Valley Store or Degnan's Deli for supplies. You also can pick up picnic supplies at the Crane Flat store at the intersection of Big Oak Flat Road and the Tioga Road.

Tioga Road runs through this area from Crane Flat in the west to the Tioga Pass Entrance Station in the east.

Yosemite Museum and Indian Cultural Exhibit
Yosemite Village

This attraction traces the park's cultural history. The Indian Cultural Exhibit explains the lives of the Ahwahneeche, Miwok, and Paiute tribes that once lived in the area. You occasionally find Native Americans speaking here or giving demonstrations of long-forgotten arts, such as basket weaving. A replica of an Ahwahneeche village is behind the museum. Its exhibits guide you through the tribe's transformation in the years after whites discovered the valley. A ceremonial roundhouse, which is still used, is also on site.

Near the Valley Visitor Center. Admission: Free. Open: Daily 9 a.m.–4:30 p.m.

Yosemite Pioneer Cemetery
Yosemite Village

This cemetery is the final resting place of some of the valley's homesteaders. It's worth a visit, if for no other reason than to examine the headstones, some of which bear rudimentary or fading writing that identifies the grave. On your way over to the cemetery, stop at the Valley Visitor Center to pick up a copy of the *Guide to the Yosemite Cemetery*. Among the souls buried here is James Lamon, an early settler considered to be the first white man to winter in the valley, back in 1862 to 1863. He also lived here year-round and planted apple trees, which still bear fruit.

Near the Valley Visitor Center.

Yosemite Valley

If you're primarily interested in Yosemite's waterfalls and granitic domes, spend the bulk of your trip (if not all of it) on the valley floor, which runs 7 miles west-to-east and barely a mile wide at its broadest point. Here you see Yosemite's main attractions — **Bridalveil Fall, El Capitan, Yosemite Falls, and Half Dome** — simply by driving into the valley. But you really need to get out and do a little exploring. Perspective is a funny thing. Although viewing Yosemite Falls from a distance is captivating, you have a vastly different experience when you stand near its base and feel the thundering waters crashing down.

Yosemite Valley's best vantage point is from atop **Glacier Point,** which juts out 3,200 feet above the valley floor. Sure, any trail that gains some elevation provides stunning valley views, but they can't hold a candle to the ones from this outlook. An easy 30-mile drive from the valley floor, the overlook offers stellar views of **Half Dome, Vernal and Nevada falls, Yosemite Falls,** and the lazy meanders of the **Merced River.** You can even see 9,926-foot-tall **Clouds Rest** far off to the northeast.

A great way to combine a hike and a visit to Glacier Point is to take one of the hikers' shuttles to the point and then hike down to the valley via the **Panorama Trail.** (Call ☎ **209-372-1240** for information on the shuttle.) This 8½-mile trail provides views of three waterfalls: Vernal, Nevada, and Illilouette. Other hiking trails in the valley include Bridalveil Fall, Half Dome, The Mist Trail to Nevada Fall, The Mist Trail to Vernal Fall, and Upper Yosemite Fall Trail. See "Taking a hike," later in this chapter, for descriptions of these.

For a bit of human history in the valley, see the listings in this section for the Ansel Adams Gallery, the Yosemite Pioneer Cemetery, and the Yosemite Museum and Indian Cultural Exhibit.

 When you arrive in the valley, park your car and walk to the places you want to see, or ride the free shuttle buses that go just about everywhere on the eastern end of the valley floor.

Take Big Oak-Flat Road, El Portal Road, or Wawona Road to Southside Drive, which runs into the valley.

Taking a hike

Waterfalls are great from a distance, but they're even more mesmerizing when you're standing close enough for the spray to wash over you. With waterfalls in every direction you look in the valley, and 840 miles of hiking trails throughout the park, you'll probably want to spend at least a little time getting up close to the scenery. Sometimes you only need to go a quarter-mile to get near a waterfall. Backcountry treks, on the other hand, can cover dozens of miles over numerous days.

Bridalveil Fall

This short hike takes only 10 minutes from the time you leave your car to the time you're snapping pictures. You see the fall when you drive into the Yosemite Valley, so you may as well get up close — and wet — too.

Distance: ½ mile round-trip. Level: Easy. Access: Bridalveil Fall Parking Area 3 miles west of Yosemite Village.

Cathedral Lakes

This trail quickly leaves the Tioga Road and gets you into a spectacular backcountry setting of granite domes, conifer forests, and shimmering lakes. From the trailhead, you encounter a gentle, but steady, climb that rises 1,000 feet en route to Upper Cathedral Lake. Before you reach the upper lake, a half-mile spur drops to the southwest and Lower Cathedral Lake, which is surrounded by the soaring granite walls of Cathedral and Tresidder peaks. The work of glaciers long-since melted can be found in highly polished patches of granite along the lake shores and the U-shaped valley.

Distance: 7 miles round-trip. Level: Easy to moderate. Access: Cathedral Lakes Trailhead just west of Tuolumne Meadows complex. Shuttles are available from Tuolumne Meadows.

Clouds Rest

The trail starts off with a short downhill stretch to Sunrise Lake. From there, you head up out of Tenaya Canyon. At the junction, bear right. Killer views abound, and with 9,926-foot-tall Clouds Rest filling the horizon, losing your way is hard. The final push to the summit tests your mettle, thanks to the precipitous dropoffs on either side. That's the Yosemite River on your right and the Little Yosemite Valley on your left.

Distance: 14 miles round-trip. Level: Moderate. Access: Take Tioga Road to Tenaya Lake. The trailhead is at a parking lot down a closed road that crosses an outlet of the lake.

Half Dome

Mounting this dome makes for a long day but offers a view almost as breathtaking as the one from Glacier Point; the difference is you don't get to see Half Dome in the background. Along the way to the top, you pass Vernal and Nevada falls and cross the Little Yosemite Valley. Make sure you pack plenty of water, just in case you miss the spring located just off the Half Dome Trail. This hike isn't for those afraid of heights. Along the final 900 feet to the top you're assisted by cable railings that aren't as daunting as they first appear.

Distance: 16½ miles round-trip. Level: Moderate to strenuous. Access: Mist Trail trailhead near Happy Isles Nature Center. Shuttle bus stop #16.

The Mist Trail

This kid-friendly trail is one of the valley's classic, must-do hikes. Why? If you follow it to the top, a 7-mile round-trip, you get great views of the Yosemite Valley and the spot where the Merced River leaves the Little Yosemite Valley and tumbles out of the high country. Plus, on hot, sultry summer days, you get a wonderfully cool drenching from the falls' spray. The first half of this hike leads to Vernal Fall. The trail up to the footbridge that crosses the Merced River below the falls is paved, and it turns into an expressway during the high season. Trust me, though, the experience — if you continue on to the top of Nevada Fall — is worth facing the crowds. At the footbridge, after snapping a few pictures up- and downstream, you can choose between turning back and going forward, first to the top of Vernal Fall and then on to the top of Nevada Fall. Which choice you make determines whether you get wet.

Choose to continue upward, and after you leave the footbridge over the Merced River, things get interesting. The asphalt is gone and the trail takes on a decidedly uphill nature. Before too long, you're huffing up a series of granite steps. Pack a raincoat to deflect the sheets of mist and spray coming from 317-foot Vernal Fall, and be careful — the steps can be incredibly slick and you should hold onto any small children in your party. Just below the lip of the falls, where you gain protection from the mist, is a great place to take pictures of the rainbows that form in the canyon below you.

A few more steps lead to the brink of Vernal Fall. From here, the trail heads upstream for a short period before crossing a bridge to the north side of the river and then ascending to the top of Nevada Fall. Although the Merced River certainly looks refreshing, be careful and watch your footing. Hikers have slipped on algae-covered rocks and been swept over the 594-foot falls.

Distance: 3 miles round-trip to Vernal Fall; 7 miles round-trip to Nevada Fall. Level: Strenuous. Access: Happy Isles Nature Center, shuttle stop #16.

Upper Yosemite Fall Trail

Standing in the valley gazing at Yosemite Falls, you may be tempted to make this hike. You can do it — just plan accordingly. The hike takes between six and eight hours, round-trip, and the 2,700-foot elevation gain can suck the life from your legs. But after you're on top, the views, and the pictures, make the trip worthwhile. As with any long, steep hike, the key is to pace yourself. Walk a little, rest a little, and walk a little more. One mile into the hike, you reach Columbia Point, which offers a decent view of the valley. The rest of the way doesn't have as many good views because the trail bobs and weaves. The last quarter-mile is the real gut-buster, because you're faced with what seems like an endless series of switchbacks. But after you get to the top, you'll probably agree that the trek was worth it.

Distance: 7¼ miles round-trip. Level: Strenuous. Access: Camp 4 Campground, shuttle stop #8.

LeConte Memorial

In 1870, Joseph LeConte became one of the first geologists to support John Muir's theory that the Yosemite Valley had been carved out by repeated glaciations. LeConte died of natural causes in July 1901 during a visit to Yosemite. In 1903 the Sierra Club built a memorial to him on the south side of the Merced River across from the Housekeeping Camp. The building actually served as the park's first visitor center. Today the LeConte Memorial Lodge (☎ 209-372-4542) has a library, with a children's corner, and a variety of evening programs. See "If you have more time," later in this chapter, for information on programming.

One-day wonder

To get the most out of Yosemite in one day, you need to change your focus as often as possible, moving from the valley to the high-country lakes. But that would be a very full day and you're on vacation, right? In this section, I suggest a more leisurely approach that focuses on the valley's highlights.

If money is no object, spend the night prior to exploring Yosemite at **The Ahwahnee.** If you're budget-minded, choose **Yosemite Lodge** or even a **Curry Village** tent cabin. (See "Where to Stay," later in this chapter, for information on all three options.)

Be sure to start your day early. If possible, sit down to breakfast by 7:30 a.m. so you can be on your way before 9 a.m. Make your first stop the **Mist Trail** (see "Taking a hike"). Early morning is the best time of day to take this popular hike; you'll see the sun generating rainbows in the mist as it climbs into the sky while most other folks are still lingering over breakfast. To reach the trail, either park your car at the Curry Village day-parking area and walk to the trailhead at the Happy Isles Nature Center, or take a shuttle bus to stop #16 near the nature center.

When you finish the hike, it'll no doubt be time for lunch, so either head to **Curry Village, Yosemite Lodge,** or **The Ahwahnee** for a well-deserved meal (see "Where to Eat," later in this chapter). If you're not staying at The Ahwahnee, make sure to pay a visit before, after, or during lunch. To reach the hotel, you can walk, drive, or take a shuttle bus to stop #3. A walk through the imposing hotel gives you a hint of what park life was like in the 1920s when rich Easterners made summer-long excursions to national parks and stayed in opulent structures such as this.

After lunch, why not spend time boning up on the park's history? Stop by the **Yosemite Pioneer Cemetery** and the **Yosemite Museum and Indian Cultural Exhibit** (see "Exploring the top attractions," earlier in this chapter).

Next, it's time to make a decision about how to spend the rest of the day. If you don't mind heights and are determined to coax the most out of your day, plan on having an early dinner and then heading up to **Glacier Point.** Not only does this towering promontory offer an incomparable panorama of Yosemite Valley, but it's also a wonderful spot for some sunset photographs of Half Dome. If a full moon is scheduled to rise, you can get shots of it rising as well as some of the soft light bathing the valley below. Plus, the moonlight highlighting Half Dome is priceless. If the moon doesn't rise, well, you can gaze at a few billion stars overhead. Whatever the case, rest assured you'll have a perfect ending to an incredible day.

If you aren't interested in sunset photos, head up to Glacier Point after you've toured the cemetery and then return to the valley floor for a relaxing dinner.

Capturing Yosemite on film

Yosemite, with its waterfalls and bulbous rock mounds, is one big photograph waiting to be taken. Springtime is the best time to capture Yosemite Valley's waterfalls, because they're often raging with snowmelt and surrounded by wildflowers. Colorful sunrises and sunsets likewise make for wonderful pictures in the valley, because the gray granite provides an outstanding contrast to the reds, oranges, and yellows in the sky.

When in the park's high country, make sure your camera is loaded with film and accessible. You never know when a bear or some other wildlife will come into view. Along that line, a good telephoto or zoom lens comes in handy, too. Also think about experimenting with some black-and white film. Some guy named Adams made quite a name for himself with black-and-white park portraits.

The Ansel Adams Gallery offers a 90-minute photography walk and class. These classes are limited to 15, so make sure you sign up in advance at the gallery. The Yosemite Concession Services also offers 90-minute photography walks, which start from The Ahwahnee hotel or Yosemite Lodge. For more information and to register for these classes, which are limited to 35, check at the front desk of either lodge.

If you have more time

If you really want to see giant sequoias, stop by **Mariposa Grove,** near the park's South Entrance. Divided into the Upper and Lower groves, Mariposa holds 500 sequoias, some as old as 3,000 years. They stretch almost 300 feet tall into the air, are 50 feet in circumference, and weigh an average of 2 million pounds. You can walk or take a tram (for a fee) through the groves.

Don't drive out of your way to visit Mariposa Grove — driving back and forth from the Yosemite Valley consumes 2½ to 3 hours. If you want to stop here, organize your trip so that you exit or enter the park from the South Entrance. However, if you really want to experience sequoias, my advice is to visit Sequoia National Park (Chapter 15) on your next vacation, because it has many, many more sequoias than Yosemite.

The valley's **LeConte Memorial Lodge** (☎ 209-372-4542), open Wednesday through Sunday during summer months, has a variety of free evening programs run by the Sierra Club. Throughout the summer on Friday, Saturday, and Sunday evenings at 8 p.m., you usually find poets, environmentalists, and writers making presentations. If you're bringing kids to the park, you may want to check out the center's free family events, which range from 90-minute programs that delve into the park's bears (and include time in the field searching for signs of the bruins) to twilight "discovery walks" at Mirror Lake discussing topics such as the Ice Age or Native Americans. For current schedules, call the lodge or check out the activities boards at the campgrounds, the lodge, the Valley Visitor Center, or the post office. Yosemite Concession Services also offers free evening programs at The Ahwahnee, Yosemite Lodge, and Curry Village.

Ranger programs

Throughout the summer, rangers lead walks throughout Yosemite to explain aspects of the park's natural and cultural history. These programs, offered at various times throughout the day, touch on geology, forest ecology, wildlife, waterfalls, human history, or current park management issues. Programs on Yosemite's bear population are particularly informative and are popular with children.

In winter, rangers on snowshoes lead hikes into the forests surrounding the Badger Pass Ski Area.

Yosemite's birds and beasts

Okay, Yosemite's bear problems are famous among national park goers, and you may already know the story, so let's get through this quickly. Yes, **black bears** live in Yosemite. These guys are easy to spot because they unfortunately have figured out that where people congregate, they can usually find a meal. During my stay at Tuolumne Lodge, one of the bruins trotted determinedly out of the woods shortly before our dinner and inspected each and every bear locker in search of one that wasn't closed properly. Fortunately, even though the park's bears can smell a jelly donut from a good distance, they still haven't figured out how to get into the bear lockers, so use them during your stay. Bears are adept, though, at peeling open your car like a can of tuna, so don't store any food — not even a pack of gum — in your rig.

By the way, black bears come in various shades. Whether brown, cinnamon, blond, or just black, they're all black bears. Once upon a time, grizzlies lived in the region, too, but the last one spotted *in the entire state of California* was in 1922 near today's King's Canyon National Park. The last known grizzly in Yosemite was killed near Crescent Lake east of Wawona in 1895.

Mountain lions also call this park home, but these big cats are usually hard to spot because of their scarcity and natural reclusiveness. Although their numbers have been on the upswing, consider yourself extremely fortunate if you spy one trotting through a meadow or stalking some mule deer — it's a sight few people ever see. To avoid unpleasant encounters with mountain lions, don't leave any pets outside and unattended, because they seem like menu items to the lions. Also, when you go on a hike, go in a group, if possible, and don't let your children get too far ahead or behind.

In the unlikely event that you do find yourself face-to-face with a mountain lion, don't even think about running. You can't win this footrace. Instead, extend your arms over your head, preferably while holding a pack, to make the lion think you're a pretty big dude not worth messing with. If this still doesn't faze the cat and it begins to stalk you, throw rocks and sticks at it and shout. You want to try to convey the message that you aren't food, and that you can be pretty dangerous, too.

Another reclusive animal that makes its home in the park is the **bighorn sheep**. Yosemite's mountains and alpine meadows once hosted hundreds of them. Over the years, however, poaching, disease, and competition for food by domestic sheep wiped out the park's bighorn population. Fortunately, transplant efforts started in 1986 by the park service, U.S. Forest Service, the California Department of Fish and Game, and the Yosemite Fund, have built a herd of roughly 40 bighorn sheep in the park. Your best shot at spotting one of these nimble creatures is in the rocky slopes along California 120 just outside the park's east entrance.

Coyotes are very commonly seen in the park. You sometimes hear them howling and yipping at night, or spot them pouncing on **mice** and **voles** in meadows. Like the bears, these guys know that people pack food. Please don't feed the beggars.

Although they're timid, you can often spot **mule deer** in the park's meadows. Don't be fooled by their Bambi-ish looks. Over the years, deer have attacked people more often than bears have. Their antlers are sharp and so are their hooves. As with all the other creatures, don't tempt deer with handouts.

Yosemite is home to a few **peregrine falcons**. These dive-bombing birds love to nest on high ledges and prey on white-throated **swifts** that dart about the granite domes. Look for peregrine falcons near El Capitan and Glacier Point.

Other birds you may spot in the park include **prairie falcons, kestrels,** and **merlin falcons,** as well as **golden eagles** and **great gray owls**. Always looking for handouts are dark-blue colored birds known as **Steller's jays.** These characters aren't bashful about landing on your picnic table in search of a crumb or two.

You don't need to look too far for something to do at night. The Park Service, Yosemite Concession Services, Sierra Club, and Ansel Adams Gallery all offer hour-long programs that may include talks, film and slide presentations, storytelling, and music. Rangers also lead stargazing programs atop Glacier Point during summer months.

For information on all the programs mentioned here, check the park newspapers as well as bulletin boards at visitor centers.

 If you have kids, pick up information on the Junior Ranger Program ($3.50; see Chapter 7) at the visitor center. The program is active in Yosemite from late June through August.

Keeping active

Yosemite offers numerous opportunities for outdoor fun. In addition to hiking (see "Taking a hike," earlier in the chapter), you can bike, ski, rock climb, fish, and even golf. Here's what you need to know for each sport:

- **Biking:** You can rent bikes by the hour ($7.50) or the day ($24.50) at Curry Village or Yosemite Lodge. Both shops are open from 8 a.m. to 7 p.m. daily in summer, but the one at Curry Village closes in winter. Hours may vary slightly depending on weather and season. For information, call ☎ **209-372-8319.** Helmets are required for riders under age 18 and are provided to riders of all ages free of charge. Cyclists have access to special bikeways in the eastern end of Yosemite Valley, as well as shuttle bus roads and thoroughfares for general traffic. Biking is prohibited on all trails.

- **Fishing:** Yosemite's stream fishing season runs from the last Saturday in April to mid-November, although you can fish in lakes and reservoirs throughout the year. Anglers ages 16 and older need a California fishing license. For information on where to obtain these licenses, and park-specific fishing regulations, stop at one of the visitor centers.

- **Golf:** Wawona sports a nine-hole golf course; call ☎ **209-375-6572** to book a tee time.

- **Horseback riding:** Yosemite offers two-hour, four-hour, and all-day rides from stables in Yosemite Valley (☎ **209-372-8348**) and Wawona (☎ **209-375-6502)** from spring through fall, weather permitting. In summer, rides also depart from Tuolumne Meadows (☎ **209-372-8427**). Prices range from $51 for two hours and $94 for all-day to $1,155 for a six-day guided trip into the backcountry. Backcountry trips are available only with advance reservations from May to September. These lead to Yosemite's High Sierra camps, and trips include meals.

- **Ice skating:** The ice rink at Curry Village (☎ **209-375-8319**) is open from early November to March, weather permitting. One 2½-hour session costs $6.50 for adults and $5 for children. Skate rental is another $3.25. There are four sessions daily.

- **Rock climbing:** If you've been bitten by the climbing bug, Yosemite is the place to be. The park is one of the world's premier playgounds for experienced climbers. The **Yosemite Mountaineering School** (☎ **209-372-8344**) provides experienced instruction for beginning, intermediate, and advanced climbers in the valley and Tuolumne Meadows from April through October. Classes last anywhere from a day to a week.

✔ **Skiing:** Yosemite's **Badger Pass Ski Area** (☎ 209-372-8430) is open from mid-December through Easter Sunday with alpine and nordic skiing, snowboarding, and tubing. Lessons for all skill levels are available and prices are reasonable: A half-day beginner's lesson with all equipment and all-day lift ticket runs about $50. Snow boarders are welcome on the slopes; boards and boots are also available for rent.

✔ If you prefer **cross-country skiing,** try the guided excursions that go from the Badger Pass Ski Area to Glacier Point. For information, call ☎ 209-372-8444. You can rent skis at Badger Pass. For more independent sorts, there are 90 miles of marked trails and 25 miles of groomed tracks for both classic and skate skiers. Heartier mountaineers can journey into the backcountry.

Where to Stay

Are you a blue blood or a frontiersman? Are you adamant about getting cozy each night in a king-sized bed with thick comforter, or are you willing to stoke the woodstove and pile into a cot with two wool blankets? Do you want to soak in a tub or sleep under the stars? You can have any of these experiences in Yosemite, or choose from a variety of accommodations in between.

At one extreme are the rooms at The Ahwahnee, a National Historic Landmark with great halls, a cavernous dining room, gracious rooms, and stellar views. You pay dearly for a night here. At the other extreme (not counting backcountry camping under the stars) are the tent cabins at Curry Village, White Wolf Lodge, or Tuolumne Meadows. No more than canvas tossed over a frame set on a wood or concrete floor (with bathrooms and showers in a communal bathhouse), these cabins recreate what camping was like in the 1920s. And, frankly, sleeping in one of these with a woodstove is fun.

Yosemite Concession Services (YCS) oversees all lodging in the park — except some private homes at Wawona. You can make reservations by telephone (☎ 559-253-5635) or online (www.yosemitepark.com). Although the Wawona Hotel is operated by YCS, there are more than 100 private homes available for rent nearby through **Redwood's in Yosemite** (☎ 209-375-6666; www.redwoodsinyosemite.com). Addresses aren't included in the listings below for the park hotels. Upon entering the park, you receive a map that pinpoints the location of each one.

Lodging in the park

The Ahwahnee
$$$$$ Yosemite Valley

The Ahwahnee is one of the crown jewels of the park system. This elegant hotel, which marked its 75th anniversary in 2002, is the place to come for a pampering experience in the wilderness. The guest list is formidable: Queen Elizabeth, President Kennedy, 49ers quarterback Steve Young, and Clint Eastwood have all stayed here. You can add your name, too, if you're willing to pay the price, which can get quite steep for multiple-day stays.

Walk into the Great Lounge, a 77-x-51-foot reading room with a 24-foot-high ceiling, and you find not only overstuffed couches and armchairs but back-to-back fireplaces big enough to walk into. The monstrous dining room has a 34-foot-high ceiling, is 130 x 51 feet, and seats 450 people. During breakfast and lunch, light streams in through the 11 full-length windows, but at dinner, tapers set in wrought iron holders illuminate the tables. You also find a small swimming pool outside the bar.

The rooms are among the best in the national park system. Suites feature two rooms, whereas regular rooms provide either two double beds or one king-sized bed, a couch, plush towels, and wonderful comforters. The stencils that frame the walls date to 1927 — when the hotel was built.

See map p. 318. Parking available or take the shuttle bus to stop #3. 95 rooms, 4 suites, 24 cottages. A/C TEL. Rack rates: $373 double and cottages, additional charge for extra adults, specials during off-season; up to $822 for suites. Rates include coffee and pastries for breakfast. DC, DISC, MC, V.

Curry Village
$–$$$ Yosemite Valley

This tent and cabin village, which marked its centennial in 1999, was designed to offer an economical lodging alternative to the now-defunct Sentinel Hotel. Although it's economical, I strongly recommend against a stay in Curry Village unless you have no other option. The furnishings in each tent cabin are pretty spare — a couple of cots, a dresser, and warm blankets, plus the restrooms and showers are a short walk away. Some of the wooden cabins have baths; the rest use communal facilities, which are stressed by the 2,000 or so guests who stay in the village each night of the high season. Curry Village can be overrun with kids, it's noisy (the tent walls do little to muffle sounds from other tents and the nearby parking lot and the quiet hours of 10 p.m. to 6 a.m. are too short and not well-enforced), and its tiny bath houses aren't cleaned often enough. About the only plus, aside from the price, is that the location is close to the village's pizza parlor, cocktail lounge, taco stand, coffee corner, sports shop, general store, cafeteria, ice cream stand, swimming pool, and sundeck.

See map p. 318. Parking is available or take the shuttle to stops #1, #13, or #14. 183 wooden cabins, 427 canvas cabins, 18 hotel rooms. Rack rates: $64 tent cabin; $80 *wooden cabin without bath; $88 wooden cabin with bath; $114 hotel room; all cabin rates are double occupancy, extra charge for additional adults. Lower rates off-season. DC, DISC, MC, V.*

Housekeeping Camp
$ **Yosemite Valley**

These interesting units are concrete and canvas — three walls and the floor are concrete, and the roof is a double layer of canvas. A canvas wall in the units separates the sleeping quarters from a cooking/dining area that centers around a picnic table. Some folks find these accommodations charming, others view them as a step above a shanty town. A laundromat is nearby, as are communal restroom and shower facilities.

See map p. 318. Parking is available or take the shuttle to stop #12. 266 units. Rack rates: $67 per site for 1–4 people; $5 for each additional person. DC, DISC, MC, V. Open: Mid-April to mid-Oct.

Tuolumne Meadows Lodge
$$ **Tuolumne Meadows**

Although Spartan, these tent cabins provide a memorable and highly affordable lodging option for adventurous visitors. Beds are simple bunks with reasonable mattresses covered by wool blankets. Woodstoves supply heat on cool nights and mornings, and a table stands ready for a game of cards. A short trail leads to a nearby communal bathhouse/restroom. Although these tent cabins are identical to those in Curry Village, the difference here is the number — there are far, far fewer than in Curry Village so you don't encounter the same noise and cleanliness problems. Meals at the lodge are served family style, ensuring that you get to know your fellow travelers. The lodge also has a tour desk and dining room.

This place is similar to White Wolf Lodge, although a bit more crowded.

See map p. 318. Tioga Road (California 120). 69 canvas tent cabins. Rack rate: $71 double, with additional charge of $9 per extra adult or $4 per child. DC, DISC, MC, V. Open: Mid-June to mid-Sept.

Wawona Hotel
$$–$$$ **Wawona**

Next to The Ahwahnee, this lodge is the most elegant in the park. The rooms are housed in a cluster of six Victorian-style buildings set in a forest clearing. You can relax on wide porches or play tennis or golf. Like The Ahwahnee, the hotel is a National Historic Landmark. Rooms are comfortable and quaint and come with a choice of a double and twin bed, a king bed, or a double bed. Fifty rooms have private baths; those without have access to a communal facility. All rooms open onto wide porches and overlook sprawling green lawns. A pianist plays in the downstairs lobby of the main hotel each night.

See map p. 318. Wawona Road (California 41). 104 rooms. Rack rates: $115 double without bath, $170 double with bath; additional charge for extra adults. Lower winter rates. DC, DISC, MC, V.

White Wolf Lodge
$–$$ White Wolf

Not only does this small area offer a welcome escape from the valley crowds, but it's a bargain, too. The tent cabins are typically cleaner than those in Curry Village, and the wood-burning stoves and candles for light add a dash of charm on cool nights. You find a small general store and restaurant here. The location is popular with hikers and those seeking a weekend getaway. The canvas cabins share communal restroom and shower facilities, but the wooden cabins have their own bathrooms and small porches with chairs to plop into. Things really get quiet here at 11 p.m., when the generator is turned off. Those staying in tent cabins must stash their food in bear-proof lockers.

See map p. 318. Tioga Road (California 120). 24 canvas tent cabins, 4 wooden cabins. Rack rates: $67 double without bath, $84 with bath; additional charge of $9 for extra adults and $4 per child. DC, DISC, MC, V. Open: Late June to early Sept.

Yosemite Lodge
$$$ Yosemite Valley

Dating to 1915, this lodge has become a mishmash of accommodations over the years. You can't beat the location, at the base of Yosemite Falls, but the elegance of The Ahwahnee has not rubbed off. On the bright side, neither have The Ahwahnee's prices — Yosemite Lodge is much more reasonable. The accommodations range from cabins and motel-style rooms to suites. Some offer views of the waterfalls, some have patios, others balconies. The lodge also has helpful services — a post office, bicycle rental stand, gift shops, and swimming pool. The amphitheater in the middle of the lodge is a good place to attend ranger programs and slide presentations.

See map p. 318. Parking available or take the shuttle to stop #8. 245 motel rooms and suites. Some with A/C TEL. Rack rates: $114–$161 double, with additional charge for extra adults. Lower rates off-season. DC, DISC, MC, V.

Lodging outside the park

Yosemite West Lodging
$$–$$$$$ Sierra National Forest

Although these accommodations aren't in Yosemite, you have to drive through the park to reach them. From here it's 10 miles to the Yosemite Valley floor and just 8 miles to Badger Pass, making this a great spot to base yourself for a winter ski trip in the park. These private homes range in size and accommodate families as well as couples. All cabins come with kitchenettes, whereas homes have full kitchens, and most have fireplaces or wood-burning stoves. Homes are equipped with oversize beds.

Off Wawona Road (California 41), 12 miles north of Wawona, near Chinquapin. ☎ *559-642-2211.* www.yosemitewestreservations.com. *A fluctuating number of cabins and private homes are available throughout the year. TV. Rack rates: $85–$215 and up. No credit cards.*

Runner-up lodgings

Best Western Yosemite Way Station

$–$$ **Mariposa** Clean, comfortable, and kid-friendly thanks to the outdoor pool, this chain motel includes continental breakfast in its rates. *4999 Hwy. 140.* ☎ *888-742-4371 or 209-966-7545.* www.yosemitemotels.com/bestwesternmariposa/index.htm.

Cedar Lodge

$$$ **El Portal** Just 8 miles west of Yosemite's Arch Rock Entrance, this lodge is set on 27 mostly wooded acres, offers standard motel rooms as well as suites, and has a pizza parlor and lounge on the property. *9966 Hwy. 140.* ☎ *888-742-4371 or 209-379-2612.* www.yosemite-motels.com/cedarlodge/index.htm.

Comfort Inn of Oakhurst

$–$$ **Oakhurst** Located 15 miles south of Yosemite's South Entrance, this chain property offers a pool, Jacuzzi, and Continental breakfast, and is near a golf course. *40489 Hwy. 41.* ☎ *888-742-4371 or 559-683-8282.* www.yosemite-motels.com/comfortinnoakhurst/index.htm.

Groveland Hotel

$$$–$$$$$ **Groveland** Twenty-three miles west of Yosemite's Big Oak Flat Entrance, this gracious two-story hotel dates to 1849 and names most of its 17 rooms after women of the Sierra. Not exactly kid-friendly, but adults admire the antiques and candlelit dining room. *18767 Hwy. 120.* ☎ *800-273-3314 or 209-962-4000.* www.groveland.com.

Campgrounds

In Yosemite you can choose from the park's 13 front-country campgrounds and 5 High Sierra camps, the latter offering a somewhat pampered back-country experience. Read on for details on these options.

Camping in the front country

Yosemite has 13 front-country campgrounds — a baker's dozen, or is that a camper's dozen? Anyway, the one you choose depends on where you want to be in the park, and whether or not you want to arrive with a reservation or jockey for one of the first-come, first-served sites.

To reserve a site at any campground — later I tell you which ones accept reservations — call ☎ 800-436-7275 between 7 a.m. and 7 p.m. Pacific standard time. You can also place your reservations online by visiting http://reservations.nps.gov. You can make reservations up to five months in advance of your trip, starting on the 15th of each month. Nightly fees range from $8 to $18, with no extra charge for reservations.

For road warriors traveling by RV, none of the 13 campgrounds has a utility hookup, although sanitary dump stations are available in Yosemite Valley, Wawona, and Tuolumne Meadows (summer only).

The campgrounds have most of the amenities of home . . . within walking distance. All valley campgrounds offer showers and flush toilets nearby, as well as laundry facilities, groceries, swimming, fishing, and even horseback riding. Head out of the valley, though, and the amenities begin to dwindle. For example, only campers at White Wolf or Tuolumne Meadows enjoy nearby showers, and only those at Wawona, Crane Flat, and Tuolumne Meadows have a grocery within easy distance. For details on a specific campground, visit www.nps.gov/yose/trip/camping.htm.

If the valley floor and its attractions are the focus of your trip, find a spot in either the **Upper Pines Campground,** open year-round; the **Lower Pines Campground,** open from March through October; or the **North Pines Campground,** open from April through October. Reservations are required at these popular sites, so you can guarantee yourself a spot if you plan properly. The three campgrounds have comparable settings, but if you like to fall asleep to the sound of rippling waters, aim for a site in the North Pines campground, located along the Merced River.

If you fail to land a spot in these three campgrounds, your only other option in the valley floor is the **Camp 4 Campground** located west of Yosemite Lodge along Northside Drive. However, this walk-in campground is very popular with climbers and backpackers and can be on the rambunctious side. This facility operates on a first-come, first-served basis, and often fills before 9 a.m. each day May through September.

Outside the valley, only the **Wawona** and **Hodgdon Meadows campgrounds** are open year-round. Both campgrounds are quiet and more secluded than those on the valley floor. Reservations for these sites are required from May through September; the rest of the year they go on a first-come, first-served basis.

The **Tuolumne Meadows Campground** is open July through September. You can reserve half the sites; the other half are available for walk-ins.

Reservations are always required at the **Crane Flat Campground,** which is open from June to September.

Sites at the **Bridalveil Creek, Tamarack Flat, White Wolf, Porcupine Creek,** and **Yosemite Creek campgrounds,** which are open during the summer months, are filled on a first-come, first-served basis. If you want a more out-of-the-way spot, **Yosemite Creek Campground,** which is located at the end of a steep, 5-mile unpaved road just east of White Wolf, fits the bill.

Camping in the backcountry

If a pampered backcountry experience is what you want, consider spending a few nights at one of Yosemite's five **High Sierra camps.** Unlike your usual backcountry treks, here you can sleep on a reasonably soft mattress in a tent cabin and relish great meals that *someone else* prepares. The five camps are **Merced Lake, Vogelsang, Glen Aulin, May Lake,** and **Sunrise.** The dormitory-style canvas cabins can sleep between 32 and 60 people. You get more than just a soft place to bed down, too, because each camp is complete with restroom and shower facilities.

The price for this camping experience may seem steep — $112 per adult per night, $87.55 per child but when you consider the high-country setting and the meals included in the price (filet mignon, chicken dishes, pork loin, fish, or pasta for dinner, and pancakes, eggs and bacon, Danish, and cereals for breakfast), it starts to seem more reasonable.

These accommodations, which are available late June to Labor Day, are popular. For this reason, a lottery determines who lands a bed. Camp applications are accepted between October 15 and November 30; winners are notified the following March. If you have questions or want an application, call the **High Sierra Desk** at ☎ **559-253-5674.**

If you're seeking a more traditional backcountry experience, see "Planning Ahead," earlier in this chapter for information on obtaining a mandatory wilderness permit.

Where to Eat

When you're wondering what to pack for your trip, rest assured that if you toss your tux or cocktail dress into your suitcase, you'll have a place to wear it. Being overdressed for dinner at The Ahwahnee hotel is impossible, although you probably want to leave the tux behind if you're chowing down on pizza at Curry Village, which has a number of inexpensive cafeterias, grills and pizza joints not listed below.

You find plenty of dining options in Yosemite Valley, although they narrow considerably when you head to the high country of Tuolumne Meadows and White Wolf Lodge. And although menu prices throughout the park may raise your eyebrows, you'll be satisfied when you push away from the table.

The Ahwahnee Dining Room
$$$$ Yosemite Valley **AMERICAN**

Don't be surprised if it takes you a little while to get around to reading the menu after you're seated. This cavernous hall deserves a once- or twice-over. With its 34-foot-tall beamed ceiling, its candelabra chandeliers, and the thin tapers that dress your table, this room epitomizes national park stateliness. The menu is similarly impressive, with dinner entrees ranging from Pacific black cod and smoked duck Carbonara to roast organic pork tenderloin and lamb sirloin. For breakfasts, you can pick and choose from a sumptuous buffet with made-to-order omelets, waffles, cereals, pastries, and fresh fruit. Pasta salads, trout dishes, and a variety of sandwiches hold down the lunch menus. Gentlemen (and boys over 12) are required to don jackets, preferably with ties, and slacks for dinner.

See map p. 318. In The Ahwahnee. Shuttle bus stop #4. ☎ 209-372-1489. Dinner reservations required. Main courses: $3.50–$18.00 breakfast; $11.25–$14.50 lunch; $24.75–$38 dinner. DC, DISC, MC, V. Open: Daily 7–10:30 a.m., 11:30 a.m.–3 p.m., 5:30–9 p.m.

Degnan's Deli
$ Yosemite Valley **DELI SANDWICHES**

Ah yes, your typical deli. Not a complete New York deli, but Degnan's has a good selection of sandwiches that will keep you going through the afternoon. The lines can get long at the height of the lunch hour, but they move pretty quickly, so don't despair. You also find plenty of premade salads, sandwiches, and snacks to toss into your pack for that meal somewhere down the trail. They have a decent wine and beer selection, too. If you still have room after your meal, you can head next door to Degnan's Café for ice cream, an espresso, or a smoothie.

See map p. 318. Yosemite Village. Shuttle bus stops #2, #4, and #10. No phone. Main courses: $4–$7 breakfast, lunch, and dinner. DC, DISC, MC, V. Open: Daily, 7 a.m.–6 p.m.

Degnan's Loft
$$–$$$ Yosemite Valley **ITALIAN**

This pizza place is a great spot to take your family for a quick, reliable meal. The atmosphere is light and cheery, and the food is filling. The breadsticks, salads, and desserts are all made daily. You can build a pizza, or order a calzone and enjoy your meal over a cold beer. While waiting for your meal, cozy up to the fireplace that anchors the center of the restaurant.

See map p. 318. Yosemite Village. Shuttle bus stops #2, #4, and #10. No phone. Main courses: $4.25–$21.25 lunch and dinner. DC, DISC, MC, V. Open: mid-April to Oct, Mon–Fri, noon to 9 p.m.

Mountain Room Restaurant
$$$$ **Yosemite Valley** **AMERICAN**

Perhaps the best meal I've had in Yosemite was here at the Mountain Room. My wife claims it was because I was starving following a hike to the top of Half Dome, but I like to give the chef credit. Not as pricy as the Ahwahnee, the Mountain Room's menu is diverse and tasty from beginning to end. You don't enjoy the sprawling opulence of The Ahwahnee's dining room, but you get fantastic views of Yosemite Falls through the restaurant's floor-to-ceiling windows. The prices are a tad gentler on the wallet than at The Ahwahnee, and the menu is good, ranging from traditional steaks to the untraditional — my meal was the sesame ahi fillet seared rare and accompanied by Wasabi mashed potatoes and a cucumber-radish salad served with soy glaze.

See map p. 318. In Yosemite Lodge. Shuttle bus stop #8. ☎ *209-372-1281. Main courses: $18–$28 dinner. DC, DISC, MC, V. Open: Daily 5:30–9 p.m.*

Tuolumne Meadows Lodge
$$$–$$$$ **Tuolumne Meadows** **AMERICAN**

The food here is surprisingly good, considering how far from civilization you are. One night I ordered the lamb chops and they ran out, so instead I got tenderloin of lamb. Talk about roughing it. But that brings up a key point — sometimes they run out of dishes, so make an early dinner reservation. Seating is family style, so you never know who may end up at your table. The only meals are breakfast and dinner.

See map p. 318. Tioga Road (California 120). ☎ *209-372-8413. Reservations required for dinner. Main courses: $4.50–$7.25 breakfast; $10.75–$24.50 dinner. DC, DISC, MC, V. Open: Mid-June to mid-Sept, 7–9 a.m. and 6–8 p.m.*

Wawona Hotel Dining Room
$$$–$$$$ **Wawona** **AMERICAN**

For a laid-back, relaxing, and dignified dining experience, come here. The dining room, like the rest of the hotel, is wide open with lots of windows and sunlight. The menu is not only affordable but delectable. Breakfasts feature eggs and grill items as well as hot and cold cereals; lunches offer everything from BLTs and tuna melts to ratatouille; and dinners revolve around thick slabs of prime rib, pan-roasted chicken breast with prosciutto saltimbocca or pot roast. On Sundays, schedule your day around brunch. You have a choice of two seatings: one ($13) from 7:30 to 10:30 a.m. that is built around traditional breakfast items, and another ($18) from 10:30 a.m. to 1:30 p.m. that infuses a few more lunch-type offerings. Both give you a wide choice of egg dishes, fresh fruit, fruit breads, juices, blintzes, and meats. The second adds pan-fried trout and a carving station with roast beef, turkey, and pork roast.

See map p. 318. Wawona Road (California 41). ☎ *209-375-1425. Reservations recommended. Main courses: $2.50–$8.50 breakfast; $7–$9 lunch; $17–$26.75 dinner; $13 and $18 Sun brunch. DC, DISC, MC, V. Open: Easter week to early Oct, daily; late-Oct to Thanksgiving, weekends only; Christmas to New Years Day, daily; Jan to March weekends; Mon–Sat 7:30–10 a.m., noon–1:30 p.m., and 5:30–8:30 p.m.; Sun brunch seatings 7:30 and 10:30 a.m., Sun dinner 5:30–8:30 p.m.*

White Wolf Lodge
$$–$$$$ White Wolf   AMERICAN

By now you probably have breakfast menus memorized: pancakes or French toast, cereals and eggs, biscuits and gravy. Dinners are also pretty predictable at most national park restaurants, and this place is no exception. The menu always has a beef, chicken, fish, pasta, and vegetarian offering. After a long day on the trail, you'll appreciate the large portions and the fun, enthusiastic staff. You can't sit down to lunch here, but the lodge has a store where you can buy food.

See map p. 318. Tioga Road (California 120). ☎ *209-372-8416. Reservations required for dinner. Main courses: $3.85–$7 breakfast; $10.75–$24.50 dinner. DC, DISC, MC, V. Open: Late June to early Sept, daily 7–9 a.m. and 6–8:30 p.m.*

Yosemite Lodge Food Court
$$ Yosemite Valley   PIZZA/DELI/GRILL

This cafeteria offers the option of enjoying a sit-down meal or grabbing a quick bite before heading out into the park. Hot and cold food stations offer a varied selection ranging from a pasta station; pizza station; deli station with salads, and cheese and fruit plates; wrap and deli sandwiches; and a grill serving burgers, hot dogs, fries, and chicken and fish sandwiches. You also can choose vegetarian or meat-based entrees. Breakfast fare ranges from grilled items to cereals. Prepackaged picnic items are also available.

See map p. 318. In Yosemite Lodge. Shuttle bus stop #8. No phone. Main courses: $3–$9.35 breakfast, lunch, and dinner. DC, MC, V. Open: Daily 6:30 a.m.–8 p.m.

Fast Facts: Yosemite

Area Code
The local area codes are **209** and **559**.

ATM
ATMs are available at Yosemite Village (just south of and inside of the Village Store), Yosemite Lodge, the gift shop in Curry Village, and the Wawona store.

Emergency
In an emergency, dial **911**.

Fees
Entrance fees are $20 per vehicle per week and $10 per week for those on foot, bicycle, or motorcycle.

Fishing License

A California license is required for those ages 16 and older. Regulations are available at visitor centers.

Hospitals

Healthcare is available at the Yosemite Medical Clinic on Ahwahnee Drive (☎ 209-372-4637). If you require dental services, you can find them adjacent to the medical clinic (☎ 209-372-4200 or 209-372-4637).

Information

For information, write Yosemite National Park, P.O. Box 577, Yosemite, CA 95389, call ☎ 209-372-0200, or look on the Internet at www.nps.gov/yose.

Pharmacies

The Yosemite Medical Clinic on Ahwahnee Drive has a limited pharmacy (☎ 209-372-4637).

Post Offices

You'll find post offices in Yosemite Village, Yosemite Lodge, Curry Village, Wawona, and Tuolumne Meadows.

Road Conditions and Weather

For road conditions and weather, call ☎ 209-372-0200.

Time Zone

The park is on Pacific time.

Chapter 18

Zion National Park

● ●

In This Chapter

▶ Going into the redrock canyon
▶ Planning your trip
▶ Hiking the trails to high peaks and lush pools
▶ Finding the best beds and meals

● ●

Southern Utah's canyon-riddled redrock country is so fantastic that one national park alone can't capture its beauty, which is why you find five national parks and two national monuments displaying this marvelous and rugged landscape. But squeezing in stops at all seven during a typical vacation is impossible if you want to do them all justice.

That's where Zion National Park comes in. More than any other Utah park, Zion offers an intoxicating primer on redrock country. Whereas one part of the park is a stark, high-desert landscape, the other immerses you deep into canyons teeming with lush oases that erupt with blooms of wildflowers in the spring.

Towering cliffs cut by deep side canyons are the first things you notice as you enter the heart of the park, via Zion Canyon Drive. The rugged landscape doesn't seem very nurturing. But take a little time to explore this mazelike park and you discover flourishing hanging gardens fed by cascading streams, narrow slot canyons with sandstone walls fluted by millions of years of rushing waters, and glimmering emerald green pools stepping their way down mountainsides.

Although Zion doesn't boast the incredible number and diversity of rock arches that define Arches National Park (see Chapter 9), its **Kolob Arch** is one of the world's largest freestanding arches. And even though nearby Bryce Canyon National Park is the world champion when it comes to sheer numbers of rocky spires, pinnacles, and hoodoos, time spent on Zion's eastern flanks reveals enough mushroom-shaped **hoodoos** to sate your curiosity about these intriguing rock outcrops. Utah's Capitol Reef National Park may boast ship-sized rock formations, but Zion counters with the Great White Throne and the Watchman, two of the biggest **sandstone monoliths** known on Earth. Although Zion can't compete with

Canyonlands National Park when it comes to sprawling canyons that swallow the landscape, trek through Zion Narrows, a narrow and towering **slot canyon,** and you'll come away with a life-long memory of a 24-foot-wide, 1,000-foot-deep crack in the earth.

Must-See Attractions

After you enter Zion Canyon, you'll find your head tilting back. That's the only way to take in all the incredible palisades that frame this canyon cut by the Virgin River. But after you venture inside, where should you aim your sights? Let me give you some ideas:

✔ **Angels Landing:** King of the World, anyone? Stand atop this outcrop, and you've won that title. Below you, the park spills away in all directions. Prominent landmarks surround you: Cathedral Mountain, Observation Point, Cable Mountain, and the Great White Throne. Of course, to reach this summit you must negotiate a trail that, at points, is quite precipitous and not for everyone. But hey, you want to experience Zion, right?

✔ **Emerald Pools Trail:** In a land as arid as Utah, just about any water is worth a visit. Hike this trail during the spring and early summer, or after a midsummer's cloudburst, and you'll return home talking about towering waterfalls that leapfrog down the mountainside, creating a series of pools and lush, hanging gardens.

✔ **Great White Throne:** This is Zion's version of Yosemite's El Capitan (see Chapter 17). A large rectangular block of white Navajo sandstone set on end, the throne rises 2,344 feet above the Zion Canyon floor and is thought to be one of the world's largest upright masses of sandstone. You find this monolith about 3 miles upriver from the Zion Canyon Visitor Center.

✔ **The Watchman:** This column of sandstone guards the park's south entrance like a stony sentinel, climbing 2,555 feet above the road.

✔ **Weeping Rock:** This rock grotto at the end of a short walk is a great place to beat the summer's heat. The lush, colorful hanging gardens that drape the cliffside with Zion columbines, shooting stars, Maidenhair ferns, and scarlet gilia make it hard to believe you're surrounded by desert.

Planning Ahead

For general information before you go, write Superintendent, Zion National Park, Springdale, UT 84767 or call ☎ **435-772-3256.** You can also check the park Web site at www.nps.gov/zion.

When to go and how long to stay

Late spring, when ephemeral springs nourish hanging gardens and feed cascading rivulets down canyon walls, is a great time to visit Zion. So, too, is fall, when the weather is cooling and low stream flows make Zion Narrows easier to negotiate.

A three-day stay in Zion Canyon is adequate. However, if you want to also visit Kolob Canyon, scramble across the slickrock near the east entrance, or linger in various areas of the main canyon, plan on adding another two or three days. Similarly, if you want to visit Bryce, add another night and two days.

Advance reservations

You must plan well in advance to secure a room in Zion. Although the park may not be as popular as Yellowstone or Yosemite, let alone next-door-neighbor Grand Canyon, Zion's rooms fill quickly because there just aren't that many of them. The same is true for campsites in the developed campgrounds. As a result, if you're planning to visit in June, July, or August — when most tourists head to Zion, make room reservations at least six months ahead of your arrival. Even the shoulder seasons are becoming more popular, so don't wait until the last minute if you're planning a late spring or early fall visit.

You can reserve campsites at the Watchman Campground (open year-round), between April 2 and October 31; call ☎ 800-365-CAMP.

What to pack

There's no need to pack for a night out on the town. Zion and tiny Springdale (the town just outside the South Entrance) are laid back, and khaki and other earth tones feature prominently among the shorts and casual shirts that dominate the human scenery during the high season. If you're planning on heading down some of the trails, be sure to have a comfortable, broken-in pair of light or midweight hiking boots. (There's nothing worse than the blisters a pair of boots right out of the box will produce during a hike.) If you think you may venture into Zion Narrows from the Temple of Sinawava, pack a good pair of sneakers or hiking boots with good ankle support that will provide good footing in the Virgin River. Sandals, such as Tevas, won't protect your toes and ankles when you slip on the bowling-ball sized rocks and other cobbles in the river. For more tips on what to pack, see Chapter 8.

Getting There

Zion is near the bottom of Utah in the state's southwestern corner where canyon country runs far and wide. The park could have been made much larger — that's how much spectacular countryside there is in this part of the state. In fact, Bryce Canyon National Park is just 85 miles northeast, Cedar Breaks National Monument is 80 miles north, and the Grand Staircase-Escalante National Monument is only 60 miles east.

Driving in

Southwestern Utah is sparsely populated, so traffic jams are nonexistent. In fact, your greatest challenge is keeping your speed down. Thanks to Interstate 15, just 25 or 31 miles west of the park's **South Entrance** (depending on whether you're coming from the north or south), getting to Zion is easy. If you're heading north from St. George, take Exit 16 and drive 11 miles north on Utah 9 to La Verkin, where you turn right and continue to Springdale. If you're coming from Salt Lake City, 325 miles to the north, get off at Exit 27 and head 5 miles east along Utah 17 to La Verkin. Then turn left onto Utah 9 and continue 20 miles to Springdale and the South Entrance. (If you're coming from the north, you can't use the **Northwest Entrance** to get to Zion Canyon. This entrance leads to a dead-end road.)

The roads between I-15 and the park aren't the most scenic approach to Zion (an experience that is reserved for those who travel Utah 9 from U.S. 89 to the East Entrance), but they do offer the most expedient route. If you use the **South Entrance**, you avoid delays that often occur at the East Entrance, where traffic enters through the Zion-Mt. Carmel Tunnel that was built during the 1920s. Plus, if you can't find a room inside the park, Springdale offers a nice variety of possibilities.

The ride to the park's **East Entrance** runs 24 miles from Mt. Carmel Junction on Utah 9. The canyon country along this route is striking thanks to the aptly named Checkerboard Mesa (a sandstone mountain crisscrossed with grooves etched by erosion) and beautiful views into canyons that fall away from the road. The road tests your brakes a bit as it drops 2,400 feet and slips through the mile-long **Zion-Mt. Carmel Tunnel** before negotiating six switchbacks. Driving a large rig — one at least 11 feet, 4 inches tall or 7 feet, 10 inches wide — into the park via this route costs $10 extra because you need an escort through the tunnel. (Tall vehicles have to drive down the middle of the tunnel to keep from running into its arched walls.) Vehicles taller than 13 feet, 1 inch, are banned from the tunnel, as are pedestrians and cyclists.

Flying in

The nearest airports are in **St. George, Utah** (☎ 435- 634-3480), 45 miles away from the South Entrance, and **Cedar City, Utah** (☎ 435-586-3033), 15 miles from the Kolob Entrance and 59 miles from the South Entrance. Both airports are small, but you can get service to them on **Delta-Skywest Airlines.** (See the Appendix for the toll-free numbers of all airlines and car-rental agencies mentioned in this section.)

Zion National Park

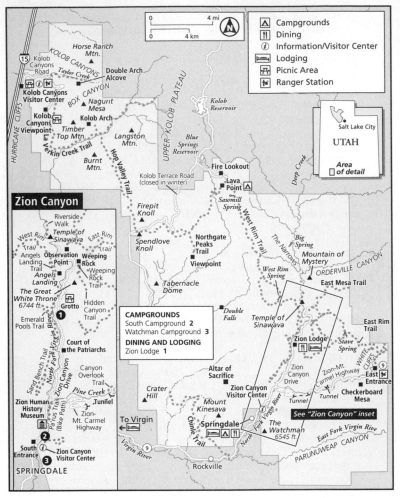

Car-rental agencies with offices in St. George include **ABC** (33 N, 400 East; ☎ 435-628-7355). **Avis** (☎ 435- 627-2002), **Budget** (☎ 435-673-6825), and **National** (☎ 435-673-5098), all have outlets at St. George Municipal Airport. **Avis** and **National** provide car rentals at the Cedar City airport.

The closest major airport is **McCarran International Airport** (☎ 702-261-5743) in Las Vegas, which is about 110 miles southwest of St. George via I-15. Most major airlines fly into McCarran, and most major car rental agencies have outlets at the airport. The **St. George Shuttle** (☎ 800-933-8320 or 435-628-8320; www.stgshuttle.com) provides daily service between St. George and Las Vegas.

Orienting Yourself in Zion

Zion National Park, which sprawls across nearly 150,000 acres, is block-shaped, except for a small peninsula off the park's northwestern corner. For most visitors, the heart and soul of the park centers on and around **Zion Canyon**. Seven-mile-long **Zion Canyon Drive** traverses the canyon. Paralleling the drive is the North Fork of the Virgin River. Within the canyon are several trailheads, cascading streams, and the Zion Lodge, the only accommodations inside the park.

Unless you have a reservation at the Zion Lodge, you can't drive along Zion Canyon Drive from April through October. Instead, you must park your car in Springdale or at Zion Canyon Visitor Center on the south end of the park. From here, you can take a seat in one of the free, propane-powered **shuttle buses** that run all the way to the Temple of Sinawava, a tight canyon surrounded by rock walls located at the north end of the canyon floor. See "Getting around Zion National Park," later in this chapter, for shuttle information. *Note:* If you do have a room at the lodge, be sure to tell the rangers at the entrance gate so they will give you a permit to drive to the lodge.

Enter the park via the East Entrance along **Zion-Mount Carmel Highway** and you encounter the intriguing **Checkerboard Mesa** with its slashed and grooved sandstone face dotted with ponderosa pines. Horizontal grooves in Navajo sandstone are common, but the vertical ones on this mountain are thought to have been cut by freezing and thawing processes and enlarged by erosion.

Just beyond Checkerboard Mesa, you wind through a colorful garden of red, orange, tan, and white rock formations in all shapes and sizes before entering two narrow tunnels. On the east end of the second tunnel is a pullout for the mile-long **Canyon Overlook Trail** that offers a great view into Zion Canyon. Exiting the second tunnel, you quickly exchange a landscape of rugged mountains for the broad and deep Zion Canyon with its abrupt cliffs.

After negotiating a series of switchbacks leading to the valley floor, you arrive at the junction of Zion-Mount Carmel Highway and Zion Canyon Drive. Turn right if you have a room at Zion Lodge. If not, continue on south down the road to the **Zion Canyon Visitor Center.** Less than a mile south of the visitor center is the **South Entrance,** and just beyond that is **Springdale** with its many restaurant and lodging options.

For the adventurous, roughly 45 minutes from the Zion Canyon Visitor Center via Interstate 15 is the park's **Northwest Entrance** station, where you find the **Kolob Canyons Visitor Center** and realize that you left most of the park's crowds back in Zion Canyon. This marks the start of **Kolob Canyons Road,** which creeps 5 miles into the park to several overlooks that show off Zion's red and orange landscape with canyons 1,500-feet deep. The small visitor center offers many of the services found at the main visitor center back in Zion Valley.

Before ending at an overlook, Kolob Canyons Road leads you past viewpoints of **Horse Ranch Mountain,** which, at 8,726 feet, is the park's highest point; of the deep and narrow **Box Canyon** through which the South Fork of Taylor Creek flows; and of **Timber Top Mountain,** which, as its name implies, is capped by a stand of fir and ponderosa pine. Also along this short stretch of pavement is **Rockfall Overlook,** which shows off a large scar gashed into the mountainside in July 1983, when a 1,000-foot-long chunk of stone came tumbling down.

Many backpackers head to the Kolob Canyons Entrance for overnight trips to magnificent **Kolob Arch;** day hikers can head to **Double Arch Alcove.**

Between Zion Canyon and Kolob Canyons lies the park's other road, **Kolob Terrace Road.** This route, which closes in winter, heads north off Utah 9 from the village of Virgin, about 15 miles west of the park's South Entrance. The road leads to two reservoirs just beyond the park's northern border, as well as to the primitive **Lava Point Campground.**

Finding information after you arrive

The **Zion Canyon Visitor Center** (open daily 8 a.m. to 5 p.m.) that anchors the park's South Entrance is the best place to get oriented. Inside this handsome building you'll find guidebooks, maps, interpretive materials, film, postcards, and backcountry information. Outside the building are exhibits that detail some of the park's natural history. You'll also find a separate building with restrooms and drinking water. The shuttle buses board outside the center. Although the **Kolob Canyons Visitor Center** isn't nearly as big, it also offers guidebooks, maps, posters, postcards, and backcountry information and permits. Hours are daily 8 a.m. to 4:30 p.m.

Paying fees

Entry into the park (for up to seven days) includes unlimited use of the shuttle buses and costs $20 per private vehicle and $10 per individual on motorcycle, bicycle, or foot. *Note:* If you stay in Springdale and ride one of the shuttle buses to the park, you'll be charged $10 per person, but no more than $20 for a family, for entry.

If you're just going into the Kolob Canyons entrance, the fee is $10 per vehicle. If you have a park pass, you don't need to pay the entrance fee; see Chapter 8 for information on the National Park Pass and Chapter 7 for the lowdown on Golden Age and Golden Access passports.

In addition to the entrance fee, drivers of oversized vehicles (see "Getting There") must pay $10 to pass through the Zion-Mount Carmel Tunnel on the stretch of highway from the East Entrance to the Zion Canyon Drive.

Permits are required for all overnight hikes in the park and for all slot canyon routes. They range from $10 for 1 or 2 persons to $20 for groups of 8 to 12 for the length of your trek and are available at the visitor centers.

Getting Around Zion National Park

Zion's propane-propelled **shuttle buses** are a godsend to a park prone to "over-automobilization." Not only can you avoid the hassle of finding a parking spot in Zion Canyon, but you can also feast your eyes on the magnificent rockscape instead of watching the road. There are no express shuttles; each opens its doors at every one of the eight stops in the canyon. Along the way, the knowledgeable drivers provide running commentaries on the canyon's natural and human history. From April through October, if you're not staying at Zion Lodge, you board these buses at the Zion Canyon Visitor Center. If you are staying at the lodge, unless you obtain a handicap pass, you must leave your car in the parking lot and board a shuttle if you want to explore farther north.

By car

Cars aren't the best way to traverse Zion. For starters, during the height of the season — from April through October — they're prohibited in Zion Canyon unless you have a room at Zion Lodge. And if you do have a room, you must leave your car there and take the free shuttles farther north into the canyon. Although this may seem outrageous to some, it's a wonderfully logical answer to what once were perennial traffic jams. Plus, the lack of personal vehicles in Zion Canyon makes the road a treat for cyclists, roller bladers, and even roller skiers.

So what do you do if you drove your car to the park? Stay in Springdale and hop aboard the free town shuttles that stop near most motels and take you to the park's main visitor's center, where more shuttles are ready to take you into the canyon.

On foot

You can't do justice to a Zion visit without walking away from the road. You can go long distances spread over several nights, or take short strolls to delicious vistas.

Remembering Safety

If you're coming from a low elevation, keep in mind that Zion's base elevation is about 4,000 feet, so you may feel a bit winded your first or second day. You may even get a headache or experience insomnia. Combat these maladies by taking it easy your first day and by making sure to drink plenty of water.

Remember, too, that Zion is in the desert. During summer's heat, which often surpasses 100 degrees Fahrenheit, you can easily and quickly become dehydrated, particularly if you're hiking, so continue to drink water; a gallon a day isn't too much. If you haven't been to the desert before, comprehending the heat, dryness, and intensity of the sun can be difficult. Bring some moisturizing lotion whether you're prone to dry skin or not; you'll probably end up using it.

It's bright in the park thanks to the general lack of trees, wide-open expanses, and reflective rock, so treat yourself kindly with sunblock, a wide-brimmed hat, and sunglasses with full ultraviolet protection.

Utah health officials also warn outdoor enthusiasts to take precautions against Hantavirus, a rare but often fatal respiratory disease. About half of the country's confirmed cases have been reported in the Four Corners states of Colorado, New Mexico, Arizona, and Utah. The disease is usually spread by the urine and droppings of rodents. Health officials recommend that campers and hikers avoid areas with signs of rodent occupations. Symptoms of Hantavirus are similar to flu, and lead to breathing difficulties and shock.

Watch your youngsters. Not only do some trails feature precipitous drops, but kids like to throw rocks off high ground and hikers coming up the trail behind you could become unsuspecting targets.

For more tips on how to ensure a safe park visit, see Chapter 8.

Exploring Zion

Most Zion visitors spend all their time on the floor of Zion Canyon. And that's okay, because the canyon has enough attractions to fill your entire stay in the park, whether it's one day or several days. However, to reach some of the best sights — such as Emerald Pools, Angels Landing, and Weeping Rock — you must hit the trails.

 Although crowds descend on Zion in summer, you can avoid them. First, don't sleep in. (If you do, you miss seeing the park in one of its prettiest settings, with the rays of the slowly rising sun casting wonderful shadows and dazzling highlights across the redrock.) Because most people do sleep in, or simply have a hard time energizing themselves, if you get out in the park at least by 8 a.m., you won't have to jostle with others to enjoy the overlooks. Plus, hikers who hit the trail right around sunrise increase their odds of seeing wildlife before the animals bed down for the day. The next best way to avoid the crowds is to flee them. Head down a trail, not merely 50 yards, but a mile or more.

Taking a hike

If you've never hiked through a narrow slot canyon with walls towering 100, 200, 300, or more feet above you, put this activity at the top of your to-do list. Sculpted by countless years of water erosion, slot canyons are cool, dark, and even haunting as they twist and turn through the landscape. They're also beautiful, thanks to the colorful fluting erosion imparted on the sandstone.

 Slot canyons can also be dangerous because you never hear the approaching thunderstorms that can generate flash floods through the canyons. Also, many of the slots require technical equipment and practiced skills to negotiate. The key to safety is to employ common sense. If you're not sure of your ability, seek out a guide.

 Before you start down a slot canyon trail, check the region's weather forecast (posted at the Zion Canyon Visitor Center) and chat with a ranger. Although skies may be blue overhead, thunderstorms 10 miles away can send torrents of water down slot canyons, which serve as the "drains" for the high country. After you're inside a slot canyon, if there's a stream running through it, pay attention to the water. If the water level suddenly starts rising, you need to start rising, too, to higher ground. If you see clouds building overhead or hear thunder rumbling off in the distance, and if you're not far from one end of the canyon, get out as quickly as you can. A flash flood may not result, but if one does, you'll be glad you're out of the canyon. If you're too far from one of the entrances to leave the canyon, search for high ground.

Also, pay attention to the weather when you're hiking to Zion's high spots. You can become a lightning rod standing atop a peak if thunderstorms come into range.

 No matter what type of hike you take, **carry water.** A hiking staff is a good idea, too, especially if you're going to wade through streams. Don't forget to pick up a **backcountry permit** at a visitor center for any overnight or slot canyon hikes.

Zion has a variety of hikes, from those that wind through tight slot canyons to others that run along canyon rims. Stop by a visitor center to learn more about the park's hiking opportunities. This section includes my recommendations.

 ## Angels Landing Trail

If you like a challenging hike, one that tests your fear of heights, this is it. The trail climbs 1,488 feet — at one point traversing 21 short switchbacks known as "Walter's Wiggles" — to a summit with incredible views of Zion Canyon. But be prepared: The final ½-mile to the top crawls along a narrow, knife-edge trail where footing can be dicey under even the best of conditions. To help you along this section, the park has mercifully added chains that you can cling to. But the view from the top is worth the work. You can gaze in all directions, taking in the Virgin River sweeping through the bottom of the canyon, the Great White Throne, Red Arch Mountain to the southeast, and the entrance to the Narrows beyond the Temple of Sinawava to the north.

Think twice about hiking to Angels Landing if you have young children or if you dislike heights. The last ½-mile of the trail is particularly harrowing due to its precipitous nature.

Distance: 5 miles round-trip. Level: Difficult. Access: Grotto Picnic Area along Zion Canyon Drive.

 ## Chinle Trail

The first few miles of this quiet desert trail are fairly easy going along a wide sandy path. Ahead you have views of Mount Kinesava and the Three Marys formation. To the south behind you, and outside the park, rise a series of peaks known as the Eagle Crags. A gradual 150-foot incline brings you to the petrified forest denoting the top of the Chinle Formation, a sedimentary rock layer. While inspecting the rock-like logs, don't forget that removing anything from the national park is illegal; leave the lovely pieces of petrified wood as you find them. After crossing Huber Wash, the trail heads for Scoggins Wash through more desert terrain, which is dotted by juniper, pinyon, and sagebrush. To the northwest, you can see Cougar Mountain, and looking east allows views of the Towers of the Virgin, the West Temple, and the Sundial — all craggy rock formations. After you're on the mesa beyond Scoggins Wash, the trail heads for three knolls, passing through several small *saddles* (ridges between two peaks), traversing a meadow, and crossing the Old Scoggins Stock Trail, built by the area's early pioneers. Continuing west, the trail passes between two knolls and bends to the north, where you'll have no trouble finding an attractive campsite. The final descent into Coalpits Wash brings Cougar Mountain, Smith Mesa, and Lambs Knoll into view, and at the bottom you find a pretty waterfall a bit upstream from Coalpits Spring — the end of the trail.

 This hike can be uncomfortably hot in summer but is an absolute delight from November to May (blankets of wildflowers please the eye in spring). The elevation gain of this hike is a gradual 550 feet over the first 5 miles, after which you drop about 250 feet over the last 3 miles.

Distance: 16¼ miles round-trip. Level: Easy to moderate. Access: From the South Entrance to the park, drive west on Utah 9 for 3½ miles to a parking area on the right side of the road. From here, a four-wheel-drive road heads north 1½ miles to the park boundary and the trailhead. Close all gates behind you.

 ## Emerald Pools Trail System

You get to decide how much of a workout you want on this route. You can enjoy a leisurely one-hour walk or a somewhat strenuous two-hour hike. The first ⁹⁄₁₀ mile of this trail is paved and suitable for people in wheelchairs, with some assistance. This stretch leads from the trailhead through a forest of oak, maple, fir, and cottonwood to several waterfalls, a hanging garden, and the dazzling Lower Emerald Pool. From here, a steeper, rocky trail continues for a ¼-mile to Middle Emerald Pool and then climbs another ⅓-mile past cactus, yucca, and juniper to Upper Emerald Pool, with still another waterfall. After you see the pools, you'll understand how they were named. Elevation gains are 69 feet to the Lower Emerald Pool, 150 feet to the Middle Pool, and 400 feet to the Upper Pool. *Note:* In late summer, the waterfalls may vanish (barring torrential downpours), because they're dependent on snowmelt and runoff.

 If you do embark on this wonderful hike, leave your swimsuit behind; swimming and wading in the pools are strictly prohibited. Look east from this trail for great views of Red Arch Mountain and the Great White Throne.

Distance: 1¼–2½ miles round-trip. Level: Easy to moderate. Access: Trailhead across from Zion Lodge.

Weeping Rock

This hike is short, but beautiful. Along the way to the rock grotto, you pass interpretive signs explaining the natural history of the area. The path leads through a mixed forest to a rock alcove with lush hanging gardens of ferns, golden columbines, shooting stars, and other colorful wildflowers. The mist (groundwater that's taken several thousand years to percolate through the sandstone cliffs) that sprays from the Weeping Rock will please everyone in your group on a hot day. There's even a trail down to the stream so you can dip your feet. In the fall, the colorful vegetation along the trail is striking.

Distance: ½-mile round-trip. Level: Easy. Access: Weeping Rock parking lot on Zion Canyon Drive.

West Rim Trail

If you're interested in getting away from the crowds, head down this trail, which runs across the Horse Pasture Plateau (offering wonderfully panoramic views) before dropping down into Zion Canyon. The good news is that this trail drops 3,560 feet on the way from the trailhead to the Grotto Picnic Area. The bad news is that you have to climb 3,560 feet up and out if you're on a round-trip hike. (Most folks just go one way.)

You need to arrange transportation to the Lava Point Trailhead. The names of various shuttle companies are available at the park's main visitor center. You can catch the shuttle back to your car at the Grotto Picnic Area at the end of the trail.

Distance: 28½ miles round-trip. Level: difficult for round-trippers, moderate for one-way. Access: Lava Point Trailhead.

Zion Narrows

Backcountry trekkers familiar with Zion talk almost reverently about the Narrows. The "trail" is actually the North Fork of the Virgin River, which flows through a 1,000-foot deep chasm that is a confining 24 feet wide in places. As you work your way downstream, you pass through fancifully sculpted sandstone arches, hanging gardens, and waterfalls. The Narrows is a magical place, but you must be in good shape for the hike but to cope with strong currents that you may encounter.

The entire Narrows experience can be had in one long day, or you can break it up with an overnight in the backcountry. Before your trip, check at the visitor center for information on arranging a shuttle both to the trailhead and from the **Temple of Sinawava,** where you leave the canyon. Before you head out, make sure to pick up a permit (required for slot canyon hiking) from the Zion Canyon Visitor Center and, if you plan an overnight trip, receive a campsite assignment.

When you first start hiking from the trailhead at **Chamberlain's Ranch,** the hike bears no resemblance to its name. From the trailhead on private land, you ford the river and follow a dirt road downstream. Please remain on the road and leave all gates as you find them. The road ends a short distance beyond an old cabin, and then you hike either along or in the river, which has cut a deep V into the Navajo sandstone. Occasionally, you may spy a lone conifer dangling from the cliffside at some bizarre angle. When you come up against a 12-foot waterfall, the path circumnavigates this barrier by leading you through a slot in the rock.

After you pass the waterfall, you're within the park, and in another 1½ miles, you arrive at the confluence with **Deep Creek,** where the canyon opens up a bit to swallow this stream of water. In the next 2 miles lie the designated (and assigned) campsites. The current here is faster due to the increased flow of water, and the rocks underfoot are slippery, so step carefully and, if you brought one, use your hiking staff. **Kolob Creek** is the next tributary you see, although it flows only when waters are released from Kolob Reservoir for downstream irrigation. Then comes **Goose Creek,** which leads to a deepening of the water and, in some places, requires waist-deep wading. Soon you see **Big Springs** pouring over moss-covered stone on the right wall of the canyon, which signifies the beginning of the Narrows.

For the next 3 miles, there is no place to climb out of the water in the event of a flood. There is also practically no vegetation to grab onto, because any small seedling is periodically ripped from the walls by the raging waters. The river spreads from wall to wall, forcing you to wade in a deep canyon with little light. The water has even undercut the walls near the confluence with **Orderville Canyon.** Runoff from above oozes from the canyon walls, providing moisture for hanging gardens and habitat for the teeny Zion snail, found nowhere else in the world. About a mile farther, where the canyon opens up, a narrow ribbon of water slips out of **Mystery Canyon** above and skims down the rounded canyon wall. Just beyond, you can finally climb out of the water onto the paved Riverside Walk that takes you to the Temple of Sinawava and the end of the hike.

If you don't have time for a full day, or overnight, hike, consider hiking into the Narrows from the **Riverside Walk.** The access is at the Temple of Sinawava, and you can hike as few as 2 miles (round-trip). The walk is paved all the way to the Narrows. When you reach the Narrows, how far up you walk is up to you. Just remember to pay attention to the water level and the weather forecast.

When preparing for this hike, you may want to slip a pair of sneakers or sturdier boots with good ankle support into your backpack. You can wear these in the water and keep your hiking boots dry. To keep your balance in swift currents, you may also want to bring along a hiking stick.

Distance: Up to 16 miles one-way. Level: Moderate to difficult. Access: Chamberlain's Ranch (outside the park) or via the Riverside Walk.

One-day wonder

The bulk of Zion's highlights are within the confines of Zion Canyon, which makes seeing the park in one day a pretty easy task. To come away with the best impression, start the day early and bring along a picnic lunch, a good hiking staff and boots, plenty of water, and lots of film. For descriptions of the trails I mention here, see the previous section.

 I always include a trip to **Angel's Landing** when I visit Zion, both for the challenge of reaching the top and for the payoff — an incredible panorama of Zion Canyon. And I always do this hike early in the day, to avoid the high heat of afternoon. If you're up for the climb, either take a shuttle to the Grotto Picnic area or walk to the area from Zion Lodge on the connector trail. (If you'd prefer something less strenuous, or if you're traveling with young children, either tackle the 2-mile-round-trip **Watchman Trail,** an overlooked trail that offers nice views of the lower end of Zion Canyon and the town of Springdale, or visit the **Zion Human History Museum.**)

After descending from Angel's Landing, take a shuttle bus to the **Temple of Sinawava** at the northern end of Zion Canyon Drive. Follow the **Riverside Walk** a mile into the southern gateway of **the Narrows,** the park's most famous slot canyon. You don't need to hike all the way through this slot, but at least take some time to travel into it to get the feel of being surrounded by towering rock walls. The experience is unforgettable.

After returning to the shuttle stop, ride back down Zion Canyon Drive to the **Weeping Rock Trail.** Follow this short, easy trail that quickly delivers you to a memorable rock alcove where, in spring and summer, lush hanging gardens thrive on the drenching they receive from the water draining out of the high country. Several places along the stream below the trail are perfect for a picnic.

Continue to work your way back down canyon on the shuttle to the **Zion Lodge.** Check out the lodge if you're not staying there; then cross the Virgin River and spend a couple hours working your way up the **Emerald Pools Trail,** a 2½-mile round-trip hike. The three shimmering pools of water that give the trail its name are gorgeous and worth some film. The Upper Pool, although reached via the steepest stretch of the trail, is a good place to rest and enjoy the view amid the maples.

By the time you return from this hike, you'll most likely be ready to return to your room for a shower and a quick power nap before heading out to dinner.

If you have more time

Most tourists confine their visit to the highlights of Zion Canyon, but those with a bit more ambition also see **Kolob Arch,** one of the world's longest freestanding arches with a span of 310 feet. You can hike to the arch and back in one long day on the **La Verkin Creek Trail,** a 14-mile round-trip hike from Lee Pass along Kolob Canyons Road in the park's northwestern extension.

A shorter, but worthwhile, hike in this area leads to **Double Arch Alcove,** an arched alcove topped overhead by an arch in the cliff. You reach the formation on the **Creek Trail,** a 5½-mile round-trip hike that crosses the Middle Fork of Taylor Creek and passes two log cabins before arriving at a viewpoint of the arch. You can access the trailhead from Kolob Canyons Road.

 Should you add Kolob Arch, or even Double Arch Alcove, to your itinerary? If you enjoy backcountry hiking, the answer is probably yes. But if you've been to Arches National Park, or plan to go there, then these two sights aren't must-sees.

Ranger programs

Zion has rangers, but you won't find as many ranger-led activities here as you do in Yosemite, for example. Still, they lead short, 1- to 2-mile hikes most mornings and afternoons. Also in the afternoon, you usually see rangers on the Zion Canyon Visitor Center patio, the Zion Human History Museum patio, and the Zion Lodge lawn, talking about the various aspects of the park. You can figure on finding an evening slide show or talk at the campground amphitheaters as well as in Zion Lodge. If that's not enough, a guided shuttle tour, requiring free tickets, is conducted each morning from Memorial Day weekend through mid-September.

The best way to find out what's going on during your stay is to look for the weekly schedules posted at the visitor centers and on bulletin boards throughout the park. These notices tell you when ranger-led activities are scheduled, what they're about, and whether you need to make a reservation to attend.

 To keep your kids interested in the park, enroll them in the Junior Ranger Program at the Zion Nature Center. For details, see Chapter 7.

Keeping active

In addition to hiking, Zion offers opportunities for the following:

✔ **Biking:** You can't ride your bike outside of designated trails in the national parks, and biking is prohibited from many Zion trails. Despite this fact, Zion remains one of the most bike-friendly parks in the Western U.S. The **Pa'rus Trail** runs a little under 2 miles along the Virgin River, from the South Entrance as far north as the Zion Mount-Carmel Highway. This trail crosses the river and several creeks and provides good views of the Watchman, West Temple, the Sentinel, and other lower canyon formations. Cyclists can also ride on the park's main roads, although not through the Zion-Mount Carmel Tunnel. For bike rentals in Springdale, log onto www.utahsdixie.com/biking.html.

✔ **Horseback riding:** Guided rides in the park are available March through October from **Canyon Trail Rides** (☎ 435-079-8665; www.canyonrides.com). Ticket sales and information are available at the horse corrals across from Zion Lodge. A one-hour ride along the Virgin River costs $30 and a half-day ride on the Sand Bench Trail that leads farther into the southern end of the park and closer to some of the major formations costs $55. Riders must weigh no more than 220 pounds, and children must be at least 7 years old for the one-hour ride and 8 years old for the half-day ride. Reservations are advised.

✔ **Rock climbing:** Expert technical rock climbers love the tall sandstone cliffs in Zion Canyon, although rangers warn that much of the rock is loose, or *rotten*, and climbing equipment and techniques suitable for granite are often less effective here. A permit is required for overnight climbs, and because some routes may be closed at times, such as during peregrine falcon nesting from early spring through July, climbers should check at the visitor center before setting out.

A side trip to Bryce Canyon National Park

If you want to explore more of southern Utah, check out **Bryce Canyon** (☎ 435-834-5322, www.nps.gov/brca), just 85 miles from Zion National Park's East Entrance via Utah 9 to U.S. 89 to Utah 12. Although a fraction of the size of Zion, Bryce's 35,835 acres are just as spectacular. You'll see **rock gardens** comprised of cream- and orange-colored spires, hoodoos, and goblins jutting out of the main canyon. Your options here include hiking down below the canyon rim and through the rock gardens, or staying atop the rim and gazing down into the maze of pinnacles. If you have the time, go down below and into the deep amphitheaters with their cliffs, windows, and arches. The **Navajo Loop Trail** is a great, and short (1½ miles round-trip), way to experience Bryce Canyon. From the Rim at Sunset Point, the trail runs 521 feet to the canyon floor and loops back up. Along the way you get great views of Wall Street, the Twin Bridges, and Thor's Hammer, a precariously balanced rock.

Spotting the local wildlife

Within Zion's borders there are 75 species of mammals, 271 bird species, 36 species of reptiles and amphibians, and 8 kinds of fish. This means that if you're hoping to see some wildlife during your visit to the park, don't worry — you will. If you're specifically hoping to see one of the park's mountain lions, also known as cougars, don't get your hopes up. Yes, a few of these cats prowl Zion's backcountry, but because they're reclusive, your chances of spotting one are slim. You can try to enhance the odds by sticking to the east side of the park beyond the Zion-Mount Carmel Tunnel, but I'm not guaranteeing anything when it comes to mountain lions. They're also known to lurk around the backcountry in the park's northwestern corner near Kolob Terraces Road, so if you strike out on the eastern side and are determined to search for one of the big cats, try up there.

Where you find mountain lions, you also find **mule deer,** probably the most visible large animals in the park; they love to browse on the Zion Lodge lawn during the evenings.

Zion also is home to a number of **desert bighorn sheep.** As with mountain lions, your best chances of spotting one of is to pan your binoculars around the east side of the park.

Among the smaller animals that roam the park are **gray fox, desert cottontail rabbits, coyotes,** and even **beaver,** which ply the smooth waters of the Virgin River. One of the more unusual park critters — that is, if you're from the East or West coasts or the northern tier of states — is the **ringtail cat.** These skittish cousins to raccoons lurk around the park after dark, looking for campsites or backpacks they can raid for munchies. Although seeing these long, bushy-tailed cats working their way through a bag of pretzels or chips may be cute, your food isn't good for them. Do your best to maintain a clean campsite.

Overhead, you may catch a glimpse of a speedy **peregrine falcon.** At one time thought to be on their way to extinction, these swift raptors are making a comeback around the country. In Zion, at least 15 pairs of peregrine falcons have been seen nesting. You stand a chance of spotting one of these birds along the Angels Landing and Cable Mountain trails and in the area around the Great White Throne. **Bald eagles** have also been spotted in the park, but usually only during the winter, so if you're planning a spring, summer, or fall trip, you're probably out of luck.

Wild turkeys are often visible on the lawns surrounding Zion Lodge and occasionally in the meadows along the Virgin River.

Red-tailed hawks are very common in the park; you usually can spot them high overhead drifting on the wind currents. Among the dozens of other birds that pass through the park are **American kestrels, doves, great horned owls, ravens, pinyon, Steller's jays,** and even **American robins.** You may also spot great **blue herons** along the Virgin River. If you're a dedicated birder, you may want to plan a year-end trip to Zion and participate in the park's Christmas bird count.

Being canyon country, Zion is also home to creepy-crawly critters like the **great basin rattlesnake, tarantulas,** and even **scorpions.** The park also has quite a good selection of amphibians, including the **Arizona tiger salamander** and **red-spotted toad,** and reptiles, such as the **chuckwalla lizard,** which, with a mature size of 20 inches, is the park's largest lizard.

Escaping the rain

Where do you head when rains fall on Zion? Well, if they come during the height of summer, you just may want to stay outdoors and enjoy the refreshing drenching and watch the cascading waterfalls that lace some of the cliffs from the runoff. But if the cloudburst turns torrential, consider heading to **Zion Canyon Theatre** (145 Zion Park Blvd.; ☎ **888-256-3456** or 435-772-2400) in Springdale to get out of the rain for an hour or so. This 60-x-82-foot big-screen theater shows movies about the park. *Zion Canyon: Treasure of the Gods,* for example, not only captures much of the park's physical beauty but also delves into its Native American legends. At night, the theater offers some of the latest Hollywood releases. The theater is open from April through October daily, with showings starting at 11 a.m.; the last showing begins at 8 p.m. Admission is $8 for ages 12 and older, $6 for seniors over the age of 60, and $5 for ages 3 through 11.

 Another option is the **Zion Human History Museum**. The museum, located along the park's shuttle bus route, in part chronicles the park's human activity through exhibits and short video presentations. You find displays on wildlife, geology, and plants and discover how the environment has affected Native Americans, settlers, and visitors. A small bookstore with maps, videos, postcards, and posters is on the premises. Summer hours are from 8 a.m. to 7 p.m., with shorter hours the rest of the year.

Where to Stay

 Lodging options within Zion's boundaries are restricted to either the Zion Lodge, a comfortable facility that offers both motel-style rooms and charming cabins, or campgrounds. High-season rates usually arrive in April and run through October. During the winter months, you can find great deals both at the lodge and throughout nearby Springdale's accommodations. See Chapter 6 for more tips on finding a place to stay.

 ### Zion Lodge
$$$ Zion Canyon

Renowned park architect Gilbert Stanley Underwood designed the original Zion Lodge in the 1920s. Unfortunately, that building, which exuded rustic charm, burned down in 1966. Although rebuilt later that year, the reincarnation didn't completely capture Underwood's vision. In 1990, the lodge's exterior was remodeled to reflect its original appearance. You can't beat the location: The Virgin River is across the road, and a trail from the lodge leads to the West Rim Trail.

 Because this is the only lodging option inside the park, call far in advance if you want a room during the spring, summer, and fall seasons. Call early enough and you can choose between the rooms and the cabins. Although the rooms are nice and well-kept, opt for the cabins — there's nothing quite like returning from a day in the park and lighting the fireplace to ward off the evening chill. The fireplaces are gas-powered, so you don't have to mess with wood. The cabins, although small, feature two double beds, log beams, and small porches to relax on before you call it a day.

The rooms inside the two-story lodge annexes are nothing to turn your nose up at, but they can't match the charm and privacy of the cabins. They come with two queen-size beds and a private balcony or porch. The suites are large, feature a king-size bed, a separate sitting room with a queen-size hide-a-bed, and a refrigerator.

See map p. 348. On Zion Canyon Drive. ☎ *435-772-3213.* www.zionlodge.com. *For reservations, contact Xanterra Parks & Resorts* ☎ *307-344-7311;* www. xanterra.com. *75 rooms, 40 cabins, 6 suites. A/C TEL. Rack rates: $124 double; $146 suites; $132 cabins. AE, DISC, MC, V, CB.*

Lodging outside the park

Best Western Zion Park Inn
$$–$$$ Springdale

This sprawling complex sits less than 2 miles beyond the park's south entrance and offers tremendous views of 7,285-foot Mount Kinosava. Just about everything you need for a park visit can be found here: lodging, a restaurant, gift shop, and a state liquor store. There's also an outdoor pool to fight off the summer's oven-like heat, a hot tub, and rooms complete with dataport connections.

1215 Zion Park Blvd. ☎ *435-772-3200 or 800-934-7275. Fax: 435-772-2449.* www.zion parkinn.com. *114 rooms, 6 suites. A/C TEL TV. Rack rates: April to Oct $89–$105 double; $95–$150 suites; Nov to Mar $60–$72 double; $75–$125 suites. AE, DISC, MC V.*

Desert Pearl Inn
$–$$$$ Springdale

It's not often that you find a motel room with nicely polished wood floors, but that's the case at the Desert Pearl. This property, which backs up to the Virgin River, also offers beautiful native stone rockwork, dataport phones if you need an Internet fix, and a swimming pool. The spacious rooms also have in-room safes, microwaves, refrigerators, and private balconies for kicking back on after a day in the park.

707 Zion Park Blvd. ☎ *888-828-0898 or 435-772-8888. Fax: 435-772-8889.* www.desert pearl.com. *61 units. A/C TV TEL. Rack rates: April to Mid-Oct $103–$123 double; Dec to April $78–$103 double. AE, DISC, MC, V.*

Flanigan's Inn
$$–$$$ Springdale

This gorgeous inn just beyond Zion's South Entrance features rustic beams and natural rock-work surrounded by decks and terraced lawns and gardens. Although parts of the inn date to 1947, all the rooms were renovated in the early 1990s and have a Southwest decor. Some of the rooms feature whirlpool tubs and bidets. Kitchenettes are available, but if you want a fireplace, call early because only one room has this feature. You also find a pool and nature trail on the grounds, as well as a wonderful restaurant that sports a greenhouse/garden atmosphere.

428 Zion Park Blvd. ☎ *800-765-7787 or 435-772-3244. Fax: 435-772-3396.* www. flanigans.com. *39 units. A/C TV TEL. Rack rates: Mid-March to Nov $99–$209 double; Dec to mid-March $79–$139 double; $5 extra person. AE, DISC, MC, V.*

Under the Eaves
$$ **Springdale**

This B&B boasts "the best front porch in Utah," and while it may not actually be the best, it *does* offer great views. Inside, this beautiful 1931 cottage displays antiques and local artworks, creating an inn that is both attractive and comfortable. The main floor has two guest rooms, decorated in early-20th-century style. Each features a double bed and private sink, although the two rooms share a bath (shower only). If sharing a bath doesn't appeal, consider the huge (1,200 square feet) upstairs suite, which features vaulted ceilings, a cathedral window through which you can view the terraced gardens, a kitchenette, a claw-foot tub with shower, a sitting room, and a wood-burning stove. Another option is the Garden Cottage, a small cottage built in the 1920s inside the park, which was relocated behind the B&B in 1989. The cottage has three guest rooms, each with a private entrance, bathroom, and shower. Breakfasts usually include freshly baked goods, fresh fruit, and main dishes such as omelets or pancakes. Children ages 8 and older are welcome.

980 Zion Park Blvd. ☎ *866-261-2655 or 435-772-3457. Fax: 435-772-3324.* www.under theeaves.com. *5 rooms (2 with shared bath), 1 suite. A/C. Rack rates: March–mid-Nov $75–$95 double; $145 suite, $10 extra person; mid-Nov to March $65–$75 double; $125 suite, $10 extra per person. AE, DISC, MC, V. Rates include full breakfast.*

Runner-up lodgings

Driftwood Lodge
$–$$$ **Springdale**   Large rooms decorated with Southwestern art, an outdoor pool, surrounded by a shady lawn and complimentary Continental breakfast make this a popular place to stay. *1515 Zion Park Blvd.* ☎ *888-801-8811 or 435-772-3262.* www.driftwoodlodge.net

Harvest House Bed and Breakfast
$$–$$$ **Springdale**   Each of the inn's four rooms comes with a private bath. Those with balconies have great views of the park. *29 Canyon View Dr.* ☎ *435-772-3880.* www.harvesthouse.net.

Novel House Inn
$$$ **Springdale**   Each of the ten rooms in this inn is dedicated to a famous writer; downstairs you find some of their works in the library. *73 Paradise Rd.* ☎ *800-711-8400 or 435-772-3650.* www.novelhouse.com.

Campgrounds

Sites at the **South Campground** are available between mid-March and the end of October and are doled out on a first-come, first-served basis. The remote **Lava Point Campground,** usually open from late May through mid-October, offers six free sites that are located on the pine-covered Kolob Plateau and which provide sweeping views into the heart of the park. You can reserve sites at the **Watchman Campground,** which is open year-round, between April 2 and October 31 by calling ☎ **800-365-CAMP.**

Where to Dine

Despite Springdale's small size, the culinary scene near Zion is diverse and contains several outstanding options. Making advance reservations by mid-to-late afternoon or even the day before is a great idea during the high season.

Restaurants inside the park

Red Rock Grill, Zion Lodge
$$$–$$$$ Zion Canyon AMERICAN

Gazing through the dining room's large windows at the park's towering rock formations makes concentrating on your meal difficult. Among the lodge's specialties are slow-roasted prime rib, New York strip steak, and Southwestern grilled chicken. You also find fish and vegetarian items on the menu. For dessert, try the Chocolate Ecstasy Cake (with the understanding that you'll need a good hike to work off the calories). For lunch, the kitchen serves up burgers, wraps, and sandwiches and offers a salad bar. Breakfast ranges from hot and cold cereals to egg dishes, fresh fruits, and bagels. They offer a hot-and-cold buffet, which I find generally offers the best bargain ($8.50 adults, $4.50 kids 12 and under.) The kitchen also prepares sack lunches for hikers; place your order at least one hour in advance for these.

See map p. 348. In the Zion Lodge. ☎ 435-772-3213. Dinner reservations required. Main courses: $3–$8.50 breakfast; $2.75–$8.25 lunch; $12.95–$20.95 dinner. AE, DC, DISC, MC, V. Open: Daily 6:30–10 a.m., 11:30 a.m.–3:30 p.m., 5:30–9 p.m.

Castle Dome Café
$ Zion Canyon AMERICAN

This snack bar on the Zion Lodge's north end is for the grab-and-go crowd. It offers hot dogs, chicken sandwiches, hamburgers, and made-to-order pizzas for lunch. Perhaps the hottest items on the menu during the summer are the ice creams.

See map p. 348. $3–$14 lunch and dinner. Cash only. Seasonal hours; Memorial Day through Sept, 10 a.m.–7 p.m.

Restaurants outside the park

Bit & Spur Restaurant and Saloon
$$–$$$ Springdale   MEXICAN/SOUTHWESTERN

Rough wood-and-stone walls and an exposed beam ceiling give this restaurant the look of an Old West saloon, but it's an unusually clean saloon that also features a family dining room, patio dining, original oil paintings by regional artists, and live entertainment. The food is also a notch or two above what you may expect, closer to what you would find in a good Santa Fe restaurant. The menu ranges from Mexican standards — burritos, flautas, chile rellenos, and a traditional chile stew with pork — to more unusual creations like *pollo relleno* (grilled chicken breast stuffed with cilantro pesto and goat cheese and served with smoked pineapple chutney) and smoky chicken (a smoked, charbroiled game hen with sourdough stuffing and chipotle sauce).

1212 Zion Park Blvd. ☎ 435-772-3498. Reservations recommended. Main courses: $9.50–$23.50. DISC, MC, V. Open: March to Oct daily 5–10 p.m. (bar open until midnight); Nov to Feb Thurs–Mon 5–9 p.m. Closed: Dec.

Flanigan's Inn-Spotted Dog Cafe
$$–$$$$ Springdale   AMERICAN/REGIONAL

Flanigan's Inn feels like an escape to a lush oasis. This award-winning restaurant has a greenhouse/garden atmosphere that's refreshing after a day in the park's dry air, and you can take in the incredible scenery through the large windows. Flanigan's uses fresh local ingredients and herbs from the inn's garden whenever possible. The dinner menu ranges from simple burgers, a chicken breast sandwich, and a grilled vegetable burrito to more creative entrees, such as Tournadoe of Beef Tenderloin with smoked tomato chutney and vegetable parfait. A menu staple is the Utah red trout. To refresh your palate, try one of the region's fine microbrews or sample the inn's 2,000-bottle wine cellar.

428 Zion Park Blvd. ☎ 435-772-3244. Reservations recommended. Main courses: $5–$10 breakfast; $10–$25 dinner. AE, DISC, MC, V. Open: Daily summer 5–10 p.m. Closed: Dec to Jan.

Switchback Grill
$–$$$$ Springdale   AMERICAN/ITALIAN

Step into the Switchback Grill and you find a menu as diverse as the park's landscape. Spit-roasted chicken, steaks, and hickory-smoked ribs contrast with French-influenced and Italian dishes. You can eat heartily with a USDA prime filet or go light with honey pecan–encrusted Utah trout or a wood-fired pizza or salad. The atmosphere is just as delicious as the menu, thanks to heavy timbers, vaulted ceilings, and a wall of glass that lets diners gaze at the park's southern ramparts.

1149 Zion Park Blvd. ☎ *435-772-3700 or 877-948-8080.* www.switchbackgrille. com. *Reservations recommended. Main courses: $4–$7 breakfast and lunch; $14–$30 dinner. AE, DISC, MC, V. Open: May to Oct daily 7–11 a.m., 11:30 a.m.–2:30 p.m., 5–10 p.m.; Nov to April hours shorter.*

Zion Pizza & Noodle
$$$ Springdale   PIZZA/PASTA

Sometimes you just want to kick back with a pizza or some pasta and a cold brew. Swap out that beer for a soda, and your kids will probably agree wholeheartedly. Here, the whole family can be happy. In an old Mormon Church built in 1930, the setting is informal, with small, closely spaced tables and black-and-white photos on the walls. You order at the counter, grab a drink at the beverage bar, and sit back and relax until your meal is delivered. The gourmet pizzas, with wonderfully chewy crusts, are baked in a slate stone oven and come with a variety of unusual toppings. You can have a barbecued chicken pizza with red onion, cilantro, and Gouda and mozzarella cheeses; a six-cheese pizza with asiago, Parmesan, mozzarella, feta, Romano, and cheddar cheeses; or even a Thai chicken pizza. Oh yeah, the menu also includes your run-of-the-mill cheese pizzas. You'll also find fettucines, stromboli, and manicotti marinara. For lunch, the menu also includes veggie burgers and brats. Some of Utah's finer microbrews are available and can be enjoyed in the shaded beer garden out back.

868 Zion Park Blvd. ☎ *435-772-3815.* www.zionpizzanoodle.com. *Reservations not accepted. Main courses: $7.95–$13.95 dinner. No credit cards. Open: Mid-Feb to Thanksgiving, daily, noon to 10 p.m.; closed late Nov to mid-Feb.*

Fast Facts: Zion

Area Code

The local area code is **435**.

ATMs

There are ATMs in Springdale at Zion Bank (921 Zion Park Boulevard) and Sol Foods Market & Deli (95 Zion Park Boulevard).

Emergencies

In an emergency, dial **435-772-3322** or **911**.

Fees

Entrance fees are $20 per vehicle per week and $10 for those on foot, motorcycle, or bike.

Hospitals

The Zion Canyon Medical Clinic is in Springdale (☎ 435-772-3226).

Information

For information, write Zion National Park, Springdale, UT 84767; call ☎ 435-772-3256; or look on the Web at www.nps.gov/zion/

Internet Access & Cybercafes

Two computers with free Internet access are in the Zion Lodge lobby.

Newspapers/Magazines

USA Today, the Salt Lake Tribune, and other papers are available at the gift shop in Zion Lodge and at various locations in Springdale.

Pharmacies

The local drug store is Zion Drug in Hurricane, 72 S. 700 W. (☎ 435-635-4456).

Police

Call the local police at ☎ 435-772-3322 or 911.

Post Office:

A post office is at 624 Zion Park Blvd. in Springdale (☎ 435-772-3950).

Restrooms

Restrooms can be found at the Zion Park Visitor Center, South Entrance.

Road Conditions

For information on road conditions, call ☎ 800-492-2400.

Smoking

State law prohibits smoking inside most public buildings and facilities. If fire danger is high, there can be restrictions on smoking outdoors as well. If in doubt, check with a ranger.

Taxis

No taxis are available. From April through October shuttle buses operate from 6:30 a.m. until 11 p.m., linking Springdale to the park's South Entrance.

Time Zone

The park is on mountain time.

Weather Updates

For weather updates, call ☎ 435-772-0120 or look on the Internet at www.zionpark.com/weather.htm.

Part IV
The Part of Tens

The 5th Wave   By Rich Tennant

"The scenery here is just magnificent. The trees, the plants, and I've never seen so many soaring eagles in one place."

In this part . . .

So many parks, so many vistas, so many places to stay. As you make the rounds of the park system, you'll surely develop your favorites. (I know I have, to the detriment of parks that I haven't yet visited.) But if you're a national parks newbie, where do you begin? This part gives you the bottom line on great park vistas, why a national park vacation beats visiting a theme park hands-down, and how you can get the most out of the national parks without taking out a second mortgage. Best of all, this part is organized in a quick, easy-to-read, top-ten format.

Chapter 19

Ten Incredible National Park Vistas

* * *

In This Chapter

▶ Viewing rain forests, river bends, and canyon narrows

▶ Looking across a salt pan

▶ Gazing up at sequoias

▶ Eyeballing canyon walls and mountain tops

* * *

*B*y their very nature, national parks are incredibly scenic places. The old saying "Beauty is in the eye of the beholder" doesn't seem to apply. You get a beautiful view just about everywhere you look. Sunsets? Parks virtually have a monopoly on the breathtaking ones. Purple mountain majesties? Got 'em by the truckload. Forests by the Brothers Grimm? Yep, you find these, too. The parks have so many wonderful views that you don't even need to get out of your car to enjoy them — but do pull over and get out. Take a short walk, pull up a rock or downed tree trunk, and look around. You can thank me later.

 If you want to capture these incredible vistas on film, but are a bit unsure of your camera skills, check out the latest edition of *Photography For Dummies*, by Russell Hart (Wiley), for the lowdown on how to become an expert shutterbug.

Badwater, Death Valley National Park

Imagine Badwater in August: The sun's glare off the dazzlingly white salt pan pains your eyes, and while you peer upward at a sign on a cliff indicating sea level 282 feet *above* you, the 120-degree Fahrenheit temperature slowly bakes your body. Pretty intense, eh? This spot is great for photographers any time of year. Just as the temperatures are unusual on the bottom floor of North America in summer, so are the lighting conditions year-round. Early mornings and late afternoons are perfect for experimenting with the play of light across the salt pan's jigsaw puzzle construction. (And it's a heckofa lot cooler at these times than at high noon, too!) Even if you're not a shutterbug, the chance to inspect the ornate fractures that riddle the salt pan and to gaze up at 11,049-foot Telescope Peak is worth a stop. See Chapter 10.

Delicate Arch, Arches National Park

Curving gracefully over the redrock landscape, Delicate Arch seems to defy gravity. Even in this land of sandstone cliffs and fins, the arch that long has graced Utah's license plates seems utterly out of place. How can you explain the freestanding arch that is perched near the edge of a cliff? Okay, a geologist could offer some technicalities, but that doesn't stop you from marveling at this setting in Arches National Park. Adjacent to one leg of the arch is a massive sandstone sinkhole, a whirlpool time has frozen in place. Although it takes a mile-and-a-half hike to reach the arch, you'll agree the effort is certainly worth it when you're standing at Delicate's base. See Chapter 9.

Giant Forest, Sequoia National Park

Big, bigger, and biggest. That pretty much sums up the trees in this corner of Sequoia National Park. How do you measure up in comparison? Not even the word tiny accurately describes your diminutive size when you stand next to these trees that soar more than 300 feet and have waist lines measured in tens of feet, not inches. Want even more perspective? Compare your own age to the age of one of these wooden giants, which can live to be 3,200 years old. You won't find just one mighty sequoia in the Giant Forest, but nearly 9,000 of them standing tall over 1,800 acres. See Chapter 15.

Glacier Point, Yosemite National Park

The drive from the Yosemite Valley floor to the top of Glacier Point is long, and the hike is even longer, but the view is awesome. To the east, the thin ropes of white that seem to dangle from a cliff are Nevada and Vernal falls. Just a bit north of them stands the rock structure known as Half Dome, which resembles a huge loaf of bread. A few thousand feet below your toes is the valley floor, which is not-so-neatly divided by the Merced River, The Ahwahnee hotel, and Curry Village. Keep scanning the horizon, and you find Yosemite Falls and, way off to the northeast in Yosemite's backcountry, the mountain called Clouds Rest. If you want some isolation, check out the view in the winter, when cross-country skis or snowshoes are about the only means of travel to the overlook. See Chapter 17.

Grand Canyon of the Yellowstone, Yellowstone National Park

Whether you stand on the lip of one of the two waterfalls in the Grand Canyon of the Yellowstone or simply view this majestic crack in the earth from one of the numerous observation points, you experience a thing of beauty. When the sun shines, it tints the mist of the falls with rainbows. In winter, the icy setting is enchanting (and dangerous, so watch your footing!). Any time of year, add the falls' frothy might to the yellows, buffs, oranges, chalky whites, and tans of the deep and rugged canyon, and you get an incredible setting. Most visitors get their initial view of the canyon from North Rim Drive (found near Canyon Village), but a more-spectacular view is from Artist Point on South Rim Drive. And don't be shy about walking beyond Artist Point on the South Rim Trail, because most folks usually return to their cars after snapping some pictures from the point's overlook. By taking a short walk, you can enjoy the canyon with a bit more solitude. See Chapter 16.

Hoh Rain Forest, Olympic National Park

The Hoh Rain Forest doesn't have hobgoblins or fairies, but you may feel that something eerie is watching your every move from a hiding spot in this densely vegetated realm. Lush, dark, and green, this corner of Olympic National Park is North America's largest undisturbed temperate rain forest. Each year, 12 to 14 feet of rain drench the forest, producing trees of astounding size. And blankets of vegetation not only coat the forest floor but also hang like veils from the canopy high overhead. Spongy mosses, ropelike vines, and delicate ferns add to the dazzling scenery. See Chapter 14.

Oxbow Bend, Grand Teton National Park

A beer commercial was filmed at Oxbow Bend, so you know the setting has to be stupendous. Snow-capped Tetons are off in the distance, and thick forest is all around, but to me, the view of wildlife is the big attraction. Moose, bald eagles, osprey, trumpeter swans, white pelicans, playful river otters, and oodles of ducks crowd this stretch of the Snake River that meanders below Jackson Lake Dam. Plenty of overlooks allow you to pull over in your car and take in the setting, although the best view is from a raft or canoe drifting slowly downstream. Photographers will want a long lens to capture the river corridor's critters (especially the eagles hauling fat trout out of the river) on film. See Chapter 12.

Paradise, Mount Rainier National Park

Paradise isn't lost in Mount Rainier National Park, where a nicely paved road leads to the Paradise Inn. If you agree that a rustic inn backed up to a snow- and ice-covered mountain has something special, you'll understand what makes this place one of the most gorgeous settings in the park system. Paradise is beautiful in late spring, when wildflowers blossom in the meadows surrounding the inn, or in fall, when the forest blazes with orange and red leaves. (Summer is pretty, too, but with all the people milling about, the natural beauty can be difficult to fully appreciate.) See Chapter 13.

Point Sublime, Grand Canyon National Park

My high school track coach often told me that nothing worthwhile is ever easily attained. That's definitely the case with Point Sublime, which is located off the beaten path so you won't run into throngs of camera-toting tourists. The view south and southwest into the many-colored gorge of the Grand Canyon is unforgettable, particularly when far-off thunderstorms are rocking and rolling over some distant corner of the canyon. The sunsets imprint themselves on your memory (in case you forget your film). See Chapter 11.

Zion Canyon Narrows, Zion National Park

There are slot canyons and then there are *slot* canyons. Zion Canyon Narrows is one of a kind. Walking even a little way into this cliff-lined passage is sort of like entering the bowels of a mountain; in some areas, the sandstone walls tower 2,000 feet overhead, and the passage is only 20 feet wide. What created these dramatic slots? Lots of water and time. Over the course of centuries, the Virgin River cut through the Navajo sandstone and into the Kayenta sandstone. In some places, the polished sandstone was delicately fluted. And the river hasn't finished its job. The water nourishes beautiful hanging gardens and continues to carve away the canyon walls. To truly appreciate the entire slot, you need to make a 16-mile trek that takes you through the canyon. But if you're pressed for time, you can see stunning vistas on a short, 2-mile round-trip walk into the slot from the Temple of Sinawava. See Chapter 18.

Chapter 20

Ten Reasons a National Park Is Better

*1*f you're having difficulty deciding between a national park and theme park, listen up. I can give you ten reasons why a national park visit beats a trip to a theme park — hands down.

Stretch Your Dollar

For $20 (or $10 in some parks and nothing in a select few), you and everyone in your car can enjoy a national park for a week. When was the last time you encountered that kind of fee at a theme park? Heck, most high-tech entertainment centers cost at least $40 per person, per day. In the national parks, 20 bucks (tops) gets you the grandest canyon in the world, the greatest collection of thermal features on Earth, animals roaming free, and rivers wild. And that's just for starters.

Expand Your Mind

Unlike theme parks, national parks can enlighten you about the world. Pay attention to the park surroundings and you'll learn about conservation, environmentalism, and zoology. In Yellowstone, the Wolf Recovery Program is an excellent example of species conservation and ecosystem preservation, and the Grand Canyon is one of the world's largest geologic classrooms. Olympic offers biologically rich rain forests and glaciers. Best of all, these lessons reach all ages. Most kids learn best when they don't realize that they're in a learning environment. And in national parks, they're too busy having fun to realize that they're exercising their minds as well as their muscles.

Tour a Real Wild Kingdom

You won't find anything artificial about the wild kingdoms in national parks. The animals aren't behind bars (which is not always a good thing, so beware), no trainers make them beg for food or make them do tricks, and the parks don't have cages to hose down. Yellowstone, for example, hosts vast herds of bison, numerous black and grizzly bears, and elk, wolves, and other animals — all in their natural settings. At Olympic, you may spot a seal or whale cavorting in the waters off the shores.

Stay after 9 p.m.

Theme parks have closing times; national parks don't. A ranger won't kick you out at closing time because there isn't a closing time. If you didn't need to sleep, you could roam a park 24 hours a day, 7 days a week, 365 days a year. The parks have been managing themselves pretty darn well for the last few thousand years, so they don't need to be shut down each day so the custodial crews can clean 'em up.

Avoid Lines

Yes, some park attractions attract crowds. Old Faithful in Yellowstone and the Mist Trail in Yosemite are two good examples, but you probably won't stand in line for over a half-hour for anything. And if you don't want to commune with the masses, you can leave them behind by taking a hike, a nap, or a lunch break in a secluded spot.

Spend the Night

When was the last time you stayed overnight in an amusement park (unless you were stranded on a broken-down ride)? Most parks provide lodges and campgrounds inside their borders where you can bed down at the end of a day. And if you feel like getting up in the middle of the night to make sure that everything is okay outside, that's okay, too.

Enjoy Vendor-Free Zones

Is anything worse than having a little kid stand in line next to you getting his cotton candy on your clothes? This won't happen in a national park, 'cuz parks don't have cotton candy vendors (or lines, remember?). You also won't find candy apple hawkers, popcorn peddlers, or even midway barkers — thank goodness.

Weather Any Storm

Neither rain, nor snow, nor dark of night can shut down a national park's attractions because weather conditions are part of the package. If an earthquake changes the dynamics of Yellowstone's geysers, or a dry summer idles Yosemite's waterfalls, or high runoff makes some backcountry trails inaccessible, well, that's part of life in the natural world. Sometimes, Mother Nature's whims can make a park's natural setting even more interesting, and no one will ask you to pay more money for the privilege of seeing the spectacle.

Pick Your Pace

Theme parks generate most of their amusement by scaring folks with rides that defy gravity or whip you around at high speeds, but national parks take a gentler approach: Natural beauty is the main source of entertainment, and you can enjoy it at your own pace. If you're a thrill-seeker, climb the Grand Teton, raft the Colorado River, or take a paddle on Yellowstone Lake. If you're not adventurous, you can take a nap beneath a sequoia or stroll to a waterfall.

Encourage Exercise

National parks are good for your physical well-being. Why? Because they encourage you to leave your couch-potato ways at home to explore the park on foot. At Yellowstone, you'll want to walk along the boardwalks that wind through the geyser basins. In Yosemite, you'll feel the urge to stroll the Mist Trail. In Olympic, your feet will guide you through a dense rain forest or along a sandy beach. And while you walk, your body will feel healthier with every step, and you won't pass a single booth selling greasy or fattening foods.

Chapter 21

Ten Incredibly Cheap Ways to Enjoy a National Park

· ·

In This Chapter

▶ Watching the sky — sunrise, sunset, and stars
▶ Getting active — hiking, camping, climbing, and fishing
▶ Expanding your mind — ranger talks, kids' activities, and more

· ·

*W*ay back in the front of the book, I mention that national parks are a bargain. If you doubt me, check out this top-ten list of cheap thrills. I guarantee this list will convince you that a national park is the best buy around. And just in case you forgot, or if you skipped the introductory chapters, keep in mind that one small fee (no more than $20!) gets you and your entire family into a park. You won't pay extra for parking, and tickets aren't required for hiking the trails.

Watch the Sun Rise

Along with sunsets and mountains, sunrises are free. In Grand Teton National Park, you can enjoy the sun and the mountains at the same time. Get up before dawn and head out to Teton Park Road and park at any of the pullouts and fix your eyes on the toothy peaks just to the west. As the sun's dawning rays pierce the morning sky, they practically ignite the Tetons' peaks and snowfields. If Grand Teton isn't your park pick, check with the visitor center for the exact time of the sun's rise. Then simply get up early in whichever park you're visiting, drive to a picturesque location, sit back, and enjoy the show. You won't be disappointed.

Hike Down a Trail

One of the best ways to unwind is to hike a trail, preferably one that leads over a ridge and around a few bends. You can't completely experience a national park through a windshield. You need to get out on the ground, walk through the forests, climb a ridge, and dip your toes in a stream.

Watch Wildlife

In many ways, parks are open-air zoos. Some parks, such as Yellowstone, are teeming with animals. Others, such as Death Valley, make you spend a little time looking for the locals. But the critters are out there, and occasionally, they reveal a comical side. Doubt me? Bears fresh out of hibernation like to have a little fun in between scavenging for meals. Head to Yellowstone's Lamar Valley in spring and, with a good pair of binoculars or a spotting scope, you just may see grizzlies whiling away an hour or so sliding down a snowfield. You can watch wildlife in all national parks throughout the year. You can spot seals off the coast of Olympic, California condors in the Grand Canyon, or moose in Grand Teton.

Go Camping

For a small fee, usually less than $20, you can venture into a park's backcountry, pitch your tent in a grove of trees, on a sandy beach, or in a sandstone alcove, and just relax. Leave radios, television, phones, and wake-up calls behind. Most likely, an incredible setting will surround your campsite. You can enjoy some peace and quiet while you gaze at bright stars and spot animals in their natural environments. And, you don't have to worry about checking out with a gargantuan hotel bill.

Involve Your Kids

Why spend $50 on some hand-held computer game when you can entertain your kids with a contest of who can spot the most animals, or the most types of animals, or the most birds? Not only is this type of fun cheap, but it's educational, too. Think about the essays your kids can write when their teachers ask them what they did during their summer vacation. Who knows, they may even be inspired to pursue careers as park rangers, wildlife biologists, or nature writers.

Climb a Mountain

Mountains are free to climb. And you don't have to climb Grand Teton or Mount Rainier to have a great experience. The parks have plenty of smaller, more assailable, mountains with incredibly awesome scenery. Not only will you be rewarded with wonderful vistas, but you'll get some exercise, too!

Listen to a Ranger

Before criminals started coming to parks to see what loot they could score from naive tourists, rangers actually spent most of their time talking to park visitors. Even though law enforcement is a disappointingly high priority in parks these days (see Chapter 7), rangers still organize hikes and gather around campfires to share their knowledge of the parks — for free. Rangers tell you about interesting things, such as the geothermal machinations of Yellowstone, how Yosemite's Half Dome rock formation got its unusual shape, and how the Grand Canyon became so grand. The talks are almost like college seminars (without the fear of follow-up quizzes!).

Go Fishing

As a young boy, I spent quite a few days fishing in the lakes, rivers, and oceans of the national parks. Plenty of adults continue to spend their days this way — and I'm one of them. Many parks have wonderful fisheries, and fishing licenses are free or cost only a small fee. (See the individual park chapters for information on obtaining licenses.) If you're a successful angler, dinner gets less expensive, too.

Count Stars

Ever try to count stars in a city? You can't see them very well because of all the light pollution. That's not a problem in national parks, which usually are far from urban areas and generate only a minimum amount of light. As a result, the Milky Way sparkles overhead on moonless nights. In some northern parks, such as Yellowstone, you can occasionally spot the Northern Lights dancing across the sky in winter.

Watch a Sunset

Sunsets are free. Always have been, probably always will be. Watching the sun go down behind a mountain, beneath the ocean, or below a desert is not only beautiful but is also a great way to reconnect with simple pleasures.

Appendix

Quick Concierge

Fast Facts

American Automobile Association (AAA)

For emergency road service, call ☎ 800-AAA-HELP (800-222-4357). To locate the AAA office nearest the park you're visiting, log on to www.aaa.com.

American Express

For cardholder services, call ☎ 800-528-4800; for lost or stolen travelers checks, call ☎ 800-221-7282.

ATMs

Most national parks have ATMs within their borders. For parks that don't, you can usually find an ATM in a gateway community. Call ☎ 800-424-7787 or 800-4CIRRUS for Cirrus, and ☎ 800-843-7587 for Plus.

Business Hours

Parks are open all the time. The front desks of lodges are usually open around-the-clock, and restaurants typically open by 7 a.m. and usually stay open at least until 10 p.m. Grocery stores and gift shops often stay open until 9 p.m.

Credit Cards

MasterCard's general information number is ☎ 800-307-7309. For Visa, call ☎ 800-847-2911.

Drug Stores

You won't find drug stores inside the parks. Gift shops often have a very small collection of over-the-counter remedies (aspirin, antacids, and sunscreens), whereas in-park groceries or camp stores have a somewhat larger selection.

Emergencies

Call ☎ 911 to report a fire, contact a ranger, or get an ambulance. Additionally, the park newspaper you receive when you enter a park contains a phone list for medical services in the park.

Health

I can't emphasize this too much: Wear sunscreen and drink lots of water when traveling in a national park. The sun can be surprisingly strong — because you're outside all day at a higher elevation where the thinner air lets through more rays or because you're near water that reflects the rays. Before you know it, you can get sunburned and dehydrated. Some of the bigger parks — Yellowstone, Yosemite, and Grand Canyon, for example — have well-stocked and staffed medical clinics within their borders, but in most cases, you have to reach a gateway community for medical facilities.

Liquor Laws

Liquor laws for the individual parks are determined by their location. Depending on the prevailing state law, convenience stores may carry beer and hard liquor, or just beer.

Mail

You can find mail drops in most lodges, visitor centers, and park headquarters.

Maps

Upon entering each park, you receive a free copy of a National Park Service map. National Geographic's *Trails Illustrated* series publishes incredible maps with all sorts of information, such as hiking trails, mountain bike routes, scenic points, and more. If you need driving directions to a park, AAA members can get excellent maps in advance at their local AAA office. Free of charge, Mapquest (www.mapquest.com) will plot a route from point A to point B for you, if you know your exact points of departure and arrival.

Newspapers/Magazines

Park gift shops carry a decent selection of magazines as well as newspapers. Each park also publishes its own newspaper, which usually comes out seasonally and is given to you when you enter the park.

Photography

National parks offer a widely varied range of photographic conditions — such as the bright light of Death Valley, the low light of Olympic National Park's rain forests, and the shimmering conditions found in the Grand Canyon. Brighter conditions require slower films — that is, films with a low ASA, or ISO, number — to produce sharper pictures. In general, an ASA of 100 or 200 is good for most daytime situations, whereas early morning or late afternoon and evening settings demand a faster film, say an ASA of 400. Serious shutterbugs with more than point-and-shoot cameras may also want to invest in a *polarizer*, which reduces contrast, deepens colors, and eliminates glare.

Film is heat sensitive. Never leave your camera or film in a car in the sun because your images can be damaged. In Yellowstone, be vigilant around geysers, hot springs, and other thermal features by quickly wiping spray or steam from your lens. This moisture is mineral-rich and can leave lasting marks behind if you don't remove it quickly.

Safety

You need to take the usual common-sense precautions for your personal safety and your belongings. See Chapter 4 for information about what to do if your money gets lost or stolen, and see Chapter 8 for tips on safely sharing the parks with wildlife.

Smoking

Lodges in more and more parks are becoming smoke free, although some lodges do have a small number of rooms for smokers.

Tipping

Tipping in national parks is no different than tipping in your favorite restaurant. See Chapter 4 for details.

Weather Updates

Although TVs are few and far between in national parks, most lodges post three-day forecasts near their front desks. If you're staying in a gateway community, your accommodation's cable TV service probably offers a weather channel — either *the* Weather Channel or a local station.

Toll-Free Numbers and Web Sites

Airline carriers

Air Canada
☎ 888-247-2262
www.aircanada.ca

Alaska Airlines
☎ 800-252-7522
www.alaskaair.com

American Airlines (American Eagle)
☎ 800-433-7300
www.aa.com

American Trans Air
☎ 800-225-2995
www.ata.com

America West Airlines (America West Express)
☎ 800-235-9292
www.americawest.com

Continental Airlines (Continental Express)
☎ 800-525-0280
www.continental.com

Delta Air Lines
☎ 800-221-1212
www.delta.com

Frontier Airlines
☎ 800-432-1359
www.frontierairlines.com

Midwest Express
☎ 800-452-2022
www.midwestexpress.com

Northwest Airlines
☎ 800-225-2525
www.nwa.com

SkyWest
☎ 800-221-1212 (Delta Connection flights)

☎ 800-241-6522 (United Express flights)
www.skywest.com

Southwest Airlines
☎ 800-435-9792
www.southwest.com

Sun Country
☎ 800-359-6786
www.suncountry.com

United Airlines (United Express)
☎ 800-241-6522
www.united.com

USAirways (USAirways Express)
☎ 800-428-4322
www.usairways.com

Car-rental agencies

Advantage
☎ 800-777-5500
www.advantagerentacar.com

Alamo
☎ 800-327-9633
www.alamo.com

Avis
☎ 800-331-1212
☎ 800-TRY-AVIS in Canada
www.avis.com

Budget
☎ 800-527-0700
www.budgetrentacar.com

Dollar
☎ 800-800-4000
www.dollar.com

Enterprise
☎ 800-325-8007
www.enterprise.com

Hertz
☎ 800-654-3131
www.hertz.com

National
☎ 800-CAR-RENT
www.nationalcar.com

Payless
☎ 800-PAYLESS
www.paylesscarrental.com

Rent-A-Wreck
☎ 800-535-1391
www.rentawreck.com

Thrifty
☎ 800-367-2277
www.thrifty.com

Concessionaires

Aramark Parks
Olympic National Park
www.aramarkparks.com

Delaware North
Yosemite and Sequoia/
Kings Canyon national parks
www.visitsequoia.com
www.yosemitepark.com

Grand Teton Lodge Company
Grand Teton National Park
www.gtlc.com

Guest Services Company
Mount Rainier National Park
www.guestservices.com

Xanterra Parks & Resorts
Death Valley, Grand Canyon,
Yellowstone, and Zion national parks
www.xanterra.com

Hotel and motel chains

Best Western International
☎ 800-528-1234
www.bestwestern.com

Clarion Hotels
☎ 800-CLARION
www.clarionhotel.com
www.hotelchoice.com

Comfort Inns
☎ 800-228-5150
www.hotelchoice.com

Courtyard by Marriott
☎ 800-321-2211
www.courtyard.com
www.marriott.com

Days Inn
☎ 800-325-2525
www.laquinta.com

Doubletree Hotels
☎ 800-222-TREE
www.doubletree.com

Econo Lodges
☎ 800-55-ECONO
www.hotelchoice.com

Fairfield Inn by Marriott
☎ 800-228-2800
www.marriott.com

Hampton Inn
☎ 800-HAMPTON
www.hampton-inn.com

Hilton Hotels
☎ 800-HILTONS
www.hilton.com

Holiday Inn
☎ 800-HOLIDAY
www.basshotels.com

Howard Johnson
☎ 800-654-2000
www.hojo.com

Hyatt Hotels & Resorts
☎ 800-228-9000
www.hyatt.com

La Quinta Motor Inns
☎ 800-531-5900
☎ 800-241-3333
www.lq.com

Marriott Hotels
☎ 800-228-9290
www.marriott.com

Motel 6
☎ 800-4-MOTEL6 (800-466-8536)
www.motel6.com

Quality Inns
☎ 800-228-5151
www.hotelchoice.com

Radisson Hotels International
☎ 800-333-3333
www.radisson.com

Ramada Inns
☎ 800-2-RAMADA
www.ramada.com

Red Roof Inns
☎ 800-843-7663
www.redroof.com

Residence Inn by Marriott
☎ 800-331-3131
www.marriott.com

Ritz-Carlton
☎ 800-241-3333
www.ritzcarlton.com

Rodeway Inns
☎ 800-228-2000
www.hotelchoice.com

Sheraton Hotels & Resorts
☎ 800-325-3535
www.sheraton.com

Super 8 Motels
☎ 800-800-8000
www.super8.com

Travelodge
☎ 800-255-3050
www.travelodge.com

Westin Hotels & Resorts
☎ 800-937-8461
www.westin.com

Wyndham Hotels & Resorts
☎ 800-822-4200
www.wyndham.com

Where to Get More Information

If you're like me, when you decide to go someplace, you want to do as much research as possible so you're somewhat familiar with your destination before you arrive. After all, that's why you bought this book, right?

Well, thanks to computers, rounding up information on national parks is a snap (or is that a click?). The place to start — after reading this book, of course — is at the **National Park Service** Web site: www.nps.gov. Log on, and the park system becomes an open book. You can find Web sites for each park, make your lodging and campground reservations online, delve into the park system's cultural and natural history, and even see what jobs are available.

After you've plumbed the site for information, check out the **American Park Network** (www.americanparknetwork.com). These folks print many of the small, glossy, park guidebooks you receive for free at the parks. At this site, you can pull up an electronic version of these guides for some of the more popular parks. You find, among other things, information on the park's lodgings, sites worth visiting, hiking suggestions, and history.

You won't find every unit of the national park system represented, but most of the major ones are here, and you can build on the information you gained at the National Park Service site and in this book.

If you haven't yet entered the computer age, write to the National Park Service, Office of Public Inquiries, 1849 C Street, NW, Room 7012, Washington, D.C., 20240, and request general information on the park system as well as brochures about a specific park. If you don't like waiting on the mail system, call the office at ☎ 202-208-4747 Monday through Friday from 9 a.m. to 3 p.m. eastern time, and place your request.

Another publication that can help you get a feel for the national park landscape is *America's National Parks,* published by the **National Park Foundation,** 11 Dupont Circle, NW, Suite 600, Washington, D.C., 20036 (☎ 202-238-4200). This beautifully illustrated coffee table–style book, which costs about $50, can be purchased through the foundation's Web site (www.nationalparks.org) and often can be found in bookstores as well.

Index

Notes

....

_____

_____

_____

_____

_____

_____

_____

_____

_____

_____

_____

_____

_____

_____

_____

_____

_____

_____

_____

_____

_____

_____

_____

_____

BUSINESS, CAREERS & PERSONAL FINANCE

0-7645-5307-0   0-7645-5331-3 *†

Also available:

- Accounting For Dummies †
  0-7645-5314-3
- Business Plans Kit For Dummies †
  0-7645-5365-8
- Cover Letters For Dummies
  0-7645-5224-4
- Frugal Living For Dummies
  0-7645-5403-4
- Leadership For Dummies
  0-7645-5176-0
- Managing For Dummies
  0-7645-1771-6

- Marketing For Dummies
  0-7645-5600-2
- Personal Finance For Dummies *
  0-7645-2590-5
- Project Management
  For Dummies
  0-7645-5283-X
- Resumes For Dummies †
  0-7645-5471-9
- Selling For Dummies
  0-7645-5363-1
- Small Business Kit For Dummies *†
  0-7645-5093-4

HOME & BUSINESS COMPUTER BASICS

0-7645-4074-2   0-7645-3758-X

Also available:

- ACT! 6 For Dummies
  0-7645-2645-6
- iLife '04 All-in-One Desk Reference
  For Dummies
  0-7645-7347-0
- iPAQ For Dummies
  0-7645-6769-1
- Mac OS X Panther Timesaving
  Techniques For Dummies
  0-7645-5812-9
- Macs For Dummies
  0-7645-5656-8
- Microsoft Money 2004 For Dummies
  0-7645-4195-1

- Office 2003 All-in-One Desk
  Reference For Dummies
  0-7645-3883-7
- Outlook 2003 For Dummies
  0-7645-3759-8
- PCs For Dummies
  0-7645-4074-2
- TiVo For Dummies
  0-7645-6923-6
- Upgrading and Fixing PCs
  For Dummies
  0-7645-1665-5
- Windows XP Timesaving
  Techniques For Dummies
  0-7645-3748-2

FOOD, HOME, GARDEN, HOBBIES, MUSIC & PETS

-7645-5295-3   0-7645-5232-5

Also available:

- Bass Guitar For Dummies
  0-7645-2487-9
- Diabetes Cookbook For Dummies
  0-7645-5230-9
- Gardening For Dummies *
  0-7645-5130-2
- Guitar For Dummies
  0-7645-5106-X
- Holiday Decorating For Dummies
  0-7645-2570-0
- Home Improvement All-in-One
  For Dummies
  0-7645-5680-0

- Knitting For Dummies
  0-7645-5395-X
- Piano For Dummies
  0-7645-5105-1
- Puppies For Dummies
  0-7645-5255-4
- Scrapbooking For Dummies
  0-7645-7208-3
- Senior Dogs For Dummies
  0-7645-5818-8
- Singing For Dummies
  0-7645-2475-5
- 30-Minute Meals For Dummies
  0-7645-2589-1

INTERNET & DIGITAL MEDIA

-7645-1664-7   0-7645-6924-4

Also available:

- 2005 Online Shopping Directory
  For Dummies
  0-7645-7495-7
- CD & DVD Recording For Dummies
  0-7645-5956-7
- eBay For Dummies
  0-7645-5654-1
- Fighting Spam For Dummies
  0-7645-5965-6
- Genealogy Online For Dummies
  0-7645-5964-8
- Google For Dummies
  0-7645-4420-9

- Home Recording For Musicians
  For Dummies
  0-7645-1634-5
- The Internet For Dummies
  0-7645-4173-0
- iPod & iTunes For Dummies
  0-7645-7772-7
- Preventing Identity Theft
  For Dummies
  0-7645-7336-5
- Pro Tools All-in-One Desk
  Reference For Dummies
  0-7645-5714-9
- Roxio Easy Media Creator
  For Dummies
  0-7645-7131-1

SPORTS, FITNESS, PARENTING, RELIGION & SPIRITUALITY

0-7645-5146-9   0-7645-5418-2

Also available:

- ✔Adoption For Dummies
  0-7645-5488-3
- ✔Basketball For Dummies
  0-7645-5248-1
- ✔The Bible For Dummies
  0-7645-5296-1
- ✔Buddhism For Dummies
  0-7645-5359-3
- ✔Catholicism For Dummies
  0-7645-5391-7
- ✔Hockey For Dummies
  0-7645-5228-7

- ✔Judaism For Dummies
  0-7645-5299-6
- ✔Martial Arts For Dummies
  0-7645-5358-5
- ✔Pilates For Dummies
  0-7645-5397-6
- ✔Religion For Dummies
  0-7645-5264-3
- ✔Teaching Kids to Read
  For Dummies
  0-7645-4043-2
- ✔Weight Training For Dummies
  0-7645-5168-X
- ✔Yoga For Dummies
  0-7645-5117-5

TRAVEL

0-7645-5438-7   0-7645-5453-0

Also available:

- ✔Alaska For Dummies
  0-7645-1761-9
- ✔Arizona For Dummies
  0-7645-6938-4
- ✔Cancún and the Yucatán
  For Dummies
  0-7645-2437-2
- ✔Cruise Vacations For Dummies
  0-7645-6941-4
- ✔Europe For Dummies
  0-7645-5456-5
- ✔Ireland For Dummies
  0-7645-5455-7

- ✔Las Vegas For Dummies
  0-7645-5448-4
- ✔London For Dummies
  0-7645-4277-X
- ✔New York City For Dummies
  0-7645-6945-7
- ✔Paris For Dummies
  0-7645-5494-8
- ✔RV Vacations For Dummies
  0-7645-5443-3
- ✔Walt Disney World & Orlando
  For Dummies
  0-7645-6943-0

GRAPHICS, DESIGN & WEB DEVELOPMENT

0-7645-4345-8   0-7645-5589-8

Also available:

- ✔Adobe Acrobat 6 PDF
  For Dummies
  0-7645-3760-1
- ✔Building a Web Site For Dummies
  0-7645-7144-3
- ✔Dreamweaver MX 2004
  For Dummies
  0-7645-4342-3
- ✔FrontPage 2003 For Dummies
  0-7645-3882-9
- ✔HTML 4 For Dummies
  0-7645-1995-6
- ✔Illustrator cs For Dummies
  0-7645-4084-X

- ✔Macromedia Flash MX 2004
  For Dummies
  0-7645-4358-X
- ✔Photoshop 7 All-in-One Desk
  Reference For Dummies
  0-7645-1667-1
- ✔Photoshop cs Timesaving
  Techniques For Dummies
  0-7645-6782-9
- ✔PHP 5 For Dummies
  0-7645-4166-8
- ✔PowerPoint 2003 For Dummies
  0-7645-3908-6
- ✔QuarkXPress 6 For Dummies
  0-7645-2593-X

NETWORKING, SECURITY, PROGRAMMING & DATABASES

0-7645-6852-3   0-7645-5784-X

Also available:

- ✔A+ Certification For Dummies
  0-7645-4187-0
- ✔Access 2003 All-in-One Desk
  Reference For Dummies
  0-7645-3988-4
- ✔Beginning Programming
  For Dummies
  0-7645-4997-9
- ✔C For Dummies
  0-7645-7068-4
- ✔Firewalls For Dummies
  0-7645-4048-3
- ✔Home Networking For Dummies
  0-7645-42796

- ✔Network Security For Dummies
  0-7645-1679-5
- ✔Networking For Dummies
  0-7645-1677-9
- ✔TCP/IP For Dummies
  0-7645-1760-0
- ✔VBA For Dummies
  0-7645-3989-2
- ✔Wireless All In-One Desk Reference
  For Dummies
  0-7645-7496-5
- ✔Wireless Home Networking
  For Dummies
  0-7645-3910-8